CW01099947

Sanctions, Statecraft, and Nuclear Proliferation

Some states have violated international commitments not to develop nuclear weapons. Yet the effects of international sanctions or positive inducements on their internal politics remain highly contested. How have trade, aid, investments, diplomacy, financial measures, and military threats affected different groups? How, when, and why were those effects translated into compliance with nonproliferation rules? Have inducements been sufficiently biting, too harsh, too little, too late, or just right for each case? How have different inducements influenced domestic cleavages? What were their unintended and unforeseen effects? Why are self-reliant autocracies more often the subject of sanctions?

Leading scholars analyze the anatomy of inducements through novel conceptual perspectives, in-depth case studies, original quantitative data, and newly-translated documents. The volume distils ten key dilemmas of broad relevance to the study of statecraft, primarily from experiences with Iraq, Libya, Iran, and North Korea, bound to spark debate among students and practitioners of international politics.

ETEL SOLINGEN is Chancellor's Professor in the Department of Political Science, University of California, Irvine and President-elect of the International Studies Association. Her most recent book *Nuclear Logics: Contrasting Paths in East Asia and the Middle East* (2007) was awarded the APSA's Woodrow Wilson Foundation Award and the Robert Jervis and Paul Schroeder Award for Best Book on International History and Politics. She is also author of *Regional Orders at Century's Dawn: Global and Domestic Influences on Grand Strategy* (1998), among other books.

Sanctions, Statecraft, and Nuclear Proliferation

Edited by
Etel Solingen

CAMBRIDGE UNIVERSITY PRESS
Cambridge, New York, Melbourne, Madrid, Cape Town,
Singapore, São Paulo, Delhi, Mexico City

Cambridge University Press
The Edinburgh Building, Cambridge CB2 8RU, UK

Published in the United States of America by Cambridge University Press,
New York

www.cambridge.org
Information on this title: www.cambridge.org/9780521281188

First published 2012

Printed in the United Kingdom at the University Press, Cambridge

A catalogue record for this publication is available from the British Library

Library of Congress Cataloguing in Publication data
Sanctions, statecraft, and nuclear proliferation / [edited by] Etel Solingen.
  pages   cm
  Includes bibliographical references and index.
  ISBN 978-1-107-01044-4 (hardback) – ISBN 978-0-521-28118-8
  (paperback)
  1. Nuclear nonproliferation.   2. Economic sanctions.
  3. International relations–Economic aspects.   I. Solingen, Etel, 1952–
  editor of compilation.
  JZ5675.S245 2012
  327.1'747–dc23
  2011052387

ISBN 978-1-107-01044-4 Hardback
ISBN 978-0-521-28118-8 Paperback

To Ruby and Benjamin, who master the art of positive inducements

Contents

Figures

Tables

Contributors

DANIEL W. DREZNER is Professor of International Politics at the Fletcher School of Law and Diplomacy at Tufts University, a contributing editor for *Foreign Policy*, and a senior editor for *The National Interest*. Prior to Fletcher, he taught at the University of Chicago and the University of Colorado at Boulder. Drezner is the author of four books including *All Politics is Global*. He has published articles in numerous scholarly journals as well as in the *New York Times*, *Wall Street Journal*, and *Foreign Affairs*. He received his B.A. from Williams College and his Ph.D. from Stanford University.

STEPHAN HAGGARD is the Krause Distinguished Professor at the Graduate School of International Relations and Pacific Studies. He is the author of *Pathways from the Periphery: The Political Economy of Growth in the Newly Industrializing Countries* (1990), *The Political Economy of the Asian Financial Crisis* (2000) and, with Bob Kaufman, *The Political Economy of Democratic Transitions* (1995) and *Development, Democracy and Welfare States: Latin America, East Asia and Eastern Europe* (2008). His work on the political economy of North Korea with Marcus Noland includes *Famine in North Korea: Markets, Aid and Reform* (2007) and *Witness to Transformation: Refugee Insights into North Korea* (2011).

SARAH KREPS is an Assistant Professor of Government at Cornell University. Her research focuses on issues of international security, particularly questions of conflict and cooperation, nuclear proliferation, alliance politics, and international peacekeeping. Her first book is called *Coalitions of Convenience? United States Military Interventions after the Cold War* (2011). Her work has appeared, among other places, in the *Journal of Conflict Resolution*, *Security Studies*, *Journal of Strategic Studies*, *Political Science Quarterly*, *Foreign Policy Analysis*, the *Duke Journal of Comparative and International Law*, and *Intelligence and National Security*.

ALIREZA NADER is an International Policy Analyst at the RAND Corporation. His research has focused on Iran's political dynamics, elite decision-making, and Iranian foreign policy. His RAND publications include "Saudi-Iranian Relations Since the Fall of Saddam: Rivalry, Cooperation, and Implications for U.S. Policy"; "The Rise of the Pasdaran: Assessing the Domestic Roles of Iran's Islamic Revolutionary Guards Corps"; and "Mullahs, Guards, and Bonyads: An Exploration of Iranian Leadership Dynamics." His commentaries and articles have appeared in a variety of publications, including *Foreign Policy* and *The World Today*.

MIROSLAV NINCIC is Professor of Political Science at the University of California, Davis. He has written eight volumes on topics of international relations and on the proper relation of pure theory to policy relevant research. His newest book is entitled *The Logic of Positive Engagement*.

MARCUS NOLAND is the Deputy Director of the Peterson Institute for International Economics and a Senior Fellow at the East-West Center. He was a Senior Economist at the Council of Economic Advisers in the Executive Office of the President of the United States, and has held research or teaching positions at Yale University, the Johns Hopkins University, the University of Southern California, Tokyo University, Saitama University (now the National Graduate Institute for Policy Studies), the University of Ghana, and the Korea Development Institute. His latest book, co-authored with Stephan Haggard, is *Witness to Transformation: Refugee Insights into North Korea*.

DAVID PALKKI is Deputy Director and Senior Research Fellow at the National Defense University's Conflict Records Research Centre (CRRC). Mr Palkki is the co-editor of *The Saddam Tapes: The Inner Workings of a Tyrant's Regime, 1978–2001* (Cambridge University Press, 2011) and has published in the journals *International Security and Diplomatic History*. He is also a Ph.D. candidate in political science at the University of California, Los Angeles. His dissertation is on "Deterring Saddam's Iraq: Theory and Practice."

ZAIN PASHA is a graduate of Cornell University, where he was a Meinig Family Cornell National Scholar, an Irwin and Joan Jacobs Scholar, and won both the John F. Kennedy Memorial Prize and the Meinig Family Excellence in Leadership Award. His research interests include international political economy, nonproliferation studies, and political science methodology. Zain has conducted research on the causes and consequences of China's nuclear modernization and the relationship between peaceful nuclear assistance and nuclear proliferation.

CELIA L. REYNOLDS received her M.A. in political science from the University of California, Irvine in June 2011 and is a Nonproliferation and International Security analyst at Lawrence Livermore National Laboratory (LLNL). Prior to her graduate studies, Celia worked as a nuclear nonproliferation analyst with the National Geospatial-Intelligence Agency in Washington, DC. During her graduate studies, she also served as an International Nuclear Safeguards summer intern at LLNL in 2010 as part of the US Department of Energy, National Nuclear Security Administration's Next Generation Safeguards Initiative.

SHANE SMITH is a Research Fellow at the National Defense University's Center for the Study of Weapons of Mass Destruction and Director of the Center's Program for Emerging Leaders. He is also an Adjunct Professor at Johns Hopkins University, where he teaches courses on US nuclear policy. Prior to joining the WMD Center, he worked at the Harvard-Stanford Preventive Defense Project and the Council on Foreign Relations.

ETEL SOLINGEN is Chancellor's Professor of Political Science at the University of California, Irvine and President-elect of the International Studies Association. Her book *Nuclear Logics: Contrasting Paths in East Asia and the Middle East* was awarded the American Political Science Association's Woodrow Wilson Foundation Award and the Robert Jervis and Paul Schroeder Award. She is also author, among others, of *Regional Orders at Century's Dawn: Global and Domestic Influences on Grand Strategy*. She served as Chair of the Steering Committee of the University of California's system-wide Institute on Global Conflict and Cooperation.

ARTHUR A. STEIN is Professor of Political Science at UCLA and co-editor of the *American Political Science Review*. He received an A.B. from Cornell University and a Ph.D. from Yale University. He is author of *The Nation at War* and *Why Nations Cooperate: Circumstance and Choice in International Relations*, and co-editor of *The Domestic Bases of Grand Strategy* and *No More States? Globalization, National Self-Determination, and Terrorism*. He has served on the Policy Planning Staff of the US Department of State and consulted for US defense and intelligence agencies. He has also been a Guest Scholar at the Brookings Institution, a Senior Fellow of the University of California's Institute on Global Conflict and Cooperation (IGCC), and an International Affairs Fellow of the Council on Foreign Relations. He has worked extensively on the bases of international cooperation, on the construction of international regimes and institutions, and on the relationship between domestic and international politics.

WILFRED T. WAN is a Ph.D. candidate in political science at the University of California, Irvine, and a Stanton Nuclear Security Research Fellow with the Belfer Center for Science and International Affairs. He spent the 2011–2012 academic year at the Harvard Kennedy School, with a joint appointment with the International Security Program and the Project on Managing the Atom. He was a 2010–2011 Institute on Global Conflict and Cooperation Dissertation Fellow. His dissertation, titled "Institutions, Change, and the Nuclear Non-Proliferation Regime," examines the sources, loci, and modalities of change in that security institution.

Preface and acknowledgments

This book seeks to illuminate dilemmas of statecraft in the prevention of nuclear proliferation. It focuses largely – but not uniquely – on experiences in the last two decades, primarily with Iraq, Iran, North Korea, and Libya. These dilemmas make it clear that we are far from reaching a final word on the subject and that our efforts to unpack the paths and effects of external inducements within target states may introduce more questions than can be answered in this salvo. Far from seeking to reach unanimity on a subject ridden with quandaries, the primary aspiration of this volume is to reflect on those cases and experiences with an eye on improving our knowledge of the scope conditions, processes, and causal mechanisms that link inducements to specific outcomes. This entails a better understanding of the domestic distributional costs and benefits of external inducements on target states. At the very least, the effort to concentrate on those causal mechanisms connecting sanctions and positive inducements to outcomes broadens a more typical focus on whether or not such inducements "work." Not only can assessments of outcomes be overly simplistic but too narrow a focus on outcomes often comes at the expense of a deeper and productive inquiry into why different instruments may or not yield expected effects under particular circumstances.

The main objective was thus not to take sides in the sanctions pessimism–optimism debate. Although there is plenty of that here as well, there is also ample divergence among authors over whether or not comprehensive sanctions work, targeted sanctions are less or more effective, positive inducements are any more efficient than negative ones, what should a right mix of both consist of, and whether or not all types of inducements may have proven futile. We aim not at definitive conclusions – given contested readings of the evidence – but rather at redirecting attention to the anatomy of inducements, the causal processes they unleash in the domestic politics of target states, and the intended, unintended, and unexpected outcomes inducements can yield.

That focus helps clarify what this book is not. First, it is not primarily a study of motivations and justifications for acquiring nuclear weapons, although it does build on conceptions of the "demand-side" for nuclear weapons analyzed in previous work.[1] The focal theme here, however, is the "supply-side" of inducements, or instruments used by international actors (individual states, groups of states, international institutions) to persuade those states that violate international nonproliferation commitments to comply with them. Second, neither is this a study of nuclear restraint, or why states with adequate capabilities nonetheless chose to forgo nuclear weapons. In other words, the "non-demand" side is also beyond our focus here, for the most part, although it is briefly discussed in the context of "selection effects" in the study of sanctions. Third, this is not an exhaustive study of nonproliferation statecraft over the last six decades, which would have entailed many more cases than the focal ones addressed in this volume: Iraq, North Korea, Libya, and Iran. The world has changed in significant ways, particularly after 1989, and our spotlight is on the last twenty years. Over that period there was a surge in the belief in the power of comprehensive sanctions initially, and targeted sanctions subsequently, as alternatives to war. Circumscribing the analysis to this period also enables a more controlled comparison of those four cases under a world-time that differs significantly from the Cold War era. Fourth, this is not a comprehensive exploration of all strategies vis-à-vis proliferating states, including military action, deterrence, containment, and others. Although some chapters address those strategies, in some cases tangentially, the heart of the analysis relates to sanctions and positive inducements primarily – but not solely – of the economic type. One chapter does examine military threats more directly but even there the focus is on domestic distributional consequences of such threats on target states, the volume's leitmotif.

Our main audiences are scholars, students, and practitioners with an interest in international relations, international studies, national and international security, international political economy, international security institutions, nuclear proliferation, international sanctions and economic statecraft, comparative politics, the inner workings of autocratic regimes, the links between domestic and foreign policy, and East Asian and Middle East politics. The different chapters place the study of statecraft within a broader framework, taking stock of contemporary theoretical and empirical work on sanctions and positive inducements beyond the area of nuclear proliferation, relying on different methodologies and speaking to a wide audience of experts and non-experts.

---

[1] Solingen (2007a).

From that perspective, the dilemmas of statecraft identified here can hopefully contribute to a broader understanding of causal mechanisms linking external inducements to changes in state behavior in various issue areas, including human rights.

I am indebted to the Carnegie Corporation of New York, particularly to Steve Del Rosso, who helped fund two meetings, and to Carl Robichaud. This support enabled a group of contributors and discussants to gather in Laguna Beach in March 2009 to discuss a preliminary memo on distributional effects of external inducements by Etel Solingen and Albert Wolf. Participants met as a group for a second time in Washington, DC in September 2010. I am especially grateful to Robert S. Litwak, Vice President for Programs at the Woodrow Wilson International Center for Scholars, for hosting a discussion of findings with an audience of Washington, DC scholars and practitioners. Together with Joe Pilat, Rob Litwak offered both very useful substantive advice and warm hospitality.

The project would have hardly been the same without the extraordinary commitment of Wilfred Wan and Celia Reynolds, graduate students at the University of California Irvine and nonproliferation experts in their own right, who helped steer the process along while contributing an original chapter of their own. As Dean of Social Sciences, Barbara Dosher provided the proper research environment for collaborative projects and for graduate student participation; I am especially grateful for her support and encouragement. I also thank the University of California Irvine's Center for the Scientific Study of Ethics and the Center for Global Peace and Conflict Studies, and their respective directors Kristen Monroe and Cecelia Lynch, for hosting the project and supporting student participation as research assistants. Wilfred Wan, Celia Reynolds, Helen Klein, Adam Martin, and Albert Wolf were involved in different capacities and I thank them all for their contributions.

I would also like to acknowledge the comments and suggestions of participants at workshops in Laguna Beach, the Woodrow Wilson Center, and a panel at the 2010 American Political Science Association meetings, especially Miles Kahler, Steve Krasner, Jim Lebovic, and Kim Elliott. I also benefited from participation at seminars and Track Two meetings sponsored by the Institute on Global Conflict and Cooperation. My special thanks to Susan Shirk and T.J. Pempel. The volume also benefited from helpful observations from audiences at the University of California Berkeley, University of California Los Angeles, Massachusetts Institute of Technology, Columbia University, Fudan University, Peking University, Oxford University's Centre for

International Studies, Georgetown University's School of Foreign Service in Doha (Qatar), ETH-Swiss Federal Institute of Technology, University of Hong Kong, Keio University, Fundação Getulio Vargas, the East Asia Institute in Seoul, and the 2011 ASAN Plenum sponsored by the Asan Institute for Policy Studies in Seoul. For their valuable recommendations and helpful advice on different aspects of this project I would also like to thank two anonymous reviewers for the Press and David Baldwin, Steve Brams, Jeff Richelson, Shelly Bennett-Burns, Natalie Cook, and Gillian Cummings.

It has been a particular pleasure to work with John Haslam at Cambridge University Press. A thoughtful editor with a clinical eye, John steers the arduous process of transforming a manuscript into an actual book with a reassuring and cheerful smile. Particularly helpful at the production stage were Gillian Dadd, Gail Welsh, and Rob Wilkinson.

As always, I owe my family the most, for their love, encouragement, and support, which makes anything possible and everything worthwhile.

Part I

Anatomy of inducements

1 Introduction: the domestic distributional effects of sanctions and positive inducements

Etel Solingen

In June 2009 the streets of Tehran were burning, literally and figuratively. The Obama administration faced a crucial dilemma in its effort to prevent Iran from acquiring nuclear weapons. Should President Obama openly support the persecuted opposition, as some argued, and if so, what language should he use? Should he abstain from any response, so as to avoid intruding in the internal turmoil brewing within Iran's regime? Should the US administration "talk" to Ahmadinejad or to his competitors within Iran's ruling coalition? Should the nuclear issue be raised in the repressive post-election context to signal the economic and other opportunity costs of the regime's behavior for the Iranian public? Could positive outreach by the president toward the Iranian regime yield any fruit? Were positive inducements offered too little or too much? Were sanctions too punitive or toothless? Was support extended to Iran's (and Syria's) opposition adequate considering stronger endorsement of popular uprisings in Egypt, Libya, and Tunisia in early 2011? Are security assurances to nuclear proliferators a proven means to obviate their quest for nuclear weapons?

The intractability of these dilemmas is the subject of extensive public discussion worldwide.[1] Notably, the international relations scholarly literature on sanctions and nuclear nonproliferation offers limited answers to most of these questions and has largely neglected more systematic analysis of the domestic distributional consequences of external attempts to influence target states' nuclear postures.[2] A domestic distributional focus requires particular attention to *cui bono* (who gains) and

---

[1] Opposition to Iran's nuclear program was very strong across most countries surveyed by a Pew (2010) public opinion poll.

[2] For important exceptions in the broader literature dealing with human rights and terrorism, see Crawford and Klotz (1999) and O'Sullivan (2003) inter alia. Work specific to sanctions in nuclear proliferation includes Litwak (2007), Lebovic (2007), Jentleson and Whytock (2005/2006), and Solingen (1995). To conform to the general

cui malo (who loses) from sanctions and positive inducements, and how those, in turn, affect the outcome. This volume thus seeks to contribute to the study of nonproliferation statecraft in several ways.[3]

First, it looks primarily and systematically into domestic distributional costs and benefits. This focus follows a turn to domestic politics as a major influence on the demand-side for nuclear weapons in the nonproliferation literature, a turn that replaced an over-concentration on presumed external security "imperatives."[4]

Second, it seeks to identify the specific causal mechanisms or paths connecting international sanctions and inducements to their outcomes. One set of mechanisms, among others, derives from the assumption that leaders presiding over different domestic political economy models respond differently to international sanctions and inducements.[5] Another set stems from differences in regime type (democracies vs. autocracies).

Third, replacing a more common focus on the effects of sanctions alone, this book also examines the effects of positive inducements on domestic actors in target states.

Fourth, it begins to explore whether different stages in the development of a nuclear program are more amenable to different types of external inducements, as expected from principles of prospect theory and arguments about audience costs. Whereas the North Korean regime would have to give up tested nuclear weapons, the Iranian regime would have to retreat from a program that has not yet yielded nuclear weapons, at least according to published reports as of 2011 (though many assert that Iran has certainly been pursuing capabilities to build nuclear weapons).[6] Clearly, the two circumstances could have different implications for domestic receptivity to different kinds of inducements.

---

literature we adopt the term "sender" to refer to states extending inducements (sometimes referred to as "sanctioning" states), and "target" to refer to the state to which inducements are being extended (sometimes referred to as "sanctioned" states).

[3] Statecraft can be defined as a government's use of various instruments – diplomatic, economic, military – in the service of foreign policy objectives. See, inter alia, Mastanduno (2008).

[4] See, inter alia, Lavoy (1993), Solingen (1994a, 2007a, 2010), Sagan (1996/1997), Liberman (2001), and Potter and Mukhatzhanova (2008).

[5] The primary focus of Solingen (2007a) was to identify domestic patterns of motivations to acquire or renounce nuclear weapons as the main "dependent variable," addressing only indirectly how different states respond to sanctions and positive inducements.

[6] On Iran's violations, see the February, May, and November 2011 IAEA reports discussing new evidence of Iran's weaponization activities at www.iaea.org. See also "New Hints Emerge of Iranian Nuke Drive: Experts," NTI, *Global Security Newswire*, July 6, 2011. US Defense Secretary Gates argued that he "personally believe(s) [Iranian leaders] are intent on acquiring nuclear weapons" (quoted in "Military Action Won't Stop Iranian Nuclear Program: US," *AFP*, November 16, 2010). Admiral Mullen said

Fifth, it considers the relative effectiveness of targeted versus comprehensive forms of both sanctions and inducements, particularly in the context of varying domestic political economy models and regime types.

Sixth, it reflects on the gap between intended and unintended or unforeseen domestic distributional effects of sanctions and inducements.

Seventh, it revisits the problems of collective action among senders, on the supply-side of sanctions and inducements, a well-known barrier to achieving objectives. The fact that multilateral sanctions tend to be more effective than unilateral ones is not a particularly novel insight, nor one subject to much contention. Furthermore, given the prominence of this topic in the literature and much less emphasis on domestic distributional considerations in target states, this volume pays special attention to the latter. It also raises the possibility, however, that the organization of collective action under US primacy may be altered by new underlying reconfigurations of international economics and politics, including the rise of China and regional powers such as Turkey, Brazil, India, and others.

Eighth, it relies on a variety of analytic and research methods, novel conceptualizations, new quantitative data, comparative historical analysis based on newly declassified archival evidence, and detailed process-tracing of in-depth case studies.[7]

In line with Baldwin's (1985, 1998) conceptualization, sanctions and inducements are instruments of statecraft specifically geared to change the target state's behavior. A working definition of sanctions (which might also be labeled negative inducements) refers to international instruments of statecraft that punish or deny benefits to leaders, ruling coalitions, or broader constituencies in a given state, in an effort to dissuade those targets from pursuing or supporting the acquisition of nuclear weapons. The literature often refers to negative inducements as sanctions and the two terms are sometimes used interchangeably in

---

he has no doubt Iran is trying to develop nuclear weapons (Pessin 2010). Assistant Secretary of State for Verification and Compliance Rose Gottemoeller (2007: 106) declared "Iran's evident drive toward nuclear weapons is the other major proliferation crisis the international community has been grappling with for well over a decade." Ahmadinejad's spiritual mentor Ayatollah Mohammad Taqi Mesbah Yazdi has repeatedly called for producing the "most advanced" "special weapons" that are a monopoly of a few. Ayatollah Ali Khamenei has denied Iran's pursuit of nuclear weapons. A hardline Iranian website called Yazdi an "Imam," a title not awarded to Khamenei (Associated Press, "Top Cleric: Iran Has Right to 'Special Weapons,'" June 14, 2010).

[7] George and Bennett (2005) describe process tracing as the effort to link a series of hypothesized interrelated causal processes and observed outcomes.

this volume as well. Conversely, positive inducements are benefits or rewards extended to leaders, ruling coalitions, or broader constituencies in target states, with the expectation that they will persuade recipients to eschew nuclear weapons. Chapter 3 includes a fine-grained listing of sanctions and positive inducements, and provides data and historical context to these different forms. The body of work addressing positive inducements in various issue areas – but particularly in nonproliferation – is generally smaller and more recent than the one on sanctions.[8]

Notwithstanding our particular concentration on external mechanisms geared to dissuade states from pursuing nuclear weapons, this volume is informed by a broader literature exploring other objectives of statecraft such as improving human rights, preventing ethnic cleansing and civil conflict, or curtailing support for terrorism.[9] However, the tendency to aggregate results of sanctions and inducements in different issue areas can also conflate effects; obscure causal mechanisms specific to the issue we seek to understand; and perhaps even perpetuate the high level of disagreement over whether or not sanctions or inducements "work."[10] This volume thus limits the scope of inquiry to nuclear proliferation, which can partially circumvent the problem of heterogeneity in desired objectives that affects many studies of sanctions. Work with such specific focus is rare, only a small subset of comprehensive studies across different issue areas. It is also often unguided by a coherent set of hypotheses and prone to plunge into policy prescriptions even as conditions presumed to maximize the chances for success remain ambiguous. Disagreements regarding the effectiveness of sanctions and inducements on Iraq, Iran, Libya, North Korea, and others before them are far from settled; the lessons learned are still unclear and often

---

[8] Among precursors, see Baldwin (1971a), Solingen (1995), Davis (1999), Davis, Jr. (2000), Bernauer and Ruloff (1999), Wallensteen and Staibano (2005), and Kahler and Kastner (2006). For more recent efforts, see Reardon (2010) and Nincic (2011).

[9] The broader literature focusing largely on sanctions includes, inter alia, Galtung (1967), Doxey (1971), Baldwin (1985), Nossal (1989), Kaempfer and Lowenberg (1992), Kirshner (1995), Haass (1998), Pape (1997), Crawford and Klotz (1999), Haass and O'Sullivan (2000), Chan and Drury (2000), Davis, Jr. (2000), Rowe (2001), Cortright and Lopez (2002), O'Sullivan (2003), Mansfield (2004), Biersteker et al. (2005), and Hufbauer et al. (2007), among many others.

[10] Hufbauer et al. (1990a) found that sanctions were partially effective in 40 out of 115 cases (34 percent) between 1914 and 1990. Pape (1997) found that only five of the cases listed in Hufbauer et al. (1990a) met his own definition of success, which is at odds with studies by Baldwin (1985), Martin (1992a), and Cortright and Lopez (1995). As Elliott (1998) and Baldwin (1998) argued, coding the effects of sanctions dichotomously – as either a success or failure – is a mistake. A focus on causal mechanisms helps transcend findings that imply correlations but are less concerned with the process linking cause and effect.

subject to debate. Our effort here certainly does not end this debate but hopefully helps advance it.

The cases unfolding over the past two decades, in particular, offer the opportunity to explore in greater detail the domestic distributional effects of external instruments, including both intended and unintended ones, on target states and nonproliferation efforts. Academic research on globalization and democratization in the post-1989 world has deepened our understanding of general distributional effects of international influences on the domestic politics of states.[11] Globalization acts as an incentive for some constituencies to support engagement with the global political economy but as a disincentive for others who might be adversely affected by such engagement. This creates different sets of motivations underlying domestic responses to international inducements and threats of punishment. Those who stand to lose from economic openness pressure governments for protection and import-substitution. Those who stand to gain from openness pressure governments for liberalizing trade, investments, and financial exchanges with the rest of the world. Both positions have implications for the kinds of trade-offs that different actors are likely to tolerate with respect to external sanctions or inducements regarding their nuclear policy. International sanctions imposed on account of non-compliance with the nonproliferation regime can deprive domestic actors of goods, services, and international access to markets and technology. Sanctions can also, by contrast, benefit other actors by enhancing their control over the domestic economy. Whether or not positive inducements have the polar opposite effects of sanctions remains contested. There is far more agreement on the fact that democracies tend to be more vulnerable to sanctions than autocracies.

Elucidating how these instruments of external influence work in the nuclear area may benefit the broader study of sanctions and inducements in international relations. The latter encompasses a sizeable literature which has only recently addressed more systematically who the precise targets of such instruments ought to be, and how the issue of *cui bono* and *cui malo* within target states affects outcomes. That broader literature highlights several difficulties that carry over into the more discrete arena of dissuading proliferators from developing nuclear weapons. One such difficulty is the proper identification of the precise objective stipulated by sender states, or the benchmark against which outcomes can or should be evaluated. Objectives can change over time, may have a hierarchical structure, and can be divided into tactical and

---

[11] For an overview of that wave of research, see Solingen (2009a).

strategic components. Several objectives may be pursued at once – some truly and privately, some ostensibly and publicly – leading to elusive estimations of success or failure.[12] The policies of the United States, Japan, China, and South Korea vis-à-vis North Korea, for example, are overtly directed at rolling back the latter's nuclear weapons and sensitive exports program. Yet unstated objectives of either replacing the regime altogether or, at the other extreme, acknowledging its nuclear status, occasionally surface. Senders' ultimate objectives may not even be the target's policy reversal in and of itself but rather to signal to third parties that non-compliance with the NPT or with IAEA safeguards obligations carries a heavy price. If so, the precise benchmark for evaluating the policy's success would be the extent to which additional potential proliferators desist from such designs in light of sanctions endured by other targets.

But the path not traveled by others is not easy to assess and raises an important methodological difficulty that afflicts some of the literature on sanctions more broadly, particularly – but not only – its quantitative branch. The problem of selection effects entail the plausibility that sanctions are only applied in instances where targets estimate (correctly or incorrectly) that sanctions will not work in their own particular case.[13] This would exclude from the analysis the many potential cases where targets estimate that they are too vulnerable to sanctions, and hence refrain from pursuing the proscribed behavior, biasing results. If included, those cases would have been counted as "success." When others discontinue nuclear weapons programs because they estimate a priori that the cost (raised by sanctions) may be too high to bear, this arguably constitutes *ex ante* compliance. Sanctions are not necessary in such cases, but their imposition on others might have had consequential effects that should be factored in.

The nonproliferation literature makes sporadic reference to such demonstration effects but a proper assessment of how other countries weighed the effects of sanctions applied to Iraq, Iran, Libya, or North Korea, among others, is elusive and beyond the scope of this volume. As Rowe (2010) notes, the non-event (no sanction) is often unobservable. Furthermore, evidence for its putative effects is even harder to get (and interpret) than is evidence from cases that had endured sanctions. Indeed, the causes for why some states abandoned nuclear ambitions

---

[12] Baldwin (1985, 1999/2000). Furthermore, it is difficult to differentiate between states that "found it good policy to resist the temptation to mobilize those nuclear resources [and those that] were not tempted" (Schelling 1976: 80).

[13] Drezner (1999), Nooruddin (2002), and Lacy and Niou (2004).

have never been easy to determine, and can rarely be simply traced to the potential threat of sanctions. There is extensive disagreement over what effectively accounted for restraint in cases where the capability was there but nuclear weapons were nonetheless renounced.[14] The problem is aggravated by cases that were over-determined, where many factors influenced the decision to abstain from acquiring nuclear weapons, including potential sanctions, the nature of domestic ruling coalitions and political economy models, public opinion opposed to nuclear weapons, or the preferences of a crucial ally. A final, related source of selection bias is the inability to ascertain the precise universe of cases that should be taken into account.[15]

Summing up the point on selection bias, many targets might want to avoid sanctions to begin with, and they are usually excluded from the relevant universe of cases under analysis in studies of sanctions. The secretive nature of nuclear weapons discussions, decisions, and actual programs exacerbates the barriers to inclusion of all relevant cases.

Domestic distributional effects in target states: understanding causal mechanisms

Many of the difficulties afflicting both the broader study of sanctions and inducements and work focusing primarily on nonproliferation stem from the limited attention paid to the causal mechanisms linking external instruments to outcomes.[16] In his pioneering study Johan Galtung introduced what he considered a "general theory of economic sanctions," in an effort to map what he labeled the "mechanisms of economic boycott."[17] Galtung defined the general theory as a causal process leading from the imposition of a partial or total boycott to

---

[14] See, inter alia, Reiss (1988, 1995), Reiss and Litwak (1994), Dunn (1998), Solingen (1994a, 2007a), and Rublee (2009) for cases that historically abstained from acquiring nuclear weapons (arguably Egypt, Taiwan, South Korea, Japan, Brazil, Argentina, and others), because they were self-deterred by the threatened or hypothetical application of sanctions or because they relied on positive security assurances from the United States to come to the target's defense, or for other domestic reasons. Nuclear weapon states can also offer negative security assurances that they would not attack the target state. For a more detailed analysis of distributional consequences of security assurances, see Solingen and Wolf (2009).

[15] Collier (1995).

[16] Causal mechanisms explain phenomena by opening up the black box and showing the cogs and wheels of the internal machinery, the continuous and contiguous chain of causal or intentional links between *explanans* and *explanandum* (Elster 1989). Causal mechanisms are probabilistic rather than deterministic and they may or may not be observable (Hedström and Ylikoski 2010).

[17] Galtung (1967: 378).

value-deprivation, political disintegration, and eventual compliance. However, all three terms – value-deprivation, political disintegration, and compliance – are hard to operationalize. The thresholds required for each to have their expected causal effects are thus undefined, a problem that continues to plague the analysis of sanctions and inducements. Furthermore, as Baldwin suggests, rather than a single theory there are many different causal mechanisms through which economic sanctions can and have worked, and there are many causal logics that can lead to various theories of economic sanctions.[18] This point is particularly apt for a volume concerned with a wider range of inducements, not just sanctions, which compounds the range of causal mechanisms deserving attention.

Sanctions and inducements affect individuals (leaders, producers, consumers, rent-seekers, and others) who respond to them in ways that shape collective outcomes. *Agent-based* models in the social sciences focus on the incentives of individuals, their estimation of others' incentives (including senders), their responses, and the effects of those responses on others, all of which result in some aggregate outcome. Other models emphasize *institutional* effects on individual choices (the absence of democratic checks and balances, for instance) that, in turn, may or may not lead to compliance with external instruments of statecraft. Yet other models emphasize *structural* constraints and opportunities that can skew outcomes toward or against compliance (availability of substitutes or natural resources, for instance). Agent-based, institutional, and structural models help map the range of causal mechanisms that may be at work in responses to sanctions and inducements. At the same time, differentiating between agent-based, institutional, and structural models is not always straightforward.

A focus on such causal mechanisms demands a departure from what has been an excessive reliance on the assumption that states are coherent actors, an assumption that has handicapped both our understanding of the demand for nuclear weapons and of sanctions more generally.[19] In both cases the unitary actor assumption has precluded a proper appreciation of the complexity entailed in mapping target states' responses to sanctions and inducements. The rather recent relaxation of the unitary actor assumption leads naturally to proper attention to domestic

---

[18] Baldwin (1998: 193). Political disintegration, for instance, may be neither necessary for attaining compliance, as the 2003 Libyan nuclear reversal suggests, nor sufficient. See also Crawford and Klotz (1999).

[19] For exceptions, see Kaempfer and Lowenberg (1988, 1992, 1999), Morgan and Schwebach (1996), Kirshner (1997), Baldwin (1998), and Rowe (2001).

distributional effects of inducements, or to their differential impact on different internal constituencies.

There are many ways to slice the domestic landscape influencing nuclear decisions. The underlying foundation for exploring *cui bono* and *cui malo* from external influence attempts builds on the basic premise that (1) political leaders and regimes build supportive coalitions to gain and survive in power; (2) for that purpose, leaders craft favored models of political survival across constituencies with preferences bearing on political economy and national security matters; (3) given their favored model, leaders and regimes vary in their tolerance for the relative political and economic (including opportunity) costs that their nuclear policies might entail. Beyond these basic building blocs, the relative domestic receptivity to external sanctions and inducements is conditioned by four specific attributes of the domestic political landscape that provide the context against which different causal mechanisms operate.

Models of political survival

The first relates to prevalent models of political survival in power. At the heart of those models is a particular definition of what a state's relation to the global economy should be. Among those countries entertaining the possibility of nuclear weapons since the 1960s, leaders who rejected the global economy as a driver of industrialization have been more prone to develop such weapons than those advocating economic growth through global integration.[20] Inward-looking leaders emphasizing economic nationalism – sometimes dressed in rigid religious or ethnic identities – have cast ambiguous nuclear programs as tools of modernization and symbols of defiance against perceived dominant global political and economic orders. From Perón in Argentina to Nasser in Egypt, Saddam Hussein in Iraq, Kim Il-sung and Kim Jong-il in North Korea, Muammar Qaddafi in Libya, and Ahmadinejad and other radical strongholds including the Revolutionary Guards (Pāsdārān, or IRGC henceforth) in Iran, nuclear policies have been nested in broader economic nationalism and critiques of the global political economy and associated international regimes. Leaders advancing inward-looking models shielded favored constituencies including internationally uncompetitive and protected industries, military-industrial enterprises, state bureaucracies, the underemployed intelligentsia, and segments of the

---

[20] For the general argument, elaborations, and limiting cases, see Solingen (2007a, 2009b), Potter and Mukhatzhanova (2008, 2010a, 2010b), and Ford *et al.* (2009).

scientific community highly dependent on state subsidies and military procurement. Nuclear weapons' programs provided ideal technological allies of such models because they enabled vast scientific, technological, industrial, and bureaucratic complexes which are often beyond formal budgetary oversight. These complexes are portrayed to domestic publics as putatively leading to actual or imaginary outputs – "self-reliant program," "independent program," "parallel program," or simply "the bomb," depending on the degree of secrecy about its ultimate objectives – that play out as powerful sources of myths germane to inward-looking models of political survival.

By contrast, leaders relying on economic growth through internationalization and global integration have largely shied away from nuclear weapons. Such leaders require political and economic stability to reduce uncertainty and maximize access to foreign markets, resources, capital, investments, aid, and technology. Such access, in turn, requires expanding private economic activities, contracting military expenditures, progressively reducing barriers to trade, and abiding by international institutions that validate and promote those economic choices. Leaders advancing internationalization, together with their political allies and beneficiaries, have thus been more receptive to economic restructuring and more attentive to macroeconomic and political stability that attract, or at least enable, foreign investment. Internationalizing leaders perceived little benefit from a policy of nuclear assertion or ambiguity, both for domestic and international reasons, and have been more amenable to relinquishing nuclear programs that might have placed barriers to international economic access and political support. Large-scale, ambiguous, and unbounded nuclear programs were thus devalued for their potential to sap the domestic economy, strengthen domestic opponents of global integration, place valuable external resources in jeopardy, build international reputations detrimental to their preferred objectives, and contribute to unwanted regional tensions and instability. Yoshida Shigeru's "merchant nation" in Japan, Park Chung Hee's "economic miracle" in South Korea, and various Taiwanese leaders, all emphasized economic growth via exports and global integration, as did others in Argentina, Brazil, and Egypt, among others, once they chose to abide by the nonproliferation regime and abandon nuclear ambiguity or weapons aspirations. Their favored political economy models made them far more receptive to sanctions and positive inducements geared to dissuade them from developing nuclear weapons programs. Indeed, sanctions were not even threatened in some cases although would-be targets might have implicitly considered them in their decision-making. Internationalizing models of political survival thus acted as self-deterrents, foiling potential temptations to embark on nuclear weapons programs.

These two models of political survival (inward-looking, internationalizing) are only ideal types, whereas real types can be far more eclectic or hybrid. Furthermore, these models entail only proclivities or probabilistic tendencies rather than law-like generalizations. Yet an overview of all cases of nuclear aspirants since 1968, when the Non-Proliferation Treaty (NPT) was concluded, validates the association between approaches to the global economy and nuclear policies. Of all nuclear aspirants in the past four decades, not one endorsed denuclearization – fully and effectively – under domestic regimes that shunned integration in the global economy. Only leaders/ruling coalitions advancing their own political survival through global integration undertook effective commitments to denuclearize (Japan, Egypt under Sadat, South Africa, Taiwan, South Korea, Brazil, and Argentina, among others). Nuclear decisions were nested in a broader shift toward internationalization in economics and security. Where internationalizing leaders and coalitions became stronger politically, the departure from nuclear claims was maintained even as their security context deteriorated (as in the Korean peninsula and the Taiwan Straits, at various points). Where leaders and coalitions favoring internationalization were weaker, as in Argentina and Brazil until the early 1990s, the more politically constrained they were in curbing nuclear programs. This has been particularly the case in Iran, where a coalition of *mullahs, bonyads* (protected state "foundations"), and the IRGC, among others, advanced a nuclear program in violation of NPT commitments, IAEA obligations, and United Nations Security Council (UNSC) resolutions, while blocking – often through heavy repression – a counter-coalition advancing Iran's reintegration in the global economy. Tensions in North Korea between dominant *juche*-oriented *ancien régime* forces on the one hand, and much weaker would-be reformers on the other, are harder to discern in a closed and rigid authoritarian hierarchy but have implications for nuclear preferences nonetheless.[21]

None of this suggests that either North Korea or Iran is necessarily ripe for a regime overhaul in an internationalizing direction. Only that those internal divisions are a variable worth considering in the design of sanctions and positive inducements. A recently-published two-volume study by Potter and Mukhatzhanova finds the argument that competing models of political survival indeed shaped positions

---

[21] For an early stipulation of links between economic reform and nuclear preferences in North Korea, see Solingen (1994a, 2007a).

on nuclear weapons particularly convincing for Egypt, Saudi Arabia, Turkey, South Korea, Japan, and to a large extent for Iran, South Africa, Taiwan, and Ukraine.[22] A political economy focus on outward versus inward oriented models or ruling coalitions, they argue, is helpful in accounting for much of the variation in nuclear restraint across states and within states over time. Furthermore, they find that the evidence from in-depth case studies offers more support for this mode of analysis than is explicitly suggested in some cases. A proper analysis of internal politics is not always easy to conduct, particularly but not only in autocratic contexts, a point that leads naturally into the next category.

Regime type

A second factor influencing receptivity to sanctions and positive inducements is the nature of domestic institutions, or the type of regime within which competing models of political survival vie for power. As several chapters argue, there is some agreement over the fact that democracies tend to be more vulnerable to sanctions than autocracies. Democracies have also been less subjected to sanctions across all issue areas.[23] These differences across regime type may be due to the fact that democratic and autocratic leaders are assumed to vary in their relative exposure or vulnerability to domestic challenges. Democratic leaders arguably require broader supportive coalitions to gain and maintain power than autocratic leaders. The broader the supportive coalition leaders require for surviving in power, the more pressed they are to provide public goods to those constituencies. According to this same logic, autocratic leaders require much smaller supportive coalitions that they can reward with private benefits rather than public goods. Assuming these different incentives to provide private versus public goods, democratic and autocratic leaders would be expected to react differently to external instruments of influence. Democratic leaders arguably weigh inducements according to their impact on the pool of resources available for the provision of public goods among broad constituencies. Autocratic leaders arguably weigh inducements according to their impact on the pool of resources available for the provision of private benefits among their relatively smaller coterie of political allies.

---

[22] Potter and Mukhatzhanova (2010a, 2010b: 343).

[23] Bueno de Mesquita *et al.* (2003). Allen (2008b) argues that democracies are more susceptible to sanctions whereas the responses of mixed and authoritarian systems are more difficult to predict. Over 78 percent of sanctions in the past three decades were imposed on authoritarian target states. For the argument that regime *intentions*, not regime type, are more accurate indicators of proliferation patterns, see Litwak (2007).

There are numerous studies of incentives and disincentives to acquire nuclear weapons but no dedicated, inclusive, and systematic cross-regional comparison of regime-type differences in receptivity to external influence attempts in the area of nonproliferation.[24] Some focused studies on Argentina and Brazil address the role of democracy in the shift toward NPT membership and nuclear transparency.[25] However, Argentina and Brazil were not subjected to the kinds of sanctions applied to some other nuclear aspirants precisely because, as non-NPT members until the 1990s, they were technically not under the same legal international obligations as were NPT members. Furthermore, the joint renewal of democracy in the 1980s in Argentina and Brazil overlapped with periods of ambiguous nuclear programs until the early 1990s. Democratic presidents Raúl Alfonsín and José Sarney made joint declarations of peaceful intentions and exchanged visits to sensitive facilities but did not join the NPT, ratify the regional nuclear-weapons-free-zone Treaty of Tlatelolco, or abandon rights to peaceful nuclear explosions and development of delivery systems. The words "inspection," "control," and "safeguards" were absent from documents signed by 1980s democratic administrations, and unsafeguarded facilities with military potential remained in place.[26] Explicit denuclearization and NPT membership came about only with the inception of internationalizing models in both countries in the early 1990s; and they had far more to do with domestic incentives to engage fully in the global economy and its political institutions than with external pressures per se.[27]

Other studies addressed the case of South Africa, a unique one in the sense that it had already produced several nuclear weapons by the time leaders opted to destroy them and join the NPT. South Africa was no democracy and, as Liberman suggests, changing preferences within the ruling coalition toward internationalization in the 1980s, compatible with their efforts to end strong sanctions against apartheid, eroded whatever value preceding inward-looking hyper-nationalist leaders had assigned to nuclear weapons.[28] Surrendering nuclear weapons, joining the NPT, and restoring a badly damaged reputation enabled the new leadership to advance South Africa's integration in the global economy. Kazakhstan, Belarus, and Ukraine are a very different case insofar as they inherited nuclear weapons from the former Soviet Union. Yet they

---

[24] Solingen (2007a) suggests that democracies may be less prone to acquire nuclear weapons amidst disputes with fellow democracies but questions other propositions regarding the relationship between regime type and nuclear behavior.

[25] Goldemberg and Feiveson (1994), Sotomayor (2000).

[26] Redick *et al.* (1994).   [27] Solingen (2011a).

[28] Liberman (2001), Harris *et al.* (2004).

opted to return them to Russia in accordance with their ruling coalitions' incentives to deepen integration in the global political economy or abide by Russian preferences, rather than in response to a democratic process.

India and Pakistan were never NPT members. Their 1998 nuclear tests attracted international sanctions that dissipated rather quickly, and indeed were followed by agreements with various nuclear suppliers in the nuclear energy field. Under stable democratic rule India, as Israel, deflected any influence attempts to abandon its nuclear weapons program.[29] The cases of India and Israel also support the hypothesis that democracies surrounded by non-democracies may have a lower disposition to abandon nuclear weapons than democracies surrounded by fellow democracies.[30] This, in turn, may arguably explain higher international tolerance for nuclearizing democracies than for autocracies. Pakistan, intermittently under democratic and autocratic rule and subject to far greater control by its military establishment than India or Israel, has never been receptive to sanctions or positive inducements either. Finally, multilateral sanctions following the Lockerbie terrorist attack eroded Qaddafi's ability to maintain political control, pushing him into a new model of political survival – requiring him to open Libya up to the global economy – and a decision to abandon nuclear weapons. Alas, democratization was clearly not part of that conversion.

The predominance of autocracies among NPT members which violated nonproliferation commitments is evident throughout the different chapters in this volume. But while both Iran and North Korea are autocratic, they also differ in the nature and degree of political closure and the size of the selectorate (those who have a say in the selection of leaders). North Korea remains highly centralized yet interest groups – the military, the party, the cabinet, the security apparatus, technocrats, and managers of export-processing zones – are estimated to play a far more important role today than has been hitherto understood.[31] The distributional implications of sanctions and positive inducements across these and other relevant actors have received very little attention, largely as a result of the dearth of information trickling out of that country.[32] But deep internal cleavages within a far more pluralistic Iran

---

[29] Israel is said to have developed nuclear weapons even prior to the NPT, although it never tested or acknowledged such capabilities.
[30] Solingen (2007a).
[31] See North Korea chapter in Solingen (2007a) and McEachern (2008).
[32] Haggard and Noland (2007).

have been underestimated as well, until rather recently.[33] The June 2009 elections led to reassessments of the nature and depth of those fissures and of the extent to which sanctions and increased international isolation may have played some role in deepening them.[34] The repression of the opposition by radical elements of Iran's regime has also triggered significant reconsideration of the role of positive inducements, including engagement.[35] Regime transformation in Iran or North Korea may not necessarily be imminent; sanctions and positive inducements could have different effects contingent on the evolving size, nature, and special interests of the selectorate in each case, and on the domestic costs of repression for different regimes.

Regime type may influence the effectiveness of external instruments through varying audience costs. Leaders incur audience costs − such as removal from office or no-confidence votes − when they renege on their own public commitments.[36] Such commitments may be expressed in the form of promises to grant (or deny) international access to their nuclear facilities, to accept (or reject) a certain external proposal, or to protect the country with a nuclear deterrent. Because domestic audiences operating in democracies can organize politically to overcome collective action problems and are endowed with the legal authority to remove leaders from office, democratic leaders are expected to be more vulnerable to audience costs than non-democratic leaders.[37] This assumption suggests that the costs of reneging on commitments might be particularly high for democratic leaders. Yet, as Weeks (2008) suggests, those costs may also be high for authoritarian ones, a possibility examined by various chapters in this volume.

---

[33] A November 2008 letter by sixty Iranian economists urged a change in the "tension-creating" foreign policy of Ahmadinejad that, in their view, prevented foreign investment and damaged the Iranian economy heavily (Borzou Daragahi, "Economists in Iran Criticize Ahmadinejad," *Los Angeles Times*, November 10, 2008, A3). Some of the signatories were subsequently imprisoned, following the 2009 protests.

[34] Nader (2009). According to Shahram Chubin, the political unrest since June 2009 increases the number of Iranians likely to blame the regime for imposed sanctions (quoted in "Iran Still Welcome to Accept Uranium Proposal, U.S. Says," *Global Security Newswire*, January 5, 2010).

[35] Iran expert Karim Sadjadpour (Sadjadpour *et al.* 2009), a strong erstwhile supporter of engagement, expressed that "For the first time, I no longer advocate engagement, at least in the immediate term … for the first time … the costs of engagement outweigh the benefits." Engagement would "be demoralizing for the millions of Iranians who took to the street … and sends the wrong message to the regime – that you can act with impunity … Unfortunately … the Obama administration has already made a decision to go ahead with it."

[36] Fearon (1994a).   [37] Schultz (2005).

Finally, Kahler and Kastner (2006) find conditional engagement strategies (positive inducements requiring quid pro quo) to be less likely to succeed when "senders" or initiating states are democracies, particularly when their private sectors have strong incentives to trade or invest in target states. Unconditional strategies aimed at transforming the context of target states are hypothesized to be less successful when leaders in the target state can place limits on economic exchange without paying a high political price, as in North Korea. We return to these features of inducements in the concluding chapter.

Timing and temporal sequences

A third factor influencing relative receptivity to external influence attempts relates to timing and temporal sequences. One dimension here is the extent to which different stages in the development of a nuclear program are more amenable to different types of sanctions and inducements, as expected from principles of prospect theory. Leaders may be hypothesized to accept higher risks in order to retain existing nuclear weapons than to retain programs leading to a future *potential* acquisition. Leaders (and publics) presumably value more what they already have ("endowment effect") than what they might get. They are more averse to losing what they already possess than to forgo potential future gains.[38] Another dimension of temporal sequences relates to the possibility that disincentives stemming from internationalizing models of political survival may be stronger at deliberative or incipient stages of nuclear weapons consideration than they would be once such weapons have been acquired. In other words, the incentives of a globally integrated political economy may operate more forcefully where nuclear programs have not yet yielded nuclear weapons, as suggested by the cases of Argentina, Brazil, South Korea, or Taiwan. Those incentives may have lesser impact once nuclear thresholds – often in the form of nuclear tests – have been crossed, as with North Korea, which acquired nuclear weapons prior to adopting a China-style model of political survival through export-led economic growth. As of 2011, such a shift has yet to happen in North Korea.

Prospect theory, temporal sequences, timing, and audience cost considerations may suggest that backing down from (even implicit) commitments to acquire full nuclear capabilities may be easier for an autocratic leadership that has not yet achieved weaponization, as

---

[38] McDermott (1998), Mercer (2005), Levy (2000), and Solingen (2010).

is presumably the case with Iran as of mid 2011. Audience costs, in other words, might be lower for leaders that must back down from a program before it comes to "fruition" than when they must backtrack on an already realized nuclear weapons capability. These conditions might also be affected by whether or not leaders can build on strong enough internationalizing constituencies or, conversely, are highly constrained by inward-looking ones vested on the program's complete execution and continuity. Libya may reflect a case where a program (rather than actual weapons) was relinquished with considerable support from influential figures within the regime advocating Libya's economic internationalization.[39] Timing and prospect theory considerations may also affect the extent to which regime *opponents* in some of these cases can endorse specific instruments, including sanctions. Iranian opposition leaders have, for the most part, either opposed sanctions or refrained from supporting them publicly, given the potential political costs of alienating segments of the public. Following the June 2009 disputed elections and subsequent repression, however, indirect and unacknowledged support for such measures is said to have grown.[40]

Targeted versus comprehensive instruments

The fourth major influence on domestic receptivity lies in the nature of external instruments – targeted versus comprehensive ones – and the conditions under which one might be more effective than the other. Comprehensive measures target both the macro-economy and macro-politics of states, so that punishments and benefits are extended over wide segments of the population.[41] Targeted measures are directed at leaders, their core allies in the regime's hierarchy, and/or specific enterprises and agencies engaged in the proscribed behavior. Targeted sanctions seek to minimize unintended, undesirable, or indiscriminate consequences for the broader public.[42] Both sanctions and positive

---

[39] Jentleson and Whytock (2005/2006) and Solingen (2007a, Libya chapter).

[40] Nazenin Ansari and Jonathan Paris, "The Message From the Streets of Tehran," *New York Times*, November 6, 2009; Testimony by Karim Sadjadpour and Abbas Milani, House Committee on Foreign Affairs, Iran: Recent Developments and Implications for US Policy, Serial No. 111–131, July 22, 2009. According to Maloney (2009: 3), "the public's identification of Ahmadinejad with their own personal financial constraints suggests that any intensified economic pressure that results from a stepped-up sanctions regime could create unsustainable domestic political costs for the current leadership ... the diplomatic climate for applying new pressure is unusually ripe."

[41] Brooks (2002).

[42] Cortright and Lopez (2002).

inducements can be comprehensive or targeted, leading to a four-fold typology: targeted sanctions (sometimes labeled "smart sanctions"), targeted positive inducements ("concentrated carrots"), comprehensive sanctions ("classical sanctions"), and comprehensive positive inducements ("diffuse or generalized carrots").

Different chapters examine the relative effectiveness of these categories under different conditions and whether or not comprehensive measures are more effective than targeted ones under different coalitional contexts or regime types. Cortright and Lopez (2002) and Elliott (2002) found comprehensive sanctions in various issue areas to have yielded more effective political results than targeted ones in the 1990s. Financial instruments of influence ranging from targeted to more comprehensive ones have gained greater attention in the last decade. Whereas some, including Nader and Drezner, argue that sanctions have helped concentrate control of the economy in the hands of Iran's IRGC, others suggest that this concentration also makes the Guards a more precise target of additional sanctions.[43] Conversely, the offer of comprehensive benefits to the Iranian public, largely extended by the EU-3, may have been rejected by the regime's more hardline factions precisely because such generalized benefits would undermine their own power.

Mapping causal mechanisms

As is clear from the discussion thus far, these four general factors influencing relative receptivity to external instruments often interact. Together they help map an array of causal logics and mechanisms that explain different and highly contingent pathways connecting the threat/offer of sanctions/inducements with compliant or non-compliant outcomes. For instance, Drezner views smart or targeted sanctions (financial sanctions, asset freezes, travel bans, restrictions on luxury goods, and arms embargoes) as rooted in a rather simple causal mechanism: senders deprive elite supporters of the targeted regime (individuals, agencies, or companies) from benefits, which → induces those entities to pressure the regime, → pushing the latter into concessions. This mechanism is designed to impose minimal hardship on the mass public and to minimize rally-round-the-flag effects. Though parsimonious and elegant, Drezner finds this logic "brittle" because it relies only on the stated causal mechanism, thus providing very limited policy leverage.[44] By contrast, he finds comprehensive economic sanctions – or

---

[43] Shahram Chubin, as quoted in "Iran still Welcome ...," 2010.
[44] On causal mechanisms (reputational, functional) in financial sanctions, see Feaver and Lorber (2010).

more wide-ranging inducements – to be more likely to lead to the desired policy change. Relying on "analytical eclecticism,"[45] he proposes that unleashing a wide range of causal mechanisms – including comprehensive sanctions – is more likely to yield the desired policy change in the target state. In this view, and that of Palkki's and Smith's in this volume, causal pathways of comprehensive sanctions are multiple and potentially interactive, which can lead to → general domestic instability, loss of strategic standing, fears of attack, mass unrest, and elite dissatisfaction, all of which in turn may → spur reform or regime change. Notice the dependent variable in this latter formulation shifts to regime change, an objective that differs from a change in policy.

Other chapters provide a different understanding of targeted sanctions that is harder to reduce to a single causal mechanism. Targeted sanctions can unleash second-order effects that multiply, complicate, and implicate a wider range of causal mechanisms than implied in the baseline formulation described above. Nader, for instance, suggests that targeted sanctions aimed at specific members and agencies of Iran's IRGC lead to → exacerbated internal divisions among reformist, pragmatic, and principlist members of the IRGC, which in turn → strengthen the hand of "more pragmatic and profit-minded" Guards vis-à-vis their "more ideologically committed rivals," → which makes Iran more sensitive to the effects of strengthened sanctions.[46] However, Nader does not see this mechanism as ending with a change in "the regime's thinking on the nuclear program" as the dependent variable. This causal sequence, hence, stops short of either change in policy or regime, joining Nader with Drezner in their skepticism about the policy leverage of targeted sanctions. Stein argues that in a general way even the most comprehensive type of sanctions has differential impact, and that even the most targeted sanctions generate collateral damage. Palkki and Smith make this point even starker, arguing that multilateral sanctions on Libya have often been characterized as "targeted" rather than "comprehensive" but when the targeted industry represents 95 percent of a country's economy (oil in this case) it is far more difficult to distinguish between the two.

Kreps and Pasha draw attention to a different causal mechanism triggered by negative inducements of a military kind. Their chapter explores the extent to which different domestic ruling coalitions – with different orientations to the global political economy – may respond

[45] Katzenstein and Sil (2010).
[46] Nader (Chapter 7, this volume) includes prominent former Guards such as Rezai, Qalibaf, and Larijani in the first group and Jafari, Hejazi, and Taeb in the second.

differently to the same external threats. In particular, they test the hypothesis that external military threats lead to → a strengthening of inward-looking coalitions wary of integration into the global economy, which → deepens their ability to strengthen monopolies, protectionism, import substitution, and the military-industrial complex, including the nuclear program. Conversely, they assume, credible military threats tend to → undermine the target's international environment and ability to attract foreign investment, conditions which → undercut internationalizing coalitions seeking to integrate with the global economy, thus → weakening domestic proponents of a more conciliatory nuclear policy.

Drezner identifies another causal mechanism that emerges from the literature on targeted sanctions and is specifically tailored to the target's regime type.[47] Autocratic leaders, he argues, have incentives to create private and excludable goods for their supporters (as opposed to public goods for the broader citizenry), which leads them to channel comprehensive sanctions into rent-seeking opportunities for their supporters, resulting in → a stronger grip on power by the autocrat, and → continued non-compliance. Nincic's basic causal mechanism, also in the context of autocratic states, assumes that positive external inducements offered to an insecure regime in the target state → enable the regime to coalesce support from additional constituencies, which, in turn → help catalyze a less confrontational policy. Haggard and Noland, by contrast, find the combination of authoritarian rule and the particular coalitional base of North Korea's regime to have made it relatively indifferent to various economic inducements. Positive inducements, in their view → provide the regime with resources for concentrating its power even further → thus foiling economic and political reform, which → pushes the regime to further dig its heels and avoid compliance with denuclearizing commitments, leading to → demands for additional positive inducements (hence the cycle of moral hazard).

Reynolds and Wan illustrate another causal mechanism operating in autocracies fueled by the unintended (negative) effects of positive inducements, which ended up strengthening Saddam Hussein's regime. The oil-for-food program, they argue, aimed at alleviating the conditions of Iraq's population but instead → enabled oil smuggling and illicit commissions (aided by UN corruption and mismanagement), which in turn → funneled money to Saddam and his loyalists

---

[47] See, inter alia, Wintrobe (1990), Bueno de Mesquita *et al.* (1999, 2003), Brooks (2002), Lektzian and Souva (2007), and Allen (2005, 2008a, 2008b).

who → diverted it to maintain the regime's patronage among military and civilian allies, and → enabled the regime to further entice foreign companies and states to re-establish trade relations.[48] Palkki and Smith point to two-pronged mechanisms – both in the same general direction – one where sanctions led to → increasing gaps between economic reformers and supporters of Qaddafi's original inward-looking model, which → reduced Qaddafi's ability to manage elements of his ruling coalition, thus → increasing his concern with regime cohesiveness, leading to → verifiable compliance. They also point to another mechanism whereby sanctions → eroded Qaddafi's ability to deliver on his revolutionary promises to the masses, which → raised issues of legitimacy, morale, legacies, and fears of a stronger opposition, including a radical Islamist or military coup, thus → making economic reform and an inflow of resources for compensating discontents imperative, and → pushing Qaddafi toward compliance.

Palkki and Smith also observe two different causal mechanisms leading in opposite directions. On the one hand, the standard argument suggests that sanctions enabled Saddam and his allies to monopolize smuggling routes and rationing, which were useful for → manipulating the supply of scarce commodities, which could then → be funneled to regime loyalists, thus → intensifying their dependence on Saddam and decimating Iraq's middle-class opposition → all of which strengthened Saddam's hold on power → enabling him to defy external demands. On the other hand, newly available documents also suggest that sanctions exacerbated social inequalities and class tensions, which → undermined Iraqi morale and further delegitimized the regime → heightening the possibility of popular uprising → intensifying rifts within the ruling coalition, which → raised Saddam's concern with regime survival, leading him to → partially relent on international inspections.

The concluding chapter returns to further elaborate and refine these and other causal mechanisms. It should be noted that similar mechanisms can produce different outcomes under different circumstances. For instance, some believe that the 2010 wave of sanctions would lead Iran's regime to reduce food and fuel subsidies; the latter, in turn, could lead to public alienation; which in turn would compel the regime to devise means to maintain control over a disaffected public.[49] Under conditions of high oil prices, more available resources could lower the

[48] See also Palkki and Smith (Chapter 9, this volume) and Solingen (2007a).
[49] Goldberg (2010). See also Zweiri (2010), who expects that the new round of sanctions will lead to internal upheaval and change.

need for the deepening of repression, foiling some of the expected effects of sanctions. Conversely, the fewer the compensatory resources, the greater the tendency will be to resort to repression and coercion. These different circumstances, in turn, could end up weakening the opposition further or, on the contrary, emboldening it and forcing a change in policy.

Overview of chapter contents

This chapter has introduced the common analytical focus underlying this volume. Different chapters elaborate those foundations further in different directions, some more theoretical, others through descriptive quantitative probes and yet others through empirical examinations of cases, either in isolation or in comparative perspective. Why do sanctions and positive inducements require the construction of market power; how difficult is it to achieve it; and what role do distributional considerations play in the process of constructing market power? How has the incidence of sanctions and positive inducements varied over the last two decades and across the cases of Iraq, Iran, Libya, and North Korea? How have the different authoritarian institutional contexts across those four influenced the effectiveness of sanctions and positive inducements? How have trade, aid, investments, asset seizure, or different financial measures affected different constituencies in target states, and to what effect? Have targeted sanctions worked to weaken the North Korean leadership in some instances but not others, and if so why? Can sanctions or positive inducements deepen cleavages across *bonyads*, IRGC, and *bazaari* groups? How do military threats influence domestic cleavages between inward-looking and internationalizing coalitions? When are targeted and comprehensive sanctions or positive inducements more likely to succeed? These are only some of the questions raised by different chapters.

Part I provides an overview of the literature on sanctions and positive inducements and of empirical trends observed for the most recent cases where they have been extensively applied in the area of nuclear proliferation: Iraq, Iran, Libya, and North Korea. These four had failed to meet their reporting obligations under their safeguards agreements with the IAEA or otherwise violated their NPT international commitments, thus becoming the targets of various instruments of statecraft designed to bring them into compliance.

Stein provides a theoretical foundation for understanding sanctions and positive inducements rooted in the idea that both forms constitute attempts by senders to wield market power. The chapter lays bare the anatomy of coercive economic diplomacy as a strategic interaction game between the two sides (sender and targets). Each side attempts to wield market power and gain the power of monopoly or monopsony while dividing the opponent (so as not to face concentrated market power by its opponent) and using market power to extract a political price for an economic exchange. Democratic sanctioners adopt sanctions when and where they hurt them the least, leading to the kinds of sanctions that are "designed to fail." The chapter also advances that even comprehensive sanctions have differentiated consequences, compelling attention to those distributional considerations. For sanctions to be both politically and economically successful they must undermine the foundations of state power in target states, imposing costs on the elite and its supporting coalition while strengthening opposition forces. Yet the unintended effect is that sanctions often enhance the degree of state control over the economy; and the stronger the state (i.e., the less it is penetrated by and subservient to societal forces), the more it is capable of resisting sanctions.

Reynolds and Wan provide a thorough empirical comparative analysis of unilateral and multilateral sanctions and positive inducements imposed on, or offered to, Iraq, Iran, Libya, and North Korea over the last two decades. In addition to cumulative data for all four cases, they disaggregate the data on both sanctions and positive inducements for each one of the four targets. Their detailed chronology enables fruitful comparisons across time, within and across cases. It also leads them to advance that not only was the use of sanctions quite extensive in all cases but that, counter to some conventional wisdom, there has also been a high incidence of positive inducements. These have come from different sources (the United States, the UN, China, Russia, European and other powers) and spanned several categories, from trade and diplomatic offers to technological cooperation and security guarantees. Diplomatic pressures were the most common negative inducement while comprehensive trade and financial measures were the least common ones. The United States relied more on trade and financial actions than all others, as might be expected from the sheer economic presence of the United States in the global political economy, at least until recently. The United States was also the primary sender of positive inducements. Financial measures assumed greater prominence in the last five years or so.

Part II dissects a spectrum of inducements ranging from the putative utility of positive inducements to a skeptical assessment of targeted sanctions and a differentiated impact of military threats for different kinds of ruling coalitions in target states. Nincic argues that sanctions have proven futile and counterproductive, proposing instead that positive inducements that address the interests of supporters courted by the regime are more likely to be effective. Further, they are likely to be especially effective when their support is most needed by a regime whose domestic position is insecure. His framework has some crucial scope conditions that must be met for the regime to be receptive to the kind of positive inducements that could buttress its fragile rule. First, the society and economy should be differentiated enough, so that groups with interests that differ from those of the regime are significantly large. A domestic political economy sealed from the international one cannot provide sufficient space for the emergence of independent economic actors. Second, international inducements must directly benefit those independent groups that could, in turn, shore up the regime's domestic position. Third, the regime must value the support of these new groups more than it values the policies it is asked to abandon.

Drezner's chapter is, in some ways, the mirror image of Nincic's, focusing almost entirely on the effectiveness of sanctions. Targeted or smart sanctions, which have gained much attention in the last decade and a half, are considered the precision-guided munitions of economic statecraft, designed to hurt elite supporters of the targeted regime while imposing minimal hardship on the mass public. The chapter notes that although the application of smart sanctions requires a more fine-grained analysis of domestic distributional consequences, most of the literature on smart sanctions has not provided coherent analytical tools to map those consequences. Further, Drezner argues, the promise of smart sanctions has fallen short. Only more comprehensive economic sanctions – or more wide-ranging positive inducements – are likely to lead to desired policy changes. This is the case, in his view, because comprehensive sanctions can work through multiple causal mechanisms that are not mutually exclusive.

Further along in the direction of sanctions is the threat of use of force, the focus of Kreps and Pasha's chapter. "The power to hurt is bargaining power. To exploit it is diplomacy – vicious diplomacy, but diplomacy," argued Schelling.[50] Whereas previous studies of coercive diplomacy effectively "black boxed" the target state, Kreps and Pasha assume that the domestic political-economic environment conditions the incentive structures and likelihood that the target state will respond to the political objectives – in this case denuclearization – of the sender state. Theirs is an original effort designed to probe quantitatively the effect of external military threats on the balance of power between competing

[50] Schelling (1966: 2).

domestic coalitions described earlier in this chapter. Their core assumption is that threats issued under the shadow of costly consequences would tend to reinforce inward-looking coalitions, who can wield the nuclear program as guarding against external threats. Conversely, credible military threats are hypothesized to undermine internationalizing coalitions seeking to integrate with the global economy, thus weakening the prospects of denuclearization. The hypotheses are put to work in a pilot test of the effects of US military threats on Iran.

Part III offers an in-depth examination of how sanctions and positive inducements have operated in the specific cases of Iraq and Libya on the one hand, and Iran and North Korea on the other, the latter constituting the two most prominent outstanding cases, which continue to be courted with positive inducements and punished with sanctions. Alireza Nader examines distributional consequences of targeted and comprehensive sanctions in the case of Iran. Although sanctions there appear to have contributed to the deterioration of Iran's economy, Nader argues that it remains unclear whether or not they have also weakened the regime's resolve to pursue what many, including the IAEA, consider to be an ambiguous nuclear program at best or one oriented toward nuclear weapons at worst. This program remains an important pillar for the survival and legitimacy of Iran's ruling coalition, yet competing factions within the regime differ on nuclear policy against a background of particularistic political ambitions and economic interests. The chapter maps Iran's factional terrain historically and in the aftermath of the 2009 elections, and draws implications for relative receptivity to external influence attempts.

Stephan Haggard and Marcus Noland examine the extent to which sanctions and positive inducements through the Six-Party Talks have elicited cooperative or uncooperative escalatory responses. They find that while the pressure tactics of the Bush administration clearly had adverse effects, the subsequent shift toward a more conciliatory stance produced only glacial movement along a denuclearization agenda. The authors note that growing integration with China and other developing countries, particularly in the Middle East, and a sharp retreat from economic reform – compounded by regime succession issues – have made it more difficult to influence the course of the regime using either sort of tool.

Palkki and Smith provide a comparison between Iraq and Libya relying on important evidence from newly available documents of meetings and phone conversations recording Saddam Hussein as a participant. They focus on *how*, as opposed to merely whether or to what extent, external influence attempts led to Iraqi and Libyan nuclear reversal decisions through their domestic distributional effects. Similar external inducements involving economic sanctions and other factors persuaded Libya and Iraq to end their nuclear weapon programs. However, the weapon programs, paths, and reversal outcomes were far from identical: Libya disarmed unambiguously whereas Iraq's reversal was more equivocal. Palkki and Smith elaborate the different mechanisms through which sanctions and positive inducements worked in each context but warn about the complexity and non-linearity surrounding the inducements-denuclearization connection given strategic interactions among a diverse set of actors within both sender and target states.

Finally, Part IV offers a detailed elaboration of findings, outstanding questions for further research, and a distillation of policy implications through a focused examination of ten dilemmas in nonproliferation statecraft. Those dilemmas are, to a large extent, applicable to a broader range of objectives than persuading states to abide by their nuclear nonproliferation commitments.

2 Sanctions, inducements, and market power: political economy of international influence

Arthur A. Stein

Introduction

In the international system, states have preferences over the policies other states pursue. Sometimes those preferences are about their foreign and security policies, as when the United States opposed Japanese expansion in the Western Pacific in the 1930s, when it opposed Soviet intervention in Afghanistan in 1979, and currently as the United States opposes Iran's pursuit of a nuclear weapons capability. Sometimes those preferences are about the internal policies of other countries, as when the United States and other countries opposed the internal South African policy of apartheid and as they currently object to Sudan's policy in Darfur.

Governments have an array of policy instruments with which to influence, that is change, the policies of others. Most basically they can threaten adverse consequences or they can promise benefits. They can actually punish or reward. Scholars thus talk of both positive and negative inducements, and positive and negative sanctions.

Moreover, they can use an array of influence steps, from rhetorical to material, from political to economic to military. Searching for measures that fall short of using military force but that go beyond mere diplomacy, they adopt economic measures to induce policy change by others. These measures have material consequences and are thus more than the verbal expression of disapproval. But they simultaneously are less costly than using military power.

Economic sanctions and inducements have long been recognized as such halfway instruments of national power – between war and peace (Davis and Engerman 2003), between war and commerce (Lenway 1988), between words and wars (Wallensteen and Staibano 2005).[1]

---

[1] Sanctions can be differentiated on the basis of objectives. Førland (1991) argues that although sanctions and economic warfare pursue the same means, the former aims at a policy change whereas the latter is intended to weaken an adversary. Yet, distinguishing sanctions by type of objective is problematic (Baldwin 2003).

They are one of an array of policies with which to coerce or induce or influence other countries.[2] They are expressive and thus constitute a signal, both of what has been done and of what may still lie ahead, and since they have material consequences and thus function as costly signals, as threats and punishments, but also as promises and rewards.[3]

Sanctions are as old as antiquity. The most famous economic sanction in the ancient world is the Megarian decree, in which Athens prohibited merchants from Megara from trading in Athenian markets or stopping in the port of any member of the Athenian-led Delian League. Notwithstanding the debate about the importance of this decree in causing the Peloponnesian War, it is the case that Megara complained to Sparta, which told Athens that a failure to rescind the decree would mean war. Two hundred years later, Rome imposed a trade embargo on the Gauls and applied it to non-Roman citizens. In short, sanctions predate international institutions and the industrial revolution.[4]

Sanctions are more prevalent than ever. Their use has exploded in the last half century, and especially the last two decades, coinciding with the emergence of a global economy and the end of the Cold War.[5] Whereas during the four and a half decades of the Cold War the UN Security Council only adopted sanctions in two cases, in less than the following decade and a half it imposed sanctions in more than a dozen cases.[6] Similarly, the use of unilateral sanctions by the United States also exploded. In the four years 1993–1996, the United States adopted new sanctions measures against thirty-five countries, and between 2002 and 2006 new unilateral sanctions were adopted against forty-seven countries.[7]

This chapter develops a political economy of material sanctions and inducements, one that reflects the strategic interaction of sanctioners and sanctioned and that also emphasizes the centrality of domestic politics for both. The following sections focus on sanctioning states,

---

[2] For the first discussion of the use of sanctions and rewards as regards arms control, see Bornstein (1968).

[3] For the relationship between threats and promises, see Schelling (1960) and Baldwin (1971a and 1971b).

[4] Førland (1993).

[5] Ironically, the United States, the largest employer of economic sanctions, was a latecomer to their use. On the late US adoption of economic sanctions, see Williams (1943).

[6] Targeted Financial Sanctions Project (2004: 2).

[7] National Association of Manufacturers (1997) and Malloy (2006). The Reynolds and Wan chapter (Chapter 3) beautifully demonstrates that unilateral sanctions dominate multilateral ones (302 to 149 in the four cases they study), and that the United States is ahead of other states and international institutions, especially as regards negative sanctions.

and develop the argument that sanctions constitute attempts to wield market power, that this requires the growth of state power to create monopoly or monopsony power, entails distributional consequences, requires monitoring and enforcement, and typically the construction of a multilateral cartel. The sections that then follow focus on sanctioned states and the distributional consequences of sanctions in them and the growth of state power in these countries as their rulers attempt to create countervailing market power. This is followed by a discussion of the similarity of material inducements to material sanctions, and then a conclusion.

Sanctions, inducements, and market power

Sanctions, whether positive or negative, are economic measures adopted to obtain political changes in some target country. As such, they are intended to change the price for some market exchange by including a political price in addition.

Yet such changes in price cannot be achieved in a competitive market, which by definition contains competing buyers and sellers, competing investors and traders. There are always other buyers and sellers in a competitive market and the price cannot be affected by any individual consumer's or producer's choice. In a competitive market, no one wields economic power. No consumer or producer can dictate a price different from the market price. Each is a price taker, not a price maker. There are too many substitutes.

Market power depends on the absence of alternatives. The wielding of market power is then about the creation of monopsony or monopoly and entails the concentration of consumption or production. Market power depends on the desirability for an exchange in the absence of alternatives. Market power is thus an exercise in exploitation and not coercion, it still presumes a voluntaristic exchange. No consumer has to purchase from a monopoly producer, it is simply that there is no alternative. An exorbitant price, one that a consumer would rather not pay, is extracted for the good in question. Nevertheless, the consumer accedes to the exchange.

Economic rewards and punishments can achieve political change in the absence of a competitive market. Sanctions aim to withhold selling goods to specific consumers and/or to preclude purchasing from them, and are thus about creating monopoly and/or monopsony. On the one hand, a monopoly is created that sets a price for selling goods to a country that includes policy changes. For example, an export embargo is an attempt to charge a monopolist's price for a good, a price which includes a political component. Sanctions also aim at creating monopsony power. Thus, sanctions on Iraq that prevented its sale of oil on global markets meant the creation of a monopsonist purchaser dictating a price for purchase that included policy changes by the Iraqi government.

Creating a sanctions regime then is inherently about interfering with market processes for the purpose of exercising market power by changing the price for an exchange. Sanctions are classic examples of market power in which the price under negotiation includes non-monetary components, namely policy change by the sanctioned country.[8]

Government and market power

Governments are mechanisms for arriving at policies that will bind all constituent members. Government policies that affect prices and competition are inherently exercises in the construction or destruction of market power. Government policies effectively take large numbers of producers and consumers and weld them into a cartel. The workings of economic sanctions and inducements must perforce begin with an explication of a government's role in market power.

Many government policies are about the construction and destruction of market power. Government policies to ensure a competitive marketplace are about the destruction and prevention of private market power. Anti-trust policy consists of breaking up monopoly producers or preventing mergers that would create monopolies.

But government policy also prevents competition. Government regulations forbidding the use of child labor, requiring minimum workplace standards, and so on, all prevent competition. In a competitive market, individual producers might engage in practices of which they disapprove and which they would prefer not to engage in, such as hiring children, but feel compelled to by the pressure of other producers. Government policy channels their competition, delimiting the ways in which they may compete with one another.

Government policy also creates monopsony. When a government welds together individuals in a health plan (e.g., Medicare) it creates monopsony power which can negotiate lower prices with hospitals and physicians.

---

[8] Because the price includes non-monetary terms, scholars have talked about sanctions as an example of linkage politics (Lacy and Niou 2004). For my delineation of linkage situations, see Stein (1980).

Foreign economic policy and market power

Although not often appreciated, foreign economic policy is all about the construction of market power. A tariff, in effect, transforms many individual consumers of an imported good into a single collective actor imposing a tax at the border. Some consumers might want such a tax imposed (especially if they work in import competing industries) but others might not want to pay higher prices for imported goods. But government policy transforms them into a single consumer imposing a tariff on all transactions. Similarly, an import ban transforms all of a country's citizens into boycotters.

Similarly, state policy transforms many smaller scale producers into conglomerates. Agriculture consists of many small producers. Globally, there is probably no sector with more individual producers than agriculture. Yet, in many agricultural products, the global market resembles an oligopoly. There are millions of wheat growers in the world, and there are thousands in any one country, but the combination of only a few countries that produce enough to export and the government policies of those countries effectively transform the global wheat market into an oligopoly. The big wheat exporting nations then negotiate agricultural trade policy.

Government regulatory policies, whether they prohibit child labor or the exportation of computer software and hardware, preclude actions that might be taken by private actors engaged in market exchanges. In some cases they level the playing field by limiting allowable forms of competition. But in regard to the regulated behavior, state policy effectively creates an integrated market entity acting in common.[9]

State and society

A government's ability to construct market power is a function of its relative power vis-à-vis private actors. And this relationship between state and society varies across countries. Some governments control whole industries, whereas others are barely involved in production. Governments also vary in the extent of the GNP they consume. Nevertheless, in most societies, production and consumption are largely in private hands. The economic and financial power of most

---

[9] This differs from the case in which market competition leads to the diffusion of practices and thus sameness. In this case, sameness is forced by state power and precludes competition as regards the regulated behavior.

states is dwarfed by that of private actors.[10] Thus a government's ability to undertake foreign inducements or sanctions depends upon its ability to control the activities of private actors.

Economic sanctions and inducements thus implicate the relative power of state and society. Although states have some ability to compel compliance by their ability to control cross-border flows, the foreign economic policies of sanctions and inducements typically depend on the ability of states to coerce, cajole, or induce private actors to do something (invest in a particular country) or not do something (buy from or sell to a particular country).

Table 2.1 provides a simple depiction of policies of inducements and sanctions governments can pursue as regards the movement of goods and capital. All but foreign aid and government lending are in the hands of private actors, especially in advanced industrial societies. When a country directly owns and controls state corporations (parastatals), then the government has direct control over the foreign sale of goods.[11] Only when the government controls state trading companies can it directly control the purchase of imports. Otherwise trade is in private hands. And as regards capital movements, states control the levels of direct aid and government loans they provide, and they have different voting shares in international financial institutions such as the IMF, but these resources are overwhelmingly dwarfed by those of private capital. Thus, for most exercises of foreign economic power, and most especially in open democratic societies, the state critically depends on statutory authority to control cross-border flows. In the case of the United States, for example, the government has the ability to control exports, but has much less latitude to control imports.[12]

Although not often noted, sanctions entail the growth of state power, and are thus more difficult for capitalist economies and representative governments.[13] The less the state controls the economy and the less coercive power it has, the greater its difficulty in imposing sanctions.

---

[10] Note the image of a US government able to provide some level of disaster relief to Haiti, but in which the first lady and the president (as well as former presidents) go on television asking individuals to contribute.

[11] An interesting example is provided by military industries. When governments own and run the production of military hardware, the sale of equipment is solely in government hands. Where private manufacturers produce military equipment on order from the government, there are private actors with an interest in exporting. In such cases, as discussed below, governments need the authority to control exports and must monitor compliance.

[12] Carter (1987, 1988).   [13] Knorr (1977) and Krasner (1977a).

Table 2.1 *Sanctions, inducements, and policy domains*

	Policy Domains		
	Goods	Capital	Transport and communication
Sanctions	export control, import control (tariffs, quotas, prohibitions)	capital controls, credit suspension, freeze or seize financial assets	restrict transportation and communication
Inducements	trade concessions (higher quotas, lower tariffs, MFN, etc.)	aid, loans, grants, allow FDI, technology transfer	

Exercising market power: winners and losers, supporters and critics

Government policies intended to exercise market power by the construction of monopoly and monopsony inherently have distributional consequences. Those prevented from selling their products to sanctioned countries pay a price for national policy. They bear the brunt of a foreign policy aimed at making another country pay a price for, and hoping to induce a change in, its foreign policy.[14]

Even foreign economic policies that do not succeed in creating market power can generate winners and losers in the short term. Ironically, economic sanctions are sometimes characterized as only creating costs for the country that imposes them, but the market distortions created by sanctions that hurt some also typically benefit others.

A number of implications flow from the reality that there are winners and losers from a state's attempt to create market power.[15] First, at the policy development stage, there is political opposition to economic sanctions from adversely affected groups and sectors. The resort to economic sanctions, especially unilateral ones, has generated sustained opposition by corporate interests. Concerned about the growing resort to economic sanctions in the post-Cold War world, "a coalition of small

---

[14] For the costs to the sanctioning country, or sender as it is called in the literature, see Farmer (1999, 2000).
[15] Solingen's introductory chapter signals the importance of distributional issues in this volume.

and large businesses, agriculture groups and trade associations working to seek alternatives to the proliferation of unilateral US foreign policy sanctions and to promote the benefits of US engagement abroad," established USA*Engage in 1997. The new organization "leads a campaign to inform policy-makers, opinion-leaders, and the public about the counterproductive nature of unilateral sanctions."[16]

Given the opposition to sanctions, some have even argued that political competition among domestic interest groups determines the nature of sanctions.[17] Based on such a perspective, some argue that democracies adopt sanctions when and where they hurt the sanctioning state the least, and are adopted and implemented in a form which makes them designed to fail.[18]

In short, the weaker the state relative to society, the greater the power of special interest groups, the more difficult it will be for a government to adopt and sustain a sanctions regime. This is especially the case if the costs are concentrated and the benefits diffuse.

Monitoring domestic compliance

Another implication of the distributional consequences of government policies that create market power is that private actors have incentives to circumvent government policy (after having opposed it unsuccessfully). Governments adopt anti-trust policies but large firms have incentives to collude. Governments impose sanctions and individual firms have incentives to circumvent them. At the national level, there will be firms interested in making sales from which they are precluded and which will be all too willing to evade and circumvent sanctions.

The adoption of economic sanctions or inducements is about appropriating power for the state at the expense of some forces in civil society. Firms that prefer to sell to sanctioned countries will be prevented from doing do. In the case of inducements, for example, banks that prefer to lend on commercial grounds will be pressed to lend to politically important locations, and firms will be encouraged to target their foreign investments in a particular direction.

Sanctioning countries have to be willing and able to rein in important business interests and will have to monitor their own societies for

---

[16] Cummings (2006).
[17] Kaempfer and Lowenberg (1988, 1992); for a contrary empirical assessment in the case of the United States, see Drury (2001).
[18] There is a disconnect between the sanctions literature that argues that trade disruption does not generate acquiescence, but that the existence of economic exchange predicts cooperation between states (Stein 2003).

compliance. Adopting economic sanctions thus implies institutionalizing some mechanism for monitoring compliance and entails a realization that there will be cheating.[19] Indeed, the greater the distributional
costs, the greater the incentives to cheat and the more the system must
be monitored. Moreover, the punishments for non-compliance must
exceed the gains to be realized from cheating.

Although not often emphasized, a sanctioning government, in effect,
is not only punishing another country and groups in it, it is also punishing firms and individuals in its own society. It is making some actors
bear the burden of national interests. And it must be prepared to punish
domestic interests who run afoul of its foreign economic policy.[20]

Multilateral monopsony and the creation of cartels

Of course, international economic sanctions and inducements typically
require the construction of a multilateral cartel. For most products and
sectors in the world economy, market power can only be wielded by
groupings of states. Sanctions that are readily circumvented because
of the existence of alternative buyers and sellers are not going to be
materially effective.[21]

Multilateral economic sanctions thus attempt to accomplish at the
supranational level what the state must achieve at the national level –
welding together producers and consumers in order to wield market
power. At the international level, therefore, constructing market power
implicates all the requisites of interstate cooperation, including issue
linkage, credible commitments, and the like.[22]

---

[19] The Bush administration, for example, was aware of illegal oil purchases from Iraq
prior to the 2003 US invasion and attendant kickbacks to the Saddam regime which
was at the same time being sanctioned by the United States. The administration
chose to look the other way. Indeed, US purchases were responsible for more than
half of the kickbacks received by the regime for selling oil (Julian Borger and Jamie
Wilson, "US 'Backed Illegal Iraqi Oil Deals,'" *Guardian*, May 17, 2005).

[20] It is possible to run afoul of sanctions without even knowing it. In 2006, the United
States imposed a ban on doing business with Chinese firms that had allegedly sold
missile technology to Iran. Despite the ban, a brisk business continued until exposed
through an analysis of shipping records by the Wisconsin Project on Nuclear Arms
Control. An assessment by the *Wall Street Journal* concluded "that the US firms
likely were unaware they were doing business with banned entities" (Peter Fritsch,
"Chinese Evade US Sanctions on Iran," *Wall Street Journal*, January 4, 2010).

[21] They may still matter for other non-material reasons. Kaempfer and Lowenberg
(1999) argue that unilateral sanctions can have signaling value when undertaken by a
state with close ties to the sanctioned state even as their economic irrelevance mini-
mizes the opportunity for the sanctioned state to accrue rents.

[22] Martin (1992a, 1993).

Sanctions are thus intimately linked to international institutions.[23] Economic sanctions were built into the League of Nations charter and were widely used in its short life.[24] They are embedded in the UN charter and became prominent UN measures once great power cooperation in the Security Council emerged with the end of the Cold War. Not only can the construction of multilateral sanctions be facilitated by international organizations, but international organizations embody some mechanism for collective sanctioning as a core element of obtaining compliance by their members to their obligations. The issue of this relationship was put succinctly in the title of a 1930s article, "Are Sanctions Necessary for a Successful International Organization?"[25]

Monitoring cartel compliance

The attempt to wield economic power is thus subject to challenge at the supranational level just as it is at the national level. Historically, individual countries have been prepared to sanction others on one issue or another, but they have had great difficulty getting adherence by the set of countries needed to wield effective market power. After all, the more countries that join a sanctioning regime, the greater the windfall returns to those who do not take part.

Thus, one feature of the exercise of market power is the issue of second order policy: what to do about relevant others unwilling to go along with a sanctioning (or inducing) regime. The United States has, for example, repeatedly confronted the problem of allies unwilling either to accept the general approach of US foreign policy toward another country or unwilling to use the tactics adopted by the United States.

This first arose during the early Cold War when key allies of the United States did not accept its policy of economic warfare against the Soviet Union and China.[26] Similar problems arose subsequently, even as regards sanctioning small countries with whom there was not much extensive trade. The United States' NATO allies, for example, repeatedly disagreed with US sanctions against Cuba.[27] In the case of Iran, the United States has consistently imposed unilateral sanctions more

---

[23] Wallensteen (2000).   [24] Fiedorowicz (1936).
[25] Buell (1932).
[26] For disagreements on the Soviet Union, see Adler-Karlsson (1968) and Sørensen (1989); for disagreement in dealing with China, see Engel (2005). Also see Mastanduno (1988) and Førland (1990).
[27] Morley (1984) and Wilkinson (2009).

extensive than those that others would agree to.[28] The United States has, for example, instituted secondary boycotts, boycotting companies of allies in order to coerce their compliance with US sanctions.[29]

The problems of cartel management also include dealing with countries willing to circumvent (or not enforce) sanctions that they have titularly supported. Thus countries joined in a sanctioning regime must monitor one another as well as their own and one another's citizens. In effect, states working collaboratively to sanction another state must also contemplate sanctioning one another and one another's citizens. One study concludes "multilateral economic sanctions are sabotaged not by bargaining problems, but rather by enforcement difficulties."[30]

This has meant that the United States has faced the problem of how to obtain others' agreement with its sanctioning strategy. This has proven to be a problem with great power rivals such as China and Russia, and the United States has had to choose between more lenient sanctions that others would accept and tougher sanctions adopted unilaterally.[31] China, for example, has posed a problem for the United States and its allies regarding sanctions on both North Korea and Iran. To obtain China's acquiescence in UN sanctions, for example, Western nations have watered down multilateral resolutions. In June 2010, to obtain passage of a fourth round of UN sanctions against Iran, Western nations had to bow to Chinese demands that permitted continued foreign investment in Iran's oil and gas sector, even though these nations' actions would preclude such investments by their own firms.[32]

This has also been a problem with allies of the United States.[33] And it has thus confronted the question of sanctioning those who fail to sanction, and in the process applied US law extraterritorially. In 1996, the US Congress passed the Cuban Liberty and Democratic Solidarity (Libertad) Act, more popularly known as the

---

[28] Chapter 3 by Reynolds and Wan makes clear that the United States has been ahead of others in sanctioning Iran, Iraq, Libya, and North Korea, and has often not had much support, or only received support after ever more egregious behavior by the sanctioned state.

[29] The empirical record is that one's allies are sanction-busters more than other states (Early 2009).

[30] Drezner (2000: 74).

[31] D. Crawford, R. Boudreaux, J. Lauria, and J. Solomon, "U.S. Softens Sanction Plan Against Iran," *Wall Street Journal*, March 25, 2010.

[32] Paul Richter, "West Worries China May Undermine Iran Sanctions Efforts," *Los Angeles Times*, June 28, 2010; "Factbox: EU Clamps Down on Iran's Energy Interests," *Reuters*, July 27, 2010.

[33] Turkey, a member of NATO and an applicant to the EU, announced that it would abide by UN sanctions but not by US or EU ones, thus taking advantage of the resolution watered down to meet China's objection (Ghajar 2010).

Helms-Burton Act, and it included ways in which the United States could punish other countries' citizens for doing business with Cuba. It also called for reducing US payments to international institutions which provided Cuba assistance. It was widely denounced as in violation of international law and a variety of international agreements and treaty obligations. The subtitle of one law journal article captures the general assessment: "inconsistency with international law and irrationality at their maximum."[34] Congress also passed the Iran and Libya Sanctions Act of 1996 (also known as the D'Amato Act), which gave the president the authority to impose sanctions on firms investing $40 million or more (subsequently reduced to $20 million or more) in the oil and gas sector in either country, and the options for punishment included banning imports into the United States and precluding federal government purchases from such firms. Both acts generated extensive responses from US allies including counter-legislation intended to block US actions.[35] In the end, the United States never enforced the legislation against foreign firms or foreign subsidiaries of US firms. Two *New York Times* reporters analyzed federal records and found that the US federal government had awarded over $100 billion in contracts to seventy-four foreign and multinational firms that were doing business in Iran, and this included $15 billion to companies that invested in Iran's oil and gas sector in defiance of US sanctions.[36]

With the rise of multinational corporations, countries face both a problem and an opportunity.[37] The problem is the possibility of sanction-busting behavior not just by a domestic firm but by its foreign subsidiaries. US companies, such as Halliburton, continued doing business with Iran simply by using "fully independent, foreign based" subsidiaries, which were not subject to the US embargo. Halliburton's "Dubai-based, Cayman Isles-registered Halliburton Products & Services subsidiary" entered into an agreement to do some work for Iran's oil and gas sector, and perhaps even components for a nuclear reactor.[38] Monitoring as well as evasion becomes a problem as firms

---

[34] Gierbolini (1997).

[35] Lowe (1997) and von Lutterotti (2002).

[36] Jo Becker and Ron Nixon, "US Enriches Companies Defying its Policy on Iran," *New York Times*, March 6, 2010.

[37] Rodman (1995, 2001).

[38] Guy Dinmore and Najmeh Bozorgmehr, "Iranian Has Dual Role in Nuclear and US Oil Talks," *Financial Times*, January 27, 2005; J. Leopold, "Halliburton Sold Iranian Oil Company Key Nuclear Reactor Components, Sources Say," *The Free Press*, August 10, 2005.

can also transship goods and hide the origins of fungible goods such as grains and crude oil.

On the other hand, the opportunity arises for a government to enforce its laws by applying them to extraterritorial entities linked to domestic firms or to foreign firms operating in the United States. The United States, for example, fined Barclays, Lloyds, and Credit Suisse, among others, for violating federal sanctions. Court documents revealed, for example, that Barclays "continued disguising sanctioned payments" even after the UK management was warned by its US branch. The banks evaded sanctions by a practice of "stripping" transactions of identifying information and bank officers coached foreign firms by telling them what words could not appear on payment documents.[39] Credit Suisse also helped clients keep financial transactions from being detected by US authorities. They created a pamphlet entitled, "How to Transfer USD Payments," distributed copies of payment forms showing how to fill them out, and assured Iranian clients that payment messages would be individually checked by bank employees, all in order to avoid detection.[40] The entities aided by Credit Suisse included the Atomic Energy Organization of Iran and the Aerospace Industries Organization, both of which had been designated by the United States as proliferators of weapons of mass destruction.[41] Overall, in applying just one particular statute to prevent Iranian proliferation, between 2001 and 2007, the United States imposed 111 sanctions against specific foreign parties, and fifty-two were Chinese, followed by nine that were North Korean, eight that were Syrian, and seven that were Russian.[42]

The need to create an international sanctioning cartel leads states to try to enforce their policies through the extraterritorial application of its laws and policies and to sanction those who do not join in their sanctioning effort.[43] The end result can merely multilateralize an initial bilateral conflict. Efforts on the part of the United States, for example, to obtain extraterritorial compliance with its economic sanctions have

---

[39] Michael Rothfeld, David Enrich, and Jay Solomon, "Barclays in Sanctions Bust," *Wall Street Journal*, August 17, 2010.

[40] Aaron Lucchetti and Jay Solomon, "Credit Suisse's Secret Deals," *Wall Street Journal*, December 17, 2009.

[41] Claudio Gatti and John Eligon, "Iranian Dealings Lead to a Fine for Credit Suisse," *New York Times*, December 15, 2009.

[42] US Government Accountability Office (2007: 46–47).

[43] Sometimes states compensate rather than sanction others in order to get their support for multilateral sanctions. The Security Council received appeals from twenty-one countries for financial assistance to compensate them for costs borne in sanctioning Iraq in the 1990s (Stremlau 1996: section 4).

generated conflict with its allies. One analysis of countermeasures to US sanctions concludes, "efforts by trading partners against US extra-territorial sanctions through blocking measures and other means have a long history and have been increasing in intensity."[44] Since the 1990s, the efforts to block US sanctions have come to include successful challenges within the World Trade Organization (WTO) of US measures as in violation of international obligations.

The need to weld a multinational cartel to exercise market power generates a host of problems. Some states will not go along. Some will actively undercut. Some will agree but not enforce. Enforcing one's sanctions leads to the use of extraterritorial measures which in themselves generate conflict with one's trading partners. Sanctions either create additional conflict or the necessity among a set of sanctioning states to monitor one another and sanction their own firms.

The political economy of sanctions in targeted countries

The point of economic sanctions is to impose economic costs (i.e., hardships) on a sanctioned country. There are general costs that are borne by both state and society in the target nation, and many point to aggregate indicators of costs and suffering: decline in GNP, increased unemployment, increased child mortality, and so on.[45] The broad consequences of comprehensive sanctions, captured by articles with titles such as, "Punish Iran's Rulers, Not Its People" led, by the late 1990s, to calls for targeted or smart sanctions.[46] But costs borne by a nation are not borne equally by all its citizens, not only because economic sanctions generate winners and losers in targeted nations as they do in sanctioning states, but because targeted states respond in part by shifting the burden of sanctions.[47]

Distributional politics in targeted countries

Not only do sanctions (and inducements) have distributional consequences in sanctioning countries, they have distributional consequences

---

[44] Clark and Wang (2007: 2).

[45] Like war and gun violence, sanctions have come to be assessed as public health issues by some in that community. In the words of a Harvard Medical School physician in an editorial in *The New England Journal of Medicine*, "economic sanctions are, at their core, a war against public health" (Eisenberg 1997). See also Dreze and Gazdar (1992). For a voice raising a cautionary note about treating sanctions as human rights violations because of their public health implications, see Marks (1999).

[46] Nader (2009).

[47] For discussions of the diverse economic effects of sanctions, see Kaempfer and Loewenberg (1992), Kirshner (1997), Selden (1999), Rowe (2001), and Brooks (2002).

in sanctioned countries. Targeted sanctions are intended to affect some in the society, the targeted, while leaving others unscathed. But even untargeted comprehensive sanctions have differentiated consequences. Not all are equally exposed to increasing rates of unemployment or to drops in income and wealth. Given that, the issue, whether assessing targeted or comprehensive sanctions, becomes one of thinking through the distributional consequences of specific sanctions and whether they strengthen or weaken a ruling elite's hold on power. In some cases, targeted positive and negative sanctions can generate the desired effects on the ruling elite's coalition with minimal collateral damage and thus weaken the regime.[48] In other cases, comprehensive sanctions can wreak such broad widespread economic damage as to weaken the regime.[49]

Ironically, those sectors hurt by sanctions are typically the ones that engage in exchange with the outside world and are the ones most likely to be influenced by it.[50]

Domestic cleavages and distributional consequences of sanctions

Countries are typically riddled by multiple cleavages, and distributional consequences, both within sanctioning states and sanctioned ones, can arise across any of them. Disaggregating domestic society to assess distributional consequences thus raises the issue of the relevant politico-economic cleavages in a society. Disruptions in trade and financial flows can affect a variety of different cleavages between classes, between ethnicities and religions, between generations, between regions, between urban and rural, between industries and sectors, and so on. Iraq under

---

[48] This is the purpose of the volume as described in Solingen's introductory chapter. In this sense, sanctions are like cancer treatments. Chemotherapy and radiation treatments kill cancerous cells, but they also kill some healthy ones. They are used because they have a record of being beneficial on net. The search for targeted treatments is a search for therapies that work only on cancerous cells and do not damage healthy ones. So it is with economic sanctions, and the search for targeted ones that only adversely effect those we seek to punish and do not punish the innocent (note, however, Major and McGann 2005). The problem with economic sanctions is that their consequences are a product not only of the sanctions imposed but the steps taken in response by the targeted regime.

[49] See Chapter 5 by Drezner. In Chapter 9, Palkki and Smith note that even as Saddam Hussein's regime acted to protect its supporters from the worst consequences of sanctions, they also worried about consequences of the resulting inequality and the regime being blamed for the state of the economy. They make the same point about Libya, that government leaders worried not only that sanctions reduced their ability to reward allies but also reduced their ability to provide general welfare.

[50] Hendrickson (1994/1995).

Saddam Hussein, for example, favored the minority Sunnis at the expense of Shia Iraqis. For another example, the US northeast opposed the War of 1812 because it feared being disproportionately affected by the trade disruption the war would bring.

Since sanctions are economic measures that affect the flow of goods and capital, their distributional consequences, who benefits and who loses from them, can be derived from economic theories. Political scientists have used arguments from economic theory about the winners and losers from increased economic openness to explain support for and opposition to free trade and protection.[51] Using the Heckscher-Ohlin model, they argue that the consequences of trade depend on relative factor endowments, the more abundant factor preferring openness and the more scarce factor preferring closure. Using the Ricardo-Viner model, they argue that domestic political cleavages regarding trade fall along sectoral lines: exporters prefer openness and import-competing industries prefer protection. In the former view, domestic cleavages are those between labor and capital, whereas in the latter, labor and capital within an industry are unified and the divisions are across sectors.[52]

The same models that are used to assess the distributional consequences of increased openness to the global economy can be used to assess the consequences of imposed closure. They can be used to determine the distributional consequences in targeted states and the winners and losers from sanctions.[53] When exports to a targeted nation are sanctioned, import-competing industries gain from what can be thought of as externally imposed protection. When export sanctions target items not produced in the targeted nation, they can even act as infant-industry tariffs. Sanctions hurt the relatively abundant factor of production and help the relatively scarce factor of production. Yet, assessing the distributional consequences of sanctions (both their imposition and their removal) is not straightforward.[54] First, sanctioning states rarely impose across-the-board closure but target their sanctions. Second, the predictions of economic theories rely critically on the workings of market prices, and, as noted above, sanctioned states

---

[51] Frieden and Rogowski (1996).

[52] Solingen (1998, 2007a) broadens the coalitions to include all those who benefit from internationalist outward-looking policies versus those who prefer nationalist inward-looking ones.

[53] For an example of the application of Heckscher-Ohlin to economic sanctions, see Cooper (1989).

[54] For a discussion of both the empirical limitations and strengths of Heckscher-Ohlin, see Leamer (1995).

intervene to shift the effect of sanctions, and their interventions play an important role in determining winners and losers.

In some cases, outside sanctioners are particularly concerned with the distributional consequences within the target of their policies. When assessing sanctions against apartheid, for example, there was a concern about the relative impact of sanctions on blacks versus whites in South Africa.[55] The whole point of the sanctions was to end an institution that disenfranchised and immiserated blacks and not to increase their suffering; the whole point was to punish the white beneficiaries of apartheid.

Growth of state power in sanctioned states

Yet understanding even the economic consequences of sanctions requires a political as well as economic model, because sanctions increase the state power of sanctioned states as they do sanctioning ones. Just as the imposition of sanctions by a country requires a degree of state power vis-à-vis its society and may entail a state's attempt to gain the power necessary to control the activities of private actors, so too the sanctioned state uses the external pressure of sanctions to gain new powers and control.[56]

Sanctioned states invariably increase the degree of state control over the economy as they seek to adjust to the pressures of sanctions.[57] Since sanctions lead to a divergence between the world price and the terms of trade for a sanctioned country, they provide the opportunity to earn rents through arbitrage. Governments that can organize monopolies or monopsonies can capture much of the rents, with resulting bigger budgets and resources. Through such rents and through greater economic control, sanctioned governments can minimize the impact on the political elite and the military.

Just as in wartime, the state in countries under sanction grows in power relative to civil society and comes to control and allocate more of national income.[58] Further, sanctioned states facing internal political pressures for change typically also increase their repression.[59] The

---

[55] For one example, see Becker (1987).

[56] See Chapter 7 by Nader for sanctions strengthening the Iranian regime.

[57] See Chapter 7's discussion of the IRGC in Iran for an example. Also see Wehrey *et al.* (2009).

[58] Indeed, one critique of economic sanctions is that even as they reduce the stability of the targeted state, they also allow increases in state power.

[59] In Iran, the IRGC has played a role both in increasing economic control and in increased repression (Scott Peterson, "Irans Revolutionary Guard Tightens Grip: In Post-election Crackdown, Irans Revolutionary Guard Corps has Taken a New

existence of an external threat (in the form of sanctions) may or may not increase internal cohesion, but it does provide the motive, opportunity, and means for accretions in state power.[60]

Sanctioned states and the retargeting of sanctions

The hope of targeted sanctions is that they can adversely affect particular actors and leave others unscathed, that they can pressure imports and exports of critical items while leaving food and medicine untouched. A concern with the general consequences of economic sanctions, what came to be called "comprehensive sanctions," led to a widespread interest in targeted and smart sanctions.[61] The problem is that targeted sanctions affect the untargeted as well, especially as sanctioned governments respond to shift the domestic burden of sanctions.

Unintended economic spillovers occur as actors shift their patterns of consumption and investment in response to demand and supply shifts imposed by others. This observation has come up often in debates on welfare policy. Even targeting assistance to the poor by providing stamps which can only be used for purchasing food will nevertheless result in increased consumption of non-necessary items as the poor use the stamps to replace some of the resources they previously expended on food and shift those funds to the consumption of other items. Food stamps thus increase non-food consumption.[62]

This shift in patterns of consumption (which would also apply to investment) operates as regards sanctions as well. States facing sanctions will shift some consumption from other areas to compensate. Thus sanctions that exclude food and medicines will still affect domestic consumption of food and medicine to the extent that the state has the power to shift societal purchases to reflect state priorities.

This conclusion is conditional on the power of the state to affect domestic distribution and enduring foreign sanctions lead to the growth of state power in order to effect just such changes. Thus, quite separate from the effects of sanctions in creating rally effects or in discrediting a

---

Leading Role by Tightening its Control Over Levers of State Power and Stifling Dissent," *Christian Science Monitor*, December 9, 2009). Wallensteen (2000) describes external sanctions and a rising internal opposition as the "double grip." Allen (2008b) finds that domestic structures in target states (i.e., repression by autocracies) more than mitigate any increased anti-government activity due to sanctions. For the relationship between sanctions and increased repression and human rights violations, see Wood (2008), Peksen (2009), and Peksen and Drury (2009).

[60] Stein (1976).   [61] Biersteker (2004).

[62] Governments thus labor mightily to construct policies that minimize such shifts but have a difficult time designing such measures.

political opposition or the range of consequences for regime legitimacy and support, the imposition of sanctions is met by efforts to increase state power and the state's role in controlling and allocating economic resources. Palkki and Smith note in Chapter 9 that Saddam Hussein's regime gave preferential ration allotments to government employees and regime supporters.

The results of sanctions in targeted countries

The net result of the foregoing is that the effects of sanctions run the gamut in both political and economic terms. In economic terms, sanctions can be inconsequential when sanctioning countries do not achieve market power. Yet even when sanctions are economically consequential, their political effects can run the range from strengthening the sanctioned state to leading to its downfall.

Sanctions can be economically effective and politically self-defeating when they exact economic pain but serve to strengthen the sanctioned regime. This occurs both because the state increases its power relative to society and because the factions supporting the state are strengthened relative to those opposed to it. There is no small irony and tragedy in the ability of sanctions to impose greater costs on a sanctioned regime's opponents than its supporters.[63]

For sanctions to be politically as well as economically successful they must attack the bases of state power, they must impose costs on the elite and its supporting coalition and relatively strengthen forces opposed to the government and its policies.

Just as sanctioning governments must take into account the domestic losers who might oppose or circumvent sanctions in their society and in those countries whom they hope to enlist in a sanctions regime, they must also take into account the ways in which sanctions both strengthen the sanctioned state and create beneficiaries who would then be opposed to the policy changes desired by the sanctioners. Sanctions provide opportunities for rents whose beneficiaries might want sanctions retained. In Britain, for example, the position of members of parliament on repealing an 1807 measure that had led to a US embargo was correlated with the material consequences of the embargo for their districts.[64] Similarly,

---

[63] Note that the costs borne by a regime's opponents need not simply be material ones, they can also be politically discredited (one of the reasons for the argument in Chapter 5 that comprehensive sanctions may be preferable). As Chapter 7 demonstrates, there is a complicated interaction between the material and the ideological in Iranian politics.

[64] Selden (1999).

the very sectors and factions in Iran that have benefited from sanctions, such as the Revolutionary Guard and the *bonyads*, might well prefer weak sanctions to their complete end.[65]

Two-sided divide-and-win

A sanctions game is a two-sided exercise in constructing and wielding market power. The strategy is for each side to wield market power while dividing the other side.

Sanctioners want to use their market power to induce changes in a target state's behavior. They can accomplish this most easily by dividing the target society and creating domestic pressure on the target government to change (or even to see the target government topple as part of the process of obtaining policy change by the target).

The sanctioned government can defeat sanctions by wielding its market power and dividing a sanctioning coalition and even induce noncompliance by private actors in sanctioning countries. Most basically, sanctioned governments diversify their foreign interactions and run them through front corporations.[66] Chapter 8 by Haggard and Nolan documents the economic diversification strategy of North Korea. Iran displays much the same pattern, though with different specific countries. Iran's total trade with China grew almost eight-fold between 2002 and 2008, as China replaced Germany as Iran's biggest trade partner. In the same period, Iran's trade with the UAE more than doubled, as Dubai had become a re-exporter allowing Iran to import sanctioned items indirectly.[67]

Two sides want to play divide-and-win, and both sides depend on wielding concerted economic power to achieve their political objectives.

This analysis makes it clear both why scholars should model the sanctioning situation as a strategic interaction between sanctioner and target and simultaneously attack the unitary actor assumption and talk about the role of domestic interests and sectors. On the one hand, the

---

[65] Chapter 7 provides examples of how the Revolutionary Guard benefited from sanctions and the elimination of their business competitors. In contrast, Chapter 4 argues that under certain circumstances and with the passage of time the domestic beneficiaries of sanctions can come to internalize market incentives.

[66] For a partial list of Iranian steps, see "Factbox: Tactics Adopted by Iran to Overcome Sanctions," *Reuters*, July 26, 2010.

[67] Ilias (2010: 25–26); see also Foroohar (2010) and US Government Accountability Office (2007). In the same way that regional integration can lead to trade diversion rather than trade growth, trade sanctions can lead to trade diversion rather than trade decline.

successful construction of unified market power by both sanctioning countries and the target state generates a situation of strategic inter-action between sanctioner and target.[68] On the other hand, neither side can be presumed to be a unitary actor. Both sides consist of multiple interests that must be welded into unitary market actors, and this usu-ally occurs with differential success by different countries and coali-tions facing different circumstances.[69]

Successful sanctions thus combine the use of market power and an ability to divide the constituent elements of one's opponent. Successful resistance of others' sanctions also requires an ability to weld market power and divide sanctioning actors.[70]

The importance of creating market power implicates the relative power between state and society. The stronger the state, the less it is penetrated by and subservient to societal forces, the more it is capable of imposing sanctions and of resisting sanctions. Not surprisingly, the literature on economic sanctions emphasizes the importance of regime type in imposing sanctions and withstanding them. Moreover, exercis-ing and withstanding sanctions themselves affect the power of the state, generating heightened state power (or at least attempts to increase the power of the state).

Inducements

Much of the foregoing treats inducements as the flip side of sanctions. In one sense, inducements simply reverse the process of influence. Inducers seek to obtain policy change by promising rather than threat-ening, by rewarding rather than punishing. Different terms are used – carrots, incentives, inducements, positive sanctions, positive linkage, rewards, promises – but they all point to a set of policies to influence by providing benefits rather than imposing costs.[71]

The obvious question to raise is whether inducements, like sanc-tions, require the construction of market power. A strategy of positive

---

[68] Although most work ignores strategic interaction, examples of works that do include this kind of analysis include Eaton and Engers (1992), Smith (1995), Drezner (1998), and Hovi *et al.* (2005).

[69] The number of relevant variables thus make general assessments of sanction success or failure beside the point, in any specific case. They simply point to the variable states necessary for success.

[70] The chapter by Palkki and Smith demonstrates that Saddam Hussein worked both to split the coalition of sanctioning states, but used Iraqi resources to try to generate opposition to sanctions in foreign countries.

[71] Dorussen (2001), Crumm (1995), Drezner (1999), Baldwin (1971a, 1971b), Newnham (2000, 2002), Rosecrance (1981), and Davis (2000).

sanctions would be easier if it did not entail the construction of market power, if it did not require a government to harness its domestic society and create an international cartel. The picture often presented is that economic inducements rely on market incentives and have the character of inhering in the market and not being a product of government policy.

There are two problems for an argument that incentives differ fundamentally from sanctions. The first is that absent state power and international cartels, inducements fail in the same way that sanctions do. The second is that, just as with sanctions, it often takes state power to align private interests with public ones.

Coordinating inducements

It would seem that inducements differ from sanctions in that not all outside powers who want to see change in a particular state need to provide inducements. Sanctions will fail if they can be circumvented so all relevant outsiders must agree on sanctions, whereas inducements can be provided by only a few.

Nevertheless, inducements require coordination and the creation of market power as well. Despite the fact that not all outside powers need to offer inducements, they must nonetheless coordinate their actions. If they do not, a strategy of unilateral inducements is equivalent to a policy of sanction-busting. Indeed, a state that acts as a buster of a sanctions regime can always argue that it is merely providing inducements to obtain policy change from a targeted state. What distinguishes sanction-busting from inducement is the coordination of incentives by those attempting to influence a target state. A state attempting to influence another must have all its domestic interests adopting the same policy toward a target, and a multilateral coalition must work together, otherwise a strategy of inducements by one or a few is simply a sanction-busting strategy.

Financial flows to developing nations illustrate the problem. International financial institutions (and governments) attach conditions to loans provided to debtor nations. Borrowers, however, prefer funds without conditions. When private banks entered the sovereign lending market in the 1980s and competed with the IMF as well as each other, borrowers preferred the loans that came without conditions. Conditionality changes the price for a loan by adding additional requirements to the exchange. Conditionality thus requires the absence of alternatives or coordination by lenders. In other words, conditionality can only be exercised when there is market power by those imposing the conditions.

Moreover, a strategy of inducement itself depends on sanctions. The offer of market benefits in exchange for policy change requires sanctions that preclude those benefits without policy change.[72]

A strategy of targeted benefits is also one of targeted sanctions. Providing inducements targeted toward some groups and sectors also requires that these incentives not be available to other groups and sectors.

In short, positive sanctions are also sanctions that require the construction of market power. In effect, inducing policy change requires the creation of a monopoly to provide benefits under some conditions and to some sectors.

A strategy of inducement as well as a strategy of sanctioning both rely on carrots and sticks. It is possible to adopt a sanctioning strategy in which the carrot being held out is merely that of an end to punishments once there is compliance. At the other extreme is a strategy of inducement in which the stick is merely the denial of benefits rather than a meting out of punishments.[73]

But without a common strategy, that is without market power, sanctions are merely unilateral efforts that can be undercut by other countries and non-compliant domestic interests, and incentives are merely sanction-busting by another name. What is striking in the analysis of US and non-US unilateral sanctions of Iran, Iraq, Libya, and North Korea is that, between 1990 and 2009, the United States adopted almost twice as many unilateral negative sanctions as those adopted unilaterally by others (ninety-nine to fifty-six), and in the same period, other countries unilaterally extended almost twice as many positive inducements as the United States (ninety-three to fifty-four).[74] This provides some indication of the problem of collective action and the asymmetric preferences of the United States and its allies.

Both rewards and punishments entail the construction of market power and require multilateralism, monitoring, and enforcement. And ironically can require punishing one's citizens and allies, and can result

---

[72] The chapter by Reynolds and Wan demonstrates that many inducements are about the removal of sanctions.

[73] This is linked to the finding by cognitive psychologists of the importance of the status quo point and the different ways in which gains and losses are viewed. This too has implications for sanctioning strategies.

[74] Reynolds and Wan, Chapter 3, this volume.

in greater self-punishment than that experienced by the sanctioned state.

Incentives and governmental action

Governmental involvement in an inducement regime is not limited to restraining market benefits absent policy change in a target state. The inducement of joining the global economy, of buying and selling in competitive markets, and becoming a recipient of foreign investment and the like presumes that private actors will respond in particular ways once internal changes are adopted. It presumes that only the restraints of sanctions have prevented the flow of commerce and investment. It presumes that the interests of private actors will provide the necessary blandishments once sanctions are removed. The self-interested behavior of societal actors will be sufficient. Thus, whereas the interests of producers and consumers are such that sanctions have to be state exercises in the construction of market power, inducements are often presumed to flow from the interests of societal actors and merely require the end of state-imposed sanctions.

Yet the policy changes being pressed on foreign governments are no guarantee that proffered economic inducements will follow. It is interesting that in the cases of both Libya and Iran, governments sanctioning those regimes could hold out the prospect of future investment flows if they shifted away from proliferation policies, but no such prospect is likely for North Korea. The exchange and investment prospects for North Korea are certainly dim in the short term, even if it changes its nuclear policy. In that case, inducements would have to be provided by governments.

There are then cases in which incentives require governmental involvement. This can happen directly or through government's ability to direct the actions of private actors.

Governments can directly proffer inducements, offering aid and low-interest loans. But governmental resources are typically dwarfed by those of private actors. In such cases, carrots, like sticks, depend on marshaling private action for public purpose. Private actors will not buy products from specific countries simply because their government wants to use this as a carrot. Exporters will not sell to those who need credits. Capital will not flow where rates of return are smaller or where concerns of instability and expropriation remain.

Governments also have an ability to provide positive sanctions indirectly through their ability to channel private market activity. They step in when private actors find market incentives inadequate for providing the inducements governments desire. They provide export credits and guarantee bonds and loans and provide insurance.[75]

The contingency of multiple possibilities

Sanctions depend on a multiplicity of features associated with sanctioning and sanctioned countries as well as the markets to which they are applied. The political ability to impose sanctions depends on the strength of the state relative to its society. Imposing sanctions in a democracy is more difficult than in an authoritarian system, and it is most difficult in a democracy in which the state is weak relative to the society.[76] Sanctions become more problematic when the sanctioning state does not have market power and must obtain the acquiescence of others.

The disjuncture between having and not having market power is evident in the consequences of the 1996 US attempt to prevent investment in Iran's oil and gas sector. Demand for both forms of energy has increased, especially in China and India, and as noted above, the policy has been eminently unsuccessful as foreign multinationals have simply replaced US companies as investors and developers of Iranian oil, and the United States has not been willing to punish those firms.[77] This has made it difficult to obtain much acquiescence. When John Bolton, as Undersecretary of State for Arms Control and International Security, suggested to the Japanese ambassador in 2004 that Japan might be penalized for an investment by its state-controlled oil exploration company in developing an oil field in Iran, the ambassador replied, "Well, that's interesting. How come you've never sanctioned a European Union company?"[78]

In contrast, the same bill has been eminently successful in preventing the development of a liquified natural gas industry. Iran has the world's second largest reserves of natural gas but has been hampered in expanding its export production because US firms have effective monopoly power on the equipment needed to develop the capacity. In the words of James Ball of Gas Strategies, "There has never been an LNG plant built

---

[75] For an argument of how a state's strategic needs affect its shaping of markets, see Skålnes (2000).

[76] The United States is typically characterized as a weak state, although the literature does note that state strength can vary across policy domains, and thus the US state is stronger on monetary policy than trade policy (Krasner 1977b). On the other hand, one study argues that democracies are more successful sanctioners because of their superior ability to signal credibly (Hart 2000).

[77] Pant (2010) and Hughes and Kreyling (2010).

[78] Becker and Nixon, "US Enriches Companies."

without any US component. With the sanctions, not even a 5-cent washer or bolt could come from the US." And he noted, "This is uncharted territory. It can be done, but nobody has had to do it before."[79]

On the flip side of the coin, the ability to foil, undercut, diffuse, and adjust to sanctions depends on the market power of the sanctioned country and the strength of its state relative to its society. Authoritarian regimes, targets of more than three-quarters of US sanctions, are more difficult to sanction precisely because they already reflect states with some societal control, with relatively smaller constituencies, and with the instruments to increase their control and capture the rents that accrue from sanctions successful enough to change the terms of trade of sanctioned countries.[80] Moreover, sanctioned states with substantial resources, such as oil-rich Iran, are in a position to redistribute among factions and sectors, buy off critics, and pay more for what they need.[81]

Conclusion

Sanctions are state strategies and the outcomes of sanctions are a product of strategic interaction, of the sanctioner(s) and the sanctioned. Each side in this interaction is attempting to wield market power, to gain the power of monopoly or monopsony, in the process both dividing the opponent (so as not to face concentrated market power by its opponent) and using market power to extract, or to avoid having extracted, a political price for an economic exchange.

Although sanctions are adopted by one state or coalition of states to influence the behavior of another state, and as much as they are an element of international strategic interaction, they are inherently exercises in which domestic economic cleavages are central. Each side is engaged in marshaling together domestic economic interests and other countries to wield market power. And each side is attempting to divide the other so as to defeat its attempt to wield market power. Understanding divergent domestic and international interests is essential for both sides.

The adoption, implementation, and success of both sanctions and counter-sanctions policy thus depends on relations between state and

---

[79] Hafezi *et al.* (2004); also Thomas Erdbrink, "Sanctions Slow Development of Huge Natural Gas Field in Iran," *Washington Post*, July 23, 2010, but see Gas Matters (2010) and Noël (2010).
[80] The introductory chapter by Solingen especially emphasizes the different constituencies in different types of regimes and the consequences for elites concerned with their political survival.
[81] As characterized in one microeconomic model, "Power is obtained through expenditures on repression and loyalty" (Kaempfer *et al.* 2004: 34).

society and between a state and its allies (or at least confederates). Executing a policy successfully (and quite apart from whether the policy is itself successful) requires monitoring and sanctioning one's own firms and the firms of one's allies.

Since the result of sanctions depends critically on the relationship between state and society within the sanctioner and the sanctioned, regime type is a critical factor in assessing the prospects for, and the outcomes of, economic sanctions. When the sanctioning states are democracies and the sanctioned state is an autocracy, their respective domestic governance arrangements make it harder for the former to generate the requisite collective action and make it easier for the latter to generate countervailing measures against targeted sanctions.[82] Ironically, sanctions can weaken a state absolutely but also strengthen it relatively (to its society and domestic opposition).

Even the most generic sanctions have differential effects, both because economic measures have distributional consequences and because the impact of sanctions also reflects the attendant political measures taken by sanctioner and sanctioned. There are two important consequences to note. First, even the most comprehensive sanctions have differential impact. Second, even the most targeted sanctions generate collateral damage, hurting those not targeted by the sanctioners. However precise, sanctions remain blunt instruments whose consequences depend on a complicated set of strategic interactions, including the sanctioned state's ability to retarget sanctions and to extract rents.

---

[82] Autocracies differ in their dependence on external sources of revenue and in their ability to increase tax revenue and reallocate expenditures, and as a result sanctions have different effects on leadership stability in different types of autocracies (Escribà-Folch and Wright 2010).

3 Empirical trends in sanctions and positive inducements in nonproliferation

Celia L. Reynolds and Wilfred T. Wan

Introduction

The end of the Cold War ushered in a new era of multilateralism that represented a fundamental change to the global balance of power. The exercise of statecraft to dissuade nuclear proliferation offers one example of this transformation, as countries and multilateral organizations utilized an increasingly diversified array of sanctions and positive inducements to address the issue. While past research has considered the flurry of sanctions activity in the post-Cold War environment – some declaring it a "sanctions era" – there is less in the literature that considers the general breadth of increased formal action, both positive and negative, exercised by international actors. From 1990 to 2009, four countries have been the primary targets of these coercive and persuasive tactics: Libya, Iraq, North Korea, and Iran. This chapter provides a trend analysis of sanctions and positive inducements implemented by individual countries and multilateral organizations to dissuade nuclear proliferators, and serves as an empirical foundation for subsequent chapters in this volume.[1] Our analysis proceeds as follows.

We begin by offering working definitions of sanctions and positive inducements, highlighting the conceptual ambiguity that accompanies these terms. We then proceed to a general overview of empirical trends across our four cases, followed by individual country chronologies that parse out the actions related specifically to nuclear proliferation and their associated domestic ramifications.[2] We conclude by providing a

---

Authors have been listed alphabetically to indicate equal contribution. We would like to express our gratitude to Etel Solingen for her invaluable feedback on this chapter, and for her constant support throughout this project.

[1] "Trend analysis" denotes a particular type of analysis within the fields of economics and finance, but the term here simply refers to the identification of general patterns within the data.

[2] The general trends section is accompanied by the charts in Appendix A, while the Appendix B tables complement the country chronologies.

brief overview of notable cases beyond the four countries that constitute our primary focus here, highlighting the significant differences between the two groups. We also raise several issues that warrant further study.

Working definitions

Solingen's introductory chapter provides the baseline definitions used here. Sanctions are "international instruments that punish or deny benefits to leaders, ruling coalitions, or broader constituencies," and positive inducements are "benefits or rewards" extended to those parties. While we pay special attention to those actions taken "in an effort to dissuade those targets from pursuing or supporting the acquisition of nuclear weapons," we do reach beyond nuclear-related actions.[3] A primary goal in this chapter is to provide a thorough accounting of inducements across our four country cases. Many scholars in the political science literature eschew legalistic perspectives of international sanctions in favor of a more general notion of statecraft.[4] This rather broad and loose conception of sanction, or "negative inducement," reflects the inherent difficulty in pinpointing any sort of singular legal framework given the multi-level, decentralized nature of global society. Therefore, as Solingen's definition suggests, it is the political objective at the base of the sanction, rather than its technical form, that gives the action meaning.[5] Given this, sanctions can and do vary in scope, level of authorization, and form. For instance, a report from the United States General Accounting Office (GAO) describes economic sanctions as penalties in the areas of trade, finance, and military assistance designed to influence the recipient.[6] We draw upon all of these categories, and include strictly political and military action as well, in operationalizing what Solingen terms "international instruments."

The term "positive inducement" also applies to a spectrum of activity in statecraft and diplomacy. We again consider "benefits or rewards" across several arenas, from economic resources, to security assurances, political overtures, and the lifting of pre-existing sanctions. While the

---

[3] Solingen, this volume.

[4] Nossal (1989) refers to Kelsen (1950) and Daoudi and Dajani (1985) as exceptions; according to Nossal, the latter falls back on a notion of sanctions as "legal policy instruments to enforce international law" (304).

[5] Some scholars do classify sanctions as a particular type of economic weapon wielded to apply international pressure. Wallensteen (1968: 248) distinguishes between sanctions, economic warfare, specific economic actions, and tariff wars, and defines sanctions as "general trade bans." Pape (1997) similarly equates sanctions to the politically-driven reduction of international trade.

[6] United States General Accountability Office (1992: 2).

substantive nature of such actions differs, each one reflects the general consensus that has emerged in the literature as to the representative characteristics of positive inducements.[7] First, the notion of value is based on the judgment of the recipient party. As such, positive inducement is a term used interchangeably with incentive, payment, and carrot.[8] Second, senders use positive inducements as persuasive measures to cajole the recipient into changing its behavior, even if the expected quid quo pro is not always specified. A final component concerns the notion of exclusivity, which indicates that the positive inducement has meaning because of the sender's identity and its relationship with the target. For instance, a characterization of potential diplomatic overtures from the United States toward Iran could include "assurances against attempting regime change, and 'respect' for Iran's status in the region."[9] If these overtures came from another party, their persuasive power would not be as great.

General trends

In collecting the data for this chapter, we focused on inducements, both nuclear-related and non-nuclear in nature, directed toward Iraq, Libya, Iran, and North Korea from 1990 to 2009. We compiled this dataset from numerous databases and secondary sources, ultimately identifying a total of 454 individual inducement observations that reflect formal actions either imposed or announced by the respective governmental bodies.[10] This section highlights general trends across these observations.

The first trend to note is that sanction observations slightly outnumber positive inducement observations, as shown in Table 3.1. Furthermore, senders have targeted Iran and North Korea with far greater frequency than Iraq or Libya. This is unsurprising since Iraq involuntarily and Libya voluntarily relinquished their respective nuclear programs in 2003, which effectively removed them from the list of targets.[11]

---

[7] George and Smoke (1974), Cortright (2001), and Art (2003).

[8] Cortright (2001) and Nye (2008). Limiting discussion to economic action, Baldwin (1985) divides "positive sanctions" into trade and capital categories, and includes actions such as tariff discrimination, most-favored-nation treatment, aid provision, and investment guarantees.

[9] Riedel and Samore (2008: 109).

[10] Sources include O'Sullivan (2003), Hufbauer *et al.* (2007), Arms Control Association (ACA) (2007), and James Martin Center for Nonproliferation Studies (CNS) (2010). See the individual tables in Appendix B for the full listing of the sources; those tables also relate the totality of the 454 observations, albeit in an abbreviated form.

[11] Although Iraq's nuclear weapons program was successfully terminated during the First Gulf War in the early 1990s, this revelation did not emerge until the 2003 invasion and subsequent regime change. Thus, throughout the 1990s and into the early

Table 3.1 *Sanctions and positive inducements by target country and time period*

General Type of Inducement	Iran	Iraq	Libya	N. Korea	Subtotal
Sanctions					
1990–1994	23	31	9	21	84
1995–1999	26	13	4	16	59
2000–2004	21	5	3	24	53
2005–2009	35	0	0	20	55
1990–2003 Subtotal*	65	49	16	57	187
Overall Subtotal	105	49	16	81	251
Positive					
1990–1994	19	8	0	19	46
1995–1999	14	18	15	18	65
2000–2004	22	13	4	18	57
2005–2009	22	0	0	13	34
1990–2003 Subtotal**	49	39	19	50	157
Overall Subtotal	77	39	19	68	203
Total	182	88	35	149	454

* 1990–2003 subtotals for sanctions calculated from Table A3.7 in the appendix.

** 1990–2003 subtotals for positive inducements calculated from Table A3.8 in the appendix. We provide the 1990–2003 subtotals in Table 3.1 because this is the time period during which all four countries faced inducements.

A closer examination of Table 3.1 indicates that senders utilized sanctions with the greatest overall frequency from 1990 to 1994 and positive inducements with the greatest overall frequency from 1995 to 1999, but this trend breaks down when disaggregated by target. For example, Iran experienced a relatively consistent number of sanctions from 1990 to 2005, when either pragmatic conservatives or reformists occupied the presidency. However, a spike occurred in the number of sanctions from 2005 to 2009, after Mahmoud Ahmadinejad, a principalist hardliner, became Iran's president. Conversely, the use of sanctions against North Korea fluctuated more than it did in Iran's case. During both the 1995–1999 and 2005–2009 time periods, North Korea saw modest drops in the number of sanctions it experienced. The signing of the Agreed Framework in 1994 may account for the first drop, while the ongoing Six-Party Talks that began in 2003, may account for the

2000s, the international community sanctioned Iraq based upon the presumption that it was still pursuing a nuclear weapons program.

second. Thus, it seems that those decreases followed efforts by North Korea to engage with the international community. Both countries experienced relatively consistent numbers of positive inducements over the 20 years as well, with North Korea experiencing a slight overall decrease as time progressed, while Iran's numbers fluctuated a bit and dropped temporarily from 1995 to 1999.

Understandably, Iraq experienced the greatest number of sanctions from 1990 to 1994, with the preponderance occurring in the immediate aftermath of its 1990 invasion of Kuwait and the discovery of Iraq's illicit nuclear activities. With each subsequent five-year period, Iraq experienced a greater than 50 percent drop in the number of sanctions it faced, with these dropping to zero after the US-led invasion in 2003. Iraq experienced the greatest number of positive inducements from 1995 to 1999, perhaps due to rising concerns regarding the humanitarian costs of the aggressive United Nations sanctions regime established after the Persian Gulf War. The most noticeable trend for Libya is that it experienced dramatically fewer sanctions and positive inducements than the other three countries; it experienced its greatest number of sanctions from 1990 to 1994, and its greatest number of positive inducements from 1995 to 1999. Neither Iraq nor Libya were the targets of positive inducements or sanctions from 2005 to 2009 because both of their nuclear programs had ended by that time.[12]

Our discussion of inducement strategies would be incomplete without an examination of their origins. To address this, we simply noted the source of each inducement observation. For a more parsimonious breakdown of our data, we first divided the data into unilateral and multilateral actions. We then pulled out the actions that originated from the United States in the former group, and from the United Nations in the latter group. Table 3.2 indicates that the United States has been the largest source of total inducements and the largest source of sanctions, but that other countries (i.e., unilateral actors that are not the United States) combined have provided the largest source of positive inducements. Furthermore, the United Nations utilized sanctions more than twice as often as other multilateral bodies (e.g., the European Union or the P5+1 – the five permanent members of the UNSC, plus Germany), while the reverse of this pattern is true for positive inducements.[13] When examining the periodicity of the use of sanctions and positive inducements by

---

[12] Inducements, directed at Libya and Iraq, were transcended by actual rewards following the end of their respective nuclear weapons programs in 2003.

[13] The fact that most UNSC resolutions comprise sanction strategies probably explains this observation. However, in some instances, the Security Council suspended or reversed its sanctions (partially or in totality), which account for the few positive inducements attributed to the UN in Table 3.2.

Table 3.2 *Sanctions and positive inducements by sender and time period*

General type of inducement	US	Non-US unilateral	UN	Non-UN multilateral	Subtotal
Sanctions					
1990–1994	19	35	21	9	83
1995–1999	28	12	13	6	59
2000–2004	28	5	13	7	53
2005–2009	24	4	19	8	55
Subtotal	99	56	66	30	251
Positive inducements					
1990–1994	11	30	2	3	46
1995–1999	18	29	7	11	65
2000–2004	12	29	6	10	57
2005–2009	13	5	0	17	35
Subtotal	54	93	15	40	203
Total	153	149	81	70	454

the different senders, unilateral actors fluctuated most in their usage. For example, unilateral actors utilized sanctions less often in each subsequent five-year time period, with the most dramatic drop occurring in the 1995–1999 period. Unilateral actors also followed a declining pattern – though less pronounced – in the use of positive inducements over time, with a dramatic drop occurring from 2005 to 2009.

Analyzing by the underlying intent to deter the acquisition or support for nuclear weapons, the data also reinforces one of the primary themes in this volume.[14] The past twenty years have witnessed a prevalence of inducements directed at pursuing this goal. As illustrated in Table 3.3, based on the databases we examined, approximately 79 percent of sanctions and 56 percent of positive inducements fall into the purview of nuclear-related actions.

Complexity, severity, and effectiveness

Oftentimes, a single inducement includes a litany of components. We account for this complexity at a basic level by classifying each

---

[14] We classify offers involving nuclear technological cooperation as positive inducements as well. We assume that offers of such assistance aim to prevent the target state from pursuing nuclear technology through illegitimate avenues, such as with the A.Q. Khan network. As such, it constitutes proliferation deterrence.

Table 3.3 *Inducements differentiated by intention to deter nuclear proliferation*

Deterring nuclear proliferation	Sanctions	Positive inducement	Total
No	47	83	130
Yes	198	114	312
Maybe/unclear	6	6	12
Total	251	203	454

Table 3.4 *Substantive categorization of actions*

Sanctions	Positive inducements
Comprehensive trade and financial bans	Conditional offers
Targeted trade actions	Trade-related actions
Targeted financial actions	Financial actions
Diplomatic pressures	Diplomatic initiatives
Reversal of positive inducements	Reversal of sanctions
Petroleum-sector restrictions	Petroleum and energy sector actions
Military intervention	Security-related actions
Military/defense sector restrictions	Infrastructure aid
Flight restrictions	Nuclear-related cooperation agreements
Targeted at the nuclear industry	Non-nuclear technological cooperation agreements

inducement observation into descriptive categories that reflect the substantive nature of the inducement; these are detailed in Table 3.4.[15]

It is important to note that these categories are not necessarily mutually exclusive; thus, an individual inducement observation can and often does fall into multiple categories.[16] For instance, approximately 37 percent of our sanction observations (93 of 251) and 44 percent of our positive inducements observations (89 of 203) fell into two or more categories. We explored the inherent complexity of inducement strategies further by parsing out categorical trends and filtering

[15] Even when one disaggregates inducements into their respective categories, sanctions still outnumber positive ones, 455 to 349 observations (Tables A3.5 and A3.6).

[16] One example is UNSC Resolution 748, a sanction taken against Libya in March of 1992, which included arms and air embargoes, while providing restrictions on Libyan diplomats.

them by target, sender, target-sender pairings, and periodicity (see Appendix A). Some trends worth highlighting from that analysis are as follows:

- The most common sanctions were diplomatic pressures, followed by targeted actions and actions aimed at the nuclear industry. Flight restrictions, and comprehensive trade and financial bans were the least common sanctions.
- When implementing sanctions, different senders preferred different instruments. For example, the United States used more targeted trade actions and targeted financial actions than all other senders combined, while the United Nations preferred diplomatic pressures to other instruments and to a greater extent than other senders.
- The most common positive inducements were diplomatic initiatives, conditional offers, and nuclear-related technological cooperation agreements.[17]
- Positive inducements exhibited a more balanced distribution across senders, but the United States remained the primary sender overall.
- There appears to be a shift in the strategy of sender parties in the 2005–2009 period, with the United States and the United Nations taking new aim at the financial sector.

Country cases

Libya

Sanctions The United States initially imposed sanctions on Libya for reasons unrelated to nuclear proliferation. Rather, concerns regarding its growing support for extremist groups and terrorist tactics prompted the initial imposition of sanctions, as exemplified by the US designation of Libya as a state sponsor of terrorism in 1979. The 1980s witnessed a steady escalation in these sanctions as US–Libyan relations progressively deteriorated. Prominent events include the termination of diplomatic ties with the closure of the US embassy in Tripoli (1980), US military intervention in the Gulf of Sidra (1981), the imposition of a comprehensive trade ban and the freezing of Libyan financial assets in the United States via the International Emergency Economic

---

[17] In contrast with sanctions, there is also a greater balance among the types of positive inducements. While diplomatic initiatives represent the most common type (112 of the 349 data points), such actions happen to be the most public of overtures. Thus, these tactics not only present the most accessible and known data points, but may also obscure further detail intentionally hidden from public consumption.

Powers Act (January 1986), and US air raids on Tripoli and Benghazi in response to the West Berlin discotheque bombing (April 1986).[18]

American attempts to galvanize a strong multilateral response to Libya's terrorism-related activities in the 1980s faltered until Libya's support for terrorism peaked with the 1988 bombing of Pan Am flight 103 and the 1989 bombing of French airline UTA 722. These incidents finally convinced European states to endorse more aggressive and multilateral sanctions, culminating in the passage of United Nations Security Council (UNSC) Resolutions 748 (1992) and 831 (1993). These resolutions remained in place until 2003 and represent the only multilateral sanctions implemented against Libya from 1990 to 2009. They entailed an arms embargo, an air embargo, travel restrictions, petroleum-sector restrictions, and the freezing of Libya's financial assets and funds. Combined with the US inducements from the 1980s, these bans exacerbated the dire economic conditions precipitated by Muammar Qaddafi's chosen political economy model, which isolated Libya from the global economy. By the 1990s, Libya was experiencing nearly non-existent growth and production, as well as high unemployment and inflation.[19] Despite this severe economic stagnation, the country did not experience a massive humanitarian crisis under the multilateral UN sanctions regime.[20]

Although the UNSC resolutions of the early 1990s finally satisfied the United States' call for a multilateral response to Libya's transgressions, the United States continued employing unilateral sanctions throughout the decade and into the early 2000s. Complementing the air embargo imposed by UNSC Resolution 748, President George H.W. Bush signed Executive Order 12801 in April 1992, prohibiting access to US airspace to any flights bound to or flying from Libya. Responding to increasing domestic pressure from the Lockerbie victims' families, Congress passed the controversial Iran-Libya Sanctions Act (ILSA) in 1996. This legislation mandated the sanctioning of foreign firms with significant investments in Libya or Iran's petroleum sectors (initially $40 million was the threshold for inducing sanctions; this later dropped to $20 million). Congress also passed the Antiterrorism and Effective Death Penalty Act (AEDPA) in 1996. Implications of this legislation were two-fold – it banned any financial dealings between US entities or individuals and Libya, and mandated that US aid be denied to any

---

[18] For a comprehensive review of sanctions against Libya during the 1980s, see O'Sullivan (2003).
[19] O'Sullivan (2003) and Solingen (2007a).
[20] Solingen (2007a).

third-party country that provided military assistance to Libya. The 2001 renewal of ILSA constituted the final sanction aimed at Libya during this two-decade period.

Throughout the 1990–2009 period, concerns over Libya's terrorism-related activities constituted the primary impetus behind the variety of sanctions levied against it. However, Libya also aggressively pursued multiple weapons of mass destruction (WMD) programs during the 1980s and 1990s, seeking to establish the technological infrastructure for an indigenous nuclear weapons production capability. These efforts entailed a multi-faceted approach. One strategy attempted "to exploit the chaos generated by the collapse of the Soviet Union to gain access to former Soviet nuclear technology, expertise and materials."[21] To complement that strategy, Libya also purchased gas centrifuges and parts, plans for a centrifuge enrichment plant, and nuclear weapons blueprints from the A.Q. Khan nuclear technology black market.[22] Despite Libya's efforts to acquire WMD, and in contrast to UN resolutions directed at the other countries in this chapter, neither UNSC Resolution 748 nor 883 included any restrictions explicitly targeting the nuclear sector. While any transfer of nuclear weapons or related technologies would fall under the arms embargo mandated by UNSC Resolution 748, neither resolution technically banned peaceful nuclear cooperation. This is probably due to Libya's successful concealment of its nuclear program until the 2003 reversal. Thus, Libya's efforts to acquire WMD officially provided an additional justification for sanctions only toward the end of the 1990s.

Positive inducements   Toward the end of the 1990s and during the early twenty-first century, the United States and others shifted to a strategy structured around offering Libya positive inducements. This movement did not occur spontaneously, but resulted from both strategic diplomatic maneuvers on the issue of terrorism and broader changes in the Libyan political landscape. By offering to relinquish the Lockerbie bombing suspects for a trial in the International Court of Justice (ICJ) and by actively courting its regional neighbors, Libya successfully solicited calls from the Arab League and the Organization for African Unity (OAU) for a cessation of the existing UN sanctions.[23] This erosion of support for multilateral sanctions prompted the United States

---

[21] Jentleson and Whytock (2005/2006: 61).

[22] Jentleson and Whytock (2005/2006) Purchases of the weapons plans and the centrifuge enrichment plant did not occur until 2001/2002. For more information on Libya's uranium enrichment efforts and weapons plan acquisition, see IAEA Board of Governor's Report, GOV/2004/12, February 20, 2004.

[23] O'Sullivan (2003) and Jentleson and Whytock (2005/2006).

and the United Kingdom to counter with their own proposal for the trial. With the assistance of intermediaries, a mutually accepted compromise regarding the trial resulted in the passage of UNSC Resolution 1192, which formally suspended the sanctions imposed under UNSC Resolutions 748 and 883.

Within the domestic political landscape, Muammar Qaddafi noticeably altered his policies in 1998, when he publicly sided with technocrats in the ruling coalition who favored economic reform and engagement in the world. The impetus for this policy shift seemed to come from Qaddafi's realization that his wholesale rejection of global markets had exacerbated Libya's poor economic conditions, empowered his challengers, and threatened his domestic political survival. The military was his most aggressive internal challenger. While the military initially served as Qaddafi's primary ally in securing and consolidating his power base, this relationship deteriorated as expenditures on the nuclear weapons program competed with and undermined other military priorities.[24] The peak of their resistance culminated in an unsuccessful and violently suppressed coup attempt in 1993. External challenges also arose from Islamist groups, such as the Muslim Brotherhood, whose domestic offshoots Qaddafi had suppressed during his consolidation of power throughout the 1970s and 1980s.[25] Other challengers included exiled opposition groups located within Western countries, but these were not allowed to return to Libya. Overall, these various threats to the regime spurred Qaddafi to alter his policies, which included the launching of an *infitah* (economic reform) in October 2003 that included privatization of the state oil industry.[26]

The United States cautiously embraced positive inducements toward Libya, and only after other countries pursued such strategies (see Table B3.1).[27] From 1999 to 2003, and coinciding with Qaddafi's domestic reforms, the United Kingdom brokered secret talks between the United States and Libya. While these talks primarily focused on reparations for the families of the Lockerbie bombing victims, the United States conditioned the normalization of relations upon Libya verifiably ending its WMD programs.[28] Ultimately, they laid the groundwork for the lifting of sanctions via UNSC Resolution 1506 in February 2003, and

---

[24] O'Sullivan (2003).   [25] Solingen (2007a).
[26] Vandewalle (2006), as cited in Solingen (2007a).
[27] This observation is reinforced by comments in the memoirs of former Secretary of State Madeleine Albright (2003: 329–330).
[28] Jentleson and Whytock (2005/2006).

Libya's eventual announcement relinquishing its WMD programs in December 2003.

Qaddafi's December 2003 announcement marked the end of Libya's nuclear weapons aspirations and the demise of inducement efforts to dissuade Libya's pursuit or acquisition of nuclear weapons. While we can no longer characterize them as positive inducements, the United States responded to Qaddafi's announcement by gradually rolling back its sanctions as US and IAEA inspectors confirmed Libya's abandonment of its WMD programs. Since 2004, other countries also have increased their engagement with Libya. For example, France, Russia, and Ukraine have discussed peaceful nuclear cooperation agreements with Libya.

Iraq

Sanctions   Iraq's 1990 invasion of Kuwait induced a comprehensive sanctions regime that remained in place until the United States and United Kingdom occupied the country in 2003.[29] With Resolution 661 of August 6, 1990, the UNSC isolated Iraq in an unprecedented manner, imposing "a ban on all trade, an oil embargo, a freezing of Iraqi government financial assets abroad, an arms embargo, suspension of international flights, and banned financial transactions."[30] UNSC Resolution 670 a month later established an air embargo. The US Iraq Sanctions Act of November 1990, taken in accordance with those resolutions, cemented the multilateral response. UNSC Resolution 687 of April 3, 1991, tied the issue of nuclear proliferation to the existing sanctions regime, committing Iraq to partake in the destruction of its WMD programs and to adhere to future inspections as mandated. Inspections conducted in accordance with UNSC Resolution 687 exposed the full extent of Iraq's clandestine nuclear activities, including undeclared uranium enrichment, undeclared plutonium production, and undeclared reprocessing activities.[31] The Security Council's subsequent judgment, rendered in February 1992, noted that the country had failed to comply with the conditions set by the UN Special Commission

---

[29] The United States previously imposed sanctions on Iraq for its support of terrorism, but had lifted those restraints by 1982. Furthermore, as Hufbauer *et al.* (2007) note, while the State Department publicly expressed its refusal in 1987 to sell arms to either side of the Iran–Iraq conflict (in the aftermath of the Iran-Contra affair), both the Reagan and Bush administrations rejected congressional efforts to levy sanctions on Iraq until its invasion of Kuwait.

[30] Alnasrawi (2001: 208).

[31] Albright and Hibbs (1991).

(UNSCOM, established to supervise the dismantling and destruction of Iraq's WMD programs), thus beginning the Iraqi "nuclear sanctions regime" in earnest.

The results of these actions were devastating to Iraq. Not only did Iraq's oil dependency make it particularly vulnerable, but the Persian Gulf War had also destroyed its infrastructure. The comprehensive trade ban effectively eliminated the country's foreign exchange, resulting in an estimated inflation rate that eventually exceeded 8,000 percent per year.[32] Iraq's Gross Domestic Product (per capita) fell from $2,304 in 1989 to $938 in 1990, and failed to exceed more than $507 over the next six years.[33] Large portions of the population were unable to procure basic goods and services. In 1997, more than a million children under the age of five were malnourished, according to some estimates. In 1998, 70 percent of Iraqi women were considered anemic according to other estimates.[34] While the exact nature of human costs brought about by comprehensive sanctions remains contested, the economic impact was evident in the decreased standard of living, the collapse of industry, and the absence of equipment and supplies.[35]

The sanctions directed against Iraq retained a rather consistent character through the entirety of the 1990–2003 period. Following the discovery of Chinese cruise missiles in the Gulf, the United States enacted the Iran–Iraq Act in October of 1992. The act threatened sanctions on any foreign persons or nations who transferred goods or technology to those countries' pursuit of WMD. Beyond that, the comprehensive sanctions from both the United Nations and the United States remained in place through the 1990s; the Security Council in fact chose to maintain the regime in forty separate regular reviews, held at sixty-day intervals following the deployment of UNSCOM.[36] A consistent flow of UN resolutions charted the intransigence of Iraq with regard to UNSCOM, and sanctions expanded temporarily in 1997 to ban the travel of senior Iraqi officials following several incidents with weapons inspectors. Iraq's decision to suspend (and later cease) cooperation with UNSCOM in September 1998 ensured the permanence of the comprehensive system, with the Security Council responding by lifting the

---

[32] Shehabaldin and Laughlin Jr. (1999).

[33] Duelfer (2004).   [34] Gordon (2010).

[35] Initial research provided staggering mortality figures, with up to 500,000 deaths from 1991–1997 (Baram 2000; Cortright 2001; Gordon 2010). However, Dyson (2009) argues that the most common numbers were based in part on a methodologically flawed 1999 survey. Recent UNICEF estimates, as well as two retrospective surveys, indicate no abnormal fluctuation – in child mortality rates, at least – following the implementation of the sanctions regime in 1990.

[36] Katzman (2002).

periodic reviews. Yet, the sanctions regime never affected the political landscape of the country in the manner that the international community intended. Instead, it provided an anti-US and UN propaganda tool, established a permanent "emergency" situation that Saddam Hussein's political machine co-opted (as the next section details), and limited the rise of potential political opponents by eliminating the professional middle class.[37]

Positive inducements The positive inducement strategy was rather subdued in the nuclear chronology of Iraq, especially outside of a humanitarian context, for several reasons. The contentious relationship between the Iraqi government and the UN weapons inspectors is certainly one. Given that UNSC Resolution 687 of 1991 predicated the lifting of sanctions on Iraq's compliance with UNSCOM, the Security Council's reinforcement of this compliance condition in 1999's Resolution 1284, this time with regard to the newly established UN Monitoring, Verification, and Inspection Commission (UNMOVIC), highlights that this contention continued. Some also attribute the limited offers by the Security Council to growing US sentiment for regime change, with other members "unwilling or unable to prevent the United States and Great Britain from ... maintaining a rigid and unyielding posture regarding the continuation of sanctions."[38] The UN "oil for food" program in Iraq, established in 1995, did represent a notable exception.

UNSC Resolution 986 allowed Iraq to sell up to $2 billion in oil every six months to acquire basic necessities for its citizenry (hence the moniker "oil for food"). While this action was not intended to affect Iraq's nuclear behavior, the program did lift restrictions previously set on the oil industry due to that issue. The primary impetus for this resolution was a series of reports from the UN Children's Fund (UNICEF) that began in 1993; the organization provided figures on malnutrition and disease that depicted the wide scope of the ongoing humanitarian crisis.[39] A depletion of technological and human resources accompanied the crisis and weakened the Iraqi military-industrial complex (i.e., the Military Industrial Commission [MIC] overseen by Husayn Kamil).[40] These factors, combined with the bleakness of the overall economic situation, played a critical role in Saddam's decision to accept the establishment of the program, which he had twice refused. Small

[37] Bengio (2000) and Mazaheri (2010).
[38] Cortright and Lopez (1999: 749).
[39] Cortright and Lopez (1999) also note that more than thirty major studies, many released from 1995–1997, confirmed the severity of the problem. These included reports from the World Food Programme, the Food and Agriculture Organization, and ultimately, the UN Secretary-General.
[40] Solingen (2007a).

adjustments came in the years to follow, raising the limits of oil exports to $5.26 billion every six months, easing restrictions on civilian goods, and tightening controls on military items.

Problematically, however, the controlled flow of money that came into Iraq through the oil-for-food program often ended up being diverted to Saddam and his loyalists. The regime managed to acquire $10.1 billion in illegal revenues from 1997 to 2002, largely through oil smuggling and illicit commissions.[41] Exacerbating the problem was widespread UN corruption and mismanagement; indeed, an independent UN inquiry found that over 2,000 companies were involved in the provision of illicit payments.[42] The Iraqi regime lobbied governments, enticed foreign companies, and basically used oil-for-food funds to re-establish trade relations.[43] As the international community removed further barriers to oil-for-food, MIC saw its budgets increase forty-fold from 1996 to 2002.[44] Thus, the oil-for-food program may have inadvertently served to consolidate Saddam's grip on the country, undermining the sanctions sender parties had imposed.

Other positive inducements offered to Iraq were quite limited. Russia did make several proposals within the UNSC, but with little success. Russia's most significant action was the signing of a $40 billion economic and trade pact for infrastructure modernization with Iraq in 2002. Both sides claimed that the deal fell within the confines of the sanctions regime.[45] Like Libya, the era of inducements targeted at Iraqi nuclear proliferation ended in 2003. In this case, the result was attributable to Operation Iraqi Freedom and US and UK occupation rather than any conciliatory overtures from Saddam Hussein. Again, while we can no longer characterize the actions that followed as positive inducements, the United States suspended the 1990 Iraq Sanctions Act in May of 2003, thus lifting restrictions that stemmed from Iraq's designation as a state sponsor of terrorism. That same month, UNSC Resolution

---

[41] United States General Accountability Office (2004).

[42] Volcker (2005). Most recently, in July of 2010, General Electric paid $23 million to the Securities and Exchange Commission to settle a complaint concerning bribes it provided to Iraqi government officials in 2002 and 2003; GE subsidiaries received lucrative contracts for medical and water-purification equipment as part of oil-for-food (Zachary Goldfarb, "GE to Settle SEC Charges of Bribery," *Washington Post*, July 28, 2010).

[43] Gulal (2001).

[44] Most notably, UNSC Resolution 1153 in 1998 raised the limit to $5.2 billion per six months, and Resolution 1266 in October 1999 temporarily allowed an extra $3.04 billion to compensate for a previous shortfall; Solingen (2007a: 159) discusses in detail the growth of MIC, referring also to a 2004 report from the Iraq Survey Group.

[45] Peter Baker, "Russia, Iraq Plan Deal to Bolster Ties," *Washington Post*, August 17, 2002.

1483 lifted all trade and financial sanctions. Finally, in the midst of Iraq's reconstruction a year later, President George W. Bush issued Executive Order 13350 terminating the emergency declared with the invasion of Kuwait, thus lifting the comprehensive trade ban. The post-2003 invasion and occupation uncovered no extant nuclear capabilities, thus clearing the road to Iraq's rehabilitation.

North Korea

Sanctions   The history of the comprehensive sanctions regime imposed upon North Korea dates back to the Korean War. That country's June 1950 invasion across the 38th parallel marked the beginning of conflict with the United States. However, it was not until the Chinese entry into the fray in October that the Harry S. Truman administration reacted to the conflict's geopolitical ramifications.[46] Invoking the 1917 Trading with the Enemy Act, Presidential Proclamation 2914 in December 1950 declared a state of national emergency, and formally established North Korea as a threat to US national security – a status it retained long after the war. Only a few days later, the Treasury Department issued Foreign Assets Control Regulations (FACR) that forbade financial transactions with that country. In the burgeoning Cold War context, the Marxist-Leninist ideology and the Communist government in place also made the state a target of broader US policies.[47] Moreover, following the bombing of Korean Airlines Flight 858 by a North Korean intelligence agent in November 1987, the United States designated North Korea a state supporter of terrorism and applied stringent trade controls invoking the 1979 Export Administration Act.[48]

Despite the sanctions system already in place, the United States has not hesitated to selectively target firms on the issue of nuclear weapons. Throughout the 1990s, US action against North Korea took this form almost exclusively, sanctioning companies for a variety of missile proliferation activities – most commonly, for technology transfers to Iran, Syria, Pakistan, and Yemen. As depicted in Table B3.5, the culprits often were recidivists, with sanctions imposed repeatedly on

---

[46] Jervis (1980).
[47] The Trade Agreement Extension Act effectively banned imports (1951), the International Traffic in Arms Regulations denied defense articles and services (1955), the Foreign Assistance Act denied a wide range of non-humanitarian foreign assistance (1961), and the Arms Export Control Act disallowed commercial arms sales (1968): in all instances, interactions with North Korea were restricted (Rennack 2005; Chang 2007).
[48] Takishita (2005: 516).

the Lyongaksan Machineries and Equipment Export Corporation and the Changgwang Singyong Corporation.[49] However, scholars suggest that the predominantly US sanctions regime had little meaningful impact either economically or in deterring North Korea from pursuing its nuclear weapons program. While the country experienced a severe economic crisis in the 1990s, most generally attribute it to the trade shocks associated with the collapse of the Soviet Union, the failure of agricultural policies, and the prioritization of the military sector.[50] The North Korean command economy, the presence of alternative trading partners, and the *juche* doctrine of self-reliance all helped dilute the effects of sanctions.[51]

Politically, the impact of sanctions was more uncertain. Inconsistent policies from Pyongyang suggested possible shifts within the ruling coalition; whether this resulted from external action is another question altogether. Shortly after assuming power in 1994, faced with energy and food crises, Kim Jong-il indeed advocated a more moderate approach, implementing a new "economic policy for the period of adjustment" that highlighted the value of foreign trade.[52] However, he stifled the emergence of any moderate contenders through political purges. Kim Jong-il consolidated power over the next two years, taking over as head of the National Defense Commission (NDC) and as general secretary of the Korean Worker's Party (KWP). Thus, while the devastating famine of the 1990s led Kim Jong-il to allow the establishment of some grassroots capitalism, he constrained any redistribution in political power.[53] Those disenchanted with the conditions in North Korea that had the ability to flee chose to do so, with a reported 300,000 leaving the country since the mid 1990s.[54]

The perceived role of the KWP in the economy's failure spurred Kim Jong-il to switch his power base to the military. Events in 1998 confirmed this shift, with the revised constitution officially placing the NDC as the head of military affairs, while September elections bore witness to 107 active duty military members joining the legislature.[55] Thus, even as Kim Jong-il and Premier Hong Song-nam subsequently initiated economic reforms in 2002, the role of the military in the Assembly

---

[49] The general trade bans in place rendered these company-specific sanctions redundant. During this timeframe, there were also symbolic penalties concerning non-nuclear issues, including the 1998 International Religious Freedom Act, the 2000 Trafficking Victims Protection Act, and the 2004 North Korean Human Rights Act.

[50] Yoon and Babson (2002) and Noland (2005).

[51] VanWagenen (2000) and Takishita (2005).

[52] Solingen (2007a: 133).   [53] Lankov (2009).   [54] Lee *et al.* (2009).

[55] Pinkston (2003) and Moon (2009).

confirmed the dominance of the military-first ideology.[56] During this critical moment at the beginning of the twenty-first century, scholars noted the continued absence of serious political threats to the regime. The entry requirements demanded by KWP continued to filter access to the system, while numerous state security agencies kept political intolerance to a minimum.[57] The totalitarian leader took steps to stifle economic reform shortly thereafter, suppressing market-oriented activities, restricting movement, and limiting private communication.[58] As with Iraq, sanctions seemed only to feed into nationalist misinformation, while the benefits offered through positive inducements fell under the carefully controlled purview of a select few.[59]

Actors beyond the United States were reluctant to participate in sanctions against North Korea. Even during the 1993–1994 crisis on the peninsula, South Korea, Japan, and China disregarded pressure from the Clinton administration to pursue punitive action, expressing both concern regarding the effectiveness of such actions and fear over a potential military response.[60] It was only following the deterioration of the Agreed Framework in 2002 that the character of the nuclear sanctions regime in North Korea showed greater signs of change. After North Korea revealed the presence of its clandestine enrichment program in October 2002 (to US Assistant Secretary of State James Kelly), the United States, Japan, and South Korea halted the shipments of oil and rice promised under the 1994 deal.[61] In November 2003, the parties stopped construction on the two light-water reactors. Still, resistance from two permanent Security Council members – Russia and China – muted the overall response; for instance, the United Nations abstained from issuing a resolution condemning or sanctioning North Korea's withdrawal from the Nuclear Non-Proliferation Treaty in 2003.[62]

A more aggressive sanctions regime emerged beginning in the latter half of 2005. The United States remained at the forefront of the international response, now guided by the newly passed Executive Order 13382, which prohibited transactions with and froze the assets of designees. Between June and October of 2005, the US Treasury alone targeted eleven entities for supporting WMD proliferation. North Korea's firing of long-range ballistic missiles in July 2006 triggered a severe multilateral response. UNSC Resolution 1695 required member states to refrain from transfers of any items, materials, goods, or technology to or from

[56] Solingen (2007a).   [57] Pinkston (2003).
[58] Haggard and Noland (2009a) and Lankov (2009).
[59] Lankov (2008).   [60] VanWagenen (2000) and Noland (2009b).
[61] CNS (2010).   [62] Rennack (2005).

North Korea's program. China and Russia supported this response, which "were the strongest reprimand of North Korea by the Security Council since 1950 and clearly represented an escalating response."[63] Following the nuclear test in October 2006, UNSC Resolution 1718 called for the inspection of all cargo shipments into North Korea and expanded economic sanctions to include a ban on the export of luxury goods. Japan and Australia, meanwhile, imposed sanctions on the same eleven entities specified by the US Treasury in 2005. Still, reflecting the unique nature of the North Korean case, there appeared to be minimal impact from these sanctions – with public and private sector actors from trading partners refusing to change their behaviors. In fact, the volume of trade with China increased substantially in this period, perhaps signaling that the consequences of sanctions took shape in an unexpected manner.[64] North Korea has seemingly increased its reliance on those trading partners less likely to engage in punitive action.[65]

A similar icy multilateral response greeted North Korea's incendiary actions of 2009, including its April testing of a multistage rocket and its second underground nuclear test in May. North Korea responded to international condemnation of the former action by withdrawing from the Six-Party Talks. This seemed to fit a historical pattern, in which the country responded to multilateral sanctions, or disagreeable external circumstances more generally, with escalation. For instance, in response to a November 2002 IAEA Board of Governors Resolution calling for full compliance with safeguards, North Korea declared the resumption of activities at its nuclear facilities. Repeated warnings from the IAEA Director General only pushed the country to disable surveillance cameras and cut seals from its sites, with the back-and-forth leading to North Korea's 2003 NPT withdrawal.[66] Furthermore, the 2006 nuclear test came just months after the UNSC imposed sanctions for the country's ballistic missile testing. Returning to the international response following the May 2009 test, UNSC Resolution 1874 again authorized and encouraged cargo inspection, and extended the arms embargo. Thus, the international community has expressed a growing intolerance for North Korea's belligerence, as reflected in the severity of its sanctions regime.[67] This has included a specific and intentional

[63] Noland (2009: 65).

[64] Chang (2008) and Noland (2009b).

[65] Haggard and Noland (2009b; see also their contribution in this volume, Chapter 8).

[66] See IAEA Board of Governor's Report, GOV/2002/62, December 30, 2003, and GOV/2003/3, January 6, 2003; CNS (2010) provides a timeline of the events leading up to the January 10 announcement of withdrawal.

[67] Haggard and Noland (2009b).

targeting of the financial sector as well. The eighteen-month investigation of Macau-based Banco Delta Asia not only inspired targeted sanctions upon that entity in 2007, but also supplementary penalties on the Tranchon Bank and the Korea Kwangson Banking Corp in 2009. Overall, the recent period provides a contrast to unilateral US action in the 1990s. The ramifications of such multilateral actions, however, remain unclear.

Positive inducements   As previously noted, the UNSC did not impose multilateral sanctions during the 1993–1994 nuclear crisis. Resistance by Security Council members (i.e., China) and concerns over a potentially violent response by North Korea (expressed by Japan and South Korea) ultimately overrode the vocal push of the United States for further sanctions.[68] Instead, a surprise visit to the peninsula by former president Jimmy Carter opened the way for an about-face, with the Clinton administration engaging the Kim Il-sung regime (and successor son Kim Jong-il). The Agreed Framework of October 21, 1994 promised North Korea light-water reactors (LWRs), an annual provision of heavy oil, and steps toward the normalization of relations with the United States. Over the next few years, the United States eased its existing sanctions regime on North Korea, modifying the Federal Assets Control Regulations in 1995 and 1996, and authorizing transactions related to travel, telecommunications, and humanitarianism. US allies contributed to the bilateral agreement, joining in the creation of the Korean Peninsula Energy Development Organization (KEDO) in March 1995. Ultimately, however, implementation difficulties undid the Agreed Framework. The absence of set deadlines for obligations on both sides, such as the dismantlement of reactors, the delivery of nuclear components, and the construction of LWRs, resulted in numerous delays. Meanwhile, domestic politics in the United States and events on the Korean peninsula, including the 1996 Gangneung submarine incident and a 1998 ballistic missile firing by North Korea, reignited tensions.[69]

The next stage in the relationship between North Korea and the international community came in 1998. The foreign policies in both the United States and South Korea propelled a second wave of inducements in the aftermath of a North Korean three-stage rocket launch.[70] Under the so-called Perry Policy, the United States engaged in multiple

---

[68] Dorn and Fulton (1997).
[69] Harrison (2001), Pollack (2003), and Wit *et al.* (2004).
[70] Wickman (2002) suggests that this action, combined with intransigence with KEDO and vocal complaints about the implementation of the Agreed Framework, were all part of a successful negotiating ploy by North Korea

rounds of missile talks with North Korean officials.[71] Former Secretary of Defense William Perry later issued a report in 1999 that proposed the United States "normalize diplomatic relations with North Korea, relax economic sanctions against North Korea, and 'take other positive steps' to 'provide opportunities' for North Korea."[72] That same year, President Clinton lifted a number of restrictions associated with the Trading with the Enemy Act, easing some trade and travel sanctions. Following the June 15, 2000 North-South Joint Declaration, the United States made further amendments to the FACRs, allowing limited investments, transactions, and even trade with North Korea. This coincided with the limited economic reforms taking place in that country mentioned in the previous section, reaching its apex with the 7.1 measures undertaken by the Kim Jong-il regime in 2002 – which allowed some autonomy for managers of state-owned enterprises, raised both consumer prices and official wages, and officially permitted the general markets that had appeared.[73] External positive inducements subsided, however, when George W. Bush became US president.

As with the sanctions regime concerning the North Korean nuclear issue, multilateral involvement in positive inducements has increased in the last few years. North Korea's admission of enrichment transgressions (2002), as well as its proclamations of intent to test missiles (2003), apparently instigated a swift response on numerous fronts, as seen in both Tables B3.5 and B3.6. The establishment of the Six-Party Talks in August 2003 indicated a willingness to actively engage with North Korea.[74] In February 2004, South Korea offered energy assistance to the North, with Russian and Chinese support. In June, the United States proposed a two-phase plan that included fuel oil from China, South Korea, and Russia, the drafting of a multilateral security agreement, and bilateral discussions with the possibility of sanctions removal. The process culminated with the September 2005 Joint Statement of Principles – a written security guarantee to be followed by food, energy, economic aid, and eventually diplomatic normalization. Perhaps the most significant concession from the United States involved the acknowledgment of North Korea's right to peaceful uses

---

[71] As the new North Korean policy coordinator, William Perry partook in multiple consultations with South Korea and Japan to ensure a more unified front; those three countries established the Trilateral Coordination and Oversight Group in April of 1999 for that purpose.
[72] Niksch (2002: CRS-12).   [73] Lankov (2009).
[74] Six-Party Talks participants include the United States, Japan, Russia, China, South and North Korea.

of nuclear energy.[75] However, the agreement fell through as the results from the Banco Delta Asia investigation came to light.

History seemed to repeat itself in October 2006, when Pyongyang conducted an underground nuclear test. While the Security Council promptly condemned the actions and bolstered the pre-existing sanctions regime, the Bush administration almost immediately opened bilateral discussions with North Korea in Beijing. The fifth round of Six-Party Talks began in December, resulting in a new "action plan" in February 2007. Not only did the United States seek to revive the 2005 Joint Statement, but the Bush administration agreed to begin the process of removing North Korea from the state sponsors of terrorism list. Ensuing talks resulted in Washington transferring the previously frozen North Korean funds from the Banco Delta Asia investigation to the Bank of China for humanitarian and educational purposes.[76]

The period coinciding with this most recent flurry of inducement activity (including both positive inducements and sanctions) witnessed a striking amount of cooperation by the Kim Jong-il regime on the nuclear issue. This includes the shutting down of the Yongbyon reactor, discussions with the IAEA about the resumption of inspections, and the provision of sensitive documents to China. As Pyongyang demonstrated this continued nuclear cooperation, the United States followed through with its positive inducements strategy. The second phase of the action plan took place in September of 2007. From 2007 to 2009, the United States resumed its food aid deliveries, rescinded its Trading with the Enemy Act sanctions, and removed North Korea from the terrorist black list. Of course, the presence of testing and sanctions in that same period suggests that this cooperation could be illusory, especially given the schizophrenic nature of North Korea's past nuclear policy. Perhaps the nuclear program simply continues to be a valuable tool for the North Korean regime, which has engaged in games of "nuclear blackmail" through the 1990s and 2000s.[77] For all the machinations behind the scenes, the regime has seemingly managed to ward off the pressures that have accompanied both positive inducements and sanctions.

Iran

Sanctions Like the other three countries analyzed in this chapter, the United States implemented sanctions against Iran prior to 1990 and for reasons initially unrelated to nuclear proliferation

---

[75] Fitzpatrick (2006).   [76] Arms Control Association (2009a).
[77] Lankov (2008).

concerns. Specifically, Iran's takeover of the US embassy in 1979–1980 and support for terrorism, narcotics trafficking, and money laundering throughout the 1980s prompted sanctions against its petroleum and military sectors; these subsequently expanded to a comprehensive trade and investment ban by 1987. The combined effect of these sanctions, the Iran–Iraq War from 1980 to 1988 and its aftermath, fluctuations in the global oil market, and the inward-looking political economy adopted by the Iranian Revolution contributed to the substantial economic problems Iran faced by 1990.[78]

The 1990s witnessed a reaffirmation of the US sanctions regime against Iran, with WMD proliferation concerns rising to the forefront of justifications for its continuation and escalation. Significant measures taken during this time included the Foreign Appropriations Act (1990), the Iran–Iraq Arms Non-Proliferation Act (1992 and amended in 1996), the Iran-Libya Sanctions Act (1996), and Executive Orders 12957, 12959, and 13059.[79] The United States used these measures to prevent the flow of investment to Iran, either comprehensively or within specific sectors. For example, the Executive Orders prevented Iran from accessing US technology to modernize its aging oil infrastructure. This has hampered Iran's ability to exploit the petroleum reserves that currently account for more than 80 percent of its total foreign exchange earnings and 70 percent of the government's fiscal budget.[80] Iran responded to these sanctions by diversifying their trade partners, thus mitigating some of the sanctions' negative effects.[81]

Despite the predominance of US measures, Table B3.7 shows that other countries also imposed sanctions in the 1990s, including targeted trade restrictions (often directed at Iran's nuclear sector) or the reversal of nuclear technology cooperation agreements.[82] Multilateral sanctions against Iran were relatively absent during this period, with a few exceptions typically involving collaboration between the United States and another country. The United States continued targeting Iran's nuclear program with the passage of the 2000 Iran Nonproliferation Act. The December 2002 revelation of two previously undeclared nuclear facilities, and the subsequent and ongoing IAEA investigation of Iran's

---

[78] Anbrahamin (1993) as cited by Solingen (2007a: 176); (O'Sullivan 2003: 61. For a comprehensive overview of the sanctions' economic impact, see O'Sullivan (2003: 61–73).

[79] O'Sullivan (2003).

[80] Amuzegar (2010) and Maloney (2010).

[81] United States General Accountability Office (2007).

[82] Germany, China, and Argentina repeatedly sanctioned Iran in this manner during the 1990s. Germany reneged on contracts to build the Bushehr Nuclear Power Plant which preceded the Iranian Revolution.

implementation of its safeguards agreement, spurred the United States to dramatically escalate its sanctions efforts. In 2005 the US Department of Treasury began freezing the assets and banning banking transactions of Iranian entities and individuals with suspected ties to Iran's nuclear efforts. The United Kingdom and Australia echoed US actions with targeted financial sanctions of their own. Hassan Rowhani, Iran's former nuclear negotiator, estimates that targeted financial sanctions increased the cost of Iran's imports by 10–30 percent.[83] They have also constricted Iran's ability to participate in the global economy by impeding its access to international financial markets, lines of credit, and insurance. They have disrupted its ability to ship nuclear materials as well.[84] Recent economic assessments report continued low growth, real GDP increase of less than 1.5 percent in 2009 and 2010; high unemployment; growing income disparities reflected in high GINI coefficients; over 20 percent inflation; a plummeting stock market; energy shortages; and increasing dependence on oil revenue.[85]

Since 2003, multilateral actions have become the primary complement to US sanctions against Iran, beginning with diplomatic pressures through quarterly reports by the IAEA Director General to the Board of Governors. The UNSC began sanctioning Iran in December 2006, simultaneously targeting trade-related and financial elements of Iran's nuclear program, while avoiding comprehensive trade, investment, and petroleum-sector sanctions.[86] Throughout 2008 and 2009, the European Union has also applied trade and financial sanctions that mirror those already established by the United States and the UNSC.[87]

Although not directly subjected to targeted multilateral sanctions, Iran's gas and oil exports suffered from the overall sanctions regime. China and India reduced purchases of Iranian crude by 20 to 25 percent

---

[83] Maloney (2010).   [84] Levitt (2010).

[85] Amuzegar (2010), Maloney (2010), The Economist Intelligence Unit (2010).

[86] S/RES/1737 2006; S/RES/1747 2007; S/RES/1803 2008; S/RES/1835 2008. S/RES/1835 did not impose new sanctions, but reaffirmed sanctions imposed under preceding UNSC resolutions.

[87] Since January 2010, Iran has encountered further unilateral and multilateral sanctions comprising UNSC Resolution 1929 passed in June 2010, followed by further EU, US, Australian, and Canadian sanctions in July 2010, and sanctions from the UAE in August 2010. In general, these sanctions expand efforts that were already underway (Peter Baker, "Obama Signs Into Law Tighter Sanctions on Iran," *New York Times*, July 2, 2010). While Iran responded to the UNSC resolution by banning two IAEA inspectors from the country, it is too soon to discern the effects of these recent sanctions on the domestic political situation within Iran (David Sanger and Jack Healy, "Iran Bars Nuclear Inspectors in Response to Sanctions," *New York Times*, June 21, 2010).

between 2009 and 2010.[88] Furthermore, Iranian–Chinese collaborations for developing Iran's gas reserves and refining infrastructure remain stalled in negotiations. Suppliers of Iranian gasoline imports, such as Total, BP, and Shell, pulled out of the Iranian market. Finally, sanctions have impeded Iran's access to technology that would allow it to exploit its extensive natural gas reserves, the second largest in the world.[89] In response, Iran began reducing gasoline consumption (e.g., rationing) and protecting its oil sector.[90] Sanctions have also affected Iran's overall trade and monetary policies, reorienting trade relations toward Asia, a rapidly growing regional market that tends to disassociate economic and political relations to a greater degree than Western powers. Furthermore, Iran's import portfolio shifted away from states susceptible to US pressures.[91] Iran also tried to keep the rial's exchange rate relatively stable despite increasing inflation, leading to its overvaluation and the inability of domestic producers to compete with foreign imports.[92] Ultimately, sanctions have exacerbated economic problems arising from the structural weaknesses and mismanagement of Iran's economy, especially under Ahmadinejad's presidency and since his contested re-election in June 2009.[93]

Some scholars posit that sanctions carry greater political consequences than economic ones, potentially changing the political calculus within Iran.[94] Historically, the balance of power among political elites shifted from the clerics and the *bonyads* in the 1990s to the Revolutionary Guards (IRGC or Pasdaran) in the 2000s.[95] Pragmatic conservatives who dominated in the 1990s and principalists who came to power in 2005 with Ahmadinejad's election stymied any serious attempts at reform, including the brief reformist interlude under Khatami's presidency (1997–2004).[96] Initial reformist responses to the nuclear revelations and crisis took the form of conciliatory diplomacy, in hopes of forestalling the transfer of Iran's nuclear dossier to the UNSC. For instance, in October 2003 they agreed to suspend uranium

[88] Mohamedi (2010).   [89] Sadjadpour (2010b).
[90] Maloney (2010) and The Economist Intelligence Unit (2010).
[91] Maloney (2010).   [92] Amuzegar (2010) and Askari (2010).
[93] Iran's structural economic weaknesses include: an over-reliance on oil exports for revenues; state dominance of the economy where the government or state-affiliated entities own approximately 65–70 percent of the economy; a poor tax base that provides only 7 percent of GDP; rampant tax evasion; high subsidies accounting for approximately 18–30 percent of GDP; the favoring of high-technology industries (e.g., nuclear energy and space technology) to the detriment of more traditional, labor-intensive industries; and the existence of a black market economy that accounts for approximately 20 percent of GDP (Amuzegar 2010; Sadjadpour 2010b).
[94] Sadjadpour (2010a).   [95] Naji (2008) and Wehrey *et al.* (2009).
[96] Thaler *et al.* (2010).

enrichment and reprocessing activities and to adhere to the Additional Protocol, which allows for more intrusive IAEA inspections and other strengthened safeguards measures. Yet they also disagreed with the IAEA on the actual scope of the suspension and continued to produce uranium hexafluoride, the feed material for gas centrifuges. The inconsistent implementation of the suspension might have been the result of Khatami's limited authority over the nuclear program.[97]

In contrast to reformist preferences for engagement on the nuclear issue, Ahmadinejad successfully factionalized the issue for electoral purposes in the June 2005 election to characterize his opposition as weak and susceptible to Western influence.[98] His principalist faction adopted an aggressive and confrontational stance on the nuclear issue geared to "retaliate against UN resolutions and future sanctions by threatening to cease and then actually limiting cooperation with the IAEA and its inspectors."[99] Although most targeted financial sanctions are aimed at Guard-affiliated individuals or entities, the impact is limited because of their economic dominance in Iran's black market economy.[100] It is doubtful that sanctions will change the current regime's political calculus on the nuclear issue in the near-term since it appears more willing to continue subjecting its people to economic hardship than to compromise ideologically.[101]

The political unrest that followed the June 2009 elections has been unprecedented since the Iranian Revolution. While the opposition was unable to oust Ahmadinejad, social, political, and economic discontent remains present in Iran. Whether the United States, its allies, and multilateral bodies can design and implement sanctions that capitalize upon this discontent is unclear. Multilateral sanctions are often tailored to a "lowest common denominator formula" to cater to the strategic interests of Russia and China, yet they serve a legitimating function and are an important prerequisite for getting other actors, such as the EU and individual European states, to adopt stricter sanctions of their own.[102] Some suggest that Iran's public is sensitive to the justifications used by the United States to apply sanctions and its stated goals.[103] Hence, they argue, the United States should highlight that its unilateral sanctions do not merely target individuals and entities involved in Iran's nuclear program but also those engaged in human rights violations and

[97] "Iran Still Welcome to Accept Uranium Proposal, U.S. Says," *Global Security Newswire*, January 5, 2010.
[98] Chubin (2010a).   [99] Thaler *et al.* (2010: 96).
[100] Levitt (2010).   [101] Sadjadpour (2010a).
[102] Levitt (2010) and Sadjadpour (2010a).
[103] Askari (2010).

anti-democracy crackdowns. In many cases the two groups are one and the same.[104] This linkage would help strengthen opposition forces within Iran who tend to favor greater engagement with the international community.

Positive inducements   International actors other than the United States have spearheaded efforts to engage Iran on its nuclear program via positive inducements. Throughout the 1990s, various countries signed nuclear technology cooperation agreements with Iran, primarily to exploit lucrative business opportunities rather than to influence Iran's behavior.[105] Table B3.8 also indicates an increase in the number and variety of positive inducements following the 1997 election of Khatami. For example, the United States secretly extended a diplomatic olive branch to Khatami, and the United Kingdom and the European Union restored full diplomatic ties with Iran. Possibly in response to such overtures, and to help mitigate US concerns regarding Iran's terrorist ties, Khatami considered downgrading Iran's ties with Hezbollah.[106] Subsequent bilateral business deals focused on Iran's petroleum sector.[107] However, following the 2002 revelation of Iran's undisclosed nuclear facilities, the EU-3 (United Kingdom, France, and Germany) spearheaded multilateral efforts to curb Iran's nuclear program. Negotiations between 2003 and 2005 proceeded spasmodically, with Iran vacillating to suspend all uranium-enrichment and reprocessing activities. In August 2005, Iran rejected the EU-3's final offer and resumed uranium conversion activities, terminating this phase of negotiations.

Following these lackluster results, China, Russia, and the United States joined the EU-3's multilateral efforts in June 2006. This group (P5+1) presented Iran with conditional offers of economic, technological, and security incentives to curb its nuclear program. Iran rejected the suspension of its enrichment activities and offered its own counter-proposal that omitted any details on specific steps. President Obama's inauguration to the US presidency prompted changes in the overall positive inducement strategy vis-à-vis Iran, reinvigorating US unilateral diplomatic outreach to Iran. He offered to engage in

---

[104] Levitt (2010) and Wright (2010).
[105] Most agreements were short-lived and later rescinded except for Russia's commitment to complete Bushehr.
[106] Thaler *et al.* (2010: 87).
[107] Russia is yet again an exception. As Table B3.8 indicates, it continued nuclear cooperation with Iran and became the first state to sign a cooperative security agreement with it since the Iranian Revolution.

negotiations without the precondition of an Iranian enrichment suspension, abandoning former US policy, enabling the P5+1 to invite Iran to negotiations that had stalled in 2008 due to the suspension precondition. However, new tensions arose with the revelation of yet another previously undeclared enrichment facility in September 2009. While expressing grave concern regarding this development, the P5+1 also offered Iran a uranium-for-fuel exchange proposal. Iran would receive fuel to power the Tehran Research Reactor, a 5 megawatt-thermal research reactor that requires 20 percent low enriched uranium (LEU) fuel, in exchange for sending a portion of its 3–5 percent LEU stockpile to Russia for fuel fabrication.[108] Although President Ahmadinejad initially expressed some interest, opponents in both the reformist and pragmatic conservative camps, as noted by Nader (Chapter 7, this volume), characterized Ahmadinejad's interest in the deal as "weak-kneed accommodation to the West," to gain political traction at home.[109] Ahmadinejad rejected the deal to save face domestically, thus sanctions were back on the agenda of the P5+1.[110]

Conclusion

Beyond the cases reviewed above, the circumstances of two other sets of cases differentiate them from our focused discussion of inducements in the last two decades. One set comprises states that possessed nuclear weapons before 1990 but relinquished them by the mid 1990s, including South Africa, Belarus, Ukraine, and Kazakhstan. South Africa undertook the decision to dismantle its nuclear weapons program in 1989. Belarus, Ukraine, and Kazakhstan experienced special circumstances as former Soviet states. The second set comprises non-signatories of the NPT – India, Pakistan, and Israel – who acquired nuclear weapons either prior to the NPT or abstained from signing the treaty. Their actions thus did not constitute violations of international legal obligations as with the four cases reviewed here.

Our analysis of positive inducements and sanctions used to deter nuclear proliferation in Libya, Iraq, Iran, and North Korea over these

---

[108] David Sanger, Thomas Erlanger, and Robert Worth, "Tehran Rejects Nuclear Accord, Officials Report," *New York Times*, October 29, 2009.

[109] Perkovich (2009).

[110] Turkey, Brazil, and Iran signed a trilateral fuel exchange agreement that prompted skepticism from the US and European powers. Given the collapse of an earlier fuel exchange agreement between Iran, the United States, France, and Russia in February 2010, many Western powers viewed the May 2010 trilateral agreement as an Iranian effort to forestall future multilateral sanctions.

past two decades underlines a key point: nuclear-related concerns did not prompt the initial use of sanctions in any of the four cases. For various reasons – support of terrorism being the most prevalent – complex sanctions systems were already in place prior to the inception of instruments related to nuclear proliferation. The United States, as the pre-eminent party relying on sanctions, addressed nuclear proliferation concerns by reaffirming existing comprehensive sanctions. This reaffirmation came through targeted sanctions designed to deter investment in the targeted country and financially isolate companies or individuals within the country with ties to the nuclear program. Assessing the independent impact of actions related to nuclear programs is therefore extremely difficult.

Our goal in this chapter has been to provide a comprehensive list of formal inducements taken by states and multilateral organizations, and to consider general patterns in that activity within and across the four cases. Understanding the complexity of individual inducements is consequential for assessing the severity and effectiveness of such actions. However, a trend analysis based on formally established metrics of severity and effectiveness would entail a level of detail that goes beyond the scope of this chapter. Establishing such metrics would require one to take into account the economic impact associated with a particular inducement for both the target and the sender. Raw dollar amounts may seem one obvious measure. Others include the target's trade dependence on the main sender, its economic position within the international system, its exposure to actual reduction of total trade, unemployment, and inflation rates, and changes in Gross Domestic Production (GDP).[111] Beyond the economic impact, assessing whether or not inducements affect the economic and/or foreign diplomatic policy of the target state would require a comparison between the pre- and post-inducement policies. Haggard and Noland, for instance, chart how North Korea sought out alternative trading partners in response to sanctions (Chapter 8). Finally, a systematic examination of inducements requires proper attention to the relative receptivity to different forms of inducement, as determined by domestic distributional considerations in different target states. Our chapter provides a comprehensive profile of the diverse positive and negative, comprehensive and targeted instruments that senders have relied upon in the last two decades to influence nuclear proliferators. We also began addressing the diverse response to those inducements. Subsequent chapters examine in greater detail the causal mechanisms through which inducements work their way through domestic contexts.

[111] Wallensteen (1968).

Appendix A

Table A3.1 *Categorized sanctions by target and time period*

Sanction	Iran	Iraq	Libya	North Korea	Subtotal	Total
Comprehensive trade and financial bans						
1990–1994	0	9	1	0	10	
1995–1999	4	0	0	0	4	14
2000–2004	0	0	0	0	0	
2005–2009	0	0	0	0	0	
Targeted trade actions						
1990–1994	13	7	2	4	26	
1995–1999	8	2	1	3	14	85
2000–2004	10	0	1	9	20	
2005–2009	13	0	0	12	25	
Targeted financial actions						
1990–1994	2	3	1	0	6	
1995–1999	3	2	2	0	7	52
2000–2004	2	0	1	0	3	
2005–2009	20	0	0	16	36	
Diplomatic pressures						
1990–1994	2	12	2	16	32	
1995–1999	6	8	2	10	26	111
2000–2004	16	4	1	11	32	
2005–2009	16	0	0	5	21	
Reversal of positive inducements						
1990–1994	13	0	0	0	13	
1995–1999	7	0	0	5	12	33
2000–2004	1	0	0	3	4	
2005–2009	2	0	0	2	4	
Petroleum-sector restrictions						
1990–1994	0	3	1	0	4	
1995–1999	4	0	1	0	5	15
2000–2004	1	0	1	4	6	
2005–2009	0	0	0	0	0	

Table A3.1 (*cont.*)

Sanction	Iran	Iraq	Libya	North Korea	Subtotal	Total
Military intervention						
1990–1994	1	6	4	1	12	
1995–1999	4	2	0	0	6	26
2000–2004	0	1	1	1	3	
2005–2009	3	0	0	2	5	
Military/ defense sector restrictions						
1990–1994	4	5	2	2	13	
1995–1999	0	0	0	3	3	29
2000–2004	2	0	0	9	11	
2005–2009	1	0	0	1	2	
Flight restrictions						
1990–1994	0	2	3	0	5	
1995–1999	0	0	0	0	0	5
2000–2004	0	0	0	0	0	
2005–2009	0	0	0	0	0	
Targeted at the nuclear industry						
1990–1994	18	6	4	4	32	
1995–1999	10	1	1	8	20	85
2000–2004	9	0	2	11	22	
2005–2009	5	0	0	6	11	
Total	200	73	34	148	455	455

Table A3.2 *Categorized sanctions by sender and time period*

Sanction	US	Non-US unilateral	UN	Non-UN multilateral	Subtotal	Total
Comprehensive trade and financial bans						
1990–1994	2	7	1	0	10	14
1995–1999	4	0	0	0	4	
2000–2004	0	0	0	0	0	
2005–2009	0	0	0	0	0	

Table A3.2 (*cont.*)

Sanction	US	Non-US unilateral	UN	Non-UN multilateral	Subtotal	Total
Targeted trade actions						
1990–1994	9	15	1	1	26	85
1995–1999	11	1	1	1	14	
2000–2004	18	2	0	0	20	
2005–2009	16	1	6	2	25	
Targeted financial actions						
1990–1994	4	1	1	0	6	52
1995–1999	7	0	0	0	7	
2000–2004	3	0	0	0	3	
2005–2009	20	3	9	4	36	
Petroleum-sector restrictions						
1990–1994	1	2	1	0	4	15
1995–1999	5	0	0	0	5	
2000–2004	2	1	0	3	6	
2005–2009	0	0	0	0	0	
Diplomatic pressures						
1990–1994	8	2	18	4	32	111
1995–1999	6	4	13	3	26	
2000–2004	14	2	13	3	32	
2005–2009	3	2	14	2	21	
Reversal of positive inducements						
1990–1994	0	12	0	1	13	33
1995–1999	5	5	0	2	12	
2000–2004	0	1	0	3	4	
2005–2009	2	0	1	1	4	
Flight restrictions						
1990–1994	1	0	3	1	5	
1995–1999	0	0	0	0	0	5
2000–2004	0	0	0	0	0	
2005–2009	0	0	0	0	0	
Military intervention						
1990–1994	2	6	1	3	12	26
1995–1999	1	4	0	1	6	
2000–2004	1	0	0	2	3	
2005–2009	0	0	3	2	5	

Table A3.2 (*cont.*)

Sanction	US	Non-US unilateral	UN	Non-UN multilateral	Subtotal	Total
Military/ defense sector restrictions						
1990–1994	8	3	1	1	13	29
1995–1999	3	0	0	0	3	
2000–2004	11	0	0	0	11	
2005–2009	0	0	2	0	2	
Targeted at the nuclear industry						
1990–1994	10	19	2	1	32	85
1995–1999	9	7	1	3	20	
2000–2004	18	1	0	3	22	
2005–2009	4	0	6	1	11	
Total	208	103	96	48	455	455

Table A3.3 *Categorized positive inducements by target and time period*

Positive inducement	Iran	Iraq	Libya	North Korea	Subtotal	Total
Conditional offers						
1990–1994	1	4	0	8	13	55
1995–1999	1	6	1	3	11	
2000–2004	7	0	1	5	13	
2005–2009	11	0	0	7	17	
Trade-related actions						
1990–1994	0	3	0	1	4	27
1995–1999	1	6	1	1	9	
2000–2004	5	3	0	1	9	
2005–2009	5	0	0	0	5	
Financial actions						
1990–1994	1	1	0	1	3	17
1995–1999	2	1	0	0	3	
2000–2004	2	2	0	3	7	
2005–2009	1	0	0	3	4	

Table A3.3 (*cont.*)

Positive inducement	Iran	Iraq	Libya	North Korea	Subtotal	Total
Diplomatic initiatives						
1990–1994	1	7	0	15	23	112
1995–1999	7	12	11	14	44	
2000–2004	5	6	3	12	26	
2005–2009	11	0	0	8	19	
Reversal of sanctions						
1990–1994	0	2	0	1	3	23
1995–1999	2	1	2	3	8	
2000–2004	2	3	2	1	8	
2005–2009	0	0	0	4	4	
Petroleum and energy sector actions						
1990–1994	1	3	0	1	5	36
1995–1999	1	11	2	0	14	
2000–2004	7	4	0	2	13	
2005–2009	1	0	0	3	4	
Security-related actions						
1990–1994	0	0	0	7	7	18
1995–1999	0	0	0	0	0	
2000–2004	1	1	0	4	6	
2005–2009	1	0	0	4	5	
Infrastructure aid						
1990–1994	0	0	0	2	2	4
1995–1999	0	0	1	0	1	
2000–2004	0	1	0	0	1	
2005–2009	0	0	0	0	0	
Nuclear-related tech. coop. agreements						
1990–1994	16	0	0	7	23	50
1995–1999	3	1	2	4	10	
2000–2004	7	0	0	1	8	
2005–2009	7	0	0	2	9	

Table A3.3 (*cont.*)

Positive inducement	Iran	Iraq	Libya	North Korea	Subtotal	Total
Non-nuclear tech. coop. agreements						
1990–1994	1	0	0	1	2	7
1995–1999	0	0	0	0	0	
2000–2004	1	0	1	1	3	
2005–2009	2	0	0	0	2	
Total	114	78	27	130	349	349

Table A3.4 *Categorized positive inducements by sender and time period*

Positive inducement	US	Non-US unilateral	UN	Non-UN multilateral	Subtotal	Total
Conditional offers						
1990–1994	5	4	2	2	13	55
1995–1999	5	1	3	2	11	
2000–2004	5	3	1	4	13	
2005–2009	3	3	0	12	18	
Trade-related actions						
1990–1994	1	1	2	0	4	27
1995–1999	2	1	5	1	9	
2000–2004	3	1	2	3	9	
2005–2009	2	0	0	3	5	
Financial actions						
1990–1994	2	1	0	0	3	17
1995–1999	0	2	1	0	3	
2000–2004	3	1	1	2	7	
2005–2009	1	1	0	2	4	
Diplomatic initiatives						
1990–1994	7	12	2	2	23	112
1995–1999	13	15	5	11	44	
2000–2004	8	13	3	2	26	
2005–2009	9	2	0	8	19	

Table A3.4 (*cont.*)

Positive inducement	US	Non-US unilateral	UN	Non-UN multilateral	Subtotal	Total
Reversal of sanctions						
1990–1994	2	1	0	0	3	23
1995–1999	3	1	2	2	8	
2000–2004	4	3	1	0	8	
2005–2009	2	0	0	2	4	
Petroleum and energy sector actions						
1990–1994	2	1	2	0	5	36
1995–1999	2	7	4	1	14	
2000–2004	1	8	2	2	13	
2005–2009	1	2	0	1	4	
Security-related actions						
1990–1994	4	1	0	2	7	18
1995–1999	0	0	0	0	0	
2000–2004	2	3	0	1	6	
2005–2009	0	2	0	3	5	
Infrastructure aid						
1990–1994	1	1	0	0	2	4
1995–1999	0	1	0	0	1	
2000–2004	0	1	0	0	1	
2005–2009	0	0	0	0	0	
Nuclear-related tech. coop. agreements						50
1990–1994	3	20	0	0	23	
1995–1999	3	7	0	0	10	
2000–2004	1	3	1	3	8	
2005–2009	0	1	0	8	9	
Non-nuclear tech. coop. agreements						7
1990–1994	0	2	0	0	2	
1995–1999	0	0	0	0	0	
2000–2004	0	3	0	0	3	
2005–2009	0	0	0	2	2	
Total	100	129	39	81	349	349

Table A3.5 *Categorized sanctions by target–sender pairing and time period*

Sanction	IR-US	IR-Uni.	IR-UN	IR-Multi.	IQ-US	IQ-Uni.	IQ-UN	IQ-Multi.	LY-US	LY-Uni.	LY-UN	LY-Multi.	NK-US	NK-Uni.	NK-UN	NK-Multi.	Subtotal	Total
Comp. trade and financial bans																		14
1990–1994	0	0	0	0	1	7	1	0	1	0	0	0	0	0	0	0	10	
1995–1999	4	0	0	0	0	0	0	0	0	0	0	0	0	0	0	0	4	
2000–2004	0	0	0	0	0	0	0	0	0	0	0	0	0	0	0	0	0	
2005–2009	0	0	0	0	0	0	0	0	0	0	0	0	0	0	0	0	0	
Targeted trade actions																		85
1990–1994	2	10	0	1	4	3	0	0	1	0	1	0	2	2	0	0	26	
1995–1999	7	0	0	1	0	1	1	0	1	0	0	0	3	0	0	0	14	
2000–2004	8	2	0	0	0	0	0	0	1	0	0	0	9	0	0	0	20	
2005–2009	9	1	2	1	0	0	0	0	0	0	0	0	7	0	4	1	25	
Targeted financial actions																		52
1990–1994	1	1	0	0	3	0	0	0	0	0	1	0	0	0	0	0	6	
1995–1999	3	0	0	0	2	0	0	0	2	0	0	0	0	0	0	0	7	
2000–2004	2	0	0	0	0	0	0	0	1	0	0	0	0	0	0	0	3	
2005–2009	11	2	4	3	0	0	0	0	0	0	0	0	9	1	5	1	36	
Diplomatic pressures																		111
1990–1994	2	0	0	0	2	1	5	4	1	0	1	0	3	1	12	0	32	
1995–1999	2	1	0	3	1	0	7	0	1	1	0	0	2	2	6	0	26	
2000–2004	7	1	7	1	3	0	1	0	1	0	0	0	3	1	5	2	32	
2005–2009	3	1	10	2	0	0	0	0	0	0	0	0	0	1	4	0	21	
Reversal of pos. inducements																		33
1990–1994	0	12	0	1	0	0	0	0	0	0	0	0	0	0	0	0	13	
1995–1999	2	3	0	2	0	0	0	0	0	0	0	0	3	2	0	0	12	
2000–2004	0	1	0	0	0	0	0	0	0	0	0	0	0	0	0	3	4	
2005–2009	1	0	1	0	0	0	0	0	0	0	0	0	1	0	0	1	4	

	1	2	3	4	5	6	7	8	9	10	11	12	13	14	15	16	Total
Petroleum-Sector Restrictions																	**15**
1990–1994	0	0	0	1	2	0	0	0	1	0	0	0	0	0	0	0	4
1995–1999	4	0	0	0	0	0	1	0	0	0	0	0	0	0	0	0	5
2000–2004	1	0	0	0	0	0	0	0	0	1	0	0	0	1	0	3	6
2005–2009	0	0	0	0	0	0	0	0	0	0	0	0	0	0	0	0	0
Military intervention																	**26**
1990–1994	1	0	0	1	1	3	0	4	0	0	1	0	0	1	0	0	12
1995–1999	0	4	0	1	0	1	0	0	0	0	0	0	0	0	0	0	6
2000–2004	0	0	0	1	0	0	0	0	0	1	0	0	0	0	0	1	3
2005–2009	0	0	1	0	0	0	0	0	0	0	0	2	0	0	2	0	5
Defense sector restrictions																	**29**
1990–1994	2	1	0	3	2	0	1	0	1	0	0	0	3	0	0	0	13
1995–1999	0	0	0	0	0	0	0	0	0	0	0	0	3	0	0	0	3
2000–2004	2	0	0	0	0	0	0	0	0	0	0	0	9	0	0	0	11
2005–2009	0	0	1	0	0	0	0	0	0	0	0	0	0	0	1	0	2
Flight restrictions																	**5**
1990–1994	0	0	0	0	0	2	1	0	2	0	0	0	0	0	0	0	5
1995–1999	0	0	0	0	0	0	0	0	0	0	0	0	0	0	0	0	0
2000–2004	0	0	0	0	0	0	0	0	0	0	0	0	0	0	0	0	0
2005–2009	0	0	0	0	0	0	0	0	0	0	0	0	0	0	0	0	0
Targeting the nuclear industry																	**85**
1990–1994	4	13	0	4	0	0	2	2	0	1	2	0	2	2	0	0	32
1995–1999	2	5	0	0	0	0	1	0	0	0	2	0	6	2	0	2	20
2000–2004	8	1	0	0	0	0	0	0	0	2	0	0	9	0	0	2	22
2005–2009	2	0	3	0	0	0	0	0	0	0	0	0	2	0	3	1	11
Total	90	59	29	22	27	17	20	9	16	9	7	2	75	16	42	15	455

Notes: "Uni." refers to unilateral countries, other than the United States. "Multi." refers to multilateral bodies, other than the United Nations.

Table A3.6 *Categorized positive inducements by target–sender pairing and time period*

Positive inducement	IR-US	IR-Uni.	IR-UN	IR-Multi.	IQ-US	IQ-Uni.	IQ-UN	IQ-Multi.	LY-US	LY-Uni.	LY-UN	LY-Multi.	NK-US	NK-Uni.	NK-UN	NK-Multi.	Subtotal	Total
Financial actions																		
1990–1994	0	1	0	0	1	0	0	0	0	0	0	0	1	0	0	0	3	17
1995–1999	0	2	0	0	0	0	1	0	0	0	0	0	0	0	0	0	3	
2000–2004	1	0	0	1	0	0	1	1	0	0	0	0	2	1	0	0	7	
2005–2009	0	0	0	1	0	0	0	0	0	0	0	0	1	1	0	1	4	
Trade-related actions																		
1990–1994	0	0	0	0	0	1	2	0	0	0	0	0	1	0	0	0	4	27
1995–1999	1	0	0	0	0	1	4	1	0	0	1	0	1	0	0	0	9	
2000–2004	2	1	0	2	0	0	2	1	0	0	0	0	1	0	0	0	9	
2005–2009	2	0	0	3	0	0	0	0	0	0	0	0	0	0	0	0	5	
Conditional offers																		
1990–1994	0	1	0	0	1	1	2	0	0	0	0	0	4	2	0	2	13	55
1995–1999	1	0	0	0	0	1	3	2	1	0	0	0	3	0	0	0	11	
2000–2004	1	1	1	4	0	0	0	0	1	0	0	0	3	2	0	0	13	
2005–2009	1	2	0	8	0	0	0	0	0	0	0	0	2	1	0	4	18	
Diplomatic initiatives																		
1990–1994	1	0	0	0	1	3	2	1	0	0	0	0	5	9	0	1	23	112
1995–1999	2	3	0	2	0	5	5	2	2	5	0	4	9	2	0	3	44	
2000–2004	2	1	1	1	0	5	1	0	1	1	1	0	5	6	0	1	26	
2005–2009	7	0	0	4	0	0	0	0	0	0	0	0	2	2	0	4	19	

Reversal of sanctions																	
1990–1994	0	0	0	0	1	1	0	0	0	0	0	0	1	0	0	0	3
1995–1999	1	0	0	1	0	0	1	0	0	0	1	1	2	1	0	0	8
2000–2004	2	0	0	0	0	3	0	0	1	0	1	0	1	0	0	0	8
2005–2009	0	0	0	0	0	0	0	0	0	0	0	0	2	0	0	2	4
Petroleum and energy sector action																	
1990–1994	1	0	0	0	0	1	2	0	0	0	0	0	1	0	0	0	5
1995–1999	1	0	0	0	0	6	4	1	1	1	0	0	0	0	0	0	14
2000–2004	0	5	0	2	0	2	2	0	0	0	0	0	1	1	0	0	13
2005–2009	0	1	0	0	0	0	0	0	0	0	0	0	1	1	0	1	4
Security-related action																	
1990–1994	0	0	0	0	0	0	0	0	0	0	0	0	4	1	0	2	7
1995–1999	0	0	0	0	0	0	0	0	0	0	0	0	0	0	0	0	0
2000–2004	0	1	0	0	0	0	0	0	0	0	0	0	2	2	0	0	6
2005–2009	0	0	0	1	0	0	0	0	0	0	0	0	0	2	0	2	5
Infrastructure aid																	
1990–1994	0	0	0	0	0	0	0	0	0	0	0	0	1	1	0	0	2
1995–1999	0	0	0	0	0	0	0	0	0	1	0	0	0	0	0	0	1
2000–2004	0	0	0	0	0	1	0	0	0	0	0	0	0	0	0	0	1
2005–2009	0	0	0	0	0	0	0	0	0	0	0	0	0	0	0	0	0

Table A3.6 (cont.)

Positive inducement	IR-US	IR-Uni.	IR-UN	IR-Multi.	IQ-US	IQ-Uni.	IQ-UN	IQ-Multi.	LY-US	LY-Uni.	LY-UN	LY-Multi.	NK-US	NK-Uni.	NK-UN	NK-Multi.	Subtotal	Total
Non-nuclear technological cooperation agreements																		7
1990–1994	0	1	0	0	0	0	0	0	0	0	0	0	0	1	0	0	2	
1995–1999	0	0	0	0	0	0	0	0	0	0	0	0	0	0	0	0	0	
2000–2004	0	1	0	0	0	0	0	0	0	1	0	0	0	1	0	0	3	
2005–2009	0	0	0	2	0	0	0	0	0	0	0	0	0	0	0	0	2	
Nuclear-related technological cooperation agreements																		50
1990–1994	1	15	0	0	0	0	0	0	0	0	0	0	2	5	0	0	23	
1995–1999	0	3	0	0	0	1	0	0	0	2	0	0	3	1	0	0	10	
2000–2004	0	3	1	3	0	0	0	0	0	0	0	0	1	0	0	0	8	
2005–2009	0	1	0	6	0	0	0	0	0	0	0	0	0	0	0	2	9	
Total	27	43	3	39	4	32	32	10	7	11	4	5	62	43	0	25	347	349

Notes: "Uni." refers to unilateral countries, other than the United States.
"Multi." refers to multilateral bodies, other than the United Nations.

Table A3.7 *Categorically undifferentiated sanctions by year and target–sender pairing*

Year	IR-US	IR-Uni.	IR-UN	IR-Multi.	IQ-US	IQ-Uni.	IQ-UN	IQ-Multi.	LY-US	LY-Uni.	LY-UN	LY-Multi.	NK-US	NK-Uni.	NK-UN	NK-Multi.
1990	1	1	0	0	5	10	2	6	1	0	0	0	0	1	0	0
1991	0	5	0	0	0	0	3	1	0	2	0	0	0	1	1	0
1992	2	7	0	0	1	0	1	1	1	1	1	0	3	1	1	0
1993	1	3	0	0	0	0	0	0	0	1	1	0	0	0	6	0
1994	1	1	0	1	0	0	1	0	1	0	0	0	2	1	4	0
1995	6	1	0	1	0	0	0	0	1	1	0	0	0	0	1	0
1996	1	3	0	1	3	1	1	0	2	0	0	0	1	1	1	0
1997	1	1	0	2	0	0	3	0	0	0	0	0	3	0	0	0
1998	3	3	0	1	1	0	2	1	0	0	0	0	3	1	2	0
1999	2	0	0	0	0	0	1	0	0	0	0	0	1	0	2	0
2000	3	2	0	0	0	0	0	0	1	0	0	0	1	0	1	0
2001	1	0	0	0	0	0	0	0	1	0	0	0	2	0	1	0
2002	4	0	0	0	1	1	1	0	0	0	0	0	2	1	1	2
2003	1	1	3	1	3	0	0	0	0	0	0	1	4	1	2	2
2004	1	0	4	0	0	0	0	0	0	0	0	0	3	0	0	1
2005	1	0	2	2	0	0	0	0	0	0	0	0	4	0	0	0
2006	4	0	4	1	0	0	0	0	0	0	0	0	1	2	2	2
2007	3	0	4	0	0	0	0	0	0	0	0	0	2	0	0	0
2008	5	1	2	3	0	0	0	0	0	0	0	0	0	0	0	0
2009	1	1	1	0	0	0	0	0	0	0	0	0	3	0	4	0
Subtotal	42	30	20	13	14	11	15	9	8	5	2	1	35	10	29	7

Table A3.8 *Categorically undifferentiated positive inducements by year and target–sender pairing*

Year	IR-US	IR-Uni.	IR-UN	IR-Multi.	IQ-US	IQ-Uni.	IQ-UN	IQ-Multi.	LY-US	LY-Uni.	LY-UN	LY-Multi.	NK-US	NK-Uni.	NK-UN	NK-Multi.
1990	3	5	0	0	2	1	0	0	0	0	0	0	1	1	0	0
1991	0	3	0	0	0	0	2	1	0	0	0	0	0	4	0	0
1992	0	4	0	0	0	0	0	0	0	0	0	0	1	2	0	2
1993	0	3	0	0	0	0	0	0	0	0	0	0	3	3	0	0
1994	0	1	0	0	0	2	0	0	0	0	0	0	1	1	0	0
1995	0	2	0	0	0	0	1	0	0	0	0	0	2	0	0	0
1996	0	1	0	0	0	0	0	0	0	1	0	0	2	0	0	0
1997	1	1	0	1	0	4	0	0	0	3	0	2	2	1	0	1
1998	1	1	0	1	0	5	3	0	1	1	0	2	1	2	0	2
1999	2	3	0	0	0	1	2	2	2	2	1	0	4	1	0	0
2000	1	3	0	1	0	5	2	0	0	2	0	0	3	3	0	0
2001	0	4	0	1	0	2	1	2	0	0	0	0	2	0	0	0
2002	0	1	0	1	0	1	0	0	0	0	1	0	0	2	0	1
2003	2	0	0	2	0	0	0	0	1	0	0	0	1	1	0	1
2004	0	2	2	2	0	0	0	0	0	0	0	0	2	3	0	0
2005	2	1	0	6	0	0	0	0	0	0	0	0	0	1	0	1
2006	1	0	0	4	0	0	0	0	0	0	0	0	0	0	0	1
2007	0	0	0	0	0	0	0	0	0	0	0	0	1	1	0	2
2008	1	0	0	2	0	0	0	0	0	0	0	0	5	0	0	0
2009	3	1	0	1	0	0	0	0	0	0	0	0	0	1	0	0
Subtotal	17	36	2	22	2	21	11	5	4	9	2	4	31	27	0	10

Appendix B

Table B3.1 *Libya – sanctions, 1990–2009*

Date		Party	Action	Description
–	1990	US	Foreign-aid appropriations ban	Direct aid ban expanded to loans, credits, insurance
–	1991	Germany	Seizure of furnace	German firm Leybold AG; for metal alloy production
Dec	1991	Germany	Seizure of atomic equipment	Includes laser and dual-use equipment, US-made
–	1992	Germany	Seizure of furnace	Caught again, alloys used in guided missiles/nuclear weapons
Mar	1992	UN	SC Resolution 748	Total air and arms embargo, restrictions on Libyan diplomats
April	1992	US	Executive Order 12801	Imposition of travel sanctions
April	1993	Ukraine	Seizure of chemicals	From Moscow firm, bound for nuclear fuel
Nov	1993	UN	SC Resolution 883	Ban on sale of petroleum equipment, freeze on assets
April	1994	US	Foreign Relations Auth. Act	Prohibition of certain assistance and support
Dec	1995	UK	Expels Libyan diplomat	Saudi embassy, on charges of espionage
Dec	1995	US	White House statement	Calls upon UN to tighten oil exports
April	1996	US	AEDPA	Provision banning sale, license of defense articles/services
Aug	1996	US	Iran-Libya Sanctions Act	Sanctions for >$40 mil gas and oil investment, good/technology exp.
Nov	2000	US	State Department Action	Renewal of travel ban
July	2001	US	ILSA Extension Act of 2001	Congress renews Act, lowers threshold to $20 mil

Sources: James Martin Center for Nonproliferation Studies (CNS) (2010), Hufbauer *et al.* (2007), Arms Control Association (ACA) (2007), and O'Sullivan (2003).

Table B3.2 *Libya – positive inducements, 1990–2009*

Date		Party	Action	Description
Nov	1996	Italy	ENI (state oil) deal	Development of natural-gas resources, pipeline
Mar	1997	Vatican	Full diplomatic relations	Recognition of progress in religious freedom
Aug	1997	Multi	Issues statement, meet Qaddafi	Burkina Faso, Chad, Mali, Niger leaders call UN to look into impact of sanctions; meeting re: economic cooperation
Sept	1997	Arab L.	Public resolution defies UN	Calls on Arab countries to ease sanctions, incl. travel restriction
Oct	1997	Russia	Signed accord	Nuclear cooperation, includes rehab of Tajura center
Oct	1997	S. Africa	Nelson Mandela visits	Gives Qaddafi South Africa's "Order of Good Hope" honor
Mar	1998	Russia	Business deal, $8 million	Atomenergoeksport company contract for Tajura overhaul
May	1998	US	Waiver of ILSA violations	Total SA (Fra): $2 bil contract to develop South Pars gas field
Aug	1998	OAU	Resolution re: UN embargo	Suspends compliance for humanitarian purposes
Sept	1998	Multi	Presidents defy embargo, travel	Niger, Chad, Mali, Eritrea, Sudan: mark Qaddafi's 1969 rise
April	1999	UN	SC Resolution 1192	Suspension of sanctions (Lockerbie suspects handed over)
May	1999	US	Secret talks under Clinton	Unspecified offers re: nuclear program; official meeting in June
June	1999	US	Official meeting	First in 18 years; w/ US Representative to the UN Peter Burleigh
July	1999	UK	Resumption of diplomatic ties	Libya takes responsibility for 1984 embassy shooting
Dec	1999	Italy	Prime minister visits	First by Western leader in eight years
Mar	2000	Japan	No longer a "terrorist threat"	Also considers lifting sanctions from country
July	2000	N. Korea	Acquisition of Nodong missiles	Agreement re: infrastructure and technology training
Mar	2003	US	Quid quo pro offered	Secret talks: removal of sanctions for verifiable dismantling
Sept	2003	UN	SC Resolution 1506	Formal lifting of sanctions (UTA bombing agreement)*
Feb	2004	US	Travel ban lifted	Follows December 2003 WMD abandonment
Mar	2004	UK	Tony Blair visit	Culminates in $200 mil deal w/ Shell to explore oil and gas

Month	Year	Event	Country	Description
April	2004	Termination of ILSA for Libya	US	Resumes commercial activities, investments, transactions
June	2004	Resumption of diplomatic ties	US	Formal resumption, Liaison Office opened
Sept	2004	Executive Order 13357	US	National Emergency ended, accompanying sanctions removed
Oct	2004	Arms embargo lifted	EU	Formal end to suspended UN sanctions
Oct	2004	Pledges military equipment	Italy	Intended to combat illegal immigration
Oct	2004	Chancellor Schroeder visits	Germany	First by German head, extends Qaddafi invite to Germany
Nov	2004	President Chirac visits	France	Discussion of civilian nuclear program development
Jan	2005	Cooperation accord	Poland	Disarmament and possibility of further cooperation
Feb	2005	State Department actions	US	Normalization of relations, restrictions for diplomats lifted
May	2005	Agreement announced	France	Development of peaceful nuclear energy program
Oct	2005	Fuel deal with TVEL	Russia	Providing low-enriched uranium to Tajura nuclear reactor
Mar	2006	Export-Import Bank action	US	Opens for trade with Libya; continued restoration of ties
May	2006	State terrorist list removal	US	Full resumption of diplomatic ties
June	2006	Joint Letter	UK	British aids in transformation of nuclear program
Mar	2007	Memorandum of understanding	UK	Scientific cooperation signed at British Foreign Office
April	2007	Cooperation with ROSATOM	Russia	Atomic Energy Agency on peaceful use, for medical purposes
July	2007	Memorandum of understanding	France	Nuclear and defense cooperation agreement
Dec	2007	Foreign Minister Lavrov offer	Russia	Help in pursuit of nuclear energy
Jan	2008	Science & Tech Coop Agreement	US	Bilateral action, exchange of personnel and information
April	2008	Cancels $4.5 billion debt	Russia	Military, energy, and construction contracts signed ($2.5 bil)
May	2008	President Yushchenko meeting	Ukraine	Further discussion on nuclear reactors and peaceful energy
Sept	2008	Secretary of State Rice visit	US	First US SOS to visit since 1953
May	2009	Agreement announced	Ukraine	Nuclear energy cooperation agreement

Note: * As noted in the narrative, Qaddafi's 2003 renouncement of nuclear weapons ends our consideration of the inducements era as it applies to Libya. We include subsequent data points to complete the time period and demonstrate the effects of the renouncement, but they do not factor in the tables in this chapter.

Sources: CNS (2010), Hufbauer *et al.* (2007), ACA (2007), and O'Sullivan (2003).

Table B3.3 *Iraq – sanctions, 1990–2009*

Date	Party	Action	Description
July	1990	US	Executive & Legislative action	Export controls on sensitive techs, denies agric. benefits
Aug	1990	US	Executive Order 12722	National emergency declared: ban on exports and imports
Aug	1990	Multi	Sanctions follow invasion	W. Germ, Belgium, Netherlands, Luxembourg, Norway freeze assets China joins arms embargo, USSR suspends military deliveries Japan freezes aid, stops exports, embargoes oil imports Turkey freezes aid, halts shipments of oil
Aug	1990	Multi	Denouncements of invasion	US and USSR issue statement calling for arms cutoff Arab League and Gulf Cooperation Council condemn attack Arab League resolution to send troops to Saudi Arabia
Aug	1990	Multi	Military action	Egypt sends thousands to Saudi Arabia for defensive purposes British, Soviet, and French ships join US naval forces Canada, France, Australia send ships to Gulf area
Aug	1990	UN	SC Resolution 661	Comprehensive trade and financial sanctions
Sept	1990	US	State Department Designation	State supporter of terrorism; prohibits grants, aid
Sept	1990	UN	SC Resolution 670	Air embargo on all except humanitarian deliveries
Nov	1990	US	Iraq Sanctions Act of 1990	Denies exp. licenses for goods, defense items, nuclear material
Jan	1991	US-led	Operation Desert Storm	UN-authorized military response
April	1991	UN	SC Resolution 687	Lifting of sanctions tied to WMD compliance
Jan	1992	IAEA/ UN	Rebuke of Foreign Ministry	Accusations of failure to report gas centrifuge materials
Aug	1992	Multi	No-fly zone declared	US, UK, and France, in southern Iraq
Oct	1992	US	Iran–Iraq Arms Nonproliferation	Act bars contributors to Iran/Iraq's acquisition of NCB weapons
Oct	1994	UN	SC Resolution 949	Demands that Iraq complies with UNSCOM

Jan	1996	Jordan	Halves exports to Iraq	Est. $400 mil, to alienate Hussein from business community
Mar	1996	UN	SC Resolution 1051	Demands information re: exports to Iraq, also dual-use items
April	1996	US	AEDPA	Provision bans sale, license of defense articles/services
June	1996	UN	SC Resolution 1060	Reiterates demand for full cooperation with UNSCOM
Sept	1996	US	Operation Desert Strike	Military strike follows Iraq's move north threatens Kurds
June	1997	UN	SC Resolution 1115	Condemns UNSCOM interference, lifts periodic sanctions reviews
Oct	1997	UN	SC Resolution 1134	Reiterates demand for full cooperation with UNSCOM
Nov	1997	UN	SC Resolution 1137	Condemnation, travel restrictions for involved officials
Mar	1998	UN	SC Resolution 1154	Reiterates demand for full cooperation with UNSCOM
Sept	1998	UN	SC Resolution 1194	Ends periodic sanctions review; left in place permanently
Oct	1998	US	Iraq Liberation Act	Provides arms and aid to opposition group
Dec	1998	US+UK	Operation Desert Fox	Air strikes aimed at Iraq's WMD program
Dec	1999	UN	SC Resolution 1284	Replaces UNSCOM with UNMOVIC, carries same mandate
Jan	2002	US	Rhetoric	President Bush labels North Korea part of the "axis of evil"
Nov	2002	UN	SC Resolution 1441	Demands compliance with disarmament of weapons program
Jan	2003	US	State of the Union	Threatens to lead multilateral coalition to forcibly disarm Iraq
Feb	2003	US	Colin Powell speech to UNSC	Shows evidence of Iraq's WMD procurement efforts
Mar	2003	US	Operation Iraqi Freedom	Invasion of Iraq following claim of WMD possession

Sources: CNS (2010), Hufbauer *et al.* (2007), Katzman (2002), and O'Sullivan (2003).

Table B3.4 *Iraq – positive inducements, 1990–2009*

Date	Party	Action	Description
Jan 1990	US	Pres. Determination 90–7	Waives ban on Export-Import Bank financing, allows direct aid
Sept 1990	Iran	Resumption of diplomatic ties	Includes discussion re: settlement of the war
Dec 1990	US	Secretary of State Baker	Offer for "last chance" peace talks bet. Dec 15 and Jan 15
Aug 1991	UN	SC Resolution 706	Oil-for-food program proposed, rejected by Iraq
Sept 1991	UN	SC Resolution 712	Oil-for-food program proposed, rejected by Iraq again
Nov 1991	Europe	Release of frozen assets	Funds from UK and European banks for humanitarian imports
Sept 1994	Turkey	Trade food for oil	Border embargo relaxed, trucks transport food
Nov 1994	Russia	Supports lifting oil embargo	Iraq formally recognizes Kuwait's sovereignty and borders
April 1995	UN	SC Resolution 986	Oil-for-food program ($2 bil/6 mo), begins in May 1996
April 1997	Russia	Bilateral oil cooperation	Development of Russian-owned Quma oilfield
May 1997	Turkey	Pipeline agreement	Preliminary deal for 807-mile pipeline
May 1997	Syria	Border reopens	Discussions lead to reopening; discussions of oil-for-frood
Nov 1997	Russia	Diplomacy in UN	Pushes for concessions, also sells strategic materials
Feb 1998	UN	SC Resolution 1153	Increases oil-for-food program limit to $5.2 bil/6 months
April 1998	Russia	Initiative in UN	Proposes easing of inspections connected to nuclear activity
May 1998	UN	SC Resolution 1137 lifted	Cooperation with inspections; travel restrictions removed
June 1998	UN	Allows $300 mil for spare parts	Purchase to upgrade oil production facilities
July 1998	Multi	Agreement with Jordan, Syria	Concerning oil pipelines
Sept 1998	Syria	Diplomatic overtures	Reopen trade relations, discussions re: oil pipeline
Jan 1999	Multi	Proposals to end oil embargo	France, Russia, UK, Netherlands each, rejected by Iraq
Sept 1999	UK/NED	US-backed proposal in SC	Concerns lifting of sanctions for new inspections
Oct 1999	UN	Lifting oil sale limits	Allows extra $3.04 bil in oil-for-food program by November

Dec	1999	Russia	Oil company announcement	Zarubezhneft will drill oil wells, first since sanctions imposed
Dec	1999	UN	SC Resolution 1284	Establishes UNMOVIC, allows temp. relaxing of sanctions
Mar	2000	UN	Allows $600 mil for spare parts	Budget increases for oil sector repairs
Aug	2000	Venezuela	Chavez visits Hussein	First elected head of state to visit since Gulf War
Sept	2000	Multi	Passenger flights to Baghdad	Russia, France, and Jordan argue civilian flights are not violation
Nov	2000	Syria	Damascus meetings	Bilateral cooperation: commercial exchange, imports
Dec	2000	UN	SC Resolution 1330	Oil-for-food renewal, oil sector repairs, expansion of imp. list
Jan	2001	Multi	Egypt, Syria free trade pacts	Symbolic moves against sanctions regime
Mar	2002	US	"Smart sanctions" plan	Pressure from Russia, eases restrictions on civilian goods
Mar	2002	Arab L.	Final communiqué	Rejects any use of force against Iraq
May	2002	UN	SC Resolution 1409	Eases restrictions on civilian goods
Aug	2002	Russia	$40 billion economic pact	Deal for economic cooperation (within sanctions regime)*
May	2003	US	Suspend Iraq Sanctions Act	1990 sanctions lifted for humanitarian aid, reconstruction
May	2003	UN	SC Resolution 1483	Ends sanctions besides arms embargo, US/UK as occupiers
July	2004	US	Executive Order 13350	Terminates E.O. 12722 national emergency
June	2007	UN	SC Resolution 1762	Terminates mandate of UNMOVIC

Note:

* For the purposes of our analyses, the 2003 US/UK invasion and occupation rendered the inducements era over in Iraq. As with the Libyan case, the data points that follow are unaccounted for in our tables.

Sources: CNS (2010), Hufbauer *et al.* (2007), Katzman (2002), and O'Sullivan (2003).

Table B3.5 *North Korea – sanctions, 1990–2009*

Date		Party	Action	Description
–	1990	USSR	Stops nuclear support, exports	Includes equipment and fuel, wants IAEA safeguards
July	1991	USSR	Suspends technical support	Ends supply of nuclear fuel rods for IRT-2000 reactor
Sept	1991	IAEA/UN	Board of Governors resolution	Calls for NK to ratify a Comprehensive Safeguards Agreement
Mar	1992	US	Firm-specific sanctions	Two-year action: Lyongaksan and Changgwang Credit Corp, under Arms Export Control Act and 1979 Export Administration Act
June	1992	US	Firm-specific sanctions	Lyongaksan and Changgwang Credit Corp, AECA and 1979 EAA
June	1992	IAEA/UN	BOG agreement	180 days notice of nuclear-related facilities construction
Oct	1992	US	SoD Cheney comments	Announces nuclear suspicions, delays troop withdrawal
Dec	1992	Russia	Special Forces arrests	36 senior weapons scientists en route to North Korea
Feb	1993	IAEA/UN	Formal request from Hans Blix	Ultimatum for special inspections, threatens special BOG meet
Feb	1993	IAEA/UN	Passes Resolution	30 days for inspection compliance; threatens UNSC referral
April	1993	IAEA/UN	BOG Resolution	Special meeting, calls for Security Council to intervene
May	1993	UN	SC Resolution 825	Calls for North Korea to reconsider NPT withdrawal
Oct	1993	IAEA/UN	General Assembly Resolution	Calls for full compliance with safeguards agreement
Nov	1993	UN	General Assembly Resolution	Calls for IAEA cooperation, implementation of safeguards
Mar	1994	US	Cancels scheduled talks	Resumes Team Spirit exercise, sends S. Korea Patriot missiles
Mar	1994	UN	Issues Presidential Statement	Proposed by China, urges readmission of IAEA inspectors
May	1994	UN	Security Council statement	Urges N. Korea to set aside spent fuel rods for inspection
June	1994	Russia	President Yeltsin warning	No promises of protection against sanctions, potential conflict
June	1994	IAEA/UN	Blix informs the Security Council	IAEA unable to determine whether fuel diversion has occurred
June	1994	IAEA/UN	BOG Resolution	Suspends technical aid (approximately $250,000 per year)
July	1994	US	Amendment to foreign aid bill	Bans aid w/o presidential certification of nuclear non-pursuit
Sept	1994	IAEA/UN	General Conference Resolution	Sponsored by France, urges immediate cooperation with IAEA

Month	Year	Actor	Action	Description
Sept	1995	IAEA/UN	General Conference Resolution	Calls for compliance with safeguards, preservation of info
Nov	1995	UN	General Assembly Resolution	Calls for IAEA cooperation, implementation of safeguards
May	1996	US	Firm-specific sanctions	Changgwang Sinyong Corp, under AECA and 1979 EAA (EO 12924)
Sept	1996	IAEA/UN	General Assembly Resolution	Calls for full compliance with safeguards agreement
Nov	1996	S. Korea	Suspends KEDO LWR project	Demands apology to September incursion of N.K. submarine
July	1997	US	Senate withholds $14 mil to KEDO	In response to N. Korean soldiers crossing demarcation line
Aug	1997	US	Firm-specific sanctions	Lyongaksan General Trading Corp and Korea Pugang Trading Corp
Nov	1997	UN	General Assembly Resolution	Calls for compliance with safeguards, preservation of info
April	1998	US	Firm-specific sanctions	Changgwang Sinyong Corp, under AECA and 1979 EAA (EO 12924)
Sept	1998	US	Amendment to foreign aid bill	Stipulates tougher conditions for allocating KEDO funds
Sept	1998	Japan	Suspends diplomacy	Stops food aid and nuclear reactor financing following tests
Sept	1998	US	Foreign Relations Approp. Bill	Cuts all $35 mil for 1999 heavy fuel oil deliveries
Sept	1998	IAEA/UN	General Assembly Resolution	Calls for full compliance with safeguards agreement
Nov	1998	UN	General Assembly Resolution	Calls for compliance with safeguards, preservation of info
Oct	1999	Multi	CTBT Conference Resolution	National delegates single out North Korea as non-signatory
Oct	1999	IAEA/UN	General Assembly Resolution	Calls for compliance with NPT obligations, safeguards
Nov	1999	UN	General Assembly Resolution	Expresses concern over implementation of IAEA safeguards
Nov	1999	US	North Korea Threat Reduction Act	Requires US President to certify fulfillment of NPT and Agreed Framework commitments prior to KEDO funds
April	2000	US	Firm-specific sanctions	Changgwang Sinyong Corp, under AECA and 1979 EAA (EO 12924)
Sept	2000	IAEA/UN	General Conference Resolution	Calls for full compliance with safeguards agreement
Jan	2001	US	Firm-specific sanctions	Changgwang Sinyong Corp, under Iran Nonproliferation Act
June	2001	US	Firm-specific sanctions	Changgwang Sinyong Corp, under INPA
Sept	2001	IAEA/UN	General Conference Resolution	Requests N. Korea to abide by NPT commitments, safeguards

Table B3.5 (cont.)

Date	Party	Action	Description
Jan 2002	US	Rhetoric	President Bush labels North Korea part of the "axis of evil"
Aug 2002	US	Firm-specific sanctions	Changgwang Sinyong Corp, under AECA and 1979 EAA
Oct 2002	S. Korea	National Assembly Resolution	Calls for North Korea to abandon nuclear programs
Oct 2002	Multi	Joint Statement	US, South Korea, and Japan call for dismantling at APEC
Oct 2002	Multi	Agreed Framework suspended	Stop oil supplies (US/S.Korea/Japan) and rice shipments (Japan)
Nov 2002	IAEA/UN	BOG Resolution	Reiterates call for cooperation, clarification of recent reports
Jan 2003	EU	EU Parliament Resolution	Condemns withdrawal from NPT
Jan 2003	IAEA/UN	BOG Resolution	Condemns N. Korea restarting reactor "in the strongest terms"
Jan 2003	US	USAID withholds aid	Fear of diversion of economic assistance to military
Jan 2003	IAEA/UN	BOG Resolution	Refers North Korean case to the UN Security Council
Mar 2003	US	Firm-specific sanctions	Changgwang Sinyong Corp, under AECA and 1979 EAA (EO 13382)
Mar 2003	China	Suspends oil shipments	Closes pipeline briefly, warning re: US provocation
June 2003	US	Firm-specific sanctions	Changgwang Sinyong Corp, under INPA
July 2003	US	Firm-specific sanctions	Changgwang Sinyong Corp, under AECA and 1979 EAA (EO 13382)
July 2003	Multi	Proliferation Security Initiative	Statement from 11 countries express support
Nov 2003	Multi	KEDO stops Framework action	Suspends construction of two light-water reactors
April 2004	US	Firm-specific sanctions	Changgwang Sinyong Corp, under INPA
Sept 2004	US	Firm-specific sanctions	Changgwang Sinyong Corp, under INPA
Nov 2004	US	Firm-specific sanctions	Changgwang Sinyong Corp, under INPA
Nov 2004	Multi	KEDO continues suspension	Announcement that construction will stop for another year
Dec 2004	US	Firm-specific sanctions	Paeksan Associated Corp, under INPA
May 2005	US	Cuts funding for personnel	Involves those working on LWR projects
June 2005	US	Executive Order 13382	Freezes assets of WMD proliferators, bans all transactions

Month	Year	Actor	Action	Description
Sept	2005	US	Banco Delta SARL designated	Prohibits transactions w/ bank, as money launderer for N.Korea
Oct	2005	US	Treasury Department action	Adds 7 entities to WMD proliferators list, freezes assets
June	2006	Multi	KEDO terminates project	Ends LWR project, for noncompliance w/ Agreed Framework
July	2006	JPN/S.Kor	Punishment for ballistic tests	Japan imposes sanctions, South Korea stops food/fertilizer aid
July	2006	UN	SC Resolution 1695	Condemns tests; prevents items, materials, tech. transfers
Sept	2006	JPN+AUS	Implementation of 1695	Targets 12 foreign entities (both), and 3 institutions (Japan)
Oct	2006	Japan	Implementation of 1695	Six-month ban on N. Korea ships from all ports, and imports
Oct	2006	UN	SC Resolution 1718	Bans missile materials transfers, luxury goods export and travel
Dec	2006	US	Pres. Determination 2007–7	Invokes Glenn Amendment and Atomic Energy Act sanctions
Jan	2007	US	Export Admin. Regulations	Reimposes licensing requirements on all exp./re-exports
Mar	2007	US	Treasury Dept. action on BDA	Prohibits business, freezes North Korean assets
Feb	2009	US	Firm-specific sanction	Moksong Trading Corp, Korea Mining & Dev. Corp, and Sino-Ki
April	2009	UN	Firm-specific sanction	Korea Mining & Dev, Korea Ryongbong Corp, Tranchon Bank
June	2009	UN	SC Resolution 1874	Expands arms embargoes, cargo inspection
July	2009	UN	Expands Res. 1718, 1874	Freezes assets, targets officials and firms, forbids dual-use import
Aug	2009	US	Firm-specific sanctions	Korea Hyoksin Trading Corp, Korea Kwangson Banking Corp
Sept	2009	US	State Department restrictions	General Bureau of Atomic Energy & Korea Tangun Trading Corp

Sources: CNS (2010), Hufbauer *et al.* (2007), ACA (2009a), Security Council Report Inc. (2010), Rennack (2005), and O'Sullivan (2003).

Table B3.6 *North Korea – positive inducements, 1990–2009*

Date		Party	Action	Description
Jan	1990	S. Korea	Four-Step proposal	Disarmament program, with nuclear safety agreements
Jan	1991	Japan	Two-day meetings	Negotiations to normalize diplomatic relations
Feb	1991	Cuba	Nuclear cooperation agreement	Unspecified details, as announced by Radio Havana
May	1991	Japan	Normalization talks	Conditional offer w/ full-scope safeguards required for aid
Dec	1991	S. Korea	South-North Joint Declaration	Agreement on denuclearization of peninsula
Jan	1992	US+S.Kor	High-level meetings	Suspension of Team Spirit exercises, bilateral talks
Feb	1992	US	Federal Assets Control Regs.	Modification allows resumption of telecommunications
Mar	1992	S. Korea	Joint Nuclear Control Comm.	Establishment and discussions on regular inspections
May	1992	Japan	Normalization talks	Discussions concern IAEA inspections and reprocessing facility
Nov	1992	US+S.Kor	Team Spirit announcement	Considers cancellation if inter-Korea inspections take place
April	1993	Japan	Offers bilateral talks	Rejected: concerns NPT withdrawal, N. Korea nuclear program
Aug	1993	S. Korea	Proposes JNCC resumption	Restart of dialogue rejected, Team Spirit exercise cited
Oct	1993	US	State Dept. secret talks	Suggests that Team Spirit exercises may be suspended
Nov	1993	US	Conditional offer of support	Provides personnel for 5MW(e) refuel, and US LWRs
Dec	1993	Iran	Defense Minister visit	Discussions of technological cooperation
Dec	1993	US	Continued bilateral talks	Discussions in New York concerning nuclear inspections
Aug	1994	S. Korea	Conditional offer	Supplies LWR technology with IAEA compliance
Oct	1994	US	Agreed Framework	Two LWRs and annual shipments of heavy fuel oil
Feb	1995	US	FACR modification	Authorizes travel-related transactions, telecom.
April	1995	US	Diplomatic action	Direct telephone/fax links, also allows import of N.K. magnesite
Mar	1996	US	FACR modification	Allows donation targeting basic needs; flooding/famine

Month	Year	Actor	Event	Description
April	1996	US	AEDPA	Provision banning sale, license of defense articles/services
May	1996	US	Technology transfer	For "licensing and safe operation of the reactors"
Jan	1997	Taiwan	Nuclear waste contract	Taiwan Power Company (Taipower) ships radioactive waste to NK
Feb	1997	US+S. Kor	Famine-relief aid	$16 million pledge, leads to N. Korean participation in peace talks
Mar	1997	US	High-level talks	First high-level consultation since June of 1995
April	1997	US	Famine-relief aid	$15 million pledge from State Department
Feb	1998	S. Korea	Kim Dae-jung's Sunshine Policy	Allows private investment, encourages reciprocity
April	1998	S. Korea	High-level talks	S. Korea reaffirms LWR finance, first such consultations in 4 years
Sept	1998	US	Bilateral talks resumed	US Special Envoy Charles Kartman: "substantial progress"
Oct	1998	Multi	Four-party peace talks	To replace 1953 Armistice Agreement, includes US bilateral talks
Dec	1998	EU	Discussions in Brussels	British, German, Austrian, and European Commission officials
Mar	1999	US	Joint statement	Improve political and econ. relations, agricultural project
Mar	1999	US	Bilateral agricultural project	Announcement by State Department, for humanitarian purposes
May	1999	US	William Perry visit	Unspecified package deal; US also donates 400,000 tons of food
Sept	1999	US	Trading w/ the Enemy Act lifted	Removal of export and travel restrictions
Nov	1999	Japan	Easing of travel restrictions	Charter flights resumed, first step in loosening sanctions
Mar	2000	Japan	Resumes food aid	Also reopens talks on normalizing relations
June	2000	S. Korea	Joint North-South Declaration	Leaders meet, agreement calls for cooperation, exchange
June	2000	US	FACR modification	Allows limited investments and transactions, imp. and exp.
July	2000	US	Albright meets counterpart	"Symbolically historic" meeting, highest levels since Korean War
Oct	2000	US	Joint statement	Cho Myong Rok visits US, meets with Clinton, Albright, Cohen

Table B3.6 (cont.)

Date		Party	Action	Description
Nov	2000	AUS	Foreign Minister Downer visits	Notes willingness to provide safeguards training/assistance
May	2001	US	Technology transfer renewed	Issued under Energy Dept. regulation 10 CFR 810
June	2001	US	Intention to resume talks	Follows policy review, desires comprehensive negotiations
April	2002	Russia	Signs agreement	Unspecified details, for scientific exchanges from 2002–2004
Sept	2002	Japan	NK-Japan Pyongyang Declaration	Economic assistance for continued testing moratorium
Jan	2003	Russia	Deputy Foreign Minister visits	Conditional offer of security guarantees, aid resumption
April	2003	US+CHN	Trilateral talks in Beijing	Discussions of nuclear program; meetings end a day early
Oct	2003	US	Pres. Bush makes overture	Conditional offer of multilateral written security guarantee
Jan	2004	AUS	Sends delegation to Pyongyang	Urges restart of Six-Party Talks
Feb	2004	S. Korea	Proposal, w/ CHN and RUS support	Energy assistance for freeze/dismantlement
May	2004	Japan	Prime Minister Koizumi visits	Meeting with Kim Jong-il in Pyongyang re: nuclear, security issues
June	2004	US	Two-phase plan	Fuel aid, security agreement, bilateral discussions offered
Oct	2004	US	North Korean Human Rights Act	Offers support for human rights groups in NK, and refugees
June	2005	US	Food aid	Donates agricultural commodities via World Food Program
June	2005	S. Korea	Energy aid	Unspecified offer of electrical power
Sept	2005	6-party	Joint Statement of Principles	Written security guarantee; also, food, energy, and aid
Dec	2006	US+CHN	US Proposal	Revival of September 2005 agreement
Feb	2007	6-party	Beijing Deal: Joint Statement	Action plan w/ heavy fuel, working groups, terrorist list removal

			Treasury Department Action	Lifts block on Banco Delta Asia accounts, unfreezes $25 mil
June	2007	US		
Sept	2007	6-party	Second phase of 2007 plan	950,000 tons of heavy fuel oil, terrorist list removal process
Oct	2007	S. Korea	Joint Declaration at Summit	Steps to denuclearization, ease military tensions, reunification
April	2008	US	Bilateral talks with Hill	Movement toward lifting of sanctions
May	2008	US	USAID resumes deliveries	500,000 tons of food aid in the next year
June	2008	US	Ends Trading w/ the Enemy Act	Attached sanctions removed accordingly
Oct	2008	US	Terrorist blacklist removal	Attached sanctions removed accordingly
Oct	2008	US	Extension of humanitarian aid	2004 North Korean Human Rights Act renewed
Sept	2009	S. Korea	Lee Myung-bak's speech	"Grand bargain" promises economic rewards, aid package

Sources: CNS (2010), Hufbauer *et al.* (2007), ACA (2009a), Security Council Report Inc. (2010), Rennack (2005), and O'Sullivan (2003).

Table B3.7 *Iran – sanctions, 1990–2009*

Date		Party	Action	Description
-	1990	US	Foreign Appropriations Act	Direct aid ban expanded to loans, credits, insurance
July	1990	Germany	Halts Bushehr reactor work	Kraftwerk Union stops construction, and stops Spain as well
Jan	1991	Germany	Denies export licenses	Related to Bushehr nuclear power plant components
June	1991	Germany	Denies Bushehr completion	Will not permit Siemens-Kraftwerk Union to work, or Spanish firm
June	1991	Italy	Disallows exports	Steam generators built by Breda for Bushehr nuclear plant
Nov	1991	India	Cancels technical agreement	To supply 10MW research reactor, pressured by US and others
Nov	1991	China	Cancels reactor sale	Offer for 27MW reactor, pressured by US
-	1992	Argentina	Cancels facility and plant sales	For fuel fabrication facility and uranium dioxide conversion plant
Jan	1992	Argentina	Suspends contract	$18 mil agreement for nuclear technologies with INVAP
Mar	1992	Argentina	Cancels proposed shipment	$18 mil machine tools to Iran Atomic Energy Organization
Mar	1992	US	Firm-specific sanction	Sanctions under Arms Export Control Act and 1979 Export Admin Act
April	1992	Argentina	Suspends contracts	Unspecified nuclear projects in Iran
July	1992	Germany	Reaffirms denial of license	Refuses to grant Siemens exports license for Bushehr
Aug	1992	Germany	Formal cancellation	Siemens notifies Iran Bushehr deal cancelled indefinitely
Sept	1992	Argentina	Blocks supply of equipment	For fuel fabrication, UCF, and heavy-water production plant
Oct	1992	US	Iran–Iraq Arms Nonproliferation	Act bars contributors to Iran/Iraq's acquisition of NCB weapons
-	1993	Germany	Leybold AG tightens exp. controls	Prohibits transfer of dual-use items to Iran

Month	Year	Country	Action	Description
Mar	1993	UK	Tightens export controls	On dual-use tech, military-related equipment, also licenses
July	1993	Italy	Tightens export controls	On dual-use technology
Sept	1993	US	Proposal to former socialist states	To ease export restrictions for pledge not to transfer military tech to Iran
Oct	1994	US+RUS	US and Russian agreement	Bans $1 bil of arms exports for US aid and export access
Nov	1994	US	Blocks HEU intended for Iran	Operation Sapphire, retrieves from Kazakhstan
Dec	1994	Japan	Delays loan for dam project	Intended to send $470 million, pressured by US
Mar	1995	US	Stops plans for RUS agreement	As punishment for nuclear cooperation with Iran
Mar	1995	US	Executive Order 12957	Ban on trade and investment in petroleum sector, direct export
April	1995	US	White House announcement	Ban on all direct trade, $4 bil in indirect trade
May	1995	US+RUS	Yeltsin and Clinton announcement	Russia eliminates all "military" aspects of deal, incl. gas centrifuges
May	1995	US	Executive Order 12959	Prohibition on all imports and exports, new investment
Sept	1995	China	Suspends nuclear deal	Suspends deal to sell two 300MW reactors to Iran
Dec	1995	US	Covert Intel. authorization bill	Congress earmarks $18 billion for covert action against Tehran's regime
Dec	1995	US	Iran Foreign Oil Sanctions Act	Prohibits investment >$40 mil in oil and gas industries
–	1996	Multi	Wassenaar Agreement	Stops sales of strategic dual-use items
Jan	1996	China	Cancels sale	Plans to sell two nuclear reactors, pressured by US
April	1996	US	AEDPA	Provision banning sale, license of defense articles/services
April	1996	Belgium	Shipment interdiction	Belgians seize a mortar from a German shipment of pickles bound for Iran
July	1996	UK	Port interdiction	British seize 110 lbs. of maraging steel bound for Iran

Table B3.7 (cont.)

Date		Party	Action	Description
Aug	1996	US	Iran Libya Sanctions Act	Sanctions for >$40 mil gas and oil investment, good/technology exp.
April	1997	Germany	Diplomatic sanctions	Expels four Iranian diplomats and recalls its ambassador from Iran
April	1997	EU	Diplomatic sanctions	EU declares a mass recall of ambassadors from Iran and suspends dialogue
April	1997	Multi	Diplomatic sanctions	Canada, New Zealand, Australia recall their ambassadors from Iran
Aug	1997	US	Executive Order 13059	Expansion of trade and investment bans to foreign subsidiaries
Feb	1998	China	Suspends sale	Anhydrous hydrogen fluoride from The China Nuclear Energy Ind.
Mar	1998	US+UKR	US and Ukraine agreement	Ukraine ends all cooperation with Iran for US support
April	1998	Azerbaijan	Interdiction	Seizes 22 tons of steel alloy bound for Iran
April	1998	RUS	Interdiction	Seizes nuclear missile parts destined from Russia to Iran via Azerbaijan
July	1998	US	Firm-specific sanctions	Seven Russian firms accused of selling weapons technology to Iran
July	1998	US	Targeted sanctions	Nine Russian institutes and enterprises for possibly selling missile tech. to Iran
Nov	1998	US	Petroleum-sector sanction	Treasury denies bid for oil swap from Kazakhstan with Iran
Jan	1999	US	Firm-specific sanctions	Denies three Russian entities access to US markets
Feb	1999	US	Import sanctions	Targets ten Russian entities for assisting Iran's nuclear and missile programs
Mar	2000	US	Iran Nonproliferation Act	Sanctions on countries transferring controlled goods to Iran

April	2000	Czech	Bans exports to Bushehr plant	Czech parliament approves law, pressured by US
April	2000	US	Arms Export Control Act sanctions	Sanctions five North Korean and Iranian entities
Sept	2000	Russia	Cancels sale	Laser technology, fear by US of nuclear usage
Aug	2001	US	ILSA Extension Act of 2001	Lower investment trigger to $20+ million in twelve months
Jan	2002	US	Rhetoric	President Bush labels Iran as part of the "axis of evil"
Feb	2002	US	Posturing	US blocks Iran's bid to join the WTO
May	2002	US	Iran Nonproliferation Act sanctions	Sanctions Armenian, Chinese, and Moldovan firms
July	2002	US	Firm-specific sanctions	Targets nine Chinese and one Indian firm
May	2003	RUS	Diplomatic pressure	Russia threatens to withhold fuel for Bushehr NPP
June	2003	US	Iran Nonproliferation Act sanctions	Targets five Chinese and one North Korean firm
June	2003	IAEA/UN	IAEA judgment	BOG reports Iran has failed to meet its safeguards obligations
July	2003	EU	Diplomatic posturing	Warns failure to sign Additional Protocol will preclude agreements
Sept	2003	IAEA/UN	BOG Report & Resolution	Iran must prove by the end of Oct. 2003 it has no weapons program
Nov	2003	IAEA/UN	BOG Report & Resolution	Publicly condemns Iran for eighteen years of nuclear program secrecy
Mar	2004	IAEA/UN	BOG Report & Resolution	Rebukes Iran for failing to disclose all aspects of its nuclear program
June	2004	IAEA/UN	BOG Report & Resolution	Reports Iran is still in violation of its safeguards obligations
Sept	2004	IAEA/UN	BOG Report & Resolution	Concerns remain regarding Iran's nuclear dossier
Nov	2004	IAEA/UN	BOG Report & Resolution	Rebukes Iran for continued outstanding issues
Dec	2004	US	Iran Nonproliferation Act sanctions	Targets five Chinese and four North Korean firms
June	2005	US	Executive Order 13382	Freezes assets, and bans transactions w/ Atomic Energy Org.

Table B3.7 (cont.)

Date		Party	Action	Description
Aug	2005	IAEA/UN	BOG Resolution	Outstanding issues re: Iran's nuclear dossier and concern over enrichment
Sept	2005	US+EU	Calls for IAEA action	Threatens to refer Iran to the Security Council
Sept	2005	IAEA/UN	BOG Report & Resolution	Condemns Iran's continued violations and outstanding issues
Jan	2006	US	Iran Nonproliferation Act sanctions	Target nine firms
Jan	2006	US	Firm-specific sanctions	Novin and Nesbah Energy Companies
Feb	2006	IAEA/UN	IAEA Board Resolution	Votes to report Iran to the Security Council
July	2006	P5	Foreign Ministers agreement	Decide to refer Iran to Security Council
July	2006	US	Firm-specific sanctions	Seven firms (Indian, Russian, North Korean, Cuban) for Iran deals
July	2006	UN	SC Resolution 1696	Demands suspension of enrichment, threatens sanctions
Oct	2006	US	Iran Freedom Support Act (ILSA)	Sanctions for CBN and advanced conventional weapons
Dec	2006	UN	SC Resolution 1737	Ban of nuclear-related material/technology supplies
Jan	2007	UN	Security Council action	Sixty-day ultimatum issued, limited sanctions
Jan	2007	US	Action on state-owned bank	Bank Sepah for support and services to proliferation firms
Feb	2007	US	Firm-specific sanctions	Kalaye Electric Co, Kavoshyar Co., Pioneer Energy Industries Co.
Feb	2007	IAEA/UN	IAEA suspends assistance	Stops half of projects it provides technical assistance for
Mar	2007	UN	SC Resolution 1747	Ban of Iran's arm exports, freezing of assets, travel restrictions

Month	Year	Source	Action	Description
Oct	2007	US	Action on state-owned banks	Freeze assets of Quds Force; Rev. Guards as terrorist group
Mar	2008	UN	SC Resolution 1803	Freezes foreign assets, ban dual-use sales and officials travel
June	2008	US/EU	New sanctions embraced	Seeks to target Iranian banks specifically
June	2008	EU	Action on state-owned banks	Freezes assets of Bank Melli, follows UK lead
July	2008	US	Firm-specific sanctions	Five Iranian entities/individuals, pursuit to EO 13382
Aug	2008	EU	Trade sanctions	Denies loans, export credits to companies, increases inspections
Aug	2008	US	Firm-specific sanctions	Five Iranian entities/individuals, pursuit to EO 13382
Sept	2008	US	Firm-specific sanctions	Islamic Republic of Iran Shipping Lines and affiliates
Sept	2008	UN	SC Resolution 1835	Reaffirms three previous rounds of sanctions
Oct	2008	AUS	Unilateral sanctions	Travel bans, financial restrictions on twenty individuals, eighteen orgs.
Oct	2008	US	Firm-specific sanctions	Export Development Bank of Iran and three related entities
Nov	2008	US	Treasury Dept action	Revokes U-Turn licenses that allowed funds through US banks
Feb	2009	US	Firm-specific sanctions	Shahid Bakeri and Shahid Hemmat Industrial Goods
Feb	2009	IAEA/UN	BOG Report	Notes continued concern regarding outstanding issues
June	2009	IAEA/UN	BOG Report	Notes continued concern regarding outstanding issues
June	2009	UK	Announcement of freeze	Has frozen $1.64 billion in nuclear sanctions
Aug	2009	IAEA/UN	BOG Report	Notes continued concern regarding outstanding issues
Nov	2009	IAEA/UN	BOG Report & Resolution	Notes continued concern regarding outstanding issues

Sources: CNS (2010), Hufbauer *et al.* (2007), US General Accountability Office (USGAO) (2007), and O'Sullivan (2003).

Table B3.8 *Iran – positive inducements, 1990–2009*

Date	Party	Action	Description
– 1990	US	Commerce Dept. approves sales	High-technology equipment worth $59 mil, from 1990–1991
– 1990	USSR	Cooperation agreement	Unspecified details, on nuclear cooperation
Jan 1990	China	Sign 10-year agreement	To build a 27MW plutonium production plant at Esfahan
Feb 1990	Spain	Signed protocol	Associated Enterprises of Spain as main contract at Bushehr
Mar 1990	USSR	Nuclear cooperation deal	Two VVER 440 reactors, two 1293 MW pressurized reactors
Mar 1990	USSR	Minister of transport agreement	Help Atomic Energy Org. w/ 440MW plant construction
May 1990	US	Pres. Bush "gesture of goodwill"	Re: disappearance of Iranians in Lebanon in 1982
June 1990	China	Nuclear Ind. Org. signs contract	Supplies micro-nuclear research reactor (30MW)
Nov 1990	US	Pres. Bush authorizes oil imp.	Import on a case-by-case basis, payments to escrow fund
– 1991	China	Reactor deal	Sales of 27kW research reactor and cyclotron
April 1991	Mexico	Cooperation agreement	Exchange of scientific and technical info, nuclear security
Nov 1991	India	Cooperation agreement	Scientific and technical help, and delivery of 10MW reactor
Nov 1991	China	Reactor deal	Reveals small-reactor deal, 1989 electromagnetic separator
– 1992	Argentina	Agreement to sell facilities	Fuel fabrication facility and uranium dioxide conversion plant
– 1992	Russia	Sign two agreements	"Building a Nuclear Plant," "Cooperation in… Peaceful Use"
Aug 1992	Russia	Bilateral nuclear accord	Fifteen-year cooperation agreement (announced in Sept)
Sept 1992	China	Reactor deal	Agrees to supply Iran with a 300MW nuclear power plant
– 1993	China	Reactor deal	HT-6B Tokamak fusion reactor installed at Aziz University
Feb 1993	Argentina	Uranium deal	IAEA confirms 20% enriched uranium will arrive in 1993
Feb 1993	China	Deal signed in Tehran	To construct 300MW nuclear power plants in Ahvaz
Mar 1994	Japan	Agreement w/ Central Bank	Reschedules $2.3 billion in loans from Japan
Jan 1995	Russia	$800 million contract	Building of VVER-1000 Mwe reactor at Bushehr within four years
Aug 1995	S. Africa	Bilateral agreement	Nuclear technology assistance for peaceful purposes
Feb 1996	Germany	Debt relief	Germany reschedules Iran's debt
July 1997	Italy	Diplomatic outreach	Calls for renewal of full relations with Iran
Oct 1997	US	Waives sanctions	Exempts French firm Total from sanctions
Nov 1997	EU	Diplomatic restoration	EU ambassadors return to Tehran

Feb	1998	Diplomatic outreach	EU	Lifts bans on high-level contacts with Iran
Nov	1998	Memorandum of Understanding	Russia	To expand coop, build second unit to Bushehr nuclear plant
Dec	1998	Reversal of sanctions	US	Removes Iran from the list of drug-source and transit nations
Jan	1999	Diplomatic restoration	AUS	Resumes high-level contacts with Iran
April	1999	Sanction exemption	US	Future sanctions will exempt food and medicine exports
May	1999	Diplomatic restoration	Britain	Restores full diplomatic ties with Iran
Aug	1999	Diplomatic outreach	US	Clinton sends secret letter to Khatami
Nov	1999	Aid offer	Britain	$3 million aid package to help Iran combat drug trafficking
Dec	1999	Sanctions exemption	US	Grants Boeing export license to supply airplane parts
Mar	2000	Albright lifts luxury exp. ban	US	Speech to American Iranian Council, as "good faith" action
May	2000	Putin revises 1992 decree	Russia	Broadens ability to export nuclear materials and technology
May	2000	Loan approval	Multi	World Bank approves first loan to Iran in seven years
July	2000	Trade inducements	Germany	Increases export guarantees to Iran
Aug	2000	Business deal	Turkey	Signs a twenty-five-year $20 billion natural gas agreement with Iran
Dec	2001	Duma ratifies treaty w/ Iran	Russia	Cooperation in 'military-technological sphere'
Mar	2001	Security agreement	Russia	First security agreement since the Iranian Revolution
June	2001	Oil sector business deal	Italy	$900 mil. contract to develop Darkhovan oilfield
July	2001	Oil sector business deal	Japan	Agreement to fund seismic analysis of Azadegan oilfield
July	2001	Oil sector business deal	UK+FRA	Joint contract to develop the Dorood oilfield
Dec	2002	Finalized fuel agreement	Russia	Supplies for Bushehr nuclear power plant
Dec	2002	Conditional negotiations	EU	Tied to progress on nonproliferation, HR, & terrorism
Sept	2003	Technological proposal	EU-3	Offer to share peaceful nuclear technology for IAEA demands
Oct	2003	Conditional negotiations	EU-3	Iran suspends enrichment and sign AP for tech. cooperation
Dec	2003	Humanitarian aid	US	US offers aid in response to the Bam earthquake
Dec	2003	Eases sanctions	US	Temporarily eases sanctions in response to Bam earthquake
Feb	2004	Oil sector business deal	Japan	$2.8 billion contract to develop Azadegan field
Oct	2004	Technological proposal	EU-3	Offer of "valuable technology" to abandon enrichment
Oct	2004	IAEA head ElBaradei proposal	IAEA/UN	Supplies fuel for power plants to abandon enrichment

Table B3.8 (*cont.*)

Date		Party	Action	Description
Oct	2004	China	Oil sector business deal	Prelim: natural gas purchases, develop Yadavaran oil fields
Nov	2004	EU-3	Paris Agreement	Nuclear technology, fuel, trade concessions, security help
Nov	2004	IAEA/UN	Endorsement	Endorses EU-3 agreement with Iran
Jan	2005	EU-3	Resumption of negotiations	Trade negotiations restart after nineteen-month pause
Feb	2005	EU-3	Geneva meetings/proposal	Offers to help acquire a LWR for Iran
Feb	2005	Russia	Russia-Iran Nuclear Deal	Supplies fuel for Bushehr reactor (for spent fuel rods)
Mar	2005	US	Pres. Bush lifts WTO block	In conjunction with EU-3; also to allow parts for aircraft
May	2005	Multi	WTO accession talks	WTO agrees to proceed with Iran's WTO accession talks
Aug	2005	EU-3	Framework proposal	Security coop, long-term civilian program support, fuel
Nov	2005	US+EU	Pauses reference to UNSC	Provides Russia more time to negotiate
Nov	2005	EU-3+RUS	Requests renewed negotiations	Unpublished Russian proposal with joint enrichment venture
Jan	2006	Multi	Russian offer, US/CHN support	Operation of civilian nuclear facilities by Russians/inspectors
May	2006	P5+1	Agreement on package	Package includes economic and technical assistance
May	2006	EU	Technological proposal	Help to obtain technology if Iran stops enrichment
May	2006	US	Sec. of State Rice announcement	Will join talks if Iran permits inspections, suspends activities
June	2006	P5+1	Economic proposal	Includes LWRs, enriched fuel, spare parts for civilian aircraft
June	2008	EU-3	Conditional offer	Offers another incentives package
June	2008	P5+1	Freeze-for-freeze proposal	Conditional offer for sanctions pause, rejected by Iran
July	2008	US	Diplomatic outreach	Undersecretary of State Burns participates in EU talks w/ Iran
Jan	2009	US	Pres. Obama announcement	Willing to pursue diplomacy, direct talks
Mar	2009	US	Pres. Obama video	Commits to pursuit of diplomatic solutions
Mar	2009	UK	Prime Minister Brown speech	Conditional offer to help build power stations
April	2009	US	Joins P5+1 talks	As full participant, departure from Bush administration
Oct	2009	P5+1	LEU for TRR fuel swap proposal	Offers fuel for Iran shipping LEU to Russia for fuel fabrication

Sources: CNS (2010), Hufbauer *et al.* (2007), USGAO (2007), and O'Sullivan (2003).

Part II

Competing perspectives: the range of
sanctions and positive inducements

4   Positive incentives, positive results?
Rethinking US counterproliferation policy

Miroslav Nincic

Although few issues weigh more heavily on the international community's concerns than the specter of nuclear weapons acquisition by regimes that flout core norms of international behavior, we do not sufficiently grasp how this can happen and what other nations could do about it. My aim, here, is to illuminate the intersection between this volume's concern with the domestic, political, and economic sources of nuclear weapons programs and my own developing interest in the use of positive incentives as tools with which to elicit cooperation from established adversaries.

Most research on nuclear proliferation inquires how a nuclear weapons capability can be acquired and why it might be sought in the first place.[1] The latter question often involves examining the security needs nuclear weapons could serve and their expected impact on the country's international standing. Nevertheless, the value of a focus on the international ends of nuclear weapons is limited. Because neither security interests nor concerns with national status are invariant across regimes, both can be adequately understood only when viewed in the context of the target country's domestic, as well as international, conditions. In this regard, one line of research has sought to root quests for nuclear weapons in social-psychological forces, as in a vision of national identity, or in the social norms that shape nuclear ambitions.[2] Yet norms are not formed in a political vacuum, whereas conceptions of national identity often flow from the legitimizing needs of political elites. Even apparent security imperatives are rarely as objective as their proponents profess. The virtue of this volume is that it seeks the sources of nuclear behavior in the circumstances within which all other relevant forces acquire their meaning, thus offering particularly credible insights into the levers by which security threats can best be controlled.

---

[1] For example, Meyer (1984) and Sagan (1996/1997).
[2] Hymans (2006) and Rublee (2009).

An overly narrow conception of the causes of proliferation is matched by a truncated view of the responses most likely to discourage it. Most of the national dialogue has focused on the manner in which punitive measures, mainly economic sanctions and diplomatic ostracism, may lead nations whose nuclear programs are now considered most threatening – especially Iran and North Korea – to alter their troubling behavior. Yet, it is very hard to find instances where coercive pressures have had the desired effect on proliferators, and, in the case of these two nations, it is not unreasonable to argue that a sense of being externally beleaguered has stoked the fears by which nuclear programs are justified and enhanced the domestic position of those who are their most forceful advocates. The case that these tools have been counterproductive is easier to make than the case for their effectiveness, and this alone justifies a far greater scholarly investigation of the potential, if any, of carrots rather than sticks. Despite the demonstrated failures of coercive pressures, the promise and pitfalls of positive incentives rarely are subjected to extended and rigorous analysis

Positive engagement implies that abrupt regime change via negative pressures is not in the cards, at least not within an acceptable time frame – that, consequently, the incumbent regime, or some variant thereof, will have to be dealt with in the relevant future. With that assumption, I ask how positive inducements can induce such a regime to abandon, or refrain from embarking upon, a nuclear program. The point of departure is the reasonable assumption that political leaders ultimately care most about securing their domestic position, a condition on which most other policy achievements depend; that their decisions regarding a nuclear capability are primarily driven by this concern. The aim, then, of counterproliferation policy should be to nudge the political calculus of national leadership toward the desired policy priorities by affecting their notion of what most benefits their political position. With this in mind, I address three of the questions that Etel Solingen, in her introductory chapter, has placed at the core of this volume's intellectual contribution. The first involves the domestic distributional consequences of counterproliferation policies, comparing negative pressures to positive inducements.[3] The second, related, issue involves the impact of the target regime's policy choices on the power and preferences of those domestic constituencies best placed to determine the course of proliferation policies. Both issues draw their significance from the argument developed in some of my earlier work according to which

---

[3] This includes both intended and unintended consequences (the sixth issue raised by the volume's editor).

the value of inducements to a target regime, and thus the magnitude of the counter-concession it is prepared to offer, is largely contingent on their anticipated impact on its domestic position (Nincic 2011, especially Chapter 3). The third issue addresses the extent to which the effectiveness of counterproliferation policies depends on where within the target nation's timeline they are activated. While Chapter 1 of this volume considers this in terms of the point in the proliferation process reached, my concern is with the stage in the regime's political development at which an inducements-based strategy is attempted.[4]

Although positive incentives, like sanctions, are most effective when backed by a broad coalition of nations, few measures could be fully effective when not initiated, or at least supported, by the world's sole superpower. Accordingly, I will be especially concerned with the effectiveness of positive inducements employed by the United States. It is also necessary to observe, at the outset, that the conditions that may make positive inducements successful are, as we shall see, restrictive. Accordingly, the fact that sticks do not work does not imply that carrots would be successful by default. At times, nothing works.

The political sources of successful policies: some analytic foundations

A successful strategy of positive incentives requires that difficult conditions must be met, both on the side of the sender and that of the target. In both cases, these conditions are entangled in the logic of domestic politics, and they appear most complex where the potential proliferant is concerned.

The target regime's major policy orientations generally reflect the themes (e.g., intense nationalism, commitment to a religious agenda) on which it seeks to build its legitimacy and the related preferences of the domestic constituencies on which its hold on power depends. Because governmental policies, including those involving weapons of mass destruction, are predictable on the basis of the interests and preferences of the segments of society from which backing is sought, these interests and preferences provide our analytic point of departure. We ask, in particular, how the choice of constituencies on which the target government seeks to build its political coalition (1) affects its attitudes

---

[4] One issue that this chapter will not deal with involves the respective impact of counterproliferation policies on democratic and non-democratic regimes. The regimes whose acquisition of nuclear weapons we most fear are abjectly totalitarian (North Korea) or have subverted formally quasi-democratic institutions (Iran); the future does not hold the serious prospect of any democratic nuclear threats.

toward the acquisition of a nuclear weapons capacity, and, (2) how this choice may be influenced by the policies directed at it by other nations, the United States in particular.

As both Solingen and Haggard and Noland have argued, the responsiveness of governments to external pressures and incentives is shaped by the nature of the political coalitions on which they rely.[5] The endogeneity involved is important, since the composition of the coalitions that governments may seek to build is influenced by the external treatment to which those governments are subjected. At the root of any regime's rule lie the groups whose support ensures its grip on power. These are the established political elites whose core values and tangible interests are reflected in the regime's policy priorities. In the case of the two nations whose nuclear potential worries us most, established elites share the government's apparent ideational aims – a radical version of Islam and a conception of national greatness in the Iranian case, a national commitment to *juche* and a rigorous form of communism in the North Korean case; they share a perception of rabid hostility toward their country by a US-led coalition of nations; and they benefit materially from the regime's patronage – as with the business opportunities enjoyed by the Iranian Revolutionary Guards Corps and the privileged access to scarce national resources given the military establishment under Pyongyang's Military First policy.

Etel Solingen's *cui bono/cui malo* question will largely determine the likely coalitions backing and opposing the regime, whereas, as Arthur Stein explains in Chapter 2 of this volume, external sanctions (positive or negative) have distributional consequences within the target nation, and it is this political fact that positive inducements should seek to exploit.[6] Because regime policies cannot gratify the preferences and interests of all segments of society, in fact they may impose considerable costs and suffering on certain segments of society, groups capable of opposing the regime invariably exist. They may have managed to articulate explicit alternative preferences and attained a considerable level of organization and mobilization (as in Iran), or indications of their potential existence may be almost completely and coercively suppressed (North Korea). Even in the latter case, the fact that policies impose costs on parts of society ensures that bearers of different interests and preferences can emerge, in the form of alternative elites, under appropriate political circumstances – as the examples of post-Mao

---

[5] Solingen (2007a), Haggard and Noland, Chapter 8, this volume.
[6] Stein, Chapter 2, this volume.

China and of several formerly Stalinist East European nations readily demonstrate.

One way of characterizing established versus alternative elites is in terms of Etel Solingen's view that a key to understanding a regime's nuclear decisions is to grasp its impact, especially its economic impact, on two possible political constituencies. She points out that nations unlikely to endorse the acquisition of nuclear weapons are those in which a prominent place is held by liberalizing elites which, unlike their "inward-looking, nationalist, and radical confessional counterparts are more likely to press for economic and international policies that serve their own interests."[7]

If the regime's major policy priorities, including those that bear on nuclear programs, are predictable on the basis of the values and interests of the constituencies that back it, then major policy shifts should coincide with changes in the nature of needed supporters. When the priorities of principal backers suffice to ensure the security of the regime's position, there is no reason for the latter to alter behaviors that coincide with those priorities. By extension, a changed policy trajectory suggests that the present basis of support no longer suffices to ensure regime stability and that, consequently, new ways of courting needed backing are being sought. If foreign actors are in a position to provide some of what potential backers desire, then external inducements are likely to have the greatest effect when the regime faces latent or manifest regime instability.

Faced with a slipping hold on power, or with the prospect of such a slip, the regime has two major choices: (1) to reinvigorate sources of support among traditional (usually inward-looking and hardline) segments of society, or, (2) to seek the help of previously marginalized groups (in many cases outward-looking and reformist groups), because traditional elites either cannot be mobilized or because their support would be insufficient. If the revived backing of established groups is sought then, in turn, two possibilities present themselves to the regime: (1a) deepening its commitment to the policies that had traditionally gratified such groups, or, (1b) finding new ways of making them happy. The decision will largely hinge on the extent to which the interests and preferences of traditional supporters have evolved over time, but whereas Option "1a" implies a continuation of internationally objectionable policies, Option "1b" opens the possibility of a change of government course. Accordingly, the goal of the international community is, above all, to

---

[7] Solingen (1994a: 222).

avoid Option 1a. On the other hand, Option 1b or (even better) Option 2 could encourage the desired shift in regime priorities.

From the perspective of our concerns, the question is how such choices could be affected by tools of external influence. More precisely, can positive inducements make it more likely that the government will seek new ways of addressing the evolving needs of traditional elites or of courting the support of new, reformist groups? I will begin by offering some general thoughts in this regard, following which the bulk of this chapter will discuss some of these issues with specific reference to the nuclear programs of Iran and North Korea.

Reinvigorating the support of traditional constituencies

Recent experience with Iran and North Korea indicates that the shortest path to the least desirable policy option (i.e., 1a), along with its consequences for nuclear weapons programs, is to further turn the screws of coercive and punitive pressures. The greatest advances in Tehran's uranium enrichment program (and missile tests) have occurred with the several waves of UNSC sanctions, as the Ahmadinejad regime turned firmly toward the instruments of the state's coercive power (mainly the Revolutionary Guards and the Basij militia). North Korea's nuclear and long-range missile tests correlated with the rise of the military establishment's power via the National Defense Commission, and with a sharp decline in interest in tentative economic reform.

The point is that, when the country feels externally beleaguered, support for nuclear (and other military) programs will often increase among those most firmly wedded to the values by which the regime has traditionally justified its conduct. The theme of Iranian nationalism lies largely behind support for Tehran's nuclear program, a support staunchest among hardline elements. A motif of vulnerability in a hostile world, along with the go-it-alone ethos of *juche* ideology, has provided much of the domestic rationale for North Korea's nuclear program. The more these values appear threatened, the greater, in many cases, the support offered the regime by its hardline backers. Military and intelligence establishments thrive when countries feel externally beleaguered. Acts imposing international isolation on the nation create opportunities for rent-seeking behavior, as black and gray markets flourish with the scarcities caused by economic sanctions. Gains frequently are shared with elements of the national security establishment, creating a powerful coalition of interests committed to the regime and the policies that make these riches possible. The political establishment also benefits from rally-round-the-flag sentiments stimulated by foreign hostility, and from opportunities to stigmatize domestic opponents as "traitors" serving the interests of hostile foreigners. It is unlikely that either Pyongyang or Tehran would easily abandon policies that serve its political interests.

Hardline elements of the regime's domestic coalition may, nevertheless, find that policies that once served their interests no longer do so when those interests evolve. A juncture may be reached where their new needs call for meaningfully altered policies, and the question is to what extent well-designed positive inducements can promote such developments. Several important examples illustrate the possibilities. It is generally recognized that the interests of China's military establishment have become tightly enmeshed with the country's economic growth and the globalized economic participation that has sustained it. Another, less apparent example of a hardline institution whose interests have assumed a very new complexion is provided by Cuba's armed forces.

Once considered a spearhead of revolutionary activity in the developing world, Cuba's Revolutionary Armed Forces (FAR) lost much of its international role when Fidel Castro retreated, in the 1980s, from international activism: especially as, during the 1990s, economic difficulties required further reductions in the nation's armed forces. New responsibilities were sought for the FAR, and Raul Castro, then Defense Minister, began entrusting military officers with economic responsibilities. The model was China's Peoples' Liberation Army, which had successfully carved out an economic role for itself. Military officers turned businessmen played a pivotal role in China's embrace of elements of a market economy, whereas "[China] is comparable to Cuba in terms of revolutionary experience and government and as a model of party/civil-military relations, economic reform ... and institutional involvement in the civilian economy."[8] According to one estimate, the FAR may now be involved in more than 60 percent of the economy; it has a hand in the lucrative tourist industry, owning Gaviota SA, which, in turn, owns 20 to 25 percent of Cuba's hotel rooms in partnership with foreign investors.[9] It runs the Aerogaviota airline and controls TRD Caribe SA, a chain of 400 retail stores that accept only foreign currencies. The FAR is also involved in the citrus and tobacco industries.[10] The military-economic nexus provides a reason for thinking that interests,

[8] Mora (2002: 7).
[9] Jose de Cordoba, "Cuba's Military Puts Business on Front Lines," *Wall Street Journal*, November 15, 2006.
[10] Institute for Cuban and Cuban-American Studies (2006).

directly connected to the regime and to dynamic segments of the Cuban economy could discover the benefits of economic engagement with the United States, an engagement that would lead them to favor suitably altered regime policies.

These examples demonstrate that, occasionally, even those interests that, at one time, might have been firm proponents of extreme and pugnacious external policies can, under evolving conditions, discover that their needs now require positive integration into the international community. It is intuitively plausible that opportunities for economic engagement with the international community can serve that purpose. It is similarly apparent that reductions in the nation's external security threats lessen the need of traditional elites to adhere to the values that previously had defined them. To the extent that the interests of those elites trace a new trajectory, the regime may become receptive to inducements that allow it to address these new needs, in the regime's own political interest.

Still, the opportunities implied by such scenarios are limited. Old interests might not evolve in the desired directions, reducing the scope for inducement-based foreign leverage. Also, reinvigorated support by such groups may not suffice to ensure the regime's position if its failures are substantial. Under the circumstances, it becomes necessary to attract new domestic allies, even if their interests clash with those of traditional supporters.

Enlisting new sources of support

From a counterproliferation perspective, this is a desirable scenario, since, unlike traditional supporters, those now courted by the regime would often have interests incompatible with externally confrontational policies. These generally are groups that had never been part of the regime's governing coalition, and whose interests and preferences incline them to desire socio-economic reforms and foreign policy moderation. This could involve aspiring members of a middle class whose economic interests require, not rent-seeking activities in a context of international isolation, but commercial and entrepreneurial activities in a liberalized economic setting, and who desire access to international markets and sources of investment. It could include cultural and intellectual elites who demand greater freedom of expression. It may encompass portions of the country's youth, wishing to participate in an international, youth-oriented culture.

Three conditions must be met if the regime is to be receptive to positive inducements as a way of enlisting new backing for its rule. The first is that the society and economy should be differentiated enough for there to be significant groups whose interests diverge from those of the traditional elites. A totally closed and state-run economy rarely provides enough space for the emergence of independent economic actors desiring closer links to the international economy, and it discourages development of a complex civil society. Second, external concessions must directly address the needs of the new groups; otherwise, inducements would not shore up the regime's domestic position. The third, very obvious, condition is that the support of these new groups must be more valuable to the regime than the policies it is asked to abandon.

Domestic consequences of positive engagement: two examples

A starting point is to recognize that, much as a country's domestic order often determines the course of its foreign policies, so might its international relations shape that order and the regime's domestic political calculus. In this regard, both punitive sanctions and positive incentives have consequences. Examples of a desirable domestic impact produced by external engagement are offered by two countries that might, but ultimately did not, pursue nuclear weapons: Egypt and Vietnam. Their decisions not to pursue nuclear weapons can plausibly be interpreted in terms of the regimes' need to strengthen domestic support, a project requiring fruitful engagement with the international community, including the United States. The latter's readiness to meet them halfway has, in turn, positively directed their foreign policy options.

Evidence indicates that Egypt had initiated a nuclear weapons program in 1960, abandoning it in the 1970s.[11] This nuclear program can be viewed as part of Gamal Abdel Nasser's broader policy agenda. Under his rule, Egypt moved close to the Soviet Union, adopting a *dirigiste* economy and a bloated bureaucracy, while its relations with the United States deteriorated badly. After Nasser's death in 1970, his successor, Anwar Sadat, made it a priority to curb the power of statist forces (mainly the military, and public-sector bureaucracies) that were stifling the economy, an effort that required backing from new quarters, both domestic and international, if resistance was to be overcome. Toward this end, he launched the policy of *infitah* (Arabic for "open door") in 1974, to promote private (including foreign) investment and market-oriented reform. Part of the purpose was to consolidate support for the regime among the country's landed gentry, business groups,

[11] Rublee (2006).

and also recently-enriched state elites seeking new sources of capital and outlets for their wealth in liberalized economic conditions. *Infitah* reforms stimulated "a bourgeoisie thriving on international connections and tertiary activities."[12] This assumed a reintegration into economic and diplomatic networks ruptured after 1967. Diplomatic relations with the United States were restored in 1973. The following year, the Nixon administration proposed $250 million in foreign assistance to Egypt.[13] The country has since become the second leading recipient of US economic assistance, as well as an active participant in the EU-sponsored Barcelona process. The situation appears to be that "These increasing links to, and dependence on, foreign sources of national income mean that Egypt's freedom of choice has been restrained by norms and rules dictated by the international system and the United States."[14]

Although Vietnam is seldom thought of in a context of nuclear proliferation, such ambitions would have come as no surprise. Having fought a long and immensely costly war with the United States, and another, much briefer, war with China in 1979, the Hanoi regime was largely shaped by its experience with foreign enemies. An initially Stalinist narrative could have cast it as a regime pitted against much of the international community. Moreover, with unification of the two halves of the country, a reasonable foundation of technical skills could have made a nuclear program feasible. Yet the regime's priorities, like those of China, began emphasizing material achievement over hardline ideological agendas and external truculence.

Responding to disappointing economic performance in the early years following reunification, Vietnam undertook, in 1986, significant market reforms known as Dôi Mói (Renovation): encouraging market mechanisms, economic deregulation, and private ownership of farms and companies.[15] Foreign investment was sought, especially from the expatriate community in Europe and the United States, and an export-oriented economic profile was encouraged. Although the Communist Party retains firm control, priorities have shifted from ideological objectives to the welfare aims common to most modern societies. Hanoi established diplomatic and commercial relations with the Association of Southeast Asian Nations and most of the countries of Europe and Northeast Asia. US economic sanctions were incrementally lifted with evidence of progressive Vietnamese withdrawal from Cambodia.

---

[12] Hinnebusch (1993: 160).
[13] David Binder, "US Said to Plan $250-Million Aid to Egypt in Year," *New York Times*, April 24, 1974.
[14] Gawdat (2007).   [15] Boothroyd and Nam (2000).

Diplomatic relations with the United States followed in 1995. A US-Vietnam Bilateral Trade Agreement went into effect in 2001. The country joined the World Trade Organization in 2006. Secretary of Defense William Cohen visited Hanoi in 2000, while his successor, Donald Rumsfeld, called on the government on three occasions, praising its "amazing economic achievements," amid talk of defense cooperation.[16] President Bush himself visited Vietnam in 2007, as it hosted the meeting of the Asia-Pacific Economic Cooperation summit.

In 2009, Vietnam announced that, with foreign assistance, it would undertake construction of two nuclear power plants, to become operational in 2020.[17] Remarkably little consternation greeted this announcement. As Mark Fitzpatrick, of the International Institute for Strategic Studies explained:

Vietnam's current nuclear activities and plans, its benign policy of regional engagement, and its commitment to non-proliferation all suggest that its nuclear aspirations are entirely peaceful. This is not for a lack of proliferation drivers. In fact, the combination of factors that have been identified as sparking proliferation decisions elsewhere have been historically present in Vietnam, and yet its leaders have forgone the nuclear-weapons option. Proliferation pressures are currently held in check by a network of regional organisations and institutions, and by growing bilateral relationships with the US and India.[18]

The insights provided by the experience of Egypt and Vietnam are illuminating, yet the most important issue involves the applicability of the catalytic model to two countries whose nuclear programs are well under way and whose international posture has provided justified cause for concern.

A note regarding the supply side

If the reasoning so far has been largely correct, it follows that political scientists seeking better ways of dealing with nuclear proliferators should recognize that regime decisions are largely guided by domestic political considerations, which the international community in general, and the United States in particular, can seek to influence. It should further be appreciated that this is most effectively done when an unstable political equilibrium leads the regime to search for ways to strengthen or expand its domestic support. At that point, the purpose of external

---

[16] "Rumsfeld Hails Vietnam's Economic Progress," *AFP*, June 5, 2006.
[17] Vu Trong Khanh and Patrick Barta, "Vietnam Assembly Approves Nuclear Plants," *Wall Street Journal*, November 26, 2009.
[18] Fitzpatrick (2010).

inducements should be to increase the likelihood that the government would try to extend its base of support to previously marginalized, but reformist and outward-looking, segments of society, or, failing that, that traditional elites should be encouraged to alter their interests in a way that implies better integration into the international community. In either case, the regime should be receptive to concessions that allow it to address the needs of desired supporters and more willing to abandon the nuclear policies upon which it had engaged – as long as the incentives match the value of that which it is asked to give up. This last point is important, for it is not enough to declare a willingness to engage adversaries, it often is necessary to provide genuinely substantial concessions if, from the other side's perspective, the effort is to be worth making.

At the same time, it must be recognized that even when conditions are propitious on the side of the target regime, the United States might find it hard to offer inducements of the magnitude objectively required. There is a culturally-imbedded conviction that bad parties should be treated badly, as a matter of proper moral balance. Rewarding unsavory regimes produces various forms of cognitive dissonance, and it carries domestic political risks for political leaders choosing such a course. Positive incentives also seem redolent of appeasement, with its historically unsavory connotations. Under the circumstances, inducements rarely are considered politically palatable; when offered, they tend to be modest – too modest to justify giving up a nuclear pursuit. The obstacles to a successful strategy of positive inducements are thus to be found both on the demand side and the supply side. I have examined the latter sort of obstacles in some detail elsewhere, and I will focus here on problems of the former sort in light of the experience of US policies toward Iran and North Korea.[19]

Lessons of Iran

The record of Iran's nuclear program, and the ways in which it has responded to US pressures, bolsters the analytical assumptions presented above, indicating that coercive pressures may produce consequences contrary to their intent – that they may encourage domestic configurations of power that fervently desire a nuclear weapons capability. On the other hand, and while the record of positive inducements offered Tehran is clearly insufficient to make firm statements about their effect, there is little reason to think they would make matters worse, while

---

[19] Nincic (2011: chapter 3).

there are credible grounds for thinking that they may make acquisition of such weapons less desirable to the regime or, at least, that they may reduce the danger that a nuclear-armed Iran would present to the international community. I will discuss two issues. I will first consider the effectiveness of negative pressures and the prospects for positive incentives when it comes to leverage over the regime's nuclear program; in other words, I will evaluate the outlook for quid pro quos that assume no major change in the nature of the regime. Second, I will ask whether a sustained policy of positive engagement, one that does not necessarily assume immediate counter-concessions, might alter the balance of power in Iranian politics, such as to favor a relinquishment of the nuclear program or, at least, that would make living with a nuclear-armed Iran less alarming.

The logic of leverage

Although Tehran's nuclear program dates well before the Islamic Revolution, it lost momentum after 1979, to be revived in the 1990s. Revelations in 2002 and 2003 of clandestine uranium-enrichment programs, centered in Natanz, fueled considerable international concern, especially given some of Tehran's foreign policy stances. The discovery, in 2009, of a second hidden uranium enrichment site in Qom, further heightened foreign anxiety about the regime's intentions. At the same time, the history of the program indicates that punitive sanctions have done nothing to discourage it. Unilateral US sanctions have been in force for three decades. There have been several sets of UNSC-mandate measures, beginning in 2005. In 2008, the European Union imposed its own set of sanctions on Iran. In June 2010, the United Nations Security Council issued restrictions on Iranian shipping and finance, followed by toughened US sanctions, as well as sanctions imposed by Japan. Yet, it seems that each new wave of sanctions has been coupled with Tehran's strengthened commitment to its nuclear program, and with staunch public support for it. One of the United States' leading analysts of Iranian politics has concluded that "the calculations of Iran's principal protagonists – Ahmadinejad and Supreme Leader Ali Khamenei – are largely unaffected by mounting financial penalties from the West."[20] In Chapter 7 of this volume, Nader points out that:

Like many authoritarian regimes, the Islamic Republic as a whole may thrive on a sense of political and economic isolation … sanctions may have the benefit

[20] Ray Takeyh, "Why Iran Won't Respond to Sanctions," *Washington Post*, September 19, 2010.

of not only strengthening Khamenei's claim to legitimacy – resistance against a 'bullying' United States – while serving his constituent's specific economic interests ... US sanctions and Iran's increasing isolation may also have contributed to the rise of the principlists[21] and the Revolutionary Guards.[22]

A survey of relevant developments illustrates these points.

Tehran politics have been relatively volatile since the Islamic Revolution of 1979, with an evident presence of reformist pressures during the 1990s and early 2000s, and an inflexibly conservative core since 2005. It could be argued that certain junctures during the prior period offered opportunities for effective engagement: opportunities that were not acted upon, a failure that helped consolidate the power of the nation's most refractory political groups.

By the time of Khomeini's death in 1989, much of the Revolution's initial Islamist fervor had been exhausted. This may not have mattered much to the regime's position had the Islamic Republic's first decade witnessed commendable economic performance, but it did not.[23] By the early 1990s, dissatisfaction with the regime became apparent. 1992 saw major unrest at Tehran University, where students opposed a government-appointed Dean. Workers at the Tehran Oil refinery went on strike, and work stoppages were reported elsewhere.[24] In the parliamentary elections of 1992, economic issues seem to matter more to voters than religious shibboleths. In one voter's words, "The more difficult the economic situation gets, the more people lose their religious beliefs ... I don't think any of the promises of the revolution have been met."[25]

Presidential elections in 1997 appeared to undermine the clerical power structure. The candidate backed by the Supreme Leader, Ali Akbar Nateq-Nouri, lost to the reformist Mohammad Khatami, who, four years later, won an even larger portion of the popular vote. Signs of deteriorating regime legitimacy were plentiful, culminating, in 1999, in week-long, anti-government student demonstrations during which pictures of the Supreme Leader were publicly burned.[26]

---

[21] I.e., the conservative hardliners.

[22] Nader, Chapter 7, this volume.

[23] According to economic historian Hashem Pesaran, "Over the period 1978–88, the real output and investment fell by average annual rates of 1.8 percent and 6.6 percent respectively, while the total real consumption expenditures had remained largely stagnant, with population growing at around 3.2 percent to 3.9 percent per annum ... The unprecedented falls in output and investment were accompanied by a widening gap between the official and the black (or 'free') market exchange rates, and rapidly rising prices" (Pesaran 2000: 64).

[24] Elaine Sciolino, "Iran Vote Expected to Turn on Economy," *New York Times*, April 11, 1992.

[25] Sciolino, "Iran Vote."   [26] PBS (1999).

Amid signs of political instability, the clerical regime sought to mobilize new sources of support. One consequence was its improved receptivity to gestures from abroad that could mitigate its economic problems. One cannot be sure that a favorable response from the West would have halted Iran's nuclear program, but the possibility cannot be dismissed. On just about every occasion, however, Tehran's overtures were rebuffed by the United States.

- A first indication of regime willingness to engage was President Rafsanjani's 1995 move to offer the US firm Conoco a billion-dollar contract to develop two Iranian offshore oil fields. This would have been the first contract awarded a foreign entity for oil field exploration and development since the 1979 revolution, and it could have given the United States a basis for future economic leverage over Tehran's policies.[27] The gesture was spurned by President Clinton who, pressured by a Republican-controlled Congress, issued an executive order barring US citizens from investing in or managing oil development projects in Iran.[28]
- Upon his election in 1997, President Khatami announced that he was prepared to entertain "relations with any state that respects our independence," calling for a "dialogue of civilizations."[29] He proposed, as a first step on the path to reconciliation, an exchange of "professors, writers, scholars, artists, journalists, and tourists." Again, the initiative evoked no meaningful US response.
- In the wake of 9/11, Khatami condemned al Qaeda's terrorist attacks, and when the United States took military action against Afghanistan's Taliban regime, Tehran offered to allow US pilots in distress to land on Iranian soil. It also supported Afghanistan's Northern Alliance, the United States' major military ally in the country, and it helped devise a broad-based government to replace the Taliban.[30] Tehran expected some US reciprocation; instead, a few weeks later, President Bush described Iran as part of the Axis of Evil.
- Another chance for progress presented itself in May 2003, following the successful US march into Baghdad. The new overture took the form of a letter from Tehran proposing an agenda for comprehensive talks between the two countries. The regime offered to put just about everything on the table, including its WMD programs and full cooperation with the International Atomic Energy Agency. The Bush administration did not respond to the offer.[31]

---

[27] Estelami (1999: 6).   [28] Slavin (2005).
[29] Khatami (1998: 150).   [30] Slavin (2007: 197–198).   [31] Slavin (2007: 205).

This, then, was a juncture when Iran's domestic political circumstances favored the use of positive incentives by the United States. But opportunities were not acted upon, and the circumstances behind Tehran's receptivity were not immutable. By 2005, the basis on which the regime sought to establish its domestic control shifted significantly. That year, Iran's presidential election was won by arch-conservative Mahmoud Ahmadinejad, who proceeded to build his position on a virulent and anti-Western nationalism and on the state's repressive machinery, mainly the Revolutionary Guards (IRGC) and the Basij militia.

The regime now benefited politically from its resistance to outside pressures to abandon its nuclear program. *Time* magazine reported that, as the confrontation with the United States developed in 2004, "Millions of Iranians are avidly following the showdown on Iranian TV talk shows, and the ruling clerics have earned more popular support than they have in years. Even Iranians who dislike the mullahs are showing pride at the idea of Iran becoming an atomic power."[32] Some polls indicated that over 80 percent of Iranians backed the goal of atomic energy.[33]

At the same time, the position of the regime's repressive apparatus, particularly the Revolutionary Guards, was strengthened. Former IRGC officers came to account for half of Ahmadinejad's cabinet.[34] The Guards acquired increasingly important responsibilities, including control of Iran's strategic missile force, and a growing role in the economy. In 2007, it was reported that the IRGC had ties to over 100 companies, with $12 billion in construction and engineering capital.[35] The economic role of the Guards came to encompass black market operations, such as the illegal importation of alcohol.[36]

Under these inauspicious conditions, the United States and its allies finally made their overtures. In October 2004, the EU-3 group (France, Germany, and the United Kingdom), informed Washington of its intention to offer Tehran a package of incentives to freeze its uranium enrichment activities.[37] The United States tentatively backed the European position, announcing, in March 2005, that it might endorse Iran's application to join the World Trade Organization and allow it to purchase American spare parts for its commercial aircraft. Inducements included an offer to provide Iran with light-water (and

---

[32] Macleod and Siamdoust (2004: 46).
[33] Abedin (2006: 6).   [34] Alfoneh (2008: 3).
[35] Kim Murphy, "Iran's $12-Billion Enforcers," *Los Angeles Times*, August 26, 2007.
[36] Bruno (2009).
[37] The Associated Press, "Three US Allies to Offer Iran Inducements," *USA Today*, October 15, 2004.

relatively proliferation-proof) reactors, for which the uranium would be enriched outside of Iran.[38] These countries also proposed to improve Iranian access to US and European agriculture goods.[39]

Now, however, the regime was inflexible, Ahmadinejad declaring, "whether you negotiate or not, whether you frown at us or not, and whether you stay beside us or turn your back on us, the Iranian nation will not retreat from its path of developments and achievement of advanced technology."[40] By 2007, the regime declared that it would expand this program from a single "cascade" of 164 gas centrifuges to one of multiple cascades involving 3,000 centrifuges – enough eventually to fuel several weapons each year. Sanctions since imposed by the UNSC have had little impact. In April 2009, Tehran announced it was testing two new high-capacity centrifuges, and that it now had 7,000 operating at Natanz.[41] This went hand-in-hand with advances in missile development. In early February 2009, a telecommunications satellite was launched on the Safir-2 rocket, portending a ballistic missile with intercontinental range.[42] On May 20, a medium-range, surface-to-surface, solid-fueled missile was tested, placing parts of Europe within its range.[43]

A moderate version of the Tehran regime, identifying with the pragmatic and educated middle class, yielded to a much harsher variant, seeking support from some of the most hardline elements of Iranian society. It is hard to know whether engagement with the Khatami administration would have made an appreciable difference to the regime's character and priorities, but prospects for direct leverage over Tehran's nuclear program had plainly dimmed.

Possibilities for constructive engagement

If coercive pressures have been ineffective at best, and more likely counterproductive, we must ask whether positive inducements could stimulate more desirable developments: either encouraging evolving interests

---

[38] "U.S. to Lift Objections Against Iranian Bid to Join the WTO," *Washington File*, March 11, 2005.

[39] Glenn Kessler, "Six Powers Reach Accord on Iran Plan," *Washington Post*, June 2, 2006.

[40] Kessler, "Six Powers Reach Accord."

[41] Borzou Daragahi and Ramin Mostaghim, "Iran Announces New Achievements in Nuclear Program," *Los Angeles Times*, April 10, 2009.

[42] "Iran Launches Homegrown Satellite," *BBC News*, February 3, 2009, available at: www.news.bbc.co.uk/2/hi/7866357.stm.

[43] "Iran Tests New Surface-to-Surface Missile," *CNN*, May 20, 2009, available at: www.edition.cnn.com/2009/WORLD/meast/05/20/iran.missile.test/index.html.

within the regime's coalition, developments that would lead them to favor a less confrontational international stance and a decreased commitment to nuclear weapons, or that would make the regime a less threatening member of the international community if such weapons should be acquired. We also ask whether external engagement could strengthen the position of elites that lie outside the regime's natural constituency, with the same aims in mind. Not enough is known about the manner in which key political actors conceive of their own interest to offer a confident answer, but certain observations suggest that possibilities exist.

It is, for example, significant that a sizable portion of Iran's economy (up to 20 percent of national GNP[44]) is controlled by organizations called *bonyads*. Nominally charitable organizations run by the clerical establishment, their assets mushroomed with the 1979 revolution, as the wealth of the Shah and followers was turned over to them. They possess huge holdings, enjoy a privileged fiscal position, publish no public accounts, and typically answer only to the Supreme Leader. They often enjoy preferential access to the banking system, giving them an edge when competing with firms from the private sector. And they appear to have used their wealth in a context of political patronage. A study by Rand concluded that the *bonyads* had:

"monetized" political life in a way the clerics had not during the latter's era of dominance in the 1980s; in a sense, the bonyads replaced the clerics as generators of wealth just as a fast-food chain might replace small hamburger franchises (although the clerical establishment retained political dominance).[45]

The wealthiest *bonyad* is the Shrine of Imam Reza, which functions both as a religious center and as a business conglomerate owning mines, textile factories, a bus factory, a pharmaceutical plant, an engineering company, a bakery, and dozens of other properties.[46] It is likely that many of the larger *bonyads* are torn in two directions: on the one hand, they benefit from the lack of transparency and occasional fiscal privileges they are allowed; on the other hand, they often compete with those, like the Revolutionary Guards, that have carved out large areas of licit and illicit economic activity in the nation and are powerfully supported by Khamenei and President Ahmadinejad. Since many *bonyads* encompass modern and potentially dynamic enterprises, they should benefit from direct access to international economic opportunities. The *Wall Street Journal* (2007) reported that the Shrine of the

---

[44] Klebnikov (2003).   [45] Thaler *et al.* (2010: 55).
[46] Andrew Higgins, "Inside Iran's Holy Money Machine," *Wall Street Journal*, June 2, 2007.

Imam Reza was looking abroad to find foreign investors for joint ventures. Although many of these would be regional to the Middle East, there is fear that nuclear programs might drive Gulf nations away from Tehran and into Washington's embrace.[47]

Accordingly, major *bonyads* could find that their interests are ill-served by confrontational policies, especially nuclear programs, that isolate Iran from globalized flows of economic activity. Should the regime come to view such *bonyads* as institutions whose renewed support must be courted, then external economic links that benefit these bodies could become a constraint on externally objectionable regime conduct. While such scenarios involve what we have termed Option 1b, the prospect that entirely new groups may come to extend their influence within the political system (Option 2) must also be considered.

Iran's economy is fairly differentiated, and in some areas relatively developed. *Bonyads* and the Revolutionary Guard have a significant presence in economic activity, but a vigorous private sector exists as well, much of which would benefit from economic liberalization and improved links to the global economy. Moreover, the comparatively high level of education among Iranians indicates that the foundations for a vibrant middle class exist, a class that often stands at the forefront of desire for democratization and economic opening. The relative youth of its population suggests that a significant segment of society may prefer integration into a global, youth-oriented culture. In any case, the possibility that reformist candidate Mir Hossein Mousavi actually won the disputed 2009 presidential election demonstrates that the priorities of the hardline conservatives do not necessarily reflect the priorities of most Iranians. The volume of post-election demonstrations spearheaded by what came to be known as the Green Movement (Green was the color symbolizing Mousavi's campaign) indicates a considerable social base for a reform movement.

Fissures are apparent within the religious establishment as well. After the disputed 2009 election, a leading group of religious leaders, the Association of Researchers and Teachers of Qom, declared the new government illegitimate. Abbas Milani, Director of the Iranian Studies Program at Stanford University, described this as "the most historic crack in the 30 years of the Islamic Republic."[48] In October 2010, it was reported that the regime had blocked the websites of two religious leaders holding the highest clerical rank in Shiite Islam, Grand Ayatollahs

---

[47] Takeyh and Gvosdev (2004: 42).
[48] Michael Slackman and Nazila Fathi, "Clerical Leaders Defy Ayatollah on Iran Election," *New York Times*, July 4, 2009.

Yusuf Sanei and Asadollah Bayat-Zanjani. Both had been critical of the country's leadership.[49]

Concessions that could relieve the international community's anxieties are not likely to be offered by those – especially the Revolutionary Guard, the Basij, and the hardline clergy – on whose support the regime now depends. These are the segments of the Iranian polity whose position largely requires foreign threats, and who, like Khamenei, believe that "The change of behavior [the United States and its allies] want – and which they don't always emphasize on – is in fact a negation of our identity."[50] When the nation feels externally beleaguered, we are unlikely to witness an opening up of political space that reformist groups could come to occupy. Yet, as Harvard's Stephen Walt complains, "We continue to ramp up sanctions that most people know won't work, and we take steps that are likely to reinforce Iranian suspicions and strengthen the clerical regime's hold on power."[51] In Ray Takeyh's view, "the only path out of this paradox is to invest in an Iranian political class that is inclined to displace dogma with pragmatism. And that still remains the indomitable Green movement."[52]

Opportunities for external engagement and a less-constrained participation in flows of globalized economic activity, stand to strengthen the sense of identity of reformist groups and make them more valuable to the country's future. Under the circumstances, it is possible that a virtuous feedback process could acquire traction – where the improved position of the new elites and changes in Iran's external posture encourage each other. However, and in addition to a better understanding of what domestic structures of power and preferences portend for the successful use of positive incentives, we must appreciate the domestic political obstacles that, from the US perspective, may stand in the way of acting on that understanding.

Lessons of North Korea

The North Korean case differs from Iran's in important ways. On the one hand, the Kim regime has not encountered instability of the sort experienced by Iranian rulers. On the other hand, the nature of North Korean society – the absence of a meaningful civil society and of independent economic interests – has meant that attempts to bolster

---

[49] William Yong, "In Sign of Discord, Iran Blocks Web Sites of Some Clerics," *New York Times*, October 3, 2010.

[50] Cited in Takeyh, "Why Iran Won't Respond."

[51] Walt (2010).

[52] Takeyh, "Why Iran Won't Respond."

domestic support have led Pyongyang to turn to those domestic groups least sympathetic to US aims. Option 1a currently provides a more plausible way of fortifying the regime's position than do either options 1b or 2, and choice of this least desirable option has been made more likely by US-led sanctions: they have encouraged the regime to concili-ate these domestic interests, and they have been associated with some of the biggest advances in the country's nuclear weapons and long-range missile programs. As Leon Sigal has correctly observed, "Far from making North Korea more amenable to disarming, the record shows sanctions have provoked it to step up arming."[53]

It is not the case that the foundations on which the Kim regime built its rule never seemed shaky. Marxism, a major component of the ori-ginal legitimizing narrative, lost some of its mobilizational power with the collapse of Soviet Communism and China's turn to a quasi-market economy. *Juche*, the call for complete national self-reliance that was the narrative's second strand, must have lost its luster as massive economic failures made the country dependent on China, South Korea, and the World Food Program for some of its basic needs. The North Korean economy is appropriately described as "one of the world's most isolated and bleak."[54] The massive famines of the early 1990s probably fueled additional regime concerns about its domestic standing.

There is some indication that, at the time, a reformist wing within the regime pressed for a more conciliatory international stance, espe-cially with regard to the country's nuclear program.[55] This also was the juncture at which adequate concessions, on both the US and North Korean side, seemed poised to curtail Pyongyang's nuclear program. In the context of the 1994 Agreed Framework, Pyongyang agreed to abandon its plutonium-based nuclear program. In exchange it expected to receive two proliferation-proof light-water reactors (furnished by an international consortium, the Korean Peninsula Energy Development Organization, or KEDO), fuel aid (in the form of 500,000 tons of crude oil annually), and progressively normalized economic and political rela-tions with the United States.

Much of the problem with realizing the promise of the Agreed Framework resided on the US side. From the North Korean per-spective, the United States had not lived up to its bargain. Largely due to Republican opposition, the Clinton administration could not get the congressional support and funds needed to deliver the prom-ised 500,000 tons of oil annually. It was not until fiscal year 1999 that

---

[53] Sigal (2010).   [54] Nanto and Chanlett-Avery (2009: 18).
[55] Harrison (2002: 33).

Congress provided the full $35 million requested by the administration.[56] Invitations to bid for construction of light-water reactors were not issued by KEDO until 1998, while construction of the first reactor began only in 2002. Even after a partial lifting of sanctions, North Korea remained one of the few countries not granted Normal Trading Relations (NTRs), its exports subject to the so-called column-2 rates of the Smoot-Hawley Tariff Act of 1930 (these tariffs are highest for labor-intensive products, such as textiles, in which North Korea could conceivably be competitive). Clearly, US gestures fell short of what Pyongyang had expected, doing little to address its domestic needs. Its interest in the agreement correspondingly faded. In October 2002, in response to US concerns, North Korea admitted the existence of a clandestine program for enriching uranium (an admission later repudiated); KEDO then suspended oil deliveries, while President Bush effectively withdrew from the agreement. A five-year period of renewed threats and punitive pressures was launched.

Since then, relations have traced an erratic course during which increases in US coercive pressures have gone hand-in-hand with some of the biggest steps toward a full North Korean nuclear weapons and long-range missile capability. Bitter invective between 2003 and 2005 was replaced by constructive developments in 2005, when South Korea agreed to provide significant amounts of food and electricity, and President Bush declared that the United States had no intention of attacking North Korea.[57] Prospects for an agreement again collapsed when, in response to Pyongyang's drug trafficking and counterfeiting activities, Washington pressured international banks, especially the Banco Delta Asia of Macau, to cease doing business with North Korea. In response, in July 2006, North Korea test-fired seven missiles, including the long-range Taepodong-2. In October, it conducted its first, partially successful, nuclear test. At US urging, the UNSC retaliated with sanctions against the regime. When these produced no concessions from Pyongyang, Washington once again switched to incentives, engaging in bilateral negotiations (parallel with the Six-Party Talks) and offering $25 million in food aid. North Korea responded by agreeing to shut down its Yongbyon reactor and plutonium reprocessing facility, and also to provide an inventory of all its nuclear programs. The Bush administration then ended the application of the Trading With the Enemy Act to North Korea and removed it from its list of state sponsors of

---

[56] Arms Control Association (1998).
[57] "N Korea to 'Give up Nuclear Aims,'" *BBC News*, September 19, 2005, available at: www.news.bbc.co.uk/2/hi/asia-pacific/ 4259128.stm.

terrorism. However, when newly-elected South Korean president Lee Myung-bak abandoned his predecessor's policy of unconditional food and fertilizer aid, North Korea responded with another Taepodong-2 launch, followed, in May 2009, with its second nuclear test, provoking further external sanctions.

The urgency for an agreement once expressed by the regime appears to have subsided. Partly, this may be related to Pyongyang's feeling that what it most wanted, fully normalized political and economic relations with the United States – a considerable victory to tout before the North Korean polity – could not be achieved. In a 2009 article published in *Asia Times* (online), Kim Myong Choi, considered an informal spokesman for Kim Jong-il, reported that the regime had entertained two strategic plans: Plan A and Plan B. The former involved negotiating away the country's nuclear capacity along with a rapprochement with the United States; the latter envisaged going it alone as a full-fledged nuclear weapons state. After a dozen years of seeking to induce the United States to treat it with proper respect, according to Choi, the regime decided that the only alternative was Plan B.[58]

An increasingly truculent stance was evidenced by the sinking, in March 2010 and almost surely by a North Korean torpedo, of the South Korean naval vessel, *Cheonan*, with a loss of forty-six lives. This belligerence may have been a product of Kim Jong-il's domestic political calculations. On the one hand, the failure to furnish the most basic foundations of national prosperity, the ever-looming threat of famine,[59] and the nearly complete absence of a middle class that could be mobilized on behalf of a reformist program, and, on the other hand, the inability to reduce the country's security and economic problems via international engagement, eventually led the regime to make the military establishment the cornerstone of its political support. Following the "military first" policy announced by Kim Jong-il in 1998, the armed forces came to supplant the Korean Worker's Party (the Communist party) as the country's dominant political institution, while the National Defense Commission eclipsed the Politburo as the supreme political decision-making body. A study by the Congressional Research Service observed that "The military-first policy places the army ahead of the working class for the first time in the history of

---

[58] K.M. Choi, "Kim Jong-il Shifts to Plan B," *Asia Times Online*, May 21, 2009.
[59] One of the leading studies on the predicament of the North Korea economy observes that the "ultimate and deepest roots of North Korea's food problems must be found in the very nature of the north Korean economic and political system" (Haggard and Noland 2007: 3).

North Korea's so-called revolutionary movement."[60] The regime's muscular and confrontational policies, especially nuclear and long-range missile tests, may be an attempt to gratify the priorities of the institution upon which the regime now most depends. In any case, and with dreary predictability, the *Cheonan* sinking was met with a new barrage of US sanctions.[61]

The North Korean case indicates that a closed political system with no meaningful civil society precludes the short-term emergence of independent groups with interests in reform and improved relations with the international community, and whose support the regime might seek. The latter's logical choice, then, is to turn to a subset of its traditional supporters, and, in the absence of tangible benefits from international engagement, it has turned to those whose values and interests imply a continuation of confrontational policies. Washington's tepid efforts to comply with the 1994 Agreed Framework, and its subsequent attempts at punitive leverage, have virtually guaranteed that US counterproliferation aims would be thwarted.

Although the nature of North Korea's society and polity, along with US policy, have so far led the regime to secure its domestic position via Option 1a, the long run may hold better prospects. Ultimately, positive engagement may have a more ambitious goal than a specific, albeit substantial, policy concession from the other side: the grander objective being to help reconfigure interests and preferences within that country, so that new and moderate sources of regime support emerge or are strengthened to the point where they simply cannot be ignored. The regime might then have no choice but to abandon its habitual supporters in favor of the emerging groups, aligning its policies with their interests and preferences. We are not assuming a complete regime overhaul: the goal is not to transform the architecture of power, only the foreign policies needed to maintain the regime in power.

Sixty years of a hermetically closed society and harsh Stalinist rule, preceded by decades of Japanese occupation, have deprived the country of an ability to adapt creatively to new conditions, of the rudiments of a differentiated civil society, of the skills and mindsets required by a market economy, and of any significant acquaintance with the world of developed democracies. A purpose of positive engagement, then, is not so much to capitalize on non-existent conditions for desirable change as

---

[60] Nanto and Chanlett-Avery (2009: 23).
[61] Mark Landler and Elisabeth Bumiller, "US to Add to Sanctions on N. Korea," *New York Times*, July 21, 2010.

to promote their emergence. This does not imply a progressively dem-
ocratizing North Korea. Barring complete regime implosion, a scenario fraught with volatility and regional risk, a plausible model, as in
the Vietnam and China case, is that of Market Leninism, combining
centralized political command with market liberalization, a development that assumes controlled reform under propitious international
circumstances.

The question is whether improving the position of those who would
most benefit from this development can bolster prospects for change.
A successfully negotiated deal on Pyongyang's nuclear programs, that
provided the country with access to the International Monetary Fund,
the Asian Development Bank, as well as WTO membership, could
spur meaningful market reforms and create substantial new opportunities for groups ready to embrace such opportunities. As those who
desire market reforms and foreign economic opportunities become
more important to the political authorities, and as reform is validated
by economic success, nuclear weapons lose their rationale within both
the legitimizing narrative and the regime's political calculus. This
assumes, however, foreign willingness to remove obstacles to the country's integration into the world economy and a conducive domestic
political climate within North Korea. The regime should not believe
that economic liberalization would result in a loss of political control and that external security fears justify nuclear programs: changes
in both expectations would benefit from a receptive international
environment.

Although Hanoi's approach to economic reform has had a schizophrenic, stop-and-go quality, interest in ways of improving dismal economic performance have, at times, been evident. Pyongyang's 1984
joint venture law opened possibilities for foreign investment, while
a 1986 policy allowed enterprises to retain 20 to 50 percent of earnings above their required contribution to the government.[62] In 1991,
after Kim Jong-il visited China, the regime announced the creation
of a free trade and investment area in the Rajin-Songbong area. The
notion was to create an important container port and hub for export
industries, but little foreign interest followed, due to poor infrastructure, difficult transportation, and bureaucratic interference. The more
recent Kaesong Industrial Park near the demilitarized zone fared better, attracting some South Korean investment. By the end of 2009,
Kaesong hosted 116 South Korea factories (some transplanted from
China) and employed some 40,000 North Korean workers, with plans

[62] Harrison (2002: 31).

for further expansion.[63] In 2002, Pyongyang announced additional reforms, including an increase in official prices (bringing them closer to black-market prices) and wages, increased scope for private farming, and a slightly decentralized system of industrial and agricultural management.[64] Further measures encouraging informal local markets and small-scale business were adopted in 2004.[65] Although, in 2005, the regime retreated from some of its reforms, certain changes have taken hold. Movements toward reform seems to have been inspired by evidence that it has brought prosperity to China without visibly undermining the regime's political and social control.[66] Kim Jong-il visited China on several occasions, showing particular interest in Shanghai's economic achievements. Apparently, "The Shanghai visit was clearly designed to examine the potential for the DPRK to pursue more market-oriented economic policy approaches."[67] The regime has expressed interest in Vietnamese-style economic reforms. In a November 2007 visit to Vietnam, Kim Jong-il publicly expressed his admiration of Dôi Môi.[68]

Amid new insights into the regime's succession politics, 2010 brought conflicting news on North Korea's political direction. On the one hand, it was reported that the regime would phase out its private markets, reverting to a fully state-controlled economy.[69] On the other hand, the apparent reinstatement of former prime minister Pak Pong Ju, banished in 2007 for advocating market reforms, has led to speculation that the regime might, once again, accept modest economic liberalization.[70] At the same time, appointment of Kang Sok Ju to the powerful position of Deputy Prime Minister could be taken to indicate a renewed desire for accommodation with the United States, since he was one of the architects of the 1994 Agreed Framework.[71]

The prospects for reform are not totally unfavorable, and it must be remembered that the first seeds of change were planted in both

---

[63] Yoon (2007).

[64] Nanto and Chanlett-Avery (2009).

[65] "Through a Glass, Darkly," *The Economist*, March 11, 2004.

[66] Maramoto (2008).

[67] Maramoto (2008: 107).

[68] Park Myun Hin, "Kim Jong Il Praises the Doi Moi Economic Reforms of Vietnam at a Delicate Time," *Daily NK*, October 29, 2007.

[69] Choe Sang-Hun, "North Korea to End Private Market Experiment," *New York Times*, April 2, 2010.

[70] *North Korea Leadership Watch* (2010), Choe Sang-Hun, "North Korea Reinstates Market-Oriented Official," *New York Times*, August 23, 2010.

[71] Harrison (2010).

Vietnam and China when they might have been least expected.[72] At the same time, parallels with China and Vietnam should keep in mind that both of those countries had resolved their security problems – mainly via reconciliation with the United States – before undertaking full economic reforms and integration into international economic flows.[73] The link between international conditions and domestic support for market reform must be kept firmly in mind. The need to conciliate the military has made it hard to abandon conservative hardline policies or a centrally planned economy focused on heavy industry, which has so benefited the armed forces. And it has made it politically necessary to maintain the country's nuclear program. Under conditions of international tension – especially with the United States – such choices have been easier to justify.[74] The opposite also follows. As a report by the Asia Society Center examining the case for economic engagement with North Korea pointed out,

North Korea's attitude toward the world is closely related to the underlying structure of its domestic political economy: a closed command economy that favors the military and heavy industry and is isolated from the sweeping economic and political changes that have transformed the Asian landscape in recent decades. Encouraging a more open and market-friendly economic growth strategy would benefit the North Korean people as a whole and would generate vested interests in continued reform and opening, and a less confrontational policy. In other words, economic engagement could change North Korea's perception of its own self-interest.[75]

Understanding that the political reward structure of proliferants is, to some extent, malleable from the outside is a prerequisite to understanding how, in the long run at least, many nuclear programs could be discouraged, or how those who, like North Korea, have managed to acquire nuclear weapons could nevertheless become acceptable members of the international community. This assumes that thinking about the promise of engagement can proceed from a strategic, not only tactical, perspective.

---

[72] For example, Feffer (2010).

[73] There is another reason why Vietnam's success might not be replicated in the North Korean context. A great boost to the influx of foreign capital from Vietnam came from its substantial expatriate community in the West, the United States in particular. North Korea can count on nothing of the sort.

[74] Toloraya (2008: 32).

[75] Asia Society Center on US-China Relations and the University of California Institute on Global Conflict and Cooperation 2009.

Concluding observations

Regimes facing domestic challenges may try to bolster their position either by re-energizing traditional backers or by seeking new sources of support. From the perspective of counterproliferation, the latter is preferable, since the new groups are less likely than the old to endorse confrontational foreign policies. However, if inducements that could help the regime conciliate new sources of support are withheld, it is apt to turn to its habitual allies. Here the risks are considerable, for, unless these supporters can be gratified in new ways, radical and con-frontational methods of mobilizing them will be employed – generally increasing the regime's commitment to its nuclear program. If induce-ments are attempted in a context where traditional support is sought by the regime, they can have either of two objects in mind. On the one hand, they can seek to dispel the enduring worries of the regime's trad-itional allies, especially their security concerns, making them less likely to resist the policy change desired by the initiator. In this regard, it is obvious that appropriate security guarantees to Pyongyang, including a comprehensive peace treaty, are a condition for a satisfactory resolution of the North Korean nuclear issue. On the other hand, if the interests of some of the regime's traditional allies have evolved – as, for example, with certain Iranian *bonyads* – such groups may be offered concessions (in this case, economic) that decrease their resistance to, and perhaps encourage their support of, the policy changes demanded of their gov-ernment. In any case, the inducements offered must address the inter-ests of the groups whose position we wish to encourage, and they must be proportional to what is demanded of the government. Timid and tentative concessions will rarely match the gratifications and domestic credit acquired by joining the restricted and prestigious club of nuclear weapon states.

The problem is that it is politically difficult, from the US perspec-tive, to offer meaningful concessions to a renegade regime. The fear of being charged with "appeasement" and of promoting a moral hazard, as well as the culturally-imbedded conviction that bad nations, like bad people, deserve to be treated harshly, imply serious political risks for leaders who advocate such a course. Such risks suggest that induce-ments of the magnitude required to persuade the regime to abandon its nuclear programs may not be seen.

Thus, inducements are not a universal panacea. On the part of the target regime, the conditions for success are restrictive, and there are considerable political and psychological barriers to credible concessions

on the US side. One must accept that, at times, neither positive inducements nor negative sanctions may be effective. Still, given the abys-
mal failure and frequently counterproductive character of threats and
punishments, a better understanding of the circumstances behind the
effectiveness of positive engagement is needed – to discourage, where
possible, renegade regimes' pursuit of nuclear weapons and, perhaps
even more importantly, to make living safely with them possible when
such efforts fail.

5   An analytically eclectic approach to sanctions and nonproliferation

Daniel W. Drezner

Introduction

Nuclear nonproliferation is an important priority for US national security. The nonproliferation issue rated very highly in all three National Security Strategies published over the past decade. It is curious, then, that the current US policy approach to the two most high-profile nonproliferation cases boils down to negotiations and "smart sanctions." As the data in Chapter 3 of this volume demonstrates, Iran and North Korea have been the target of multiple rounds of unilateral and multilateral economic statecraft for the past two decades.[1]

There are many explanations for this policy outcome, but one contributing factor is the renewed faith in "smart sanctions" and financial sanctions as a coercive policy tool. Rachel Loeffler recently concluded that, "it is hard to imagine any serious foreign policy issue down the line in which financial tools would not be or should not be considered as part of a comprehensive strategy."[2] US policy journals have been replete with essays arguing in favor of financial statecraft as the best policy lever available to the United States.[3]

As political scientists and policy analysts develop more fine-grained analyses of the coalition politics in targeted countries, the intellectual appeal of smart sanctions made some intuitive sense. Ostensibly, smart or targeted sanctions are the precision-guided munitions of economic statecraft. They are designed to hurt elite supporters of the targeted regime, while imposing minimal hardship on the mass public. Targeted sanctions are only implemented through an enhanced understanding of the domestic political economy of the target regime. By altering the material incentives of powerful supporters, the argument runs, these supporters will eventually pressure the targeted government into

---

[1] See also Shen (2010).   [2] Loeffler (2009).

[3] Hufbauer and Oegg (2000), Bracken (2007), Liss (2007/2008), Eckert (2008), Gottemoeller (2007), Loeffler (2009), Shen (2010), and Zarate (2009).

making concessions. As the coalition politics of targeted regimes are clearly mapped out, targeted sanctions should, in theory, yield greater bang for the buck.

This chapter argues that the theory of smart sanctions, while powerful, is also brittle. While the theory behind smart sanctions is both parsimonious and elegant, it relies on only one causal mechanism through which sanctions lead to policy concessions. As a result, targeted sanctions can be too constrained to provide significant policy leverage. Using an approach based on "analytic eclecticism,"[4] this chapter argues that more comprehensive economic sanctions – or more wide-ranging inducements – will often be more likely to lead to the desired policy change. Larger-scale influence attempts can work through multiple causal mechanisms – including coalitional politics – that are not mutually exclusive. Once the causal complexity of economic statecraft and nonproliferation is better appreciated, smart sanctions lose some of their luster. Financial sanctions that are tailored to have narrow effects will be as ineffective as smart sanctions, whereas financial measures that have broad-based economic effects will have a greater likelihood of success.

This chapter is divided into five sections. The next section process-traces the emergence of smart sanctions as a policy tool for nonproliferation. The third section reviews the empirical literature, and finds that smart sanctions have a poor track record for success.[5] The fourth section discusses analytical eclecticism and why that approach works well for understanding the interplay between sanctions and nonproliferation. The fifth section concludes by applying this framework to Iran and North Korea.

Smart sanctions as a focal point

Prior to the mid 1990s, most of the academic research treated the sender and target as rational unitary actors.[6] Little attention was paid to the causal mechanisms through which sanctions were supposed to lead the target government into acquiescing. The Iraq case, however, spurred more attention to the causal logic through which sanctions were supposed to work. Both scholars and policy-makers called for an opening up of the "black box" of the target state.

---

[4] Katzenstein and Okawara (2001/2002) and Katzenstein and Sil (2010).
[5] The next two sections are an expanded and updated version of Drezner (2010).
[6] See Rowe (2010) for a historical survey of the literature.

Intriguingly, research emanating from wildly disparate theoretical and methodological perspectives came to the same conclusion about the effect of comprehensive sanctions: they disproportionately hurt politically weak groups and benefited target regime sympathizers. Kaempfer and Lowenberg used a public choice framework to explain how sanctions had distributional effects on interest groups within the target country.[7] If the sanctions enriched – or could be manipulated to enrich – key supporters of the target regime, then the aggregate cost of the sanctions would have minimal impact on the target government. Jonathan Kirshner proposed a microfoundations approach, arguing that "instead of considering how those sanctions hurt the target state, this approach emphasizes how groups within the target are affected differently, and how these consequences change with the form of statecraft chosen."[8] He concluded that financial sanctions – aid cutoffs, asset freezes, and monetary pressures – were more likely to pressure key supporters of the target regime than broad-based trade sanctions. Buck *et al.* used a feminist approach to argue that the costs of trade sanctions are disproportionately imposed on women, who are often the most powerless political actors in the target country.[9] David Rowe's research on the effects of the sanctions regime on the Rhodesian government demonstrated how the target regime could manipulate the effects of sanctions to reward supporters and weaken opponents of the government.[10]

In the last decade, the emphasis of sanctions research has focused primarily on the political economy of authoritarian countries. As Susan Allen observes, more than 78 percent of sanctions in the past three decades were imposed on non-democratic target states.[11] As the data in Chapter 3 suggests, nonproliferation sanctions cases during the post-Cold War period are even more concentrated among closed authoritarian economies.[12] Wintrobe and Bueno de Mesquita *et al.* developed political economy models that could explain the incentives for non-democratic leaders when sanctions are imposed.[13] In authoritarian regimes, leaders had an incentive to create private and excludable goods for supporters, as opposed to public goods for the mass citizenry. Comprehensive sanctions created the opportunity for target governments to allocate

---

[7] Kaempfer and Lowenberg (1992) and Kaempfer *et al.* (2004).
[8] Kirshner (1997: 33).   [9] Buck *et al.* (1998).
[10] Rowe (2001).   [11] Allen (2008a: 269).
[12] Solingen's observation in the introductory chapter about the divergent preferences of internationalizing vs. inward-looking coalitions is salient for the broad spectrum of possible nonproliferation cases. For the cases of concern in this chapter, however, it is safe to assert that inward-looking coalitions dominate their national economies.
[13] Wintrobe (1990) and Bueno de Mesquita *et al.* (1999, 2003).

rent-seeking opportunities to those supporters. This policy response, would, if anything, increase an authoritarian regime's grip on power. Relying on this theoretical framework, a number of sanctions scholars argued that broad-based economic sanctions would have minimal effect on authoritarian targets.[14] Smart sanctions that hurt key elites, on the other hand, would have a better chance of success without hurting the target country's mass public.

This research trend dovetailed nicely with the evolution in policy-making on sanctions.[15] Smart sanctions could raise the target regime's costs of non-compliance while avoiding the collateral damage that comes with comprehensive trade embargoes. The most prominent country-wide examples included targeted financial sanctions, asset freezes, travel bans, restrictions on luxury goods, and arms embargoes. Furthermore, instead of sanctioning an entire country, smart sanctions advocates advocated the targeting of individuals, restrictions on corporations or holding companies associated with the target government's leadership. Targeted sanctions would hamper the ability of leaders to offer crucial supporters rent-seeking opportunities.

Smart sanctions were an idea that created a useful ideational focal point of agreement among key stakeholders in the international system.[16] UNSC members Russia, China, and France grew frustrated by their inability to alter the sanctions regime once the initial measures were approved. At the same time, the United States and United Kingdom wanted to keep sanctions in the policy toolkit. For recalcitrant members of the Security Council, smart sanctions offered the opportunity to cooperate with the hegemonic actor in the international system. At the same time, smart sanctions would not impose excessive humanitarian costs or threaten lucrative trading relationships with target countries. For the United States and the United Kingdom, the targeted sanctions framework seemed like a more precise policy tool. For humanitarian and human rights activists, smart sanctions seemed the best way to enforce norms in the global system without imposing needless costs on the most powerless members in target societies.

A two-track process emerged to improve the use of targeted sanctions. Within the United Nations machinery, an ongoing series of sanctions committees were formed to monitor and assess the effect of different Security Council resolutions authorizing sanctions. In 2006, for example, the Security Council formed the 1718 committee for

---

[14] Brooks (2002), Lektzian and Souva (2007), and Allen (2005, 2008a, 2008b).
[15] Cortright and Lopez (2002) and Brzoska (2003).
[16] Garrett and Weingast (1993).

North Korea and the 1737 committee after imposing sanctions against Iran. These committees had little enforcement power, and therefore acted only as a minimal deterrent against private actors engaging in sanctions-busting activity. These committees did succeed, however, in explicitly naming and shaming countries that were violating existing sanctions resolutions.[17] Given the powerful norms of diplomatic comity at the United Nations, this move in and of itself represented a significant break from past practices in Turtle Bay.

Outside the Security Council, a series of conferences were convened to figure out how to improve the implementation of sanctions. These conferences demonstrated the tight linkage between scholars and policy-makers on this issue.[18] In 1998, the Swiss government convened the "Interlaken Process," a rolling series of meetings designed to improve the practice of financial sanctions. The Interlaken Process brought together government officials, private sector experts, and academics to hammer out the technicalities of imposing sanctions. In 2001 the Swiss commissioned sanctions experts at Brown University's Watson Institute for International Studies to prepare a "how-to" sanctions manual, including a model Security Council resolution for future cases.[19] The German governments followed up Interlaken with the Bonn-Berlin Process to focus exclusively on arms embargoes and travel sanctions. The Swedish government subsequently convened the Stockholm Process to improve the sanctions machinery at the United Nations. Uppsala University's Department of Peace and Conflict Research provided significant expertise for the Stockholm Process. Scholars and other experts participated in all three of these processes, which led to significant buy-in from key stakeholders.

Bipartisan support for targeted sanctions also emerged in the United States – particularly for financial sanctions. The Clinton administration embraced the idea as part of the Treasury Department's initiative to combat financial abuse.[20] Financial countermeasures were developed to punish states and jurisdictions with lax anti-money-laundering statutes. These acts of financial statecraft proved effective in forcing target countries to alter their policies.[21] Because the United States was the epicenter of global finance, international bankers needed access to US capital markets to conduct international transactions. An advisory warning from the Treasury Department was sufficient to get foreign bankers to stop doing business with terrorist entities, for fear of losing access to

---

[17] Brzoska (2003).   [18] Biersteker *et al.* (2005).
[19] Biersteker *et al.* (2005: 17).   [20] Wechsler (2001).
[21] Drezner (2007: 142–145).

American banking services. After the 9/11 terrorist attacks, the Bush administration also embraced the smart sanctions initiatives.[22]

By 2010, both the United Nations and the United States had internalized the idea of targeted sanctions. The United Nations has not implemented comprehensive sanctions for the past fifteen years. The sanctions reform effort had a manifest impact on the ways that the UNSC authorized economic coercion. Biersteker *et al.* and Foot observe that concerns about the humanitarian and human rights effects of sanctions increased the degree of due process within existing UN sanctions committees over the past decade.[23] Even the 1267 committee, authorized to sanction individuals working with al Qaeda, grew more sensitive to minimizing the humanitarian impact of the sanctions. Hawkins and Lloyd argue that "a new norm against comprehensive sanctions has become part of the shared understanding among states."[24]

The bipartisan consensus within the US foreign policy community in favor of targeted sanctions has also deepened over time. Rose Gottemoeller, now US Assistant Secretary of State for Verification, Compliance and Implementation, concluded in late 2007 that smart sanctions "had been honed through the 'war on terror', and sanctions are hitting their targets among corrupt elites more often."[25] Juan Zarate, a deputy national security advisor in George W. Bush's administration, argued that the tools of financial statecraft "provide the United States and its allies the best source of diplomatic leverage to affect regimes' behavior and calculus."[26]

Assessing smart sanctions

There are two ways to evaluate the performance of the smart sanctions framework in world politics. First, have smart sanctions ameliorated the humanitarian costs that more comprehensive sanctions create? Second, have targeted sanctions improved target state compliance? The evidence provides moderate support for smart sanctions being more humane but less effective than more comprehensive measures.

Recent research on the impact of economic coercion in the target country would appear to support the humanitarian arguments in favor

---

[22] Zarate (2009).
[23] Biersteker *et al.* (2005) and Foot (2007). For a review of the legal due process issues raised by the sanctioning of individuals in the United Nations Security Council, see Bianchi (2006).
[24] Hawkins and Lloyd (2003: 441).   [25] Gottemoeller (2007: 109).
[26] Zarate (2009: 55).

of smart sanctions. Shagabutdinova and Berejikian examined HSE's pre-1990 sanctions data and found that financial sanctions were of shorter duration, lessening the suffering of target populations.[27] Wood analyzed the effect of economic sanctions on state repression using data from 1976 to 2001.[28] He found that comprehensive sanctions were likely to increase repression in authoritarian countries. In bivariate tests, Peksen and Drury find that the implementation of sanctions triggers drops in democracy and human rights scores in target governments.[29] Peksen also shows sanctions lead to a decline in both press freedoms and the physical integrity rights of individuals in target countries.[30] Furthermore, the decline in both sets of rights is greater if comprehensive sanctions are imposed rather than targeted sanctions.

These results suggest that, all else equal, targeted sanctions are a more humane policy tool. However, not all else is equal. Paradoxically, there are a number of conditions under which comprehensive sanctions appear to be better at ameliorating suffering in the target country. As Solingen suggests in her introduction, and as the econometric literature of the past decade confirms, comprehensive sanctions are more likely to trigger quick concessions if the target state is a democracy.[31] The goal of the sanctions episode also matters. If the sender's aim is regime change, then sanctions that impose larger costs have a greater likelihood of success.[32] Nikolay Marinov found that sanctions of any stripe tended to reduce the staying power of the target government; military action, in contrast, increased the duration of the government in power.[33] Major and McGann argue that there might be instances when sanctioning the "innocent bystanders" in the target country will be more likely to produce target concessions.[34] Most intriguingly, comprehensive sanctions were most useful in bringing about a quicker end to civil wars. Both Gershenson and Escribà-Folch found that comprehensive embargoes were more effective than targeted sanctions at ending intrastate conflicts.[35]

Smart sanctions are less promising in coercing the target government into making concessions. After reviewing the United Nations sanctions during the 1990s, Cortright and Lopez note that "the obvious conclusion is that comprehensive sanctions are more effective than targeted or

---

[27] Shagabutdinova and Berejikian (2007).
[28] Wood (2008).   [29] Peksen and Drury (2009).
[30] Peksen (2009, 2010).
[31] Bolks and Al-Sowayel (2000), Brooks (2002), Lektzian and Souva (2007), and Allen (2005, 2008a).
[32] Dashti-Gibson *et al.* (1997).   [33] Marinov (2005).
[34] Major and McGann (2005).
[35] Gershenson (2002) and Escribà-Folch (2010).

selective measures. Where economic and social impact have been greatest, political effects have also been most significant."[36] Elliott arrived at
a similar conclusion: "with the exception of Libya, the results of UN
targeted sanctions have been disappointing."[37] In their review essay,
Tostensen and Bull concluded: "the optimism expressed in some academic circles and among decision makers at national and international
levels appears largely unjustified."[38] At a 2010 International Studies
Association panel on the topic, many of the scholarly architects of the
smart sanctions approach agreed that, compared to comprehensive
sanctions, the policy results had been mixed at best.[39]

There are case studies that demonstrate the utility of targeted sanctions, including one instance of nonproliferation. The exemplar case is
the sanctions placed on Libya to renounce aiding terrorism, and, later,
its weapons of mass destruction programs. That episode, however, also
shows the limits of targeted sanctions. A welter of different policy tools
were used to get Libya to alter course, including back-channel negotiations, the Proliferation Security Initiative, and the unspoken threat
of invasion after Operation Iraqi Freedom. It was the combination of
these policy tools – as well as Muammar Qaddafi's quixotic nature –
that led to Libya's acquiescence.[40]

There have been more extensive investigations into the two most
common forms of targeted sanctions – arms embargoes and financial
statecraft.[41] The results have been underwhelming. Tierney evaluates
arms embargoes in civil wars across five criteria for success, including their symbolic impact. He concludes that "much of the impact of
UN arms embargoes in civil wars can be summarized as irrelevance or
malevolence."[42] Fruchart et al. reach a similar conclusion.[43] Brzoska offers
a slightly more hopeful assessment. He points to clear successes, such as
the 1993–2003 arms embargo of Angola. He also argues that there has
been an increasing amount of effectiveness over time in halting the transfer of weapons to armed combatants.[44] Qualifying this result as a "success," however, is problematic. As both Damrosch and Tierney observe,
arms embargoes can have malevolent distributional effects. They reward
the actor possessing the largest *ex ante* cache of weapons – which is often

---

[36] Cortright and Lopez (2002: 8).   [37] Elliott (2002: 171).
[38] Tostensen and Bull (2002: 402).
[39] "UN Sanctions: A Model of Scholar/Practitioner Collaboration?" roundtable at the
International Studies Association annual meeting, New Orleans, February 2010.
[40] Jentleson and Whytock (2005/2006).
[41] The literature assessing travel bans is much more sparse. Cortright and Lopez (2002:
133–148) provide a mixed assessment.
[42] Tierney (2005: 661).   [43] Fruchart et al. (2007).   [44] Brzoska (2008).

the actor responsible for the most egregious war crimes.[45] Brzoska also acknowledges that, over time, arms embargoes have been less successful in altering the behavior of target countries, working less than 8 percent of the time.[46] Paradoxically, however, sender country satisfaction with arms embargoes has increased over time – suggesting that the political virtues of smart sanctions trump the policy virtues.

The literature on financial statecraft is somewhat more upbeat. Hufbauer *et al.* originally found in bivariate tests that financial sanctions had a better track record of success than trade sanctions.[47] Shagabutdinova and Berejikian replicated that finding in multivariate tests, confirming that financial sanctions are more effective.[48] These results are based on pre-1990 episodes, however, and principally involve aid cutoffs – it is far from clear whether these results would carry over into modern financial sanctions.[49] There is evidence that financial sanctions have been useful in coercing countries into changing their anti-money-laundering rules.[50]

It is not clear, however, whether financial statecraft alone will be as successful on issues more highly valued by the target regime – such as a nuclear program.[51] Steil and Litan surveyed recent efforts by the United States to use capital market access to force policy changes in Sudan, Russia, and China. They found that all the targeted entities were able to find alternative sources of financing at minimal cost, concluding, "rarely has so powerful a force been harnessed by so many interests with such passion to so little effect."[52] A collaborative effort to examine efforts at monetary statecraft reached a similar conclusion: "among the central findings of our study are the substantial impediments to the efficient exercise of monetary power as a deliberate instrument of economic statecraft … The tools of monetary statecraft … are often too blunt to be effective when they would most be desired and too diffuse to be directed at particular targets without incurring substantial damage."[53]

Thinking about sanctions in an eclectic manner

Targeted sanctions have led to, at best, uneven results. If one widens the definition of success to include goals like international and domestic

---

[45] Damrosch (1994) and Tierney (2005).   [46] Brzoska (2008).
[47] Hufbauer *et al.* (1990).   [48] Shagabutdinova and Berejikian (2007).
[49] These results also suffer from omitted variable bias. Aid flows are strongly correlated with alliance relationships, which Shagabutdinova and Berejikian did not include in their regression analysis.
[50] Drezner (2007: chapter 5).   [51] Ang and Peksen (2007).
[52] Steil and Litan (2006).   [53] Andrews (2006: 25).

symbolism,[54] then targeted sanctions have been a roaring success. If one keeps the definition of success focused on the concessions made by the target country, then smart sanctions have consistently underperformed more comprehensive efforts. This is particularly surprising given that targeted sanctions rest on strong theoretical foundations. Bueno de Mesquita *et al.* represent the state of the art in terms of rational choice analyses of coalition governments.[55] Given the heavy intellectual and theoretical artillery deployed in support of targeted sanctions, why have they worked so poorly?

An approach grounded in analytic eclecticism offers some possible guidance on this question. Analytic eclecticism defines itself in contradistinction to particular research traditions or theoretical paradigms. By focusing on empirical problems rather than puzzles that bedevil a particular paradigm, an eclectic approach can draw from multiple theoretical approaches to attack a policy problem.[56] Conventional research traditions generate useful theoretical and empirical work, but can also develop conceptual blinders about causal mechanisms that do not conform to their own model's internal logic.[57] An analytically eclectic approach emphasizes explanatory power over the value of parsimony. Analytical eclecticism stresses pragmatism over rigor, focuses on substantive policy problems over analytical puzzles, and – most importantly, for our concerns – concentrates on the role that complexity and the multiplicity of causal processes plays in determining outcomes. As Sil and Katzenstein (2010: 419) put it:

[Specific research traditions], proceeding on the basis of particular ontological and epistemological assumptions, implicitly or explicitly focus attention on certain types of mechanisms while ignoring or defining away others. Analytic eclecticism, by contrast, offers complex causal stories that incorporate different types of mechanisms as defined and used in diverse research traditions. That is, rather than privilege any specific conception of causal mechanism, analytic eclecticism seeks to trace the problem-specific interactions among a wide range of mechanisms operating within or across different domains and levels of social reality.

An analytically eclectic approach to economic statecraft brings into stark relief the difference between targeted sanctions and more

---

[54] See, for example, Baldwin (1985) and Lindsay (1986).
[55] Bueno de Mesquita *et al.* (1999, 2003). In a related vein, see Acemoglu and Robinson (2005).
[56] Katzenstein and Okawara (2001/2002: 183).
[57] Analytic eclecticism also has its drawbacks. Katzenstein and Okawara (2001/2002: 184) acknowledge that "this approach may be too flexible to define by itself a research program capable of mobilizing strong political preferences and enduring professional ties."

comprehensive sanctions. To be sure, multiple research traditions criticized the notion of comprehensive sanctions. The targeted sanctions approach, however, is firmly rooted within a particular model of the target government – a foreign policy leader that needs to placate at least a majority of the selectorate with material benefits in order to remain in power. The theory behind these measures assumes sanctions will have no effect unless an authoritarian government's elite supporters are economically disadvantaged. Causal mechanisms that do not affect the target state's elite supporters – or consider whether the target state's elite supporters are internationalist or autarkic in their orientation – are summarily dismissed or ignored.

In contrast, consider the multiple causal pathways through which sanctions could lead an authoritarian target government to alter an undesired policy:

1. Sanctions harm a target country's elite supporters, forcing the government to acquiesce in order to stay in power.
2. Multilateral sanctions signal normative disapproval by the rest of the international community; the target government alters its policies so as to avoid being ostracized.
3. Sanctions lead to autarkic elite discontent, which causes the leader to engage in omnibalancing and seek supporters from internationalized interests.[58]
4. Sanctions imperils a country's strategic standing vis-à-vis its enduring rivals. Making a *realpolitik* cost-benefit decision, the target regime alters its policies.
5. Sanctions trigger popular unrest; the target regime, fearing domestic instability, alters its policies.
6. Sanctions trigger popular unrest, which leads to regime change. The new regime alters its policies.
7. Sanctions deny the target state the ability to implement its preferred policy.
8. The act of sanctions signals to a target's military that force will soon be used, leading them to force a change in policy.
9. A key ally signs onto a multilateral sanctions effort, signaling a worsening strategic position to the target leadership; it therefore concedes.

Some of these causal pathways share some of the same components, but they rest on different theoretical foundations. Some are realist, some rely on domestic coalitions, some are rational choice, some are

---

[58] See David (1991) on omnibalancing.

constructivist, and some are based on theories of political mobilization. To use the language of Lakatos, each different theoretical tradition focuses on the causal mechanisms consistent with its own negative heuristic. An eclectic, problem-oriented approach posits that all of these pathways are *possible* causal mechanisms through which sanctions could influence target behavior. It then asks how the range of sanctions (from very targeted to very comprehensive) affects the probability of each causal mechanism. An analytically eclectic approach asks *cui bono* (who benefits), but also asks *cuo modo bono* (how do they benefit).

The central insight of the targeted sanctions framework has been to point out the ways in which comprehensive trade sanctions can enrich the selectorate of an authoritarian state. As Escribà-Folch and Wright observe, "much of the sanctions literature makes the strong assumption that dictators are able to capture the rents associated with economic sanctions and that the subsequent increase in resources available to payoff political supporters stabilizes their rule."[59] It is therefore safe to assume that more comprehensive sanctions undercut the first causal mechanism listed above. If costly sanctions undercut multilateral cooperation, then the second causal mechanism would be circumscribed as well.

On the other hand, the greater the cost of the sanctions to the target state, the more likely the *other* seven posited causal mechanisms would be expected to work. Probabilistically, the effect on the outcome therefore depends on the relative probabilities of each of these causal mechanisms working. To use a numerical example, suppose that the first two mechanisms are independent, and each has a 30 percent chance of succeeding if smart sanctions are employed and only a 5 percent chance of succeeding if comprehensive sanctions are used. Six of the remaining seven causal mechanisms are independent,[60] but are more likely to work when comprehensive sanctions are imposed. Each of these mechanisms has a 5 percent chance of succeeding with smart sanctions but a 20 percent chance of succeeding with comprehensive sanctions. Note that, with these probabilities, the selectorate story is still the most causally powerful. Implementing smart sanctions would generate a probability of success roughly equivalent to 65 percent – but implementing comprehensive sanctions would lead to a success rate of more than 80 percent.[61]

---

[59] Escribà-Folch and Wright (2010).

[60] The popular revolt scenarios are clearly not independent.

[61] In the smart sanctions scenario, the probability of success equals $(1 - .7 \ast .7 \ast .95 \ast .95 \ast .95 \ast .95 \ast .95 \ast .95)$. In the comprehensive sanctions scenario, the probability of success equals $(1 - .95 \ast .95 \ast .8 \ast .8 \ast .8 \ast .8 \ast .8 \ast .8)$.

The weights in the above paragraph are purely notional – wouldn't the actual weights be more skewed in favor of smart sanctions? The econometric data suggests otherwise. Sanctions that impose significant costs on the target economy are more likely to produce concessions.[62] Indeed, in almost all of the statistical work, the cost of sanctions to the target country is positively and significantly correlated with successful outcomes. Regardless of regime type, costly sanctions are also more likely to trigger regime change.[63] Personalist authoritarian regimes are particularly vulnerable to serious sanctions.[64] Smart sanctions are likely to work via one or two causal mechanisms; comprehensive sanctions can work via five or six different causal mechanisms. It is certainly true that authoritarian regimes can use countermeasures, such as greater investments in repression and private goods for coalition supporters, to blunt the effect of sanctions. The more causal mechanisms that are in play, however, the more difficult it becomes for the target regime to block the intended effect of sanctions.

None of this is to argue that comprehensive sanctions should be used over targeted sanctions in all instances. There are two additional factors to consider. First, as Solingen points out in her introduction, the nature of domestic institutions affects the target regime's ability to effectively thwart each of these causal mechanisms. These institutions go beyond the simple dichotomy of democratic and authoritarian states. Different types of authoritarian states – one-party states, theocracies, military dictatorships, personalist regimes – might have different capabilities.[65] Personalist regimes are uniquely vulnerable to economic sanctions, while resource-rich regimes are better able to resist economic pressure.

The second factor to consider is the negative policy externalities associated with each kind of sanctions alternative. Nonproliferation is an important issue, but the initial advocates of smart sanctions were correct to point out the humanitarian costs of comprehensive sanctions. Focusing strictly on the effect of sanctions on nonproliferation outcomes leads to poliheuristic decision-making, in which one policy dimension is focused on to the exclusion of all others.[66] Beyond the humanitarian costs, comprehensive sanctions create other negative policy externalities. As Peter Andreas has demonstrated, trade sanctions encourage the creation of organized crime syndicates and

---

[62] Dashti-Gibson *et al.* (1997), Morgan and Schwebach (1997), and Drezner (1999).
[63] Dashti-Gibson *et al.* (1997) and Marinov (2005).
[64] Escribà-Folch and Wright (2010).
[65] Escribà-Folch and Wright (2010).
[66] Redd (2002).

transnational smuggling networks.[67] Sanctions do not just weaken the rule of law in the target country – they weaken the rule of law in bordering countries and monitoring organizations as well. This corruption has a path dependent quality, persisting long after sanctions have been lifted.[68]

An eclectic approach must therefore consider all of these criteria before considering the optimal statecraft approach toward potential proliferating states. The next section considers the salient facts with respect to Iran and North Korea.

Using an eclectic framework to assess Iran and North Korea

In thinking about Iran and North Korea, there are many arguments in favor of continuing a smart sanctions approach. The humanitarian disaster in North Korea appears to be worsening – sanctions of any kind will not help matters much.[69] As Chapter 7 in this volume demonstrates, Iran has a much more vibrant civil society. Ever since the June 2009 uprisings the leaders of the Green Movement have forsworn further sanctions, arguing that any further pain caused by economic coercion will be blamed on the West instead of the Ahmadinejad/Khamenei regime.

Most expert assessments place little faith in the ability of additional sanctions to end Iran's nuclear program or eliminate North Korea's nuclear stockpile. The Islamic Republic has been under some form of embargo for its entire existence, and the regime has grown comfortable with them. Saeed Jalili, Iran's lead negotiator on the nuclear, bragged to *Der Spiegel* in September of 2009: "do you really believe there are sanctions that can hit us that hard? We've lived with sanctions for thirty years, and they can't bring a great nation like Iran to its knees. They do not frighten us. Quite the opposite – we welcome new sanctions."[70] While this is pure bluster, the sanctions have accelerated the IRGC's takeover of key sectors of the Iranian economy.[71]

---

[67] Andreas (2005).

[68] For example, according to the Transparency International's 2009 Corruption Perceptions Index, the five most corrupt countries in the world were subject to trade sanctions in the 1990s.

[69] See, for example, Sharon LaFraniere, "Views Show How North Korea Policy Spread Misery," *New York Times*, June 9, 2010.

[70] Quoted in Maloney (2010: 142).

[71] Ansari (2010a).

What applies to Iran applies to North Korea with even greater force. The DPRK has been one of the most heavily sanctioned regimes in history. They have been sanctioned far longer and far harsher than the Islamic Republic. Despite this economic pressure, the personalist regime of Kim Il-sung and his progeny have persisted for more than a half-century. The nonproliferation-specific sanctions appear to have zero effect on the regime's nuclear program.

Does this mean that more comprehensive sanctions would not work? That is unclear, because two shifts have taken place in both countries in recent years. First, both regimes have mismanaged their economies even more badly than usual. Indeed, the greatest weakness of the current regime in Iran is their mismanagement of the economy. Despite an unprecedented oil boom, Iran's corruption and macroeconomic mismanagement have kept its economy in a sclerotic state.[72] Its inflation rate has climbed over 10 percent. According to *Foreign Policy*'s Failed State Index, the income of Iran's top 20 percent rose more than four times as fast as that of the bottom quintile between 2005 and 2007. The government is concerned about the popular backlash that will come from ending more than $40 billion in consumer subsidies. Iran's regime is succeeding in making itself less dependent on foreign imports of gasoline, but more comprehensive sanctions that encompass the energy sector would raise the price of gasoline.

As for North Korea, the country's economic plight has only gotten worse in recent years. The data is incontrovertible: infant and maternal mortality rates jumped more than 30 percent from 1993 to 2008. Life expectancy fell by three years during the same period.[73] The UN's World Food Program says one in three North Korean children under the age of five are malnourished.[74] The CIA estimated 2009 economic growth at -0.9 percent. All of this took place before the November 2009 currency reform, which badly roiled the economy and managed to spark public protests.[75] It also took place before the sinking of the *Cheonan*, which triggered trade sanctions from South Korea and the

---

[72] Data in this paragraph comes from Maloney (2010).
[73] LaFraniere, "Views Show How North Korea Policy Spread Misery."
[74] See www.wfp.org/countries/korea-democratic-peoples-republic-dprk (accessed July 2010).
[75] Blaine Harden, "In N. Korea, a Strong Movement Recoils at Kim Jong Il's Attempt to Limit Wealth," *Washington Post*, December 27, 2009; John S. Park, "North Korea's Currency Redenomination: A Tipping Point?" US Institute of Peace, December 3, 2009, available at: www.usip.org/resources/north-korea-s-currency-revaluation-tipping-point (accessed July 2010).

United States. North Korean analysts now expect the DPRK's economy to contract in 2011. Even elite Party officials are taking second jobs and demanding bribes in order to maintain their income.[76] While North Korea has provided plenty of bluster in response to those sanctions, it also signaled a desire for Western tourism.[77] DPRK spokesmen have also stressed their desire to preserve the Kaesong special economic zone – located on DPRK soil, using North Korean workers and South Korean capital.

The worsening economies in both countries also highlight the political fragility of both regimes. In Iran, the Green Movement highlighted the internecine conflicts within Iran. Although the current leadership has temporarily succeeded in quelling that movement, long time Iran-watchers believe that the June protests revealed deep fissures in the Iranian regime. Since the crackdown, further discontent in the Majlis and among the bazaari have been revealed.[78] In protest of proposed tax hikes by the Ahmadinejad regime, for example, the bazaar merchants went on strike for two weeks in the summer of 2010. At a minimum, this suggests that the discontent with the Iranian regime is based as much on economics as politics.

This data suggests that both regimes might be vulnerable to enhanced economic pressure. That said, an analytically eclectic approach must ask additional questions of both countries. What kind of authoritarian regime type best characterizes Iran and North Korea? What would be the regional impact of additional sanctions?

Neither regime is easy to characterize, but some distinctions can be made. North Korea now looks like a much more personalist regime than Iran. Numerous commentators have observed the extent to which Kim Il Sung and then Kim Jong Il promoted their own cults of personality while in power. This particularly affected the younger Kim's political strategy in his last years in power. Although North Korea is nominally a one-party state, in his last years Kim bolstered the power of the DPRK's military at the expense of the Korean Workers Party's power base.[79] After his reported stroke in the fall of 2008, he took hasty measures to install his youngest son Kim Jong-Un as his successor.[80] In contrast to Kim's own rise to power, however, there were minimal and belated efforts to

[76] LaFraniere, "Views Show How North Korea Policy Spread Misery."
[77] Christian Oliver, "North Korea to Allow More US Visitors," *Financial Times*, January 14, 2010.
[78] See, for example, Anderson (2010).
[79] McEachern (2008).
[80] Christian Oliver, "North Korea: Drastic Dynastics," *Financial Times*, July 6, 2010.

burnish the younger Kim's credentials. While the 2010 Korean Workers Party Congress promoted Kim Jong-Un to a four-star general, observers in Pyongyang found a decided lack of enthusiasm for the younger Kim.[81] Powerful rivals have died recently, ostensibly due to accidents.[82] Daniel Bynam and Jennifer Lind conclude that, "the regime has not laid the groundwork for a smooth transition."[83] They predict contestation among the selectorate in the wake of Kim Jong Il's death.

Iran's leadership is more decentralized than North Korea's. Clearly, multiple centers of power exist – Khamenei as Supreme Leader, Ahmadinejad as President, Ali Larijani as the head of the Iranian parliament. Although Khamenei's status as Supreme Leader suggests a personalist focus, the presence of more representative forms of government augment rather than undercut Khamenei's position in power. Iran is clearly a theocracy, and the leadership has relied increasingly on the coercive apparatus of the Iranian Revolutionary Guard Corps (IRGC).[84] The Islamic Republic is not a personalist regime, however.

The regional effect of more comprehensive sanctions is also different across the two cases. The negative policy externalities of comprehensive sanctions against Iran are greater than those involved with North Korea. Iran has borders with two very weak states – Iraq and Afghanistan. Comprehensive trade sanctions would encourage corruption in both of these countries, where large numbers of US armed forces and private contractors are located. At the same time, any sanctions that cut off Iran's oil supply would reverberate across global energy markets. Sympathizers with Iran's anti-American and anti-Israeli stance are scattered across the Arab Middle East. Despite the Sunni–Shia split, tighter sanctions could foment greater anti-Americanism across the region.

North Korea is far more isolated than Iran. It is surrounded by stronger states – China, Russia, and South Korea. Tighter sanctions would not really discomfit anyone living outside of North Korea.[85] The DPRK produces little of value to the outside world, and they do not have a large enough consumer base to provoke significant amounts of sanctions-busting. Indeed, the negative externalities of squeezing Pyongyang are largely based on what would happen if the sanctions

---

[81] "Spinning the Wrong 'Un," *Economist*, October 14, 2010.
[82] See Chico Harlan, "Kim Jong Il Appoints Jang Song Taek Caretaker for Kim Jong Eun," *Washington Post*, August 16, 2010.
[83] Byman and Lind (2010).   [84] Ansari (2010a).
[85] Haggard and Noland (2008).

worked. China is fearful of a steady exodus of refugees. South Korea is worried about the costs of rebuilding North Korea. Every other country is worried about the prospect of a reunified Korea. Many commentators have observed the growth of illicit border trade between North Koreans and Chinese. This has little to do with existing sanctions, however – and is anyway illegal in the DPRK. It would appear, however, that this corruption has only weakened the North Korean state.[86] Officials in border areas appear to receive more in bribes than they receive from Pyongyang.

A nonproliferation approach grounded in analytical eclecticism would appear to support the ratcheting up of pressure against the North Korean state. As a personalist regime in the middle of a delicate succession crisis, the DPRK is vulnerable to more comprehensive economic sanctions. Any measures should exempt the cross-border trade between China and North Korea, as that exchange benefits the North Korean people at the expense of the government. The full spectrum of financial sanctions, a shutdown of Kaesong, and the robust enforcement of the interdiction regime to prevent the exchange of illicit arms have a greater likelihood of toppling the DPRK regime than smart sanctions alone. Furthermore, because North Korea already possesses nuclear weapons, regime change is more likely to lead to concessions than negotiating with the current leadership. The negative policy externalities are limited, and the rule of law in neighboring states is unlikely to be eroded. None of this is to guarantee the fall of Pyongyang's communist dictatorship if these sanctions are imposed. We are dealing in a world of contingent probabilities, and North Korea's repressive apparatus is formidable.[87] Nevertheless, more comprehensive sanctions represent the best of a bad set of probabilities.

More comprehensive sanctions against Iran are less likely to work. Such sanctions might impose greater hardships on the regime. Nevertheless, Iran's government retains far more popular support than North Korea's. Comprehensive sanctions would weaken the rule of law in neighboring states, most particularly Iraq and Afghanistan. These are already failed states – another opportunity for corruption in these countries would not advance the interests of either the United States or the international community. If not comprehensive sanctions, then what? Perhaps comprehensive engagement. Blanketing Iran with

[86] Harden, "In N. Korea, A Strong Movement"; Park, "North Korea's Currency Redenomination."
[87] Haggard and Noland (2010a).

inducements could empower the groups necessary to advocate for policy change within the regime. Policy-makers might believe that more
targeted inducements would be better; a targeted approach would
presumably be more likely to benefit the groups most sympathetic to
policy change.

Such an approach would be shortsighted and hubristic, however. The
hubris would come from the West's belief that it can once again detect
the key Iranian moderates necessary to foment change. If past history is
any guide, it suggests that the United States and its allies have abjectly
failed at determining which moderates are reliable and which are con-
ning Western policy-makers. Such an approach would also be shortsighted. The Iranian leadership has already been able to identify and
persecute internal adversaries by accusing them of receiving support
from the United States. The Iranian leadership is extremely sensitive to
the possibility of the United States triggering a "Velvet Revolution."[88]
Now consider the implications of using a scattershot approach, bene-
fiting both regime supporters and adversaries. It would be tougher for
Iran's leadership to identify "enemies of the state" by their acceptance
of Western funds.

Advocates of targeted sanctions have been adroit in their rhetorical
tropes. By definition, "smart sanctions" sounds better than the alternative. Furthermore, advocates of smart sanctions contrasted their
theoretical model of how sanctions worked in the target country with
the "naïve theory" of sanctions that assumed greater costs equaled
greater concessions.[89] The obvious implication was that sanctions scholarship that assumed states to be unitary state actors were less sophis-
ticated than work that allowed second image variables to play a causal
role. Targeted sanctions have offered a solution for multiple political
problems, without seeming to compromise the policy effectiveness of
economic coercion.

The focus on smart sanctions also suggests the seductive danger of
focusing excessively on precise causal mechanisms and process-tracing
in the development of policy-relevant research.[90] Excessive attention
to one causal process can blind researchers and policy-makers to the
possibility that there can be substitutable causal processes at work.
Multiple pathways can exist through which an independent policy variable affects the outcome. Smart sanctions offer only one causal pathway
to success – elite dissatisfaction. If that pathway is blocked by target

---

[88] Anderson (2010).   [89] Brzoska (2003: 520).
[90] George and Bennett (2005).

countermeasures, then smart sanctions will not achieve their desired result. Sanctions that impose greater costs on the target state might offer multiple pathways – mass unrest, elite dissatisfaction, regime change – through which the target government must acquiesce. An approach grounded in analytical eclecticism would help sanctions scholars avoid the dangerous charge of policy naivety.

6 Threats for peace? The domestic distributional effects of military threats

Sarah Kreps and Zain Pasha

In June 2008, Israel's Deputy Prime Minister, Shaul Mofaz, promised, "If Iran continues its programme to develop nuclear weapons, we will attack it. The window of opportunity has closed. The sanctions are not effective. There will be no alternative but to attack Iran in order to stop the Iranian nuclear programme."[1] These threats echoed those made by US President George Bush in 2007 when he cautioned Iran that developing nuclear weapons increased the prospects for World War III, a reference to the willingness to use military force if Iran developed nuclear weapons.[2] As Alexander George notes in his study of coercive diplomacy – defined as threats of force to persuade another state to stop a particular action – "actions do not always speak louder than words." [3] Rather, they may both be important in achieving diplomatic goals especially when those threats are viewed as credible. But do threatening words or actions work? Can military threats against a suspected proliferator actually cause the state to reconsider its nuclear program?

This chapter answers those questions by looking at the domestic distributional effects of threats against nuclear programs. Whereas other studies of coercive diplomacy look at a state's incentive structures more broadly, this one takes into account the theoretical expectation that domestic coalitions may respond differently to the same outside threats. In particular, we discuss a causal mechanism showing how different coalition types may have different interests in integrating with the global economy that might make them more or less likely to respond to outside threats in a manner favorable to the threatening state.[4] Not only may certain pressuring strategies not

---

[1] Jonathan Steele, "Israel Asked US for Green Light to Bomb Nuclear Sites in Iran," *Guardian*, September 25, 2008.
[2] Brian Knowlton, "Nuclear-Armed Iran Risks 'World War III,' Bush Says," *New York Times*, October 17, 2007.
[3] George (1992: 5, 10).
[4] Solingen (2001: 524, 2007a).

work with particular domestic coalitions, these strategies might actually be counterproductive, playing into the hands of coalitions that have an interest in isolating the country from the global economy and thus making denuclearization less likely. Whereas previous studies of coercive diplomacy effectively "black boxed" the state, this analysis assumes that the domestic political environment conditions the incentive structures and likelihood that the target state will respond to the political objectives – in this case denuclearization – of the "sender" state.

To make this case, we first elaborate the theoretical argument that outlines how different coalition types might respond to outside pressures in the form of military threats. This framework generates a set of hypotheses, which we then test empirically using the case of military threats against Iran between 2002 and 2009. We consider quantitative trends in domestic responses to military threats, then trace qualitatively how the change in threat credibility from 2002 to 2009 contributed to shifts in the strength of domestic coalitions. We generally find support for the proposition that outside military threats strengthen coalitions that stymie international economic integration, resist international regimes, and privilege domestic industries, including the same nuclear program that outside threats hope to undermine. Thus, while military threats may make good politics by showing sender states' domestic audiences they are tough on proliferation, they may ultimately strengthen the domestic coalitions most hostile to international cooperation, including on nuclear issues.

Before proceeding, it is important to insert a note of caution about our findings. In particular, we recognize that states often use a number of instruments – positive and negative economic sanctions, for example – in tandem with military threats, so it is no doubt challenging to isolate the effects of each one. Therefore, our argument is that military threats *help* undermine denuclearization efforts by strengthening particular types of coalitions and undermining others is far from deterministic. Thus, we more modestly seek to identify a general causal pathway and adduce quantitative and qualitative evidence that might provide general support for this argument. Even a suggestive relationship between military threats and domestic strengthening of certain coalitions is important, as it opens up a new research agenda in which future scholarship can refine the specific causal mechanisms through which military threats operate within states and provide additional evidence. Moreover, it allows for a deeper policy understanding of why threats may not work when targeted at particular states or when being used to deal with particular issues.

The effect of threats on domestic coalitions

Despite the logic that more nuclear weapons might be better, the international community has acted with concern about the prospects of nuclear proliferation. It has accordingly crafted a number of political, diplomatic, economic, and military strategies to counter what it sees as the dangers of proliferation. Current nonproliferation strategies include diplomatically negotiated bilateral security guarantees, multilateral international treaties such as the NPT, and regional Nuclear Weapon Free Zones (NWFZs) that each aim for disarmament. More aggressive strategies include economic instruments such as strategic export controls that restrict the supply of commodities used for nuclear weapons and the imposition of economic sanctions against proliferating states. The most extreme and controversial form of opposition to proliferation is the use or threatened use of military force. A large volume of work has considered when states use force and whether the use of force has worked in historical instances, but these studies ask a different question from whether the *threat* of strikes is effective.[5] Research on coercive diplomacy does better in capturing the question of threats, but it homogenizes the issue area and regime type questions while also considering threats alongside actual uses of force.[6]

Not only are threats qualitatively different from actual uses of force, but the question of issue area matters as well. Coercive diplomacy to push Iraq out of Kuwait is necessarily different from threats of force to coerce a state to denuclearize. Moreover, while many target states are likely to be non-democratic, there are coalition types within non-democracies that might react differently to the same outside pressure. Kim Jong-il's government in North Korea and Iran under Khatami would both be considered non-democratic states, but Kim Jong-il has generally been disinterested in integrating with the global economy while Khatami was interested in a version of détente that allowed Iran to benefit from international integration and engagement.[7] Conflating these domestic polities under the heading of non-democracy misses the fundamental point that the incentive structure of each is different and therefore so is the likelihood that it will respond differently to

---

[5] Kreps and Fuhrmann (2011), Fuhrmann and Kreps (2010), Nakdimon (1987), Claire (2004), Betts (2003), Reiter (2005: 355–371, 2006), Ramberg (2006), Litwak (2002/2003: 53–80), and Burr and Richelson (2000/2001: 54–99).
[6] George (1992), Schultz (2001), and Byman and Waxman (2002).
[7] Takeyh (2003a).

external influences that can dent the state's ability to integrate with the international political economy.[8]

Military threats, for example, might be expected to have differentiated effects on denuclearization based on domestic coalition type. The basic logic follows from theories of international political economy that locate the source of international cooperation in domestic structures and the types of incentives that those structures create. Broz and Frieden write that "international coordination or cooperation may not find sufficient support within a nation if the losers are sufficiently powerful."[9] Taken in the context of financial currency decisions, the authors note that whether states join an international or regional regime depends on domestic coalitions. Whether they join depends on the coalition's preferences with respect to fixed versus floating currency, level of exchange rate, and the price at which the national currency trades in foreign exchange markets. Those groups which benefit from foreign trade and investment, such as bankers, exporters, and investors, would be expected to prefer a system with fixed currency rates, which are associated with levels of stability that favor these groups. In contrast, groups that rely on sectors that compete with imports are more likely to favor a floating currency regime that the government can more easily tweak under particular conditions. In short, the domestic distributional consequences of integration affect the propensity of the state to pursue a particular exchange rate regime.

We expect a similar logic to hold for issues that go beyond currency regimes, to include whether a state has incentives to take steps toward or away from the production of nuclear weapons. In principle, internationalizing coalitions would welcome greater integration with the global economy and favor more foreign investment, restraint on military spending, and closer ties between international finance and domestic export firms.[10] The threat of military force would likely undermine the strength of internationalizing coalitions. Their strength draws from the ability to promote economic linkages, which are far more complicated in the face of military force.[11] A strike would flag the state as an unstable place to do business. For example, after Iraqi strikes targeted Iran's Bushehr facility in 1987, Germany, which had a contract with Iran to engineer the facility, made clear that it would not do business

---

[8] This observation draws fundamentally from the logic of domestic coalitions developed in Solingen (1998).
[9] Broz and Frieden (2006: 587–597, especially 591–592).
[10] For more on the distinction between internationalizing and inward-looking coalitions, see the Introduction to this volume.
[11] Solingen (2007a).

with Iran "as long as Iran is still a global region of tension."[12] Germany concluded that the contract with Iran was "too risky" to be worth continuing and asserted, "under the present circumstances we're not going back there."[13] For a domestic coalition that touts the promise of integration with the global economy, the threat of outside military force undermines their narrative and constituency.

In contrast, inward-looking leaders tend to oppose integration because their domestic support comes from the military-industrial sector that depends on state subsidies, state bureaucracies themselves, and protected industries. Rather than favoring integration, inward-looking leaders would be more inclined to favor protectionism and import substitution models. The threat of military force would likely bolster the support of this type of domestic coalition, which is based on an insular, protectionist, autarkic stance.[14] Credible threats of military force reinforce their message that greater international integration is potentially harmful. This is particularly the case if the inward-looking coalition has built its narrative around the idea that nuclear weapons are an instrument for defending against unwanted international influence. Outside threats give these coalitions justification to increase defense budgets, acquire nuclear materials, and further advance domestic scientific and technological developments.[15]

This discussion raises the inevitable question of what constitutes a threat and how to contend with what are often high levels of uncertainty and ambiguous signals in the international environment. As James Morrow indicates, "actors deal with uncertainty by establishing conjectures about what underlying conditions, called states of the world, could produce the final outcome."[16] They do this on the basis of incoming information, which actors use to clarify underlying uncertainties. New information does not always clarify, however. A domestic coalition might have some difficulty interpreting the difference in rhetoric between French President Nicolas Sarkozy, who used his first major foreign policy speech as President to threaten Iran with military force if it developed the bomb,[17] and the Israeli Foreign Minister, who also issued belligerent threats. Even with this incoming information, the actor is faced with a dilemma, which James Fearon captures as follows: "(a) the target of the threat cannot directly observe the threatener's preferences and (b) the target knows the threatener has an incentive

---

[12] MacLachlan (1986) and Hibbs (1991).
[13] Hibbs (1987b).   [14] Solingen (1998: chapter 2).
[15] Solingen (2001: 524).   [16] Morrow (1989: 941–972).
[17] Elaine Sciolino, "Iran Risks Attack over Atomic Push, French President Says," *New York Times*, August 27, 2007.

to pretend to be 'resolved,' even if this is not the case."[18] Given the incentives to demonstrate resolve – namely that the threatener would rather achieve his objectives without having to use force – the target is faced with a situation in which he must infer the credibility of an actor's threats based on rhetoric and actions.

Strategists such as Thomas Schelling have offered clues in response to this challenge. Most fundamentally, the threatening state must have both the (1) capability and (2) resolve to carry out the threat to be perceived as credible. Capability, most fundamentally, means the "capacity for pure damage, pure violence ... the power to hurt."[19] As he wrote of the Soviets in the Cold War, no one doubted their ability to do remarkable damage in the United States; "whether they can hurt [West Germany] terribly is not doubted."[20] The balance of capabilities, according to this sub-heading of credibility, tends to be correlated with dispute outcomes, and therefore acts as a source of credibility.[21]

Determining resolve, or "the balance of motivation among the protagonists rather than the balance of capabilities"[22] is somewhat more problematic. Schelling cites "sheer character,"[23] obstinacy, and even insanity as examples of resolve, but also goes further and develops what subsequent scholars have referred to as "costly signals." The term intends to distinguish between costless signals or "cheap talk," since a "state with low resolve may have no disincentive to sending" these costless signals, and signals that can incur costs.[24] Burning a bridge constitutes a costly signal, since doing so eliminates the option of retreat. Chiang Kai-shek mobilized his strongest troops to the island of Quemoy, effectively burning a bridge since being on the island meant that retreat was not an option and the troops would have to fight.[25]

Fearon adds to these costly maneuvers physical costs such as the mobilization and deployment of troops, which are credible ways to signal a state's willingness to use force. An even stronger form of signal, since "financial costs of mobilization rarely seem the principal concern of leaders in a crisis," are audience costs – the loss of face to his domestic audience that a leader experiences by backing down after making a threat or "show of force" that is costly to the leader.[26] Shows of force are therefore costly signals in that the domestic audience concerns itself with the state's international reputation and as such punishes the

---

[18] Fearon (1997: 68–90).   [19] Schelling (1966: 4).
[20] Schelling (1966: 7).   [21] Maoz (1983: 197).
[22] Maoz (1983: 199).   [23] Schelling (1966: 42).
[24] Fearon (1994a: 579).   [25] Schelling (1966: 43).   [26] Fearon (1994a: 580).

leader who makes these threats and either does not follow through or is unsuccessful.[27]

Taken together, the preceding discussion would suggest that credible military threats would have differentiated effects on different types of domestic coalitions.[28] Threats issued under the shadow of costly consequences would tend to reinforce inward-looking coalitions that advocate for a nuclear program intended to guard against outside threats. As evidence of this strengthening, we would expect to see increased military spending, subsidies, and support for the domestic nuclear industry, and an increasingly hostile environment for foreign investment. In short:

H1: credible military threats should strengthen inward-looking coalitions and increase the likelihood of nuclearization.

By contrast, credible military threats would undermine internationalizing coalitions, seeking to integrate with the global economy. Their policy loyalties rely on the presence of a benign international environment, a point that is called into question by threats from that same setting. External threats also make the domestic economic objective of broader integration more difficult, since the possibility of military force is destabilizing for the domestic economy and discouraging for foreign investment. Therefore:

H2: credible military threats should undermine internationalizing coalitions and decrease the likelihood of denuclearization.

Research design

This analysis tests the hypotheses that credible military threats undermine internationalizing coalitions and simultaneously strengthen inward-looking coalitions. The period of interest is 2002–2009. The starting point of 2002 is appropriate since it is the time when the United States issued its first threats, Iran's covert nuclear enrichment and heavy-water facilities were revealed publicly, and the international community began exerting pressure on Iran to terminate its nuclear program. We end our analysis in 2009, the last year for which data is available, but which is too soon to investigate the effects of the 2009 election. Nevertheless, later in the chapter we offer some thoughts on the scope conditions of our propositions by taking the effect of military

---

[27] Fearon (1994a: 242).   [28] Solingen (2007a: 19–21).

threats in the broader context of factors such as domestic electoral dynamics.

We organize military threats annually as there is no obvious boundary between the termination of one threat and the initiation of another in terms of their respective effects. In addition, because threats are persistent and may have lag effects that we are interested in capturing – e.g., if former President George W. Bush issued a threat in April 2003, its impact would not abruptly end in May – we look at the effects of credible threats *over time*. Moreover, since our distributional variable is approximated using annual measures, it is appropriate to organize the independent variable at an annual interval as well. Our analysis traces the effect of outside military threats (our independent variable) on the balance of power of domestic coalitions (dependent variable). We generate quantitative measures for both the independent and dependent variables in the next section, showing how we measured them and how we collected the data. The subsequent section then traces those relationships qualitatively, assessing how changes in threat credibility affected the coalitional balance of power in Iran between 2002 and 2009.

Independent variable: threat credibility

To calculate threat credibility we independently measure and subsequently multiply the sender state's military capability and resolve.[29] We chose this approach because capability and resolve are both necessary for calculating threat credibility and are determined independent of each other.[30] A state can have sufficient military capability for following through on a threat but the threat will not be perceived as credible if the issuing state lacks the requisite resolve. For example, if the United States threatens nuclear use in response to a cyber-attack, the threat would not be credible despite the fact that the United States has one of the most advanced nuclear arsenals in the world. The incredibility of the threat arises from the lack of resolve created by the disproportionate nature of a nuclear response to a cyber-attack and the consequences of using a nuclear weapon.[31] Moreover, while it may be the case that military capability impacts a state's resolve for carrying out a threat, there are also external factors such as popular and elite opinion in the sender state that must be accounted for, which is to say that having the military capability to carry out a threat is not a sufficient condition to do so. For example, despite having substantial military resources, the

---

[29] Danilovic (2001: 343–344) and Schelling (1966: 34–43).
[30] See Ragin (2000: 90–94).   [31] Acton (2009: 2–3).

United States did not attack Iran in part as a result of negative popular opinion in the United States about taking military action against Iran.[32] Clearly then resolve and capability are both necessary components of threat credibility and as such we consider them both in our analysis. Logically, this can be represented as:

*Military Capability * Resolve → Threat Credibility*[33]

Capability as readiness

To measure military capability, we use the threatener's military readiness because it captures the availability and quality of the military resources at the state's disposal. Unless a state has military resources that are trained and equipped, a threat is less convincing since the issuing state does not have the capability to follow through. In using readiness as our measure of capability, we recognize that it has limitations as an indicator of capability because of the difficulty with which it is measured. Indeed, as one retired naval captain noted, "Measuring readiness is like nailing jello to a wall."[34]

The US Army has, however, recently generated an apt measure of readiness, the Boots on the Ground (BOG) to time at home (Dwell) ratio (BOG:Dwell). This ratio measures the total number of months a unit was deployed compared to number of months the unit was redeployed at the home station. Thus, a ratio of 1:2 implies soldiers spend twenty-four months redeployed at home for every twelve-month deployment. [35] This is a measure of global readiness based on all military deployments whether they are to Iraq, Afghanistan, or Haiti. The BOG:Dwell ratio therefore addresses the usability of US military capabilities at any given time by reflecting whether military assets are tied up elsewhere or available to be used in a new military engagement. It is also the most widely used measure of the availability of US military capabilities and corresponds with well-defined benchmarks of readiness.[36]

Though the Defense Department has established a goal of 1:2 BOG:Dwell ratio for the active duty military, the ratio was closer to 1:1 around the start of the Iraq War and increased almost to 1:1.6 between

[32] PIPA Poll, "Americans on Iran," July 31, 2003, available at: www.pipa.org/OnlineReports/Iran/Iran_July03/Iran_July03_rpt.pdf.
[33] See Ragin (2000: 94).
[34] Quoted in John Raffensperger and Linus Schrage, "A New Paradigm for Measuring Military Readiness," working paper.
[35] Casey (2009: 25–40) and Bonds *et al.* (2010).
[36] For an example of usage see www.army.mil/aps/09/addenda/addenda_e.html.

2005 and 2007. With this general range in mind, we adopt a four-point scale to assess readiness, with 1:1 corresponding with the lowest level of readiness and capability (1) and 1:2 as the highest (4). Correspondingly, a readiness level of 1:1.33 equates with a measure of 2 and 1:1.66 with 3. Deployment data is collected from the *Army Times*, which documents the number of months a unit is deployed around the world compared to redeployed at home.[37]

Resolve

Resolve is more complex to determine than readiness, as it must be measured indirectly. To deal with this complexity, we disaggregate resolve into its four measurable components: (1) international opinion regarding the sender's threatened course of action; (2) domestic popular opinion; (3) elite opinion in the sender state about the threatened course of action; and (4) mobilizations of military resources in support of the issued threat by the sender state.[38] We address each of these in turn.

International opinion

The first indicator, international opinion, is a salient measure of resolve and credibility because it imposes important constraints on a potential aggressor state. In including this measure, we assume that the sender state assigns some importance to its international standing and all other things being equal prefers to have more backing from the international community for its actions than less. This assumption is not unreasonable, as international politics is largely characterized by expectations of future and repeated interaction among states; indeed, Robert Axelrod and Robert Keohane agree that the benefits of reciprocity create incentives for cooperation and disincentives for defection among states.[39] Unilaterally undertaking internationally unpopular courses of action would be considered a form of defection, garnering a state a reputation for non-cooperation and subsequently undermining its prospects for future cooperation. The reputational costs and exclusion from future

---

[37] We borrow the ratios from Michael S. Johnson, "The Myth of the Unsustainable Army: an Analysis of Army Deployments, The All Volunteer Force, and The Army Force Generation Model," 2009, Ft. Leavenworth, Kansas. For 2009 data, see Statement by General Peter Chiarelli, Before the House Armed Services Committee Subcommittee on Readiness, May 20, 2009.

[38] Maoz (1983: 201).

[39] Axelrod and Keohane (1985: 245–246).

cooperation benefits would theoretically constrain a state from acting without international support.[40]

Even the 2003 US invasion of Iraq, which some might argue attests to the futility of international opinion as a constraint on state behavior, has two features that suggest quite the opposite: (1) the Bush administration fashioned a "coalition of the willing" to give the impression of broad-based international legitimacy, even if the contributing states themselves did not offer substantial material support in the form of troops or financial assistance; (2) the United States sought UN authorization, twice making the case for invasion to the UN, first in September 2002 and again in February 2003 before finally intervening without UN authorization. These efforts to create the illusion of a multilaterally sanctioned intervention attest to the importance the US placed on using force in a way that was consistent with international opinion.

Domestic opinion

Domestic popular opinion within a state that issues a military threat is an important determinant of resolve, as it constrains the actions of elite decision-makers through potential political costs (i.e., democratic leaders want to remain in office and carrying out an unpopular war decreases their electoral longevity).[41] Indeed "an unfavorable public opinion environment ultimately constrains the range of politically acceptable policies,"[42] which means we would expect to see low levels of public support for the use of force and thereby strong disincentives for undertaking an intervention. Because of political incentives to act in a way that is consistent with public opinion, negative popular opinion in the sender state regarding the actions prescribed by an issued threat could diminish that threat's credibility.[43] In using popular opinion, then, we try to capture the dominant public sentiments regarding the use of military force against the target state.

There are some limitations to using domestic opinion to assess a state's resolve, however. First, the public opinion poll data through time is incomplete and inconsistent. It is incomplete because public opinion data is not available for all years under consideration, and it is inconsistent because the wording of the poll questions varies depending on the year and source. This means that inferences about public opinion

---

[40] Oye (1985: 12–13).
[41] Bueno de Mesquita and Siverson (1995: 841).
[42] Larson and Savych (2005: xvii).   [43] Fearon (1994b: 236–269, 242).

should be treated with caution, as we do not have a complete, consistently worded time series of poll questions.[44]

Political elite opinion

Our third indicator of resolve is the opinion of political elites within the threatening state. These inputs are important, as elites are active within key decision-making circles and have the influence to shape the opinions of decision-makers. We define political elites as politicians and their inner circles, which include business groups, minority groups, and military leaders, all of whom wield influence over domestic decision-making.[45] For this study however, the opinions of business and minority groups are less operative because the decisions to issue and act on threats are largely matters of foreign policy that these groups do not participate in. We will thus focus on the opinions of civilian and military leaders who can influence the decision to act on a threat. As much of the civil–military relations literature suggests, civilian leadership tends to make the ultimate decision on the use of force, sometimes overriding the views of senior military officers, but these officers do provide input on whether and how to use force.[46] They base this input on a number of factors, including their related battlefield experiences, insufficient military capability to deal with the fallout of an attack and insufficient intelligence for a successful military strike.

Resource mobilization

Finally, resource mobilization by the sender state is an important indicator of resolve because it functions as a costly signal, risking audience costs in the form of domestic political censure if the sender backs down after escalating military threats and after making key military maneuvers.[47] A state that makes a threat and follows it up by placing a battle group near the target country or publicly announcing that it is increasing contingency planning efforts demonstrates resolve because it ups political ante among a domestic audience that wants its leaders to prevail in international crisis situations. A relatively costless threat and one that therefore lacks credibility and resolve is a verbal threat made without any supplementary operational changes (e.g., war planning) to reinforce it. Following this logic, we consider increased war planning

---

[44] Bennett and Paletz (1994: 194).   [45] Perry (1971: 13).
[46] Huntington (1981), Cohen (2003), and Desch (2007).
[47] Fearon (1994a: 577–592) and Tomz (2007).

and movement of military resources (e.g., troops or warships) as an indicator of resolve and a credible threat.

Since we divide resolve into four components, we chose to assign a 0 to a component if it does not demonstrate resolve and a 1 if it demonstrates resolve for acting on an issued threat. If international opinion favors the actions specified by an issued threat, we assign a 1 to international opinion. We do the same for domestic opinion, elite opinion, and resource mobilization. These indicators are somewhat less straightforward than the military measure of readiness. Elite opinion on the sensitive issue of whether to use force is often inferred through leaks in newspapers, which might introduce their own biases. We recognize these potential limitations but try to address them by being transparent with these definitions and later with sources identified in the qualitative section.

In sum, the independent variable is measured by the combination of capability and resolve. Each of these is measured based on a four-point scale, which then aggregates into an eight-point index. This effort to measure credibility has its flaws of course. The main reason is that it seeks to measure a concept that is inherently ambiguous and subjective. Credibility, according to Daryl Press, "is not tangible; it exists only in people's minds. Credibility, therefore, cannot be measured directly."[48] The indicators we propose then are indirect measures that seek to approximate credibility; they address actions on the part of the sender state and cannot speak to the ways that the target interprets the threat. Given these methodological challenges, we complement the quantitative measures with qualitative analysis. Before assessing quantitatively and qualitatively the effects of threats on domestic coalition strength, we define and operationalize the dependent variable, which we use to measure the domestic effect of credible threats.

The dependent variable: domestic distributional effects

Assessing the political economic distributional effects of military threats requires a way to capture the shifts in coalitional balance of power within the threatened (target) state. As discussed earlier, internationalizing coalitions seek to engage with the international political economy and thus advocate increased foreign investment and international trade, as well as decreased spending on the military-industrial complex. Inward-looking coalitions on the other hand seek insulation from the international political economy and accordingly advocate

---

[48] Press (2005: 11).

reduced foreign investment and international trade, as well as increased spending on the military-industrial complex. As such, if credible military threats do indeed strengthen inward-looking coalitions and at the same time weaken internationalizing coalitions we would expect to see a shift in international capital flows through the target state. In particular, we would expect to see decrease in investment freedom and trade freedom within the target state along with an increase in spending on the military-industrial complex.

Trade freedom

We use the Heritage Foundation's disaggregated *Index of Economic Freedom* for our measure of trade freedom. The dataset defines the general notion of economic freedom as "the material autonomy of the individual in relation to the state and other organized groups. An individual is economically free who can control his or her labor or property."[49] For the purposes of this study, we are particularly interested in trade freedom, since this is a key measure of economic transactions across borders; many of the other indicators in the overall economic freedom, such as the individual and corporate tax burden, government size, price stability, among others, may be relevant to starting a business domestically but are not germane to the question of economic transactions between a particular country and outside actors, which is the most salient transaction for this study.

Trade freedom assesses "the degree to which government hinders access to and the free flow of foreign commerce."[50] As such, it is measured using the tariff and non-tariff barriers that affect imports and exports of goods and services. In particular, trade barriers include taxes on imports and exports, quotas and bans on trade and regulatory behaviors, since these affect the incentives likely to drive trade flows. The trade freedom score is computed by taking into account the following measures: (1) the maximum tariff in the country; (2) the minimum tariff in the country; (3) the weighted average tariff in the country; and (4) the standardized non-tariff barrier (NTB) penalty. The function used to compute the trade freedom score is shown below.[51]

$$TF_i = \frac{Tariff_{max} - Tariff_i}{Tariff_{max} - Tariff_{min}} - NTB_i$$

[49] Beach and Kane (2007: 40).   [50] Beach and Kane (2007: 43).
[51] "Methodology for the 10 Economic Freedoms," *2009 Index of Economic Freedom* (Washington, DC: Heritage Foundation, 2009), available at: www.heritage.org/index/PDF/2009/Index2009_Methodology.pdf.

Possible NTBs captured within the standardized penalty include quantity restriction such as import quotas and export restraints, price restrictions such as anti-dumping measures, regulatory requirements such as licensing, and customs restrictions such as added clearance procedures; in some countries direct government intervention through policies may also take place.[52]

For this analysis, the trade freedom score serves as a measure of political economic distributional effects in two ways. First, it measures the ability of internationalizing coalitions to engage with the international political economy under a nation's policies, specifically with regard to international trade. A low trade freedom score would suggest that robust government tariffs and NTBs stifle the engagement of internationalizing groups such as moderate businessmen and finance ministries with the international political economy, while a high score would suggest the opposite.[53] Furthermore, that the activities of internationalizing extra-governmental groups are restricted by a state's inward-looking trade policies would suggest that those groups are weaker vis-à-vis inward-looking ones; which is to say that a low trade freedom score offers some evidence that the coalitional balance of power is in favor of inward-looking groups.

Second, because a nation's trade freedom score is determined by the robustness of the policy and regulatory barriers the government uses to control international trade, it approximates the relative influence of inward-looking and internationalizing elites on a state's policy decisions. To be clear, a low trade freedom score implies that a nation maintains robust tariffs and NTBs, which are policies we would expect to see from states in which inward-looking coalitions are stronger than internationalizing ones.[54] It logically follows then that we would expect inward-looking elites to be stronger vis-à-vis internationalizing ones in nations that are assigned low trade freedom scores. Similarly a high trade freedom score suggests that internationalizing elites are more influential than inward-looking ones.

While trade freedom is one indicator of whether internationalizing or inward-looking coalitions are strengthening or weakening, a word of caution is in order. This measure is based on countries self-reporting economic policies. In some cases, countries may have incentives to misrepresent their tariff data, which could make cross-country comparisons

---

[52] Beach and Kane (2007: 44).   [53] Solingen (2001: 522).
[54] Solingen (2001: 523).

difficult. Since this study examines one country over a number of years, however, this concern is less relevant.

Investment freedom

We use the Heritage Foundation's *Index of Economic Freedom* to measure investment freedom. Investment freedom in the dataset is defined as the number and robustness of the restrictions a nation maintains on the inflow of foreign capital.[55] For example, a relatively free and effective investment framework maintains transparency and equity, and will support all types of firms rather than those that are strategically important. Ultimately, a high investment freedom score suggests capital is permitted to flow to its most efficient use without government intervention; meaning capital will flow to organizations or individuals who will put it to most efficient use and to those whom the government believes are best.[56]

Investment freedom in the *Index of Economic Freedom* is measured on a discrete 0–100 (intervals of 10) scale with 0 being most restricted investment freedom and 100 being the least restricted investment freedom. Each level of investment freedom starting with 100 percent is associated with certain defining characteristics with each subsequent level possessing the same characteristics save a few exceptions. For example, an investment freedom score of 100 percent implies "Foreign investment (FI) is encouraged and treated the same as domestic investment … there are no restrictions in sectors related to national security."[57] The 90 percent investment freedom level is similar to the 100 percent level with the exception of increased government control on foreign investment in sectors related to national security. Subsequent levels, the 30 percent and 10 percent levels in particular, include significant domestic and international restrictions on foreign investment in the national security sector and on access to international payments and foreign exchange.[58]

In terms of this analysis the investment freedom score approximates the coalitional balance of power in two ways. First, similar to the trade freedom score, the level of investment freedom is determined by the policies imposed by a nation's government (e.g., the level of government involvement in directing the flow of capital). As such, if investment

---

[55] "Methodology for the 10 Economic Freedoms," available at: www.heritage.org/index/PDF/2009/Index2009_ Methodology.pdf.
[56] Miller and Kim (2010: 60–61).
[57] Beach and Kane (2007: 48).   [58] Beach and Kane (2007: 49).

freedom is high it is likely that the balance of power among government decision-makers favors internationalizing elites who support free capital flow. To be clear, it is not unreasonable to think that internationalizing coalitions would create policies encouraging free-capital flows if they enjoyed a larger share of the coalitional balance of power than inward-looking ones. Likewise, if investment freedom is low it is likely that inward-looking coalitions dominate government decision making for analogous reasons.

Second, the level of investment freedom as measured by the Heritage Foundation dataset approximates the degree to which capital flows are controlled to certain sectors of a nation's economy. In particular, at low levels of investment freedom, capital flows to the national security related sectors of a nation's economy (e.g., the military-industrial complex) are highly regulated by the government. If military threats strengthen inward-looking coalitions, we would expect to see increased restrictions on and government control over capital flows to the national security related sectors of a nation's economy, as inward-looking coalitions would use the narrative of an existential security threat to justify more insular economic policies; this is precisely what a low investment freedom score suggests. Moreover, under our hypotheses we would expect to see increased discrimination in terms of which individuals and organizations have access to capital; in particular, inward-looking coalitions will seek to impede those who try to engage with the international political economy while internationalizing ones would not. As such, a low investment freedom score would indicate increased discrimination in access to international payments and capital.

Admittedly, a nation's investment freedom score does not tell us who is being discriminated against, but it is likely that a government directing capital to national security related sectors of its economy will discriminate against those who seek to engage with the international political economy due to concerns about where capital flows would be directed and what they would be used for.

Military spending

As with investment freedom, under our hypotheses we would expect increased capital flows to defense-related sectors of a nation's economy because inward-looking coalitions could, for example, use the presence of an external security threat to justify increased expenditure on national security. We thus use military spending data over time as a proxy for shifts in coalitional balance of power within the target state.

Specifically, if credible military threats strengthen inward-looking coalitions, we would expect an increase in a nation's military spending around the issuance of the threat. This is because inward-looking coalitions advocate insulation from the international political economy, and as such increased flow of capital to the military complex means less capital flow to internationalizing sectors of the economy. Furthermore, increased military spending likely leads to less regional cooperation, which would also be desirable to inward-looking coalitions, as cooperation "scales back military imperatives ... and devalues nationalist confessional myth-making as political currency." Alternatively, if internationalizing coalitions dominate, we would expect to see reduced military spending as "Internationalists ... resist mobilizing resources for potential military conflict so as to both avoid unproductive, inflation-reducing investments and budgetary drain under the shroud of 'national security.'"[59]

To measure spending on military activities, we use a simple measure of military spending drawn from the World Bank's World Development Indicators. We first measure military expenditures as a percentage of GDP, then calculate total expenditures by using GDP in purchasing power parity terms. The total then is measured in constant 2005 international dollars, which reflects a measure not distorted by inflation.

Using total military spending to approximate the coalitional balance of power in a state does have the effect of aggregating both conventional and nuclear spending, but it is the best approach for two reasons. First, it captures the theoretical expectations that inward-looking coalitions would be more likely to direct capital to the military-industrial complex because it insulates them from outside actors and internationalizing coalitions would tend to reduce military investments to reduce the risk of inflation and avoid negative political economic consequences.[60] Second, there is the pragmatic point that expenditures on issues such as a nuclear program are unavailable for states such as Iran, which means that total military spending may be the only and therefore the best available data.

Admittedly, our distributional measures have some limitations that are important enough to warrant a cautionary note. First, investment freedom and trade freedom are both static measures and as such may not capture shifts in the coalitional balance of power within a nation for several years. In particular, it is possible that internationalizing coalitions come to power but are unable to eliminate inward-looking policies such as tariffs and restrictions on capital flows for several years due to

[59] Solingen (2001: 523–524).   [60] Solingen (2001).

structural barriers and possible audience costs. In such a case, investment freedom and trade freedom would not accurately reflect shifts in the coalitional balance of power in the short term, as they both rely on policy changes to adjust. Likewise, it may be the case that inward-looking coalitions come to power but are unable to enact protectionist policies for several years.

Second, all three measures may change due to external factors that are unrelated to shifts in the coalitional balance of power within a nation. For example, investment freedom may rise because of increased need for foreign capital, trade freedom may increase if there are changes in bilateral trading relationships, and military spending may increase because of increased security concerns that are unrelated to military threats (e.g., domestic terrorism). None of these changes necessitate a shift in coalitional balance of power however, and as such changes in trade freedom, investment freedom, and military spending may not necessarily be indicative of shifts in coalitional influence.

In short, the linkage between military threat and coalitional change tells a complicated story. Coalitional dynamics may be static and not immediately responsive to military threats. Moreover, when coalitional strength does change, it may do so because of factors other than military threats, such as economic sanctions. We therefore view the relationship between military threat and coalitional change with a good deal of caution and offer the correlations as suggestive rather than definitive. It is for this reason that we also trace the relationship with qualitative analysis.[61]

Results

Based on the trends depicted in our measures of threat credibility and distributional effects, we generally find support for the proposition that credible military threats strengthen coalitions that favor protectionism and garner domestic strength from the argument that greater international integration would do the country a disservice. As Table 6.1 shows, threat credibility exhibited somewhat of a bell curve, peaking between 2005 and 2007 and showing relatively lower levels on either side of that peak. Figure 6.1 shows how this trend corresponds with Iran's trend in military spending between 2002 and 2009, in which 2006 marked an inflection point before which spending had increased and after which it had decreased.

---

[61] See, for example, Chapters 2, 3, and 7 of this volume.

Table 6.1 *Effect of threat credibility on trade freedom, investment freedom, and military spending between 2002 and 2009*

Year	Threat credibility	Trade freedom[a]	Investment freedom	Military spending[b]
2002	N/A[c]	47.2	30	13.7
2003	1	72.8	30	16.7
2004	2	78.8	30	20.1
2005	6	78.8	30	24.1
2006	4	55.4	10	26.1
2007	6	55.4	10	21.1
2008	2	57.4	10	19.2
2009	2	57.4	10	N/A[d]

Notes:
[a] Trade freedom and investment freedom scores were attained from the Heritage Foundation's Index of Economic Freedom.
[b] Units: billions in 2005 international dollars.
[c] Threat credibility for 2002 is uncalculated do to the unavailability of BOG data, which we use as our measure of military capability.
[d] Military spending data not available for this year.

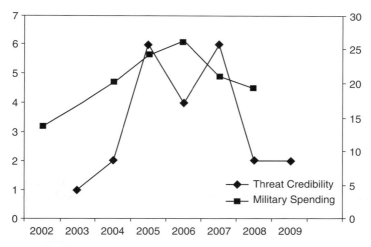

Figure 6.1 Relationship between threat credibility and military spending between 2002 and 2009

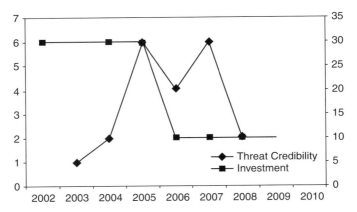

Figure 6.2 Relationship between threat credibility and investment freedom

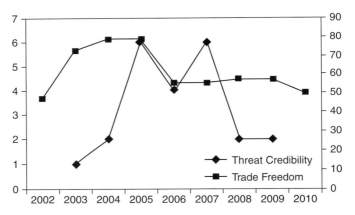

Figure 6.3 Relationship between threat credibility and trade freedom

The other two measures of domestic distributional consequences – investment freedom and trade freedom – tell a more complicated story. Once threat credibility began to decline after 2007, trade and investment freedom remained low (see Figures 6.2 and 6.3).

One reason for the lingering effects on trade and investment freedom may be the lag effect of threat credibility. To be clear a coalition determined to favor domestic industry and discriminate against outward trade and investment ties could use external military threats

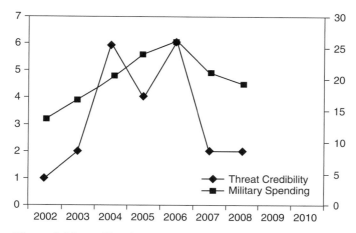

Figure 6.4 Lag effect (one year) of threat credibility on military spending

well beyond the period in which those threats were issued. A second reason may have to do with threats issued not by the United States but by Israel. As the qualitative section below discusses in more detail, while US threat credibility declined after 2007, Israel's increased. We have no reason to believe that Iran would respond preferentially to US threats and discount those of Israel. Thus, if as we expect, outside threats reinforce the preferences of inward-looking coalitions, threats from Israel may have helped sustain the power and preferences of these coalitions.

Since we have reasons to believe that coalitional effects would be felt not in the same year as the threat but perhaps in subsequent years, we also considered the lagged effects of threats. Here we found slightly more support for the proposition that threat credibility has a favorable effect on inward-looking coalitions. Here threat credibility corresponds closely with military spending, as Figure 6.4 illustrates.

Figures 6.5 and 6.6 show the lag effect of threat credibility on investment and trade freedom, which decline and remain low despite threat credibility diminishing in the latter years. The two types of economic freedom perhaps remain low for the same two reasons as cited above – enduring lag effects but also the onset of pressure from Israel.

However, additional data suggests the possibility of factors unrelated to outside military threats. Trend data that links threat credibility with various measures of the dependent variable show relatively low levels of

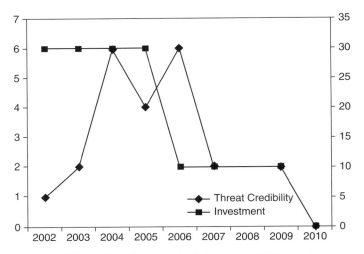

Figure 6.5 Lag effect (one year) of threat credibility on investment freedom

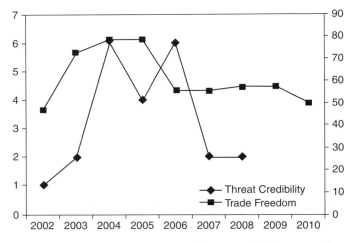

Figure 6.6 Lag effect (one year) of threat credibility on trade freedom

correlation between the two. Outside threats account for 12 percent, 21 percent, and 42 percent of variation in trade freedom, investment freedom, and military spending, respectively. This raises an important point of caution regarding the interpretation of our analysis. We make no claims about military threats being sufficient conditions for affecting the balance of power in competing domestic coalitions. Rather, military threats are just one of a number of factors that affect this balance. Factors such as economic sanctions, economic cycles more generally, and electoral dynamics all create pressures on domestic coalitions.[62] For example, we expect that the 2009 election in Iran, which generally falls outside our analysis, would plausibly shift coalitional balances, a point we return to later in the chapter. Domestic factors then may have had more to do with sustaining inward-looking coalitions in the latter years than military threats or economic sanctions.

This section provides suggestive evidence supporting the argument that miilitary threats can affect the coalitional balance of power. The limited number of years in which states have issued threats combined with the fact that states have used other inducements (e.g., economic) in tandem no doubt limits the conclusiveness of the quantitative findings, but it does offer some initial support for the way military threats might operate within certain types of states. Recognizing the limitations of the quantitative trends, the next section turns to qualitative evidence for the argument that military threats may contribute to strengthening inward-looking coalitions at the expense of internationalizing ones.

Qualitative account of the distributional consequences of military threats

The data above suggests that at a macro level credible military threats generally contributed to increased military spending, decreased investment freedom, and decreased trade freedom. In this section we further interrogate how threats affect domestic coalitions by providing qualitative explanations for the observed trends and explaining apparent anomalies.

In general, Iran's increased spending on its military-industrial complex along with its decreased investment and trade freedom scores following the issuance of a credible military threat point toward an inward reorientation of its government and dominant elites. That there is an inward reorientation is not surprising, however, as credible military threats allow inward-looking coalitions to use an external security threat (i.e., the threatener) to justify increased spending on the military-industrial complex, increased regulation of foreign and domestic capital flows, and more robust restrictions on exports and imports.

---

[62] For more on other positive and negative inducements directed at Iran, see Chapter 3, this volume.

Indeed as one Iran analyst notes, "The official line [in Iran] is that if … countries cooperate with our enemies against us, we reserve the right to defend ourselves."[63] Such thinking within Iran implies that credible military threats, which we define as threats of military force supported by moves to demonstrate capability and resolve, likely become instrumentalized to justify campaigns to reject global economic integration, support favored domestic constituencies, and indeed forge closer ties with their "ideal technological allies": the nuclear program.[64]

As Table 6.1 shows, military threats against Iran have been inconsistent since 2002, so it is worth tracing how the ebbs and flows in threat have translated into specific domestic political economy shifts over time. Early in this period, during the 2002 State of the Union address, the US administration infamously labeled Iran as part of the "Axis of Evil" for its state sponsorship of terrorism. The response in Iran was one of self-defense. The text in the *Bonyan* read: "no patriotic, independence-loving Muslim, freedom-loving, and dignified Iranian can be indifferent to the foreign threats and the intervention of the expansionist and intimidating powers and neglect the foreigners' humiliation or aggression against our country, revolution, and sovereignty."[65] The text goes on to urge that Iran undertake "preventive plans and measures that would render any possible aggression of the United States to be irrelevant." The Foreign Minister responded in a more muted way in 2002, stating, "Iran worked hard for the campaign against terrorism. But the United States is still hostile towards us. We are disappointed."[66]

Toward the end of that year, as the US focus shifted to Iraq, relations took on something of a détente – relative to historical relations between the United States and Iran – as the United States needed Iran's neutrality on both sides of its borders: Afghanistan and the forthcoming intervention in Iraq. An Iranian journalist, Mashallah Shamsolva'ezin, suggested that "in respect of Iran, America has changed its policy of axis of evil and, at least in the current situation of the Iraqi crisis, does not want to open any new fronts for evoking Iran's hostility, lest it undermines its Iraqi game."[67] By the time the United States was building its diplomatic case for invading Iraq in 2002 and in the first year of the

---

[63] Quoted in Robert Tait, "US Drops Iran Diplomacy," *Mail & Guardian Online*, February 8, 2010.

[64] See Chapter 1, this volume.

[65] Hashem Aghajeri, "Deterrence According to Which Method? War-Mongering Against Whom?" *Bonyan*, March 10, 2002.

[66] Foreign Minister Kamal Kharrazi, quoted in Japanese newspaper *Mainichi Shimbun*, January 24, 2002.

[67] Mashallah Shamsolva'ezin, quoted in *Hayat-e Now*, September 18, 2002.

2003 invasion, an imminent attack on Iran was implausible, and Iran perceived it as such, despite signals to the contrary early in 2002.

By the end of 2004 and into 2005, however, the picture began to change. The United States entered a period in which it believed major combat operations in Iraq had come to an end, before the realization that it was fighting an altogether different war: an insurgency. Military readiness levels increased and the United States appeared to shift its attention. The United States began running reconnaissance drone missions over Iran – despite resistance by Iran to the illegality of these missions[68] – and the Bush administration consistently attested to all options being on the table, leading to the perception that the United States had gone beyond basic contingency planning and was approaching a preventive strike. Media reports in Turkey and Germany cited meetings between CIA Director Porter Goss and his Turkish counterpart in which the former allegedly discussed attacks against Iran's suspected nuclear sites and Turkey's potentially supporting role.[69]

The early part of 2006 marked the peak of credible US military strikes. Commenting on the credibility of a possible strike, nuclear expert Joseph Cirioncione reported that "I previously dismissed talk about US military strikes as left-wing conspiracy theory ... But in just the past few weeks I've been convinced that at least some in the Administration have already made up their minds that they would like to launch a military strike against Iran."[70] Former National Security Advisor Zbigniew Brzezinski similarly perceived the strike to be both credible and imminent, prompting him to publish an opinion piece outlining a litany of reasons why the United States should desist.[71] While US and international public opinion were opposed to the use of force after 2002,[72] US administrations had previously undertaken limited

---

[68] Dafna Linzer, "US Uses Drones to Probe Iran for Arms," *Washington Post*, February 13, 2005.

[69] Martin Walker, "German Media: US Prepares Iran Strike," *United Press International*, December 31, 2005; "The US and Iran: IS Washington Planning a Military Strike?" *Der Spiegel*, January 2, 2006.

[70] Quoted in Tim Baldwin, "The Idea of US Nuclear Attack on Iran is Just Nuts, Says Straw," *The Times*, April 10, 2006.

[71] Zbigniew Brzezinski, "Do Not Attack Iran," *New York Times*, April 25, 2006.

[72] In a 2002 January 11–14 Gallup poll, 71 percent of Americans supported the prospect of military strikes against Iran. By 2003, Americans were generally opposed. See, for example, PIPA Poll, "Americans on Iran," July 31, 2003, available at: www.pipa.org/OnlineReports/Iran/Iran_July03/Iran_July03_rpt.pdf; an April 2003 *LA Times* poll reported that 50 percent supported strikes, 36 percent opposed, and 14 percent didn't know; in a June 2003 CNN poll, 69 percent said "US should not go to war to overthrow the government of Iran." Polls in 2004 through the present have been consistently negative on the use of force.

airstrikes without public approval, so the possibility of dissent did not appear to diminish considerably the credibility of strikes, especially between 2005 and 2006. The question appeared to be not whether the United States attacked but how and when.[73]

These escalatory measures, intended to intimidate Iran into ending its nuclear program or at least complying with provisions under the NPT, seemed to have the opposite effect. In late 2004, upon the early signals of a possible strike, General Mohammad Baqer, commander of Iranian Revolutionary Guards, said that Iran would "retaliate everywhere" if attacked. Defense Minister Ali Shamkhani similarly asserted the right of its retaliatory strikes, presumably targeted against Israel.[74] In 2005, when US signals of a possible strike against Iran's nuclear program began intensifying, "Iran [began] publicly preparing for a possible US attack, as tensions mount[ed] between the Bush administration and ... Tehran." Also during this time Iran officials boasted "Iran would respond within 15 minutes to any attack by the United States" and announced efforts to "bolster and mobilize recruits ... and plans to engage in ... 'asymmetrical' warfare."[75] Moreover, in 2006 Iran sent a letter to then UN Secretary General Kofi Annan expressing concerns about overt American threats of military force. Iran dug in its heels, staging war games, developing new defensive technology, mobilizing its own military resources, and generally using the threat to produce and rattle its own sabers.[76] Not surprisingly, this period corresponded with an increase in spending on military projects, offering perhaps the most direct evidence of credible military threats strengthening inward-looking coalitions vis-à-vis internationalizing ones for reasons discussed earlier.

These examples provide evidence of the causal relationship between credible military threats and increased Iranian military spending. In the

---

[73] Ehsan Ahrari, "Different Beat to Iran War Drums," *Asia Times Online*, March 30, 2006; Philip Sherwell, "US Prepares Military Blitz Against Iran's Nuclear Sites," *Telegraph*, February 12, 2006; David Sanger, "Why Not a Strike On Iran?" *New York Times*, January 22, 2006. As Philip Gordon, now the Assistant Secretary of State for Europe and Eurasian Affairs, wrote in 2006, "it's not easy for an American these days to convince his European colleagues that the US is unlikely to attack Iran's nuclear sites any time soon." "Will America Attack Iran?" *Prospect Online*, June 1, 2006.

[74] Youssef M. Ibrahim, "Think Twice before Targeting Iran," *USA Today*, August 24, 2004.

[75] Borzou Daragahi, "Iran Readies Military, Fearing a US Attack/Tensions with Bush Administration Surge over Tehran's Disputed Nuclear Ambition," *Chronicle Foreign Service*, February 21, 2005.

[76] AFX News Limited, "Iran Complains to UN Chief over Threat of US Attack," May 1, 2006; Reza Asafi quoted in Alan Freeman, "Canadian Prof Attends Tehran's Gathering of Holocaust Deniers," *Globe and Mail*, December 13, 2006.

earlier instance, US reconnaissance missions and increased war planning may have permitted Iran to mobilize its own military resources and increase spending on its military-industrial complex. By publicly notifying the UN about the US threats, Iran created a pretense for military mobilization within its own borders. Indeed, during this time Iran staged war games – one in April 2006 and another in November 2006 – and even funded the development of new missile technology. According to one Iranian news source, Iran "ha[s] made some changes [to Shahab missiles] installing cluster warheads in them with the capacity to carry 1400 bomblets."[77] These changes suggest that US threats may have bolstered the Iranian regime's claims about external threats, and its appeal for increased military spending.

Additionally, as Figures 6.2 and 6.5 illustrate, when military threat credibility increased substantially, there was a commensurate decline in Iran's investment freedom scores for the following years. The decline may have resulted from the 2005 election of inward-looking Mahmoud Ahmadinejad who was given a boost by the George W. Bush administration's threats against Iran in the preceding years.[78] The 2005 Iranian election result signified an "internal coup d'etat" for Iran as Ahmadinejad's economic policies represented radical shifts from those of his predecessor.[79] Indeed as one analyst at the International Atomic Energy Agency noted, Ahmadinejad's election raised "concerns [among foreign investors] about … turns inwards in … [Iran's] investment environment," as Ahmadinejad publicly advocated supporting Iran's domestic industries even at the expense of engagement with the international economy.[80] For example, in 2008 Ahmadinejad asked his economic advisors to design "an independent economic system," a strategy that was condemned in the past as having "scared off foreign investment."[81]

Iranian investment freedom behavior provides good second-order evidence in support of our hypotheses. In particular, Ahmadinejad's election in 2005 resulted in substantial changes in Iranian economic

---

[77] Quoted in Nazila Fathi, "Iran Revolutionary Guards Hold War Games after US Exercise," *New York Times*, November 3, 2006.

[78] Ahmadinejad was able to use the narrative of the US security threat to gain support for inward-looking coalitions within Iran and subsequently come to power. For example, Ahamdinejad used fiery language to frame the United States as an enemy. See Philip Sherwell, "Iranian Rails Against US over Nuclear Weapons," *Telegraph*, September 18, 2005.

[79] *Platts Oilgram Price Report*, June 29, 2005.

[80] Quoted in *Platts Oilgram Price Report*, June 29, 2005. See Chapter 4, this volume, for additional qualitative detail about Iran's regime orientation through time.

[81] Quoted in Borzou Daragahi, "Iranian Economists Condemn Policies of Ahmadinejad," *The Irish Times*, November 11, 2008.

policy that presented an obstacle to foreign investment and increased government control over domestic capital flows, which suggests that declines in investment freedom correspond to strengthening of inward-looking coalitions within government. Moreover, Ahmadinejad's policies resulted in discriminatory treatment of internationalizing domestic coalitions within Iran through increased regulation of foreign and domestic capital, which in turn hampered these coalitions' abilities to engage with the international political economy. Indeed, as a spokesman for a leading internationalizing party within Iran said, "in the current situation signs of wrong and propagandistic policies and approaches are gravely showing." The spokesman cited Ahmadinejad's policies that led to "severing economic ties and a major drop in foreign investment."[82] Finally, that a leader like Ahmadinejad who planned to develop an independent economic system – and made it publicly known during his campaign – was elected, offers some evidence that military threats strengthened inward-looking coalitions vis-à-vis internationalizing ones.[83]

By 2007, the credibility of US attacks against Iran began to diminish. Arab and Persian papers had written off the possibility of an attack, likely for two reasons. First, the situation in Iraq had clearly deteriorated and US decision-making on questions of security concentrated on whether to "surge" forces in Iraq to control violence. Launching an additional offensive, when the United States was preoccupied with the situation in Iraq and increasingly in Afghanistan, was improbable. As Parviz Sourori, a Member of the Iranian Parliament said in a visit to Pakistan, "The US is stuck up in Iraq and cannot dare attack Iran."[84] Second, media leaks suggested that high-level military leaders themselves were deeply skeptical of using force against Iran, largely because of the tenuous security situation in Iraq. Robert Gates repeatedly warned against attacking Iran and some senior military generals threatened resignation if Bush ordered an attack.[85] The United States continued dispatching warships and carrying out military exercises in the Gulf,[86]

[82] Quoted in *Agence France-Presse*, "Iran Reformists Say Conservatives Worried Ahmadinejad Policies," July 10, 2007.
[83] Indeed, his election was associated with increases in hostile language toward the United States, which likely had the effect of increasing military threats from the United States. While this may be the case, we are more interested in the consequences than cause of military threats.
[84] Quoted in *The Pakistani News*, April 11, 2007.
[85] "US Generals 'Will Quit' if Bush Orders Iran Attack," *Sunday Times*, February 25, 2007.
[86] "US Holds Navy Exercise after Iran Comments on Gulf," *Reuters UK*, July 7, 2008; "'Hostile' Iran Sparks US Attack Plan," *CBS*, April 29, 2008.

but Iran itself had rightfully arrived at the conclusion that the United States would not attack. A commentary in the popular *Resalat* Persian paper attributed the about face in the US posture toward Iran not just to the US position in Iraq but also to Iran's threats of strong retaliatory action: "The Supreme Leader of the Islamic Revolution stressed that, in the event of any invasion against Iran, the interests of the invaders throughout the world will be targeted. A while after this warning, the White House spokesman and Condoleezza Rice denied the plan to invade Iran."[87]

Admittedly, there are years during which the distributional measures – military spending, investment, and trade freedom – may seem anomalous under our hypotheses. For example, in Figure 6.5 between 2005 and 2006 and again from 2007 to 2009 investment freedom in Iran declined despite decreases in military threat credibility. Similarly in Figure 6.6, despite decreasing threat credibility from 2006 to 2008, trade freedom remained relatively constant between 2006 and 2010.

That investment and trade freedom declined or stayed the same during these years is not necessarily evidence against our hypotheses however, as credible military threats may have effects that persist and therefore create policy "stickiness." To be clear, despite changes in its external security environment, a state's aversion to risk may cause it to maintain its protectionist policies well after the decline of a military threat – a situation not dissimilar to the behavior of firms in long-term contract negotiations. As Robert Barro notes, "the motivation for long-term contracts ... derives from an insurance element. Because the owners of firms are assumed to be less risk averse (possibly due to self-selection) ... it becomes mutually advantageous to enter into a long-term arrangement." [88] Thus, wages are sticky because they are written into contracts that do not adapt to changes in the prevailing macroeconomic conditions.

By similar logic, we might expect government leaders to be risk averse, keeping policies in place long after security conditions have changed. We would therefore expect Iran's protectionist regulations and institutions to exhibit stickiness several years after the initial impetus for their creation (e.g., military threats) have disappeared. We do not, however, expect integrating policies to exhibit the same property as these policies are risky in nature, and are therefore very easily changed given an appropriate impetus.

---

[87] "Afghan, Iraq Situations Prevent US Iran Attack," *Resalat*, February 28, 2007.
[88] Barro (1977) and Baily (1974).

Policy stickiness may also result from potential audience costs leaders face in changing their policy positions. In particular, when changing their policies, leaders run the risk of being perceived as weak and unstable by their domestic audience, and thus overwhelmingly seek to maintain their original policies despite changes in the international environment. This logic particularly favors continuation of policies designed to buck international pressure and fulfill promises, such as reducing integration with those entities that had previously issued threats.[89] All of this suggests that while the increase in threats prior to 2005 had distributional consequences that strengthened inward-looking coalitions relatively quickly – as evidenced by declines in trade and investment freedom – we would not expect to see a strengthening of internationalizing coalitions following a gradual decline in military threat credibility.

It is important to note, however, that while these accounts logically apply to investment policies and regulations on trade, there is no theoretical reason to expect policy stickiness in Iranian military spending. For one thing, military spending is decided on an annual basis whereas policies and regulations tend to change at longer intervals. As John Ikenberry points out, although "rules and institutions are sticky," policies and budgets, particularly those that are re-evaluated on an annual basis, are less so.[90] Perhaps just as important is the fact that military spending affects less of the Iranian population than regulations on capital flows and trade. To be specific, changes in military spending are less observable to and consequential for the general population than adjustments in trade and investment regulations, and therefore risk fewer audience costs. In other words, the fundamental differences in the processes through which military spending decisions and changes in trade and investment policies are made mean their behaviors vis-à-vis threat credibility are expected to be different. Indeed, military spending tends to change in a way that is commensurate with threat credibility whereas regulations on investment and trade exhibit a tendency for stickiness that long exceed the original impetus for change.

Finally we feel it is important to explain what may at first glance seem to be dramatic shifts in the 2005 threat credibility and investment freedom data. The shifts are not as dramatic as they appear to be for two reasons. First, because the left-vertical axis uses increments of 1, a relatively small numerical change in the data could graphically *appear*

---

[89] Fearon (1994a: 577–592).
[90] Ikenberry (2000: 56), see also Ikenberry (1988).

too large while in reality being entirely reasonable. Similarly, the right vertical axis uses units of 10, which due to the way the investment freedom data is measured are akin to one-unit changes.[91] Second, the data is measured at discrete points in time (one-year intervals) which means (1) changes from year to year may appear dramatic (jagged) simply due to the absence of intermediate points or (2) there may be a reasonable explanation for dramatic shifts in the data.[92] It is also important to note that all other data points, which come from the same data sources as the 2005 data, behave as expected, which is to say that any dramatic shifts in the data may have plausible explanations outside of "errors in data gathering."

Conclusion

While Iran's relationship with the United States has been fraught for decades, it arguably reached new lows in the years after 9/11, when Iran secured a place in the "Axis of Evil" and revealed previously covert nuclear facilities. In response, the United States has implemented a number of measures intended to bring Iran in line with its obligations under the Non-Proliferation Treaty. Since 2001, as Reynolds and Wan documented in Chapter 3 of this volume, the United States, often in conjunction with other members of the international community, has implemented twenty-eight separate forms of sanctions intended to impose pressure on Iran's nuclear program, including the freezing of financial assets, various forms of sanctions, and tighter export controls. Attempting to escalate the pressure, the United States also resorted to coercive diplomacy, threatening the use of military force should Iran continue a nuclear program suspected of producing nuclear weapons.

With the relative cacophony of instruments implemented unilaterally, bilaterally, and multilaterally, separately and in conjunction with each other, it is difficult to identify the effect of a single type of inducement. In this chapter, we nevertheless took steps in the direction of trying to isolate the consequences of particular instruments. We do not, however, focus on the somewhat lofty question of whether these instruments "work" by eliciting denuclearization. Rather, we consider the meta-question of whether one of these measures – threats of military

---

[91] The investment freedom data is measured in increments of 10, making a 10-unit change on the graph akin to a 1-unit change.

[92] See discussion of Ahmadinejad's 2005 election for a significant event that may have caused dramatic shifts in the data.

force – affects domestic alignments that in turn affect the state's propensity to cooperate with the international community on issues of nuclear proliferation.

Our empirical analysis provides general support for the hypothesis that military threats reinforce the coalitions that are hostile to international economic integration and cooperation with international regimes more generally. Although our analysis generally focuses on the years leading up to 2009, it is useful to consider the dynamics of military threats and coalitional consequences in the context of the disputed 2009 election. As Ray Takeyh notes, "Ahmadinejad is savvy enough to recognize that his fraudulent election has eroded not just the Islamic republic's legitimacy but his own standing in Iran and in the larger Muslim community."[93] We point out in our analysis that military threats are but one of a number of factors that can affect the balance of power of domestic coalitions. In this sense, the 2009 election is potentially an important confounding variable that makes it even more difficult to isolate the effects of military threats. Because of the regime's loss of legitimacy, for example, we could imagine that there are heightened incentives to reduce international integration and enhance domestic industries as a way to insulate the regime from outside censure. This may be true independent of whether outsiders have actively issued military threats, which largely ceased in 2009. Thus, the effects of the election acted as a major shock that may have reinforced inward-looking coalitions despite the relative absence of military threats. As mentioned earlier in this chapter, factors such as economic sanctions or positive inducements may also play a similar confounding role with respect to our findings.

Despite these empirical limitations, this analysis suggests that military threats may actually reinforce the types of domestic coalitions that are inimical to the international community's nonproliferation goals. Specifically, based on the relationship between threats and military spending, trade freedom and investment freedom, as well as the detailed qualitative assessment, this chapter provides at least some support for the idea that military threats undermine denuclearization efforts by helping strengthen inward-looking coalitions. Nonetheless, this observation may be at odds with political pressures to be seen to be "doing something" with respect to Iran's nuclear program. Responses tend to take the form of an escalatory ladder, in which tough diplomacy eventually gives way to economic sanctions. Failure of economic sanctions is

[93] Ray Takeyh, "Beware of Iranians Bearing Talks," *Washington Post*, September 27, 2009.

then expected to produce implicit or explicit signals of a state's willingness to use force. These political expectations, however, are formulated essentially independent of whether those escalatory steps actually work. Issuing threats therefore may make good politics but not necessarily good strategy.

Part III

Reassessing the record: focused perspectives

7 Influencing Iran's decisions on the nuclear program

Alireza Nader

The Islamic Republic of Iran's seemingly inexorable march toward nuclear weapons capability and the failure to reach an accommodation with the Iranian regime through engagement has brought the question of sanctions into sharper focus. Though a military option is still discussed as "being on the table," an armed conflict with Iran could conceivably do more harm to US interests in the Middle East, especially given the range of US commitments in Afghanistan. An Israeli military attack on Iran could also prove to be detrimental to American interests. Hence, United Nations and US sanctions on Iran remain as perhaps the best option in pressuring the Iranian government to change its nuclear policy. These sanctions have taken the form of "smart" sanctions targeting key members of the elite, including the top echelon of the Islamic Revolutionary Guards Corps. In addition, the United States and allies have imposed broader sanctions on the Iranian energy sector, specifically targeting fuel imports, in addition to sanctions affecting shipping and the financial sector. Stronger sanctions against Iran, whether targeted or crippling, appear to have led to a substantial deterioration of the Iranian economy. Yet it is unclear if sanctions have weakened or strengthened the Iranian regime's resolve to pursue the nuclear program.

The Islamic Republic appears to be pursuing a nuclear capability as a form of deterrence against an attack by a superior military foe such as the United States. In addition, nuclear capability may lead to greater prestige and sense of self-sufficiency for an inward-looking autocratic state isolated from the global community. Hence, much like North Korea, Iran's nuclear program constitutes an important pillar of the regime's survival and even political legitimacy. However, Iran, though autocratic, is much more politically and socially open than North Korea, and more susceptible to sanctions and positive inducements.

Iran's factions, personalities, and corresponding institutions differ on Iran's nuclear policy; each also possesses competing economic interests that are uniquely affected by US and international sanctions. Much

211

depends on the political and factional landscape in Iran, and the effects of sanctions on the various components and constituents of the political system. Far from being a monolithic regime, the Islamic Republic is faced with deep internal cleavages. The distributional effects of sanctions and positive inducements among different actors will play a large role in shaping the Iranian regime's decisions on the nuclear program.

In terms of causal mechanisms, sanctions will more negatively affect certain factions that favor Iran's internationalization and global integration more than inward-looking political coalitions, perhaps leading them to pressure the regime to take a softer approach on the nuclear program, and greater engagement with the United States and the international community. Positive inducements in the form of the lifting of sanctions or Iran's entry into the World Trade Organization, for example, may also lead the same constituents and actors to advocate for Iranian engagement on the nuclear program. On the other hand, such sanctions and positive inducements may convince certain factions to take escalatory actions and continue or even accelerate the nuclear program's development.

Broadly speaking, Iran's political system today is composed of two competing camps: conservative and principlist factions led by Supreme Leader Ayatollah Ali Khamenei, President Mahmoud Ahmadinejad, and senior leaders of the Revolutionary Guards; and reformist and pragmatic conservative factions centered around 2009 presidential candidate and former Prime Minister Mir Hossein Mousavi, former parliamentary speaker Mehdi Karroubi, and former President Mohammad Khatami.

The conservatives and principlists interests are tied to a closed political and economic system dependent mostly on energy revenue, and increasingly on the use of force to maintain the status quo. The conservatives are also advocates of a strident foreign and national security policy, especially concerning Iran's nuclear program. On the other hand, the reformists and the pragmatic conservatives have long argued for a more open political and economic system that is more closely integrated into the global economy. Though supportive of the nuclear civilian program (and some are perhaps supportive of a weapons program), the reformists and pragmatic conservatives nevertheless favor a less strident nuclear policy. They form the nucleus of the Green Movement that has challenged the legitimacy of the 2009 June election and Iran's increasingly militarized system of politics.

The Islamic Republic, though a theocracy ruled by a Supreme Leader, has historically maintained a semi-participatory system of politics. The Supreme Leader is not directly elected by the people, but Iran does have regular elections for the presidency and parliament. Various factions have taken advantage of this system to implement their political, economic, and foreign policy agendas. Hence, Iran pursued more "moderate" foreign policies under the leadership of the pragmatic conservatives and reformists from 1989 to 2005. This allowed the United States and its allies some leverage over Iranian behavior in the form of negative inducements such as sanctions and positive inducements such as engagement and entry into the world economy.

The 2009 re-election of Mahmoud Ahmadinejad, perceived as fraudulent by millions of Iranians, has shattered Iran's system of participatory politics and may have broken the factional balance that sustained the political system. Khamenei's decisive support for Ahmadinejad and his use of force to crush dissent exposed the cleavages between Iran's competing factions, and greatly reduced the legitimacy of the Islamic Republic as a popularly mandated system of government. The reformists and the pragmatic conservatives, and anyone who disagreed with Khamenei's dictates, were effectively pushed beyond the regime's political and ideological framework.

Moderate voices on the nuclear program such as Khatami, Mousavi, and even chief of the Expediency Council, Ayatollah Hashemi Rafsanjani, have largely lost their ability to shape Iran's national security policy. The 2009 election and its aftermath also confirmed the Guards' political ascendancy. The Guards have a vested institutional interest in the nuclear program's ultimate success, especially in the face of US and international pressure. Hence, the 2009 election and its aftermath may have made the Islamic Republic less receptive to sanctions and even positive inducements, and more likely to pursue a nuclear weapons program regardless of the costs.

The history of sanctions and Iran's political economy

US and multilateral sanctions against Iran may have damaged its economy over the years, but it is not clear if they have changed Iran's resolve to pursue a potentially military nuclear program.

US policy toward Iran has long been shaped by the sanctions regime created after the 1979 revolution and the taking of US hostages by Iranian militants. The hostage taking led to the seizure of billions of dollars of Iranian assets in the United States, which initiated a policy of US economic sanctions toward the Islamic Republic that have continued to this day. In addition to the assets forfeitures, the United States created a sanctions regime against Iran that prohibited US investment and trade relations. US sanctions against Iran were greatly strengthened under the Clinton administration through the Iran and Libya Sanctions Act of 1996, which imposed US penalties on foreign companies investing more than $20 million in Iran's petroleum sector. The sanctions regime was expanded and strengthened under the George W. Bush administration as a result of Iran's resumption of uranium enrichment in 2005. Iranian state-owned or affiliated banks were barred from their indirect use of the US financial system, hampering their ability to transfer money internationally. Iran has also been subjected to four rounds of UN sanctions in response to its nuclear program. These sanctions require all states to block Iran's import and export of "sensitive nuclear material and equipment" and to freeze the financial assets of those involved in Iran's nuclear activities, among other measures.[1]

Iran was subjected to harsher UN, US, and European sanctions in 2010. The United States, Canada, and Great Britain also introduced additional sanctions in late 2011. These sanctions appear to have further damaged Iran's banking, shipping, and energy sectors and led to a certain amount of popular discontent.[2] The public's dissatisfaction with the economy could lead it to pressure the regime to "moderate" its nuclear policy.

Nevertheless, it is not clear if sanctions have actually impacted Iran's willingness to pursue the nuclear program. Like many authoritarian inward-looking regimes, the Islamic Republic may thrive on a sense of political and economic isolation. This is partially due to the state's ideological *raison d'être* and sense of mission: resistance to the West and the United States in particular.

The Islamic Republic's status as an authoritarian rentier state cut off from the global economy is an important factor in determining the efficacy of sanctions regarding the nuclear program. A theocratic regime, the Islamic Republic has relied on the Shia religious concept of *velayat-e faghih*[3] (rule of the supreme jurisprudent) and revolutionary nationalism to maintain its authority over Iran for the past thirty years. This has been abetted by the Iranian regime's reliance on energy revenues to sustain itself without being fully accountable to the population. According to some estimates, as much as half of the Iranian government's revenue is derived from energy exports.[4] What little private sector that exists in Iran is closely tied to the state.

---

[1] Security Council Imposes Sanctions on Iran for Failure to Halt Uranium Enrichment. UNSC. December 23, 2006, available at: www.un.org/News/Press/docs/2006/sc8928.doc.htm.

[2] Farnaz Fassihi, "Iran's Economy Feels Sting of Sanctions," *Wall Street Journal*, October 12, 2010.

[3] It should be noted that the concept of *velayat-e faghih* has shallow roots in Shia Islam and was reinterpreted by Ayatollah Khomeini to justify the creation of an Islamic state.

[4] US Energy Information Administration (2010).

Much of Iran's economy is controlled by ostensibly charitable foundations or *bonyads*. The *bonyads*, which were established through the expropriation of the former Shah's vast assets, have become giant business conglomerates serving the interests of regime constituents such as conservative clergymen and high-ranking members of the Revolutionary Guards. The *bonyads*, which account for as much as 30–40 percent of Iran's economy,[5] are not accountable to the executive or legislative branches of government. The *bonyad* directors are appointed by Khamenei and are theoretically required to report to him alone. They maintain Khamenei's authority among the Iranian population by providing benefits to the poor and casualties of the Iran–Iraq War. Many *bonyads* are controlled or staffed by current and former members of the Revolutionary Guards.[6]

One of the largest and wealthiest *bonyads*, the Imam Reza Shrine Foundation, is controlled by Khamenei's loyal acolyte, Ayatollah Vaez Tabbasi. The Imam Reza Foundation is reported to have accumulated as much as $15 billion through automobile manufacturing, real estate, and agriculture.[7] The Foundation is but one of the large *bonyads* that in some ways operate as semi-autonomous economic entities.

In addition, Iran's private sector has in recent years become increasingly dominated by the Islamic Revolutionary Guards Corps. The Guards were created after the Islamic Revolution to safeguard the revolution from internal and external enemies. The regular Iranian armed forces, or the Artesh, were viewed as being too closely linked to the Shah's regime and not sufficiently wedded to Khomeini's Islamist ideology. The Guards played a critical role in defeating leftist forces that opposed Khomeini's vision of an Islamist state. The Guards were also at the forefront of defending Iran during its long war with Iraq; the tactic of hurling thousands of Iranian soldiers at Iraqi frontlines was pioneered by the Guards and the reserve Basij forces. But despite their prominent role in the Iran–Iraq War, the Guards were not allowed to become directly involved in Iranian politics. They are supposed to function as the regime's Praetorian Guard, rather than an independent power broker.

The Revolutionary Guards' involvement in the Iranian economy took off after the Iran–Iraq War and under the presidency of Ayatollah Ali Akbar Hashemi Rafsanjani (1989–1997).[8] He viewed the Guards' involvement in reconstruction as beneficial from a practical and political

---

[5] Statement of Kenneth Katzman, Specialist in Middle Eastern Affairs Congressional Research Service, Joint Economic Committee Hearing on Iran, July 25, 2006.
[6] Wehrey *et al.* (2009).   [7] Amirpur (2006).   [8] Ansari (2010a).

viewpoint. The Guards possessed the manpower and necessary organization to work on national projects; their perceived role as defenders of Iran during the war with Iraq paved their way into a larger political and economic role after the 1989 ceasefire. Rafsanjani may have calculated that the Guards' ability to reap profits and credibility from reconstruction would tie them more closely to him and his pragmatic policies. Yet the Guards' economic role evolved to such a degree as to make them independent of any power center or political personality.

Iran's closed economic system, dominated by the Guards and various *bonyads*, has allowed Khamenei and the conservatives to pursue the nuclear program largely unfettered. If anything, sanctions may have the benefit of strengthening Khamenei's claim to legitimacy – resistance against a "bullying" United States – while serving his constituent's specific economic interests. The larger public, though dissatisfied with Iran's political and economic situation, could be further suppressed through the use of force and violence.

However, the Islamic Republic is not a monolithic or unified political entity, as one may expect from an authoritarian state. Certain key political and social constituents may benefit by economic isolation and sanctions as other political actors are undermined by the sanctions. The Islamic Republic's political make-up has been a crucial factor in determining the efficacy of positive inducements and sanctions, especially regarding the nuclear program.

The current factional landscape

Iranian politics are driven by intense factional rivalries formed by constituent economic interests and corresponding ideologies. A theocracy headed by the Supreme Leader, the Islamic Republic has nevertheless functioned as a republic with elected institutions, such as the parliament (*majles*) and the presidency. Iran's competing factions have shaped economic and foreign policies in the past three decades through their control of these elected institutions, especially the presidency.

The regime's factions can be roughly divided into two camps: the Islamist Left and the Islamist Right. These two factional groupings have competed with each other from the beginning days of the revolution and the founding of the Islamist Republic.

Both factional groupings are devoted to the Islamic revolution and the political doctrine of its leader, Ayatollah Ruhollah Khomeini. They broadly accept the concept of a theocratic state ruled according to the *velayat-e faghih*, and explicitly reject a state based on secular principles espoused by the United States. Yet they are fundamentally divided on the practice of *velayat-e faghih*, in addition to the Islamic Republic's social and economic policies.

The Islamist Left today is composed of various reformist groups such as the pro-Khatami Islamic Iran Participation Front and Karroubi's National Trust party. The Islamist Left envisions a more accountable and pluralistic political system, strengthened civil society, and more relaxed social norms favoring women and ethnic and religious minorities. Though previously espousing socialistic and statist economic policies, the Islamist Left has increasingly favored privatization and lesser state control over the economy. The Left draws support from "liberal" clerical associations such as the Assembly of Combatant Clergymen, in addition to the intelligentsia, students, women's rights groups, and the middle and professional classes.

The Islamist Right favors more conservative social and political norms. The Right views the revolution as a successful enterprise which has freed Iran from Western or US "imperialism" and enabled Iran's rise as an important regional and even global power.

The Right has a strict interpretation of the Islamic Republic as a political system based on God's laws and ruled according to the precepts of *velayat-e faghih*. The Right tends to view Khamenei as Iran's undisputed religious, political, and military authority. The extreme wing of the Islamist Right even maintains that the regime's republican and elected institutions are largely extraneous and unnecessary according the absolutist interpretation of *velayat-e faghih*. The Right, though far from united, draws support from conservative clerical groups and seminaries, the lower religious classes, traditionalist members of the Bazaar, and the security and intelligence services.

The Islamist Right can be roughly divided into three sub-factions: the traditional conservatives; the pragmatic conservatives; and the neo-conservatives or principlists. The Islamic Republic's original ruling elite, the traditional conservatives are represented by clerics such as Khamenei. The principlists share the traditional conservatives' ideology, but tend to take a more hardline and strident stance on domestic and foreign policies. Many principlists are laymen who served as the revolution's foot soldiers and were shaped by the horrors of the Iran–Iraq War. They are suspicious of clerical authority, though most accept the concept of *velayat-e faghih*. Many are Mahdists, fervent believers in the return of Shia Islam's messianic figure, the Hidden Imam. Ahmadinejad is a prime representative and leader of the principlist movement.[9]

---

[9] Ahmadinejad's challenge to the Supreme Leader in 2011 has lost him a lot of support within the principalist movement.

The pragmatic conservatives also adhere to traditional social and religious norms, but favor economic liberalization, greater integration with the global economy, and more moderate foreign policies. The pragmatic conservatives have coalesced under the leadership of former President Rafsanjani, who played a key role in the appointment of Khamenei as Supreme Leader in 1989. The pragmatic conservatives include many former and current government technocrats and Rafsanjani's Bazaari supporters.

The Iranian state has been controlled by traditional conservatives such as Khamenei through their domination of the regime's unelected institutions, including the office of the Supreme Leader; the Guardian Council, which has the power to veto legislation and ban candidates deemed "un-Islamic"; and the Assembly of Experts, which appoints the Supreme Leader. However, Iran's president, who is elected by the people, has wide constitutional authority to shape economic and foreign policies. Iran's respective factions have often functioned as a candidate's political party, though political parties are technically illegal in the Islamic Republic.

The history of politics in the Islamic Republic can be divided into three relatively distinct phases: the pragmatic conservative (1989–1997); the reformist (1997–2005); and the principlist (2005–). Each faction has determined Iran's receptivity to positive inducements and sanctions based on its specific constituent interests and ideologies.

The effects of sanctions and positive inducements on Iran's ruling factions

The pragmatic conservatives under Rafsanjani (1989–1997) pursued wide-ranging economic and foreign policy reforms that (if successful) could have led to a lessening of Iran's isolation and greater integration into the global economy. Known as the *saradar-e sazandegi* (generalissimo of reconstruction), Rafsanjani's ambition was to reconstruct Iran after the widespread destruction of the war with Iraq and even create a prosperous and "capitalistic" system of Islamic rule. To do so, Rafsanjani had to bypass the statist mentality of the Islamist Left, who desired a state controlled economy, and the traditional conservatives, who wanted to lessen the state's role in economy in favor of a monopolistic and rentist private sector. Rafsanjani was supported in his efforts by technocrats at the Central Bank and the Budget and Planning Organization.[10] He was also helped by the Executives of Construction

---

[10] Nourbakhsh (2005).

(*Kargozaran-e Sazandegi*), a technocratic and pro-privatization "party" that shared his vision within the executive and legislative branches. Rafsanjani's economic plan relied heavily on modern industrialization, a free market economy based on competition, and the privatization of state-owned industries.

In order to carry out his economic agenda, Rafsanjani pursued pragmatic foreign policies that facilitated foreign investments and integrated Iran more closely into the global economy. Under his leadership, Iran ceased its attempt to export the revolution to Shia inhabited states of the Persian Gulf. Iran improved its relations with the states of the Gulf Cooperation Council, including Saudi Arabia. Rafsanjani also sought to mend relations with Europe, though his implication in the Mikonos murders of Iranian opposition leaders set back his foreign policy agenda with Europe for many years.[11] There have been indications that Rafsanjani seeks to improve or even restore relations with the United States. However, any attempts on his part have been thwarted by hardline conservatives opposed to the normalization of relations between Iran and the United States.

Rafsanjani's efforts at economic reform were similarly blocked by the traditional conservatives, whose monopolistic control of the economy would have been endangered by greater domestic and international competition. They were aided in their efforts by Khamenei, who by the mid 1990s had accumulated enough independent power to emerge from Rafsanjani's shadow as Iran's most powerful political actor.[12]

Khatami (1997–2005) largely followed Rafsanjani's economic policies of industrialization and privatization. He favored a more pluralistic and less authoritarian state bounded by a strong civil society (*jame-e madani*). A strong private sector was an essential ingredient in achieving his model of governance.

Khatami's policies appealed to Iran's youthful population, which was largely frustrated by Iran's anemic economic growth and corresponding lack of employment under Rafsanjani. He managed to reduce unemployment and the poverty rate, and even secured World Bank loans for various development projects. Iran's external debt was substantially reduced and the financial sector was opened to privatization schemes. The World Bank reported in 2004 that "after 24 years marked by internal post-revolutionary strife, international isolation, and deep economic volatility, Iran is slowly emerging from a long period of uncertainty and instability."[13]

---

[11] Iranian Human Rights Documentation Center (2007).
[12] Moslem (2002).   [13] Siddiqi (2005).

Iran under Khatami became a more open and tolerant society. Dozens, if not hundreds, of newspapers, magazines, and other publications sprang to life to challenge the Islamic Republic's conservative social mores and values. For the first time, the Islamic Republic held nationwide local municipal elections in 1999. The reformists not only triumphed in these elections, but also emerged as the majority in parliament a year later.[14] For the first time in two decades, Iran appeared to be moving toward a more democratic system of government.

In order to achieve his socio-political and economic goals, Khatami also pursued less confrontational and more conciliatory foreign policies. He spoke of a "dialogue of civilizations" between the world of Islam and the West. Under Khatami, Iran significantly improved relations with its neighbors, including the GCC states, and especially Saudi Arabia. Iran's diplomatic and trade relations with the European Union also saw marked improvement under Khatami.

The Khatami administration also restricted Iran's support for armed "liberation" groups across the Middle East. Iran's material support of Hamas and Hezbollah was kept to a minimum, and there was even discussion of Iran accepting a future peace deal between Israel and the Palestinians, thus implicitly endorsing the Oslo peace process.

Khatami also attempted to improve relations with the United States. Iran aided the overthrow of the Taliban in 2001 and played a critical role in the establishment of the Karzai government in 2002.[15] Furthermore, Iran committed more than $500 million for Afghan economic and reconstruction assistance.

The nuclear program continued to progress during Khatami's presidency.[16] Nevertheless, Iran pursued diplomatic engagement with the European Union and the International Atomic Energy Agency in order to forestall sanctions and other forms of pressure. If anything, diplomatic engagement on the nuclear program may have built additional confidence between the EU and Iran, perhaps allowing for greater political and economic cooperation.

However, Iran's economic and political liberalization under Rafsanjani and Khatami was not to last. Despite his initial popularity, Khatami largely failed to achieve his economic, political, and foreign

---

[14] Takeyh (2003a).
[15] James Dobbins, "How to Talk to Iran," *Washington Post*, July 22, 2007.
[16] Khatami's government was largely in control of nuclear negotiations, though it may not have had full knowledge of the actual status of the nuclear program. National security decision-making was shared between pro-Khatami institutions such as the Ministry of Foreign Affairs, and anti-Khatami organizations such as the Revolutionary Guards, which has had a large role in setting the direction of the nuclear program.

policy agenda. He could not create enough jobs for the hundreds of thousands of young Iranians entering the workforce every year. High inflation continued to eat at the average Iranian's earning power, and Iran was still rated as one of the world's most closed economies.[17]

More importantly, Khatami's efforts at reform were consistently blocked by Khamenei and the conservatives who controlled Iran's unelected institutions. The Iranian constitution affords the Supreme Leader much greater power than the president, which Khamenei used effectively to thwart the reformists' agenda. The Guardian Council, directly appointed by Khamenei, vetoed reformist legislation and prevented reformist candidates from running in the 2004 parliamentary elections.

Khatami and the reformists also failed to gain control of Iran's national security bureaucracy. The conservatives operated shadowy vigilante groups that violently targeted reformist figures. The "chain murders" of pro-reform intellectuals and activists in the 1990s were traced to hardline conservative clerics and the Ministry of Intelligence, which was never fully brought under the reformists' control.[18] The Revolutionary Guards also sabotaged Khatami's rapprochement with the United States and the West by supporting armed attacks against Israel by Palestinian groups such as Hamas. The capture of the *Karin A*, a ship carrying Iranian weapons to the Palestinian Authority, effectively exposed Iran as an obstacle to US interests in the Middle East.[19]

The thwarting of the reformist agenda, which included easing Iran's international isolation, could not have happened without the explicit approval of Khamenei.

Khamenei has consistently felt threatened by the reformist agenda, which implicitly, and at times very explicitly, challenged the concept of *velayat-e faghih* and his personal authority.

The end of the reform era led to the ascent of Ahmadinejad and the principlists, and the monopolization of national security decision-making by Guards principlists. The principlists believe in a return to the "true" ideals or principles of the Islamic revolution. They view the reformists and the pragmatic conservatives, and their desires for economic and political reform as a threat to the Islamic Republic's existence.

Khamenei has strongly supported the principlists at the reformists' and pragmatic conservatives' expense, as was demonstrated by his decisive support for Ahmadinejad in the 2009 presidential election.

[17] Amuzegar (2002).   [18] Buchta (2000).
[19] Thaler and Nader (2010).

US sanctions and Iran's increasing international isolation have arguably strengthened the principlists and the Revolutionary Guards.[20] As stated, Rafsanjani and Khatami's reform efforts were significantly dependent on Iran's ability to privatize its economy, which itself was dependent on access to the global market. Positive inducements such as expanded diplomatic and trade relations with the industrialized world, including the possibility of accession to the World Trade Organization,[21] had a moderating effect on Iran's overall foreign and national security policies under Rafsanjani and Khatami. However, the failure to achieve US–Iranian rapprochement and attract sufficient Western investment and technology weakened attempts to achieve meaningful reforms.

On the other hand, Khamenei and his conservative/principlist backers, including the Revolutionary Guards, have been less affected by sanctions and Iran's international isolation. Their aim is not to enact economic or political reforms, but to maintain the status quo in the face of internal and external challenges.

Khamenei and sanctions

Khamenei will make the final decisions on the Iranian nuclear program; hence, he is the final adjudicator on factional debates surrounding the nuclear program. A stalwart conservative and proponent of *velayat-e faghih*, Khamenei has guided the regime since the death of Khomeini. He hails from the conservative or Islamist Right spectrum of Iranian politics, which continues to view the United States as Iran's traditional and necessary enemy. As a conservative, Khamenei is closely associated with segments of the Iranian clergy that view capitalism and private property as being compatible with and even beneficial for Islam.[22]

As President from 1981 to 1989, Khamenei advocated economic policies that can be roughly described as free market in nature. He came into dispute with then Prime Minister Mir Hossein Mousavi over the latter's leftist and largely statist economic policies, which favored heavy government intervention in the economy and massive state subsidies.[23] Moreover, Khamenei has been a proponent of Article 44 of the Iranian constitution, which calls for the privatization of Iran's state-owned industries.[24]

---

[20] Radio Zamaneh (2010) and Dehghanpisheh (2010).
[21] "WTO Agrees Entry Talks With Iran," *BBC News*, May 26, 2005, available at: www.news.bbc.co.uk/2/hi/middle_east/4582081.stm.
[22] "WTO Agrees Entry Talks With Iran," *BBC News*, May 26, 2005, available at: www.news.bbc.co.uk/2/hi/middle_east/4582081.stm.
[23] *BBC News Persian* (2009).   [24] *Islamic Republic News Agency* (2007).

However, Khamenei's support for privatization should not be confused with Western concepts of free enterprise or laissez-faire economics leading to Iran's integration into the global economy. Iran's economy under Khamenei continues to be largely state controlled; whatever industries or companies that have privatized have been taken over by parties affiliated with the state, and more specifically Khamenei and the Revolutionary Guards. The various *bonyads* that operate under Khamenei's watch are hardly the definition of free enterprises. Hamid Fooladghar, the head of the *majles* commission on the implementation of Article 44 recently admitted that the privatization plan under Article 44 had been unsuccessful since government capital was not reaching the private sector but circulating within the government.[25]

True free enterprise and global integration would translate into a more open society and pluralistic political system. A more globally integrated Iran would no doubt be exposed to the economic, social, and ideological influences of the world's largest and most powerful economy, the United States. This would only enhance the current opposition movement's demands for a more open, just, and accountable political system.

Khamenei remains wedded to a closed political system at odds with the United States. He has based Iran foreign policy on "resistance" to US "imperialism" across the Middle East. Iran under Khamenei continues to closely support a number of "resistance" groups, including Hezbollah in Lebanon and Hamas in the Palestinian territories. In addition, Khamenei has increasingly favored a more aggressive nuclear policy. This has been particularly true during Ahmadinejad's presidency, who Khamenei views as being better suited than his predecessors (Rafsanjani and Khatami) in resisting US hegemony.[26]

Khamenei has pursued a policy of confrontation without much apparent regard for the economic consequences. His thinking may be influenced by Khomeini's notion that the revolution was not carried out "to lower the price of watermelons."[27] Much like Khomeini, his vision for the Islamic Republic is revolutionary in nature, and defined by continued resistance to "world wide arrogance." In addition, Khamenei and his constituents do not bear the brunt of sanctions, and may in fact benefit from them financially as long as they maintain access to the state's resources, especially oil revenues. As Drezner demonstrates, autocratic regimes like Iran may benefit by providing private goods for their narrow group of supporters as opposed to the broader public. A

---

[25] Etemad Melli (2010). [26] Thaler and Nader (2010).
[27] Pollack (2004).

monopolistic and rentist economic system, even under sanctions, forms a pillar of Khamenei's political authority.

This does not mean that Khamenei and his supporters are invulnerable to Iran's economic problems and strengthened sanctions against the Islamic Republic.[28] Ahmadinejad's economic mismanagement and international sanctions have put great strain on the Islamic Republic, and may have significantly contributed to the political divisions and mass opposition movement that followed the June 2009 presidential election. Yet Khamenei and the conservatives appear to believe that they will weather such pressures through their control of state resources and the increasing use of force and repression by the Revolutionary Guards.

Sanctions and the rise of the Revolutionary Guards

The United States has identified the Revolutionary Guards as the primary target of US and international sanctions. The Guards' role in the nuclear program and their extensive involvement in Iran's economy make them a potentially effective point of leverage for US policy. To date, several Guards officers and entities, including the Guards' construction firm, Khatam al Anbia, have been designated by the US Treasury department.[29]

Such designations would make it more difficult for countries like China to do business with the Guards and affiliated companies. Such targeted sanctions on the Guards could also potentially pressure more pragmatic or profit oriented members to limit or even scale back Iran's nuclear ambitions. However, it is not clear if the top echelon of the Guards would be sufficiently pressured to change Iran's track on the nuclear program. Certain elements of Iran's ruling elite, especially the principlists within the Revolutionary Guards, derive important ideological, political, and economic benefits from the nuclear program and the resulting sanctions.

The Guards' true political ascent began under Khatami's presidency (1997–2005), whose victory came as a surprise, and a threat, to Khamenei and the conservatives. Khamenei had implicitly endorsed a close political ally and confidant, the conservative former speaker of Parliament Hojjatolislam Nateq-Nouri. Nevertheless, Khatami received an astounding 70 percent of the vote and was popular even in Qom,

---

[28] Borzou Daragahi and Ramin Mostaghim, "Iran Sanctions Ripple Past Those in Power," *Los Angeles Times*, January 20, 2008.
[29] Rozen (2010).

Iran's traditionally conservative center of religious thought and learning. Khamenei's weak religious credentials also became a great source of vulnerability, especially as some reformist intellectuals began to critique the concept of *velayat-e faghih*.

Khamenei tasked the Guards with blocking Khatami's reformist agenda and thus prevented a direct challenge to his personal authority. The Guards, along with other security, intelligence, and vigilante organizations, played an important role in preventing the institutionalization of the reformist political-social agenda. As explained above, the chain murders and the *Karin A* incident were typical of the Guards' strategy vis-à-vis Khatami and the reformists.

But more importantly, it was the Guards' expansion into the Iranian economy which allowed them to block reformist and pragmatic conservative ambitions in the long term.

In the past two decades, the Guards have used their position as Khamenei's Praetorian guard to dominate all sectors of Iran's economy, from energy to transportation, telecommunications, finance, manufacturing, and of course the military-industrial complex.[30] The Guards' position as Iran's most powerful national security organization has allowed them to bypass domestic and international business competitors. For example, the Guards used their national security powers to prevent a Turkish company from constructing Tehran's Imam Khomeini airport in 2004. In 2009, the Revolutionary Guards-controlled company Etemad Mobin took control of Iran's Telecommunications Company through a no-bid contract,[31] allowing them better to combat the "psychological warfare" that had framed the 2009 election and the creation of the Green Movement.

The economic and political rise of the Revolutionary Guards was facilitated by Ahmadinejad's 2005 election as president. A former Guards member, Ahmadinejad came to power through the backing of top Guards and Basij officers.[32] Ahmadinejad has ostensibly favored economic policies meant to address inequality and "injustice" in Iranian society. More realistically, he has positioned the principlists and the Revolutionary Guards as the real winners of his economic policies.

The Guards and affiliated companies have benefited enormously from government loans and no-bid contracts. The Guards' construction firm, Khatam al Anbia, has been engaged in numerous construction

---

[30] Wehrey *et al.* (2009).
[31] Julian Borger and Robert Tait, "The Financial Power of the Revolutionary Guards," *Guardian*, February 15, 2010.
[32] Naji (2008).

and business activities across the country. According to opposition leader Mir Hossein Mousavi's website, Khatam al Anbia controls nearly 800 companies engaged in all manner of economic activities, from the construction of oil and gas pipelines to the development of Tehran's metrorail system.[33] Since his presidency, Ahmadinejad has transferred billions of dollars of state revenues to Guards linked entities and companies, such as Khatam al Anbia.[34]

The Revolutionary Guards played a key role in Ahmadinejad's election in 2005 and again in 2009. The 2005 election was followed by allegations of voter fraud, including ballot stuffing by the Basij, a vast paramilitary organization integrated into the Revolutionary Guards.[35] The Iranian opposition Green Movement led by Mousavi has claimed that Ahmadinejad's re-election in 2009 was nothing short of a coup by the Revolutionary Guards.

The top echelon of the Guards has sympathized with Ahmadinejad for political and ideological reasons, until his falling out with Khamenei. One can argue that the Guards' support for Ahmadinejad has been motivated by profit and financial gain.

However, the Guards are hardly a monolithic force. They are faced by the same internal divisions that have shaped Iranian politics and society. Many rank and file Guards members, for example, are reported to have voted for Khatami during his presidential campaign.[36] A significant segment of active Guards are reported to have supported Mousavi in the 2009 presidential election.[37] Some prominent former Guards members have been vocal critics of Ahmadinejad and his policies. They include Mohammad Baqer Qalibaf, Tehran's current mayor; Mohsen Rezai, former chief commander of the Revolutionary Guards (1981–1997) and current secretary of the expediency council; and Ali Larijani, former national security advisor and current speaker of Parliament. Qalibaf and Rezai in particular have advocated greater technocratic know-how in government, in addition to economic liberalization and more moderate foreign policies.

Nevertheless, the military and intelligence components of the Guards appear to be effectively controlled by hardline senior officers loyal to Khamenei. They include General Ali Jafari, commander in chief; Mohammad Hezaji, former commander of the Basij and current deputy chief commander of the Guards; and Hossein Taeb, former commander of the Basij and current head of the Guards' intelligence

---

[33] Aref and Farahany (2010).   [34] Wehrey *et al.* (2009).
[35] Naji (2008).   [36] Wehrey *et al.* (2009).   [37] *Setadnet* (2010).

organization. These figures have increasingly shaped not only Iran's domestic policies, but its national security policies as well.

The Guards have arguably benefited economically from Iran's international isolation. Iran's tense relations with neighboring states and its stand-off with the international community, particularly the United States over the nuclear program, have helped eliminate the Guards' external and internal business competitors. Important economic sectors such as transportation and telecommunications, which were at one point open to international bidders, are now effectively dominated by Guards' linked companies. Increased economic pressures by the Obama administration and a fourth round of UN sanctions have also led many foreign, particularly Western, companies to abandon the Iranian energy market, increasing the Guards' involvement in that economic sector. Though Iran's nuclear drive may have damaged its economy overall, it may have nevertheless enhanced the economic interests of the principlists and their allies within the Revolutionary Guards.

The factional divide on the nuclear program

Iran's competing factions broadly favor the development of the nuclear program, but disagree on its use and future direction. Ahmadinejad has pursued a strident nuclear policy, especially as compared with his predecessors. He and his principlist supporters have framed the nuclear program as an issue of sovereignty and national pride, and a political weapon against opponents from not only the reformist and pragmatic conservative camps, but rivals from the principlist camp as well. Ahmadinejad has also portrayed the nuclear program as justified resistance to the West's "attempts" to keep Iran technologically and militarily backward.

Though supportive of the civilian nuclear program, the reformists/ pragmatic conservatives have nevertheless sought to lessen the costs associated with Iran's pursuit of nuclear capability, including increasing isolation from the international community. The reformist socio-economic agenda is hardly helped by what Solingen has described as an ambiguous and unbounded nuclear program. Khatami's national security advisor, Hassan Rowhani, has typified the reformist/pragmatic conservative approach toward the nuclear program. A Rafsanjani protégé, Hassan Rowhani skillfully conducted negotiations with the international community, including the European Union and the International Atomic Energy Agency, buying Iran sufficient time and space to avoid serious sanctions while making technological progress on the nuclear program. Rowhani, now head of the Expediency Council's

Center for Strategic Studies, based Iran's engagement strategy on the pragmatic conservative political ideology: the Islamic Republic could only survive and thrive if it liberalized its economy and moderated its foreign policy. Rowhani believes that in foreign policy

> do we want to be ambiguous or clear, do we want the region and the world to be afraid of us or to be our friends, do we want to become every day more fearful or more attractive? ... If we consider the Islamic Revolution as the top priority, then we should be aware that we will be carrying an extremely grave responsibility on our shoulders. In other words, we are the Islamic Revolution and we want to spread this culture across the region and the Islamic world as a whole. However, if we seek to be primarily the Islamic Republic of Iran, our foremost mission and priority will be the Islamic Republic of Iran, and that means we will traverse a different path.[38]

Hence, the reformists and pragmatic conservatives are less prone to pursue an aggressive nuclear policy that will jeopardize their perceived economic and political achievements in the last two decades. Iran's expansion of the program, its confrontation with the international community, and the resulting sanctions could, in their view, lead to the future collapse of the Islamic Republic.

Such thinking exists even in the principlist camp. Ali Larijani, Rowhani's successor as national security advisor and lead nuclear negotiator, also pursued a similar track vis-à-vis the international community. Larijani had been critical of the Khatami administration prior to his appointment as national security advisor. This suited his position as a conservative politician opposed to reformist aspirations. Yet Larijani, currently Iran's speaker of parliament, has positioned himself as a "pragmatist" on the nuclear program. His political and policy disputes with Ahmadinejad led him to resign from his position in 2007, to be replaced by the hardline Ahmadinejad loyalist Saeed Jalili.

Nevertheless, Larijani remains involved in nuclear policy. On a recent diplomatic visit to Japan, Larijani stated that Iran desired a nuclear program like that of his host nation, which had acquired full nuclear technology but not actual weapons. Such a "virtual" program could be more palatable than an actual nuclear armed Iran from a Western or US perspective.[39]

Larijani's pragmatic stance on the nuclear program may be attributed to several factors. It is possible that Larijani is concerned more about the overall interests of the Islamic Republic as a viable political system, rather than the narrow interests of his political/ideological constituency. But the politically astute Larijani has also positioned himself

---

[38] Rowhani (2008).   [39] *Mehr News Agency* (2010b).

as a more pragmatic and technocratic alternative to Ahmadinejad. Hence, Larijani would satisfy the Islamist Right's ideological qualifications while appealing to the more technocratic pragmatic conservative camp, including figures such as Rafsanjani. A trusted advisor to Khamenei, Larijani is believed to harbor political ambitions beyond that of his current position. A presidential candidate in 2005, Larijani may seek Iran's second highest office after Ahmadinejad's term expires, or if he is removed from office.

Larijani's position on the nuclear program demonstrates the importance of factional rivalries in shaping Iran's nuclear policy.

These rivalries have also affected the US approach toward the nuclear program, making sanctions and positive inducements either more or less effective. The US and P5 attempts to "swap" Iran's stockpile of low-enriched uranium in exchange for nuclear fuel for Tehran's medical reactor is a case in point. The agreement would have allowed Ahmadinejad to reach a compromise on the nuclear program while saving face at home. The Iranian government could plausibly claim that it had won a political victory, since the uranium swap could have been interpreted as a tacit recognition of Iran's right to enrich uranium, which the United States had sought to prevent under the Bush administration. It would have also bought the United States time by preventing Iran from weaponizing its uranium stockpile.

Ahmadinejad's political opponents from both sides of the political spectrum attacked the deal, effectively scuttling a chance at compromise.[40] Mousavi, who had advocated more moderate foreign policy positions during his election campaign, labeled the deal as a betrayal of Iran's nuclear scientists. Larijani and Rafsanjani also opposed the swap deal, in effect out-radicalizing Ahmadinejad on the nuclear issue. Subsequent Iranian requests to make the swap on Iranian territory were subsequently rejected by the United States and the P5. The failure of the swap deal demonstrated the limits of US sanctions and positive inducements in shaping the Islamic Republic's thinking and decisions on the nuclear program.

The 2009 presidential election and US policy choices

The 2009 presidential election and its aftermath was a watershed event in Iranian domestic politics, and the US approach toward Iran and the nuclear program.

---

[40] Michael Slackman, "Iran's Politics Stand in the Way of a Nuclear Deal," *New York Times*, November 2, 2009.

The 2009 election may have inhibited the effect of US sanctions and positive inducements toward Iran by marginalizing reformist and pragmatic voices from the political system. It is currently unclear if Iran will retain a system of electoral politics in which competing factions are able to use their control of the government to devise more "liberal" economic and foreign policies. A militarized and Islamist Right dominated regime may not produce a Rafsanjani or Khatami administration that can be influenced by sanctions and positive inducements such as the strengthening or weakening of the sanctions regime. Though the opposition Green Movement has not been defeated, it has limited capability in shaping Iran's decisions on the nuclear program.

The Islamic Republic and the ascendant Guards may suffer from sanctions. Khamenei reportedly derives some of his personal wealth from his family's monopoly on certain international commercial activities.[41] The Guards are also dependent on business and financial ties to Dubai, Malaysia, China, and a number of other countries. Iran's broader economic vulnerabilities may also be exploited to pressure nuclear decision-makers. These vulnerabilities include an over-reliance on energy exports and a heavy dependence on the import of refined fuel products. Up to 50 percent of the Iranian government's revenues come from oil and natural gas exports. Iran, which lacks sufficient refining capacity, also relies on gasoline imports to meet up to 40 percent of its domestic demand.[42] This has led to broad sanctions on fuel imports (among other measures) in order to persuade the Iranian government to cease its nuclear activities. However, such sanctions may hurt the Iranian population and opposition factions without forcing the Iranian government's hand on the nuclear program. Indeed, Iran's reform of its massive subsidy system may be an attempt to inoculate the government from economic pressures by shifting the costs to the population at large. Though pragmatic figures like Rafsanjani have warned the regime not to downplay the impact of sanctions, their influence within the halls of power is rather limited, especially so after the 2009 election.[43]

The application of smart or targeted sanctions may create a point of leverage vis-à-vis the Guards without hurting the Iranian population or the opposition movement. A targeted sanctions regime could also take advantage of divisions between the Guards among reformist, pragmatic, and principlist. Designation of individual Guards members and entities, and the targeting of Guards front companies, may drive a wedge between the more pragmatic and profit-minded Guards and

---

[41] Makhmalbaf (2010).   [42] *Mehr News Agency* (2010a).
[43] Fassihi, "Iran's Economy."

their more ideologically committed rivals. Prominent former Guards figures such as Rezai, Qalibaf, and Larijani may be more receptive to the effects of strengthened sanctions, as opposed to the more ideologically driven current Guards leadership, represented by such figures as Jafari, Hejazi, and Taeb. However, even targeted sanctions will not necessarily change the regime's thinking on the nuclear program.

Iran's pursuit of nuclear technology and weapons is tied to overall regime and national security objectives. Nuclear capability could potentially neutralize Western conventional military superiority and safeguard the Islamic Republic from regime change through invasion, as was the case with the Taliban in Afghanistan and the overthrow of Iraq's Baathist regime. Nuclear capability will also enhance the Islamic Republic's regional prestige and its power throughout the Middle East.

Hence, positive inducements such as the provision of spare parts for airplanes and the accession of Iran into the World Trade Organization have not been enough to affect Iranian behavior, especially given the benefits of nuclear weapons capability. Sanctions have also been ineffective to date. The regime's survival is increasingly contingent on a favorable outcome regarding the nuclear program, whether it leads to a virtual or actual nuclear weapons capability. A sanctions regime contributing to Iran's economic decline cannot alter this reality.

8   Engaging North Korea: the efficacy of sanctions and inducements

Stephan Haggard and Marcus Noland

Nowhere is the efficacy of economic inducements and sanctions more hotly contested than on the Korean peninsula. The signing of the Agreed Framework in 1994 successfully froze the operations of the Yongbyon nuclear complex but did not dismantle it.[1] Economic inducements, including the construction of light-water reactors and regular shipments of heavy fuel oil (HFO), were integral aspects of that deal. However, in November 2002 the Bush administration chose to suspend HFO shipments in response to intelligence that North Korea had a clandestine uranium enrichment (HEU) program.[2] North Korea escalated the crisis by withdrawing from the NPT and ultimately announcing a nuclear capability in February 2005. The United States also escalated, in part by using new sanctions tools designed to limit North Korea's international financial transactions.

The Six-Party Talks became the diplomatic venue for addressing the nuclear crisis and ultimately yielded an important statement of principles (September 2005) that promised – albeit in vague terms – a package of economic inducements for North Korea. The talks quickly broke down following this agreement, in part because of the imposition of new financial sanctions by the United States. North Korea tested a small nuclear device in October 2006. Despite the test, the parties reached two important interim agreements outlining a roadmap

Our thanks for comments from Etel Solingen and participants in the workshop on Positive and Negative Inducements, Woodrow Wilson International Center for Scholars, Washington, DC, September 1, 2010. We also would like to thank to the Smith Richardson Foundation and the MacArthur Foundation Asian Security Initiative for financial support and to Jihyeon Jeong and Jennifer Lee for research assistance.

[1] In addition to the five-megawatt electric research reactor, the facility also housed a fuel rod fabrication plant and a reprocessing facility disingenuously called a radio-chemistry laboratory. This facility was the source of the fissile material ultimately used in the 2006 and 2009 nuclear tests.

[2] On the question of how far along the HEU program was, see Hersh (2003), the exchange between Harrison (2005) and Reiss and Galucci (2005), and Pinkston and Spector (2007).

toward complete dismantlement of the Yongbyon facility in February and October 2007. Again, economic inducements were an integral part of the bargain: HFO shipments would be exchanged for incremental disabling of the reactor and other facilities.

Negotiations on the implementation of these agreements broke down at the end of the Bush administration in 2008 and as of this writing (October 2010) have not been revived. To the contrary, President Obama's statement of a willingness to engage in his inaugural address was reciprocated by a new round of North Korean missile tests in April 2009, a second nuclear test in May 2009, as well as the sinking of a South Korean naval vessel, the *Cheonan*, in March 2010. In response, the new administration pursued a two-track policy: mobilizing wide-ranging multilateral sanctions against North Korea while at the same time holding out an olive branch of inducements were Pyongyang to return to the talks.

As can be seen from this brief narrative, the five parties[3] have tried a variety of economic incentives – positive and negative – to dissuade North Korea from pursuing a nuclear option. Those in favor of placing constraints on North Korea have proposed options ranging from increased sanctions, to "containment," to efforts to change the regime itself.[4] However, they share the conviction that positive inducements are fraught with moral hazard and the risk of blackmail, encouraging the bad behavior they are designed to forestall.

The alternative narrative on engagement sees it as a strategy that has never consistently been put to the test. We define "engagement" to mean both a willingness to negotiate – literally, to engage – as well as to consider positive inducements, including but not limited to economic ones.[5] Even before suspicions had arisen about North Korea's HEU program, the Bush administration rejected the engagement approach of the late Clinton years and argued for a more muscular response to proliferation, manifest most clearly in the invasion of Iraq (which coincided almost exactly with the onset of the Korean nuclear crisis). The Bush administration eventually shifted to a policy of engagement, but deep divisions within the administration repeatedly undermined its credibility.[6]

---

[3] The participants in the Six-Party Talks include the two Koreas, China, Japan, Russia, and the United States. References to "the five parties" are to the six minus North Korea.

[4] Examples include Bolton (2007), Eberstadt (2004), and N. Eberstadt, "What Went Wrong?" *The Weekly Standard*, January 26, 2009.

[5] For example, non-economic inducements relevant in the Korean context include normalization of diplomatic relations and security guarantees.

[6] See particularly Mazarr (2008).

Two progressive governments in South Korea, under Kim Dae-jung (1998–2004) and Roh Moo-hyun (2004–2009), actively sought to engage North Korea and the Chinese have effectively committed to a strategy of deep engagement as well. These efforts appear to have yielded few concrete benefits, either due to North Korean fecklessness or American reticence to engage. The more hawkish posture of the conservative Lee Myung-bak administration in South Korea has even less to show than its predecessors.

As these conflicting narratives suggest, North Korea has not only been impervious to nonproliferation efforts but to analytic consensus as well. It cannot simultaneously be true that strategies of engagement are doomed to failure and that they could generate (or could have generated) denuclearization. As we will see, a central – and perhaps insurmountable – methodological problem is that the behavior predicted by the two implicit models is often observationally equivalent; the response to an engagement strategy that is not credible is indistinguishable from the behavior of an opportunist forever seeking more concessions.

Nonetheless, we seek to untangle these contradictory assessments by considering three strands of evidence. In the first two sections, we discuss two key structural constraints that operate on both sanctions and engagement approaches toward North Korea. The first is the unusually closed and repressive nature of the regime and its base of political support in the party, security apparatus, and military. Although the regime did witness a reformist moment during which economic inducements might have held out somewhat greater promise, the regime "hardened" after the onset of the crisis and particularly since 2005.

The second structural constraint on the use of both positive inducements and sanctions is the profound coordination problem among the five parties, and among the United States, South Korea, and China in particular. These coordination problems are not only a matter of conflicting policy signals; they have influenced North Korea's external economic relations as well. A fundamental consequence of the second nuclear crisis has been North Korea's growing integration with China.

In the third section, we provide an analytic narrative of the Six-Party Talks through their collapse in 2008, considering the evidence for the effects of inducements and constraints on progress in the talks. Sanctions generally induced defiance and escalation rather than cooperation, although one highly-targeted set of financial sanctions did appear to push the North Koreans back to the bargaining table.[7] To the

[7] See Nincic, Chapter 4, this volume.

extent that these sanctions "worked," they did so in conjunction with a resumption of negotiations and the offer of inducements.

However, the limited success of sanctions does not imply that positive inducements were successful. Coordination problems also plagued efforts to extend inducements, along with profound credibility and sequencing problems. When inducements are extended in advance of compliance, they generate moral hazard problems: the risk that North Korea would simply pocket benefits and not reciprocate. This criticism was raised repeatedly against both South Korea and China, both of which have had periods of relatively unconditional engagement. Yet when inducements are offered only after compliance is complete – and particularly if such compliance involves irreversible actions, such as dismantling a nuclear facility – a corresponding set of credibility problems emerge. Will the United States and other actors deliver on promises made, particularly when we take into account the political constraints on providing incentives to North Korea? These twin problems help account for the start-stop pattern of negotiations and their propensity to break down altogether.

Domestic politics in North Korea: the paradigmatic hard case

It has long been recognized that the effectiveness of sanctions efforts will depend on the political economy of the target state; in recent years several efforts have been made to extend these observations to the analysis of inducements as well.[8] Both regime type and the composition of political support coalitions are relevant factors in this regard and, on both counts, North Korea provides a particularly difficult target for economic diplomacy.

The effectiveness of economic inducements, both negative and positive, will depend in the first instance on regime type. If leaders do not face significant domestic audience costs, sanctions will only bite if sharply targeted either on the political elite itself or on politically-significant constituencies.[9] The same is true of positive inducements. Leaders of authoritarian regimes are likely to be responsive to inducements over which they exercise control, or from which they profit immediately.[10]

---

[8] See particularly Drezner (1999/2000), Brooks (2002), Kahler and Kastner (2006), and Solingen (1994a, 2007a, and this volume).

[9] Brooks (2002).

[10] This is the central reason why Milner and Kubota (2005) argue that democracies have more open trade regimes than autocracies.

Second, the responsiveness of governments to external incentives also stems from the composition of political coalitions.[11] Authoritarian regimes based on inward-looking coalitions are likely to be relatively indifferent to both sanctions and certain types of inducements. The mechanism through which such inducements work is the benefits they provide or costs they impose on firms and individuals in the foreign sector, i.e., those engaged in – or who could benefit from – foreign trade, investment, or aid. But in regimes rooted in inward-oriented political coalitions these processes are unlikely to operate. Increased economic openness may even pose risks, for example by threatening existing rents or through increased information flows.

Turning to the evidence on these two lines of argument, we should first restate the obvious: the North Korean regime is unusually repressive by any standard and its capacity to impose costs on its population is extraordinary.[12] This can be seen most clearly in the economic collapse and famine of the mid 1990s when a famine rooted in the economic policies of the regime killed between 600,000 and one million people, or roughly 3 to 5 percent of the pre-crisis population.[13]

How the regime managed to survive this shock is an intriguing tale in its own right, but one reason is that Kim Jong-il had established personal control of the state apparatus and an effective base of support in the party, military, and security apparatus prior to his father's death in 1994.[14] Following the succession, Kim Jong-il openly turned to the military for support and even went so far as to initiate an ideological innovation in the so-called "military first politics" or "*songun*."[15]

At first blush, these political developments would appear to signal a virtual textbook example of Solingen's inward-looking coalition: a rigidly state-socialist economy coupled with a highly personalist leadership relying on the party, military, and security apparatus. However, a period of political consolidation and crisis management in the immediate aftermath of Kim Il-sung's death (1994–1997) was followed by a brief period of economic reform (1998–2002) following the end of the famine before the regime reversed course in an anti-reformist direction in the mid 2000s.

---

[11] Solingen (2007a).
[12] The most comprehensive treatment of the repressive apparatus can be found in the Korean Institute for National Unification (KINU) *White Papers on Human Rights in North Korea*.
[13] Goodkind and West (2001), Lee (2003), and Haggard and Noland (2007).
[14] Lim (2009) and Haggard and Pinkston (2010).
[15] See Koh (2005) for an excellent summary.

The formal inauguration of the new political order came in September 1998 with the unveiling of a constitutional revision that further strengthened the power of the National Defense Commission and its chairman. However the new constitution also included economic changes, suggesting that the leadership was simultaneously assuring the military and setting the stage for cautious reforms.[16] In June 2002, the regime launched a set of policy changes that may have been intended to constitute part of a fundamental shift in grand strategy (Noland 2004).

Yet the timing and implementation of the program proved highly inauspicious. Within months of the launching of the 2002 reforms, the second nuclear crisis had broken. The October revelation of an HEU program, and the revelation that North Korea had indeed abducted Japanese citizens, made this gambit diplomatically unsustainable. As a result, the regime was left with the problematic legacy of the partial economic reforms of July 2002, but without the expected complementary political and economic payoffs.

What followed was "reform in reverse." An early indication of this new direction was the decision in August 2005 to reinstate the public distribution system (PDS) and to ban private trading in grain. The post-reform effort to reassert state control was not limited to the food economy, but included a wider assault on market activity and the cross-border trade. By 2008–2009, the reactionary tenor of government policy was vividly represented by a revival of the 1950s Stalinist "Chollima" movement of Stakhanovite exhortation and the initiation of "speed-battle" mobilization campaigns. The culmination of the anti-reform drive came on November 30, 2009, with the introduction of a surprise confiscatory currency reform aimed at crushing market activity and reviving orthodox socialism.[17]

This brief overview of domestic economic and political developments is designed to make several simple points. First, the capacity of the regime to absorb the adverse effects of sanctions is extraordinarily high. A regime capable of surviving a famine that killed up to a million people is not likely to be swayed by sanctions threatening marginal changes in trade and investment flows. Sanctions would have to be extraordinarily focused and "smart" to have effect and for reasons we explore in the next section such actions are difficult – although not impossible – to achieve.

---

[16] Reforms were signaled in part through constitutional provisions that granted greater scope for private activity (Article 24), for incentives within the state sector (Article 33) and for foreign trade and investment (Article 36 and 37).

[17] Haggard and Noland (2010a).

Second, the particular coalitional base of the regime also made it relatively indifferent to economic inducements, both positive and negative.
Political and policy developments in the immediate post-1998 period
suggest a brief effort to combine "military first" politics with a mild
reformism, culminating in the partial reforms of 2002. But the opening
provided by these events was completely missed by the Bush administration, and with the onset of the crisis the cost-benefit calculus with
respect to the pursuit of nuclear weapons shifted and it became harder
to secure cooperation using either inducements or constraints.

The coordination problem: North Korea's foreign economic relations

As has long been noted in the sanctions literature, the effectiveness of
sanctions is contingent on cooperation among the target state's trading
partners.[18] Throughout the course of the crisis, those parties seeking to
pressure North Korea, particularly the United States, found themselves
in conflict with those who were willing to engage with it, most importantly China and South Korea.

We also find evidence of coordination problems in a more dynamic
sense as well. Over time, North Korea has gravitated toward those trading partners that place the least restrictions on trade and investment,
making it increasingly difficult to coordinate effective sanctions.

However, the fact that South Korea and China were willing to engage
with North Korea did not necessarily mean that such engagement
achieved nonproliferation objectives. The coordination dilemma operated with respect to strategies of engagement as well. Pyongyang consistently reiterated its position that the nuclear question could only be
addressed through negotiations between North Korea and the United
States, even if conducted under the auspices of the Six-Party Talks. In
the absence of a forthcoming posture from the United States, the engagement strategies of South Korea and China proved ineffective as well.

North Korea's changing foreign economic relations

North Korea does not provide data on its own trade, meaning it must be
constructed from trading partners. This data is vulnerable to significant
discrepancies,[19] but with the appropriate caveats in mind, we present

---

[18] For example, Hufbauer *et al.* (2009).
[19] For a more detailed discussion of the technical issues involved in constructing mirror
statistics, see Haggard and Noland (2008).

(% of DPRK total trade or imports)

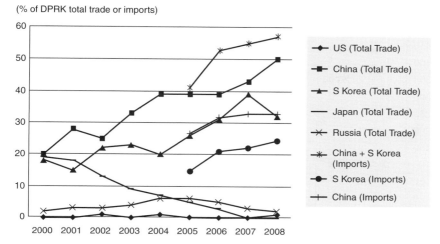

Figure 8.1 Shares of DPRK's total trade (KOTRA) and imports
Source: KOTRA (Korea Trade-Investment Promotion Agency,
available at: www.kotra.go.kr)

several estimates of the direction of North Korea's trade with select
partners. Figure 8.1 is taken directly from the Korea Trade-Investment
Promotion Agency (KOTRA) and shows North Korea's total trade with
the five interlocutors in the Six-Party Talks – the United States, China,
Japan, South Korea, and Russia – for 2000 through 2008 (Figure 8.1,
"total trade"). KOTRA has a reasonable track record in eliminating
obvious discrepancies and this data has the advantage of constituting a
consistent series for the entire period of the crisis from a single source.
However, compared to data produced by the United Nations and the
International Monetary Fund, the KOTRA data significantly under-
estimates the growth of North Korea's trade with many countries. We
therefore provide an alternative estimate of North Korean imports
from China and South Korea for the period 2004–2007 (Figure 8.1,
"imports").[20] The KOTRA estimates might be viewed as at the high-
end of the likely range for these two important trading partners, with
our estimates more likely to represent the lower bound.

The first point to note is that China and South Korea alone probably
account for between 55 and 80 percent of North Korea's trade. Second,
whatever the *level* of trade with China and South Korea, their *share* has
clearly increased since the onset of the crisis.

[20] See Haggard and Noland (2010b).

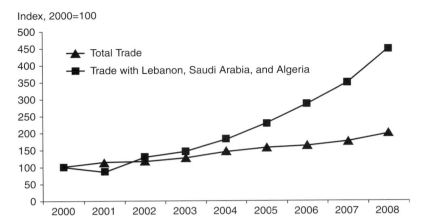

Figure 8.2 North Korean trade with the world vs. the Middle East, 2000–2008
Sources: KOTRA (Korea Trade-Investment Promotion Agency), IMF DOT (Direction of Trade Statistics)

The third point is that despite the high partner concentration of North Korea's trade, its vulnerability to sanctions has not necessarily increased, and for two reasons. First, those countries more inclined to sanction North Korea – the United States and Japan – now have negligible economic exchange with the country. Second, the countries toward which North Korea's trade has shifted – most notably China – have proven unwilling to use their leverage for nonproliferation ends.

This coordination problem becomes even more apparent if we consider possible measurement problems with the KOTRA data. In recent years, developing countries such as Brazil, Thailand, and India have increased their trade with North Korea; in 2007, according to the UN/IMF data these three countries accounted for more than 10 percent of both North Korean imports and exports. Even more revealing are developments with the Middle East. In Figure 8.2, we aggregate trade with three countries – Algeria, Saudi Arabia, and Lebanon – that report non-negligible trade with North Korea on a consistent basis, construct an index of their trade growth, and compare it to the growth of total trade. The index almost certainly understates the true growth of trade between North Korea and the region (given under-reporting and illicit trade) and does not capture foreign direct investment (particularly from the Egyptian conglomerate

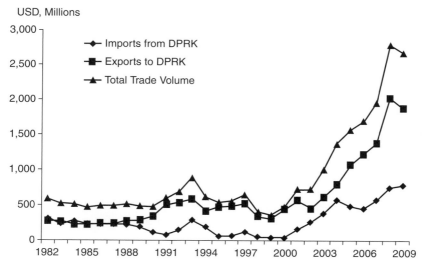

Figure 8.3 China–North Korea trade, 1982–2009

Orascom).[21] Nonetheless, the index shows a dramatic increase in relations with these three countries when compared with the growth of overall trade.

The China trade

A closer look at the China–DPRK and North–South trade provides further insights into the political dynamics of these two critical bilateral relationships. Figure 8.3 provides a long-run overview of the trade relationship with China from 1982 through 2009.

The observed growth in bilateral trade and investment in the period since the onset of the second nuclear crisis casts doubt on the likely effectiveness of multilateral sanctions. These doubts can be tested more precisely by examining the effects of the two major multilateral sanctions efforts on China–DPRK trade: those imposed in the wake of the 2006 nuclear test (UNSCR 1718) and the 2009 nuclear test (UNSCR 1874).[22] These sanctions did not directly impinge on purely commercial

---

[21] Noland (2009a).

[22] In addition, UNSC 1695 prohibits North Korea's export or import of missiles and missile-related technology and also bans any financial transactions associated with its nuclear or missile programs.

trade, in part because of Chinese reluctance to support more wide-ranging sanctions. UNSCR 1718 imposed an embargo on exports of heavy weapons, dual-use items, and luxury goods to North Korea, as well as a ban on the importation of heavy weapons systems from North Korea. UNSCR 1874, passed in the aftermath of the May 2009 test, marginally extended sanctions to include all arms-related trade as well as all training or assistance related to it (such as suspected cooperation with both Syria and Iran).

But the two resolutions, and particularly 1874, contain a number of provisions that might disrupt North Korea's broader commercial relations, including an injunction against non-humanitarian aid and a call for member states to inspect all cargo on their territory believed to contain prohibited items. UNSCR 1874 also authorizes members to inspect vessels on the high seas or to escort them to port if there are reasonable grounds to believe that they are carrying prohibited cargo, but does not authorize the use of force.[23]

Moreover, we might expect sanctions to have effects beyond trade in proscribed products: the increase in political tensions might drive up the risk premium on all trade and financial transactions with North Korea and thus discourage them at the margin.

In recent years, China has not reported the export of heavy arms to North Korea, but luxury goods are a different story. China did not publish a detailed list of sanctioned luxury goods, but a number of other countries did, and these lists exhibit considerable consistency across countries.[24] In the absence of a Chinese list of sanctioned luxury goods, Figure 8.4 reports Chinese exports of luxury goods to North Korea defined in three ways. The first variant ("Australian list – SITC") takes the Australian sanctions list and maps the verbal description of the sanctioned luxury products to Standard International Trade Classification (SITC) categories. The second variant ("Japanese list") is based on KOTRA (2006), which attempted to map the Japanese sanctions list to detailed product categories using the Harmonized System (HS). The third variant ("Australian list – HS") reconstructs the Australian list using KOTRA's HS codes, which tend to be more narrowly drawn than the SITC-defined list. Chinese exports of luxury goods to North Korea did not fall to zero in 2007 under any variant; indeed, luxury goods exports increased between 2006 and 2007 under all three definitions (Figure 8.4). Resolution 1718 appears to have had no impact on Chinese behavior.

---

[23] Haggard and Noland (2010b).
[24] Noland (2009b).

USD, Millions

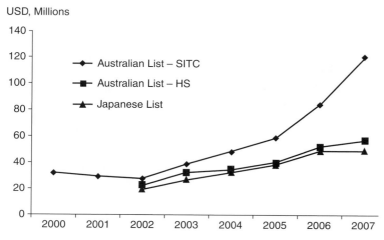

Figure 8.4 Chinese luxury goods export to DPRK

To test for these broader effects of the two nuclear tests and sanctions episodes, we estimated some simple econometric models of Chinese exports to North Korea, using quarterly data from 3Q 2001 through 2Q 2010.[25] The models include a time trend, seasonal dummies, an indicator of aggregate demand in North Korea (real GDP, which when included eliminated the significance of the time trend) and the inverse of the black market exchange rate (to capture the North Korean price level). The effects of the tests and sanctions were captured with dummies for all post-test-and-sanctions quarters (i.e., a dummy from 4Q 2006 and a second from 3Q 2009).[26]

The results of the models are striking, and confirm what one would already suspect from a visual inspection of the trade data in Figure 8.3. In the model of total Chinese exports, the coefficients on the two sanctions dummies are actually positive and significant. Far from total Chinese exports to the DPRK falling in the aftermath of the two tests, relative to the underlying economic fundamentals they actually *increased*.

North–South trade

The pattern of North–South trade since its modest beginnings in the late 1980s is similar in some respects to China–DPRK trade, with a

[25] See Haggard and Noland (2011) which updates Noland (2009b).
[26] The coefficient on the 2009 sanctions dummy can be interpreted as the effect of the second test and sanctions conditional on the existence of the first.

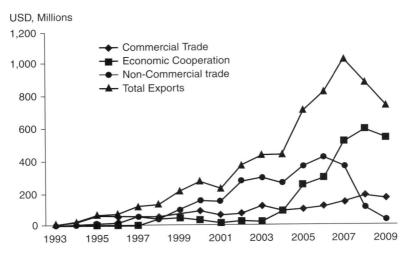

Figure 8.5 ROK exports to DPRK by type, 1993–2009
Source: Ministry of Unification, Republic of Korea (available at:
www.unikorea.go.kr)

relatively modest and constant level of trade through 1998, followed by
steady growth through the Kim Dae-jung administration and a more
dramatic upward inflection under Roh Moo-hyun. Figure 8.5 traces
these developments through the lens of South Korean exports to the
North. We divide these exports into three categories: aid, commercial
trade, and cooperation projects (primarily the Mt. Kumgang tourist
project and the Kaesong industrial park, which involved private companies but public subsidies as well).[27] Between 1995 and 2009 South
Korea's aid – primarily food and fertilizer – and economic cooperation
activities have at times accounted for almost 60 percent of total exports
and have averaged more than 40 percent of trade over the period.

Aid was an important component of Kim Dae-jung's Sunshine Policy
but became even more firmly institutionalized under Roh Moo-hyun

---

[27] Haggard and Noland (2009b). The three categories are constructed from data provided by the Ministry of Unification as follows. "Aid" is the sum of government and
civilian aid, support for the construction of the light-water reactors and fuel-oil shipments promised under the 1994 Agreed Framework, and energy assistance provided
as an inducement for agreements struck through the Six-Party Talks in 2007–2008.
"Commercial trade" is the sum of general and processing on commission trade.
"Cooperation projects" include trade in conjunction with the Kaesong industrial
park, the Kumgang tourist project, and other cooperation projects the government
has periodically launched.

when the Mt. Kumgang and Kaesong Industrial Complex came on line. Both the Kim Dae-jung and Roh Moo-hyun administrations argued that economic engagement through such projects might moderate North Korean behavior and provide a means to leverage reform in North Korea. Yet following the 2006 missile and nuclear tests, the Roh administration refused to use the projects diplomatically, and despite its more confrontational policy approach, the Lee Myung-bak administration was similarly reticent to close down Kaesong. (The Mt. Kumgang project was suspended following the killing of a South Korean tourist by a North Korean guard in July 2008.)

The coordination problems arising from the divergent strategies of Washington and Seoul are readily apparent. While the Bush administration periodically attempted to corral support for a more confrontational posture toward the North, both the Kim Dae-jung and Roh Moo-hyun South administrations remained committed to a relatively unconditional form of engagement.

The election of December 2007 fundamentally changed the nature of North–South economic relations. The Lee Myung-bak administration moved toward a more conditional concept of engagement in which expanded trade, investment, and even humanitarian assistance would follow rather than anticipate progress on the nuclear question. As Figure 8.5 suggests, these were not empty threats. From the outset of his administration, humanitarian assistance was virtually eliminated. Following the sinking of the *Cheonan* in March 2010, commercial trade outside of the Kaesong Industrial Complex was sanctioned as well. Nonetheless, for much of the second nuclear crisis, US and South Korean policies toward North Korea were pulling in diametrically opposed directions.

The Six-Party Talks: the role of inducements and constraints

In this final section, we move from broad structural constraints on economic diplomacy vis-à-vis North Korea to an overview of the role economic inducements and sanctions played in the Six-Party Talks from their inception in 2003 through their collapse in 2008, the last year of the Bush administration; in the conclusion we consider developments in the early Obama administration.[28] The narrative follows an extensive body of analysis on North Korea by Sigal (1998, 2002,

---

[28] On the Six-Party Talks see particularly Sigal (2005), Funabashi (2007), Pritchard (2007), Mazarr (2007), and Chinoy (2008).

2005, 2009, 2010) as well comparative contributions by Nincic (2005, Chapter 4, this volume) that consider whether inducements and constraints induce cooperative or uncooperative, escalatory responses. Do such policy measures "work"?

In addition, we consider two additional questions that are of theoretical interest. First, an ongoing debate in the negotiations has been whether inducements or cooperative actions would be extended in advance of, simultaneously with, or only after the other party had fulfilled stipulated obligations. Given the belief on both sides that important commitments had not been met in the past,[29] the offer of inducements was less likely to be credible if promised only after the completion of the corresponding obligation. As the North Koreans insisted throughout the negotiations, they should proceed on the basis of "words for words (or 'commitments for commitments'), actions for actions." However, North Korean proposals did not necessarily conform to this injunction. Inducements were periodically demanded simply to talk, in exchange for declaratory statements of intent, or to take actions that were easily reversible, most notably a "freeze" of existing activities.

These credibility problems were related to the nature of the inducements (and obligations) on offer; their specificity and the time frame over which they could be implemented. At the most discrete and tangible end of the spectrum were outright transfers such as the delivery of fuel oil, electricity, food, or even cash, as occurred in the context of the 2000 North–South summit. These measures provided tangible benefits and were easily monitored. Complex projects such as the construction of light-water reactors involve a much more protracted time frame, as the Agreed Framework's KEDO process demonstrated to both sides. The lifting of sanctions, or promises to lift them, have more ambiguous and less tangible effects. The effects of lifting sanctions will depend on subsequent policy developments in North Korea and on the reaction of private actors, who might still be deterred from trade and investment as a result of the controlled and corrupt policy environment in North Korea or general political uncertainty surrounding the country. Similarly, admission into the international financial institutions does not necessarily ensure lending because of the conditional nature of IFI programs. The problem with these longer-run inducements is even

---

[29] Following the onset of the crisis, the United States clearly had reason to doubt North Korean commitments under the Agreed Framework. But the Agreed Framework also called for a process of normalization of relations with the United States that made limited progress during the Clinton administration.

more pronounced if we believe that important actors in North Korea are simply seeking delay or are indifferent or even hostile to them in the first place.

A second question has to do with the nature and effectiveness of sanctions. We have already noted the coordination problem in orchestrating wide-ranging commercial sanctions, and the political imperviousness of the regime even were they to be successfully coordinated. However, sanctions on weapons sales affect particular firms and no doubt the foreign exchange earning capacity of the regime, and might strike closer to home. Certain targeted financial sanctions appear to have had surprisingly wide-ranging effects on both commercial trade and foreign accounts of direct interest to the leadership. However, as we will show these *material* effects did not necessarily translate into the desired *political* consequences.[30]

Prior to the crisis: January 2001 to October 2002

The deep divisions that existed within the first Bush administration with respect to North Korea policy have now been thoroughly documented.[31] On the one hand, the incoming administration showed a willingness to abide by formal commitments. Inducements under the Agreed Framework – fuel oil shipments to North Korea and efforts through KEDO to complete the long-delayed construction of the promised light-water reactors – continued despite efforts from within the administration to kill them, as did the provision of food aid.[32] Secretary of State Colin Powell favored a continuation of the talks initiated by the Clinton administration, and following the completion of a policy review in June 2001 appeared to gain the authority to proceed.

However, hawks within the administration bitterly opposed the Agreed Framework or any negotiations with Pyongyang. The president himself sent mixed signals with respect to engagement, most notably in his repudiation of Powell's stated intention to pursue the Clinton negotiations on missiles, in the open clash with President Kim Dae-jung during his state visit in March 2001 and in the infamous "Axis of Evil" comment in the 2002 State of the Union address.

Moreover, both the substantive agenda and the modality of engagement marked a sharp departure from the Clinton era. The difference in approach is outlined clearly in a speech by Colin Powell before the Asia

[30] Nincic (2005, Chapter 4, this volume).
[31] Mazarr (2007), Pritchard (2007), and Chinoy (2008).
[32] Chinoy (2008: 75–77).

Society in June 2002.[33] Although nominally endorsing engagement, the speech made progress in bilateral relations conditional on a number of prior actions by the North Koreans: on humanitarian issues, conventional force deployments, missiles, and obligations under both the Agreed Framework and the NPT. The earlier policy review had also put human rights on the agenda. Internal discussions did consider possible benefit, but these were publicly outlined only in the most vague terms ("the United States is prepared to take important steps to help North Korea move its relations with the US toward normalcy"), and would in any case come only after satisfactory steps were taken on the US agenda.[34]

In addition to the mixed signals with respect to North Korea policy itself, 9/11 had resulted in a much more aggressive posture toward proliferators, including the assertion of a right of pre-emption. When coupled with the administration's pointed unwillingness to reiterate the Clinton administration's statement of peaceful intent and public speeches by members of the administration outlining perceived North Korean derogations, it was certainly plausible for Pyongyang – and the North Korean military – to draw the conclusion that the United States had hostile intent that required deterrence.[35] The invasion of Iraq, which occurred precisely as the crisis was breaking, no doubt deepened these concerns.

From the onset of the crisis to the Six-Party Talks: October 2002 to August 2003

Did the Bush administration's hardened stance have effect? Although the North Koreans responded negatively to the substance of the policy review, they also signaled a willingness to negotiate.[36] These overtures were ignored. It was not until the ASEAN Regional Forum meeting in July 2002 – a year and half into office – that Secretary Powell communicated US willingness to send an envoy to Pyongyang. Tightly instructed,

---

[33] "Remarks at Asia Society Annual Dinner," June 10, 2002, available at: www.asiasociety.org/policy-politics/colin-powell-remarks-asia-society-annual-dinner-2002.

[34] Sigal (2005).

[35] Particularly John Bolton, then Undersecretary of State for Arms Control and International Security, "Beyond the Axis of Evil: Additional Threats from Weapons of Mass Destruction," The Heritage Foundation, May 6, 2001, available at: www.heritage.org/Research/Lecture/Beyond-the-Axis-of-Evil, and "North Korea: A Shared Challenge to the US and ROK," Korean-American Association, Seoul, August 29, 2002.

[36] "KCNA on US-Proposed Resumption of DPRK-US Negotiations," *Korean Central News Agency*, June 28, 2001, available at: www.kcna.co.jp/index-e.htm.

Assistant Secretary of State James Kelly's October visit focused largely on the HEU intelligence and proved highly acrimonious.

In the aftermath of the visit, the administration exerted strong pressure on both Japan and Korea to sign on to a KEDO resolution condemning the HEU program as a violation of the Agreed Framework and cutting off fuel oil shipments. The North Korean response was generally escalatory rather than compromising. In October, North Korea proposed the negotiation of an agreement that would resolve all outstanding nuclear issues in return for three concessions: respect for North Korean sovereignty; a binding US commitment to non-aggression; and that the United States not "hamper" the country's economic development, presumably a reference to the lifting of sanctions. Interestingly, this proposal made explicit reference to the economic reforms of 2002 as a sign of the regime's good intentions.[37] This proposal was revived by the North Koreans following the cutoff of oil shipments in November.

When the United States failed to respond, Pyongyang quickly escalated. In December 2002, Pyongyang asked the International Atomic Energy Agency (IAEA) to unseal the Yongbyon facilities, and when the agency asked the government to reconsider, the inspectors were ejected. North Korea formally renounced its obligations under the Non-Proliferation Treaty on January 10, 2003. Shortly thereafter, the regime resumed reprocessing from spent nuclear fuel rods and took steps to generate new fissile material by refueling and restarting the reactor.

The United States subsequently undertook a variety of other actions designed to pressure the North Koreans to reconsider, including the mobilization of military assets in the region. In addition, the administration launched the Proliferation Security Initiative (May 31, 2003), a multilateral effort to cooperate around the interdiction of trade in WMD-related materials. It also strengthened inter-agency efforts to deter and stop North Korean engagement in illicit activities, including counterfeiting, drug trade, and the financial transactions and money laundering associated with the country's weapons trade.[38] At least in the short run, these measures had little effect in moving North Korea toward negotiations.

The Six-Party Talks had their origin in a trilateral meeting hosted by Beijing in April 2003 that provided the administration a way out of the

---

[37] See the Foreign Ministry statement at "Conclusion of Non-Aggression Treaty between DPRK and US called for," KCNA, October 25, 2002, available at: www. kcna.co.jp/index-e.htm. Januzzi (2003) reports a North Korean version of the Kelly visit, and Pyongyang's expectation of an offer to negotiate.

[38] Asher (2007).

impasse created by its unwillingness to hold bilateral talks with North Korea. The expansion to six parties appeared to serve American interests by providing a venue through which the five parties could coordinate – and pressure – the North to abandon its weapons program.

However, as we have already seen, China and the new South Korean government of Roh Moo-hyun had doubts about the utility of pressure and were wedded to a wide-ranging engagement approach. Russia had doubts about the utility of pressure as well.[39] Rather than marshaling collective pressure on North Korea, the lack of progress in the Six-Party Talks gradually forced the Bush administration to consider the inducements it would be willing to offer for a settlement.

The first three rounds of the Six-Party Talks: August 2003 to January 2005

The United States came into the first round of the Six-Party Talks (August 27–29, 2003) with a clear set of demands. These became embodied in the acronym CVID; that the United States was seeking a *complete* (meaning plutonium and HEU), *verifiable* (meaning a return to the NPT and IAEA inspections if not more), *irreversible dismantlement* of all facilities at Yongbyon (in distinction to the Agreed Framework, which had frozen North Korea's nuclear program but left it intact). Although inducements for compliance were not made explicit, the sequencing of them was clear: any concessions from the United States would come only after these actions had been completed.

Pyongyang was willing to negotiate to get to CVID but had a very clear view about the sequencing of inducements and reciprocal actions.[40] As a first step, the North Koreans would declare their intention to abandon their nuclear program in return for Washington's resumption of fuel oil supply and expanded humanitarian food aid. In the second phase, North Korea would freeze its nuclear activities – but not dismantle them – and allow inspections if the United States signed a legally binding non-aggression treaty and compensated the North for lost energy supplies. In the third step, Pyongyang would accommodate US concerns about missiles in return for establishing diplomatic relations. Finally, at the point of completion of the two light-water reactors promised under the Agreed Framework, the North Koreans would verifiably dismantle the Yongbyon facilities. As with US proposals, the

[39] Funabashi (2007: 166–196).
[40] Ser Myo-ja, "North Korea Details Its Plan to End Crisis," *Joongang Daily*, August 28, 2003, available at: www.joongangdaily.joins.com/article/view.asp?aid=2025739.

North Korean approach front-loaded inducements, limited its commitments largely to declaratory policy while delaying irreversible actions until the distant future.

The first talks ended with so little progress that the Chinese had to extend bilateral inducements of their own to get the North Koreans to even return to the next round.[41] This became a pattern, as China, South Korea, and even Japan extended various inducements to North Korea, both to improve the prospects of the talks and for diplomatic objectives altogether independent of the Six-Party process.

Not until the third round of talks (June 23–26, 2004) did the United States place an offer on the table, and it constituted a virtual mirror image of the North Korean approach. North Korean commitments were heavily front-loaded, while American inducements would not be forthcoming until progress was made on a wide agenda of bilateral issues. In return for a North Korean statement of its willingness to dismantle all nuclear programs, South Korea and Japan would resume shipments of heavy fuel oil in line with the Agreed Framework commitments. The North would institute a freeze on all nuclear activities and provide the five parties with a detailed plan for disabling, dismantling, and eliminating all of its nuclear activities, including its HEU program, existing stocks of fissile material, weapons, and components; all of this work would take place under the auspices of international inspections. Once the plan was agreed to, the United States and others would provide security assurances, but other economic inducements such as meeting longer-run energy needs or removing sanctions would be phased and subject to further negotiation. The path to normalization was more distant still and would require progress on the widened agenda of the June 2001 policy review and "bold approach." The North Koreans stalled, and the fourth round of talks scheduled to take place prior to September 2004 failed to materialize.

Bush's second term I: through the "roadmap" agreements of 2007

The September 2005 statement of principles, the outcome of the prolonged fourth round of Six-Party Talks,[42] constituted a breakthrough and remains the touchstone document of the Six-Party Talks process. Both supporters and critics of the new course concur that the agreement followed changes in the US approach, although both China and

---

[41] Funabashi (2007: 320–321).
[42] The fourth round of talks consisted of two phases, July 26 to August 7 and September 13–19, 2005.

South Korea provided incentives as well. The second Bush administration ushered in a new foreign team that was more willing to engage
North Korea, including Secretary of State Condoleeza Rice herself.
Chief US negotiator Christopher Hill was granted greater latitude to
pursue specific quid pro quos.

The statement of principles lays out the broad bargain that had been
implicit in earlier rounds of negotiations. The statement is unambiguous that the denuclearization of the peninsula is a shared goal and that
North Korea is committed to "abandoning" its nuclear program, rejoining the NPT, and readmitting IAEA inspectors. In return, the United
States affirmed that it had no intention of attacking or invading North
Korea. Both the United States and Japan committed to "take steps" to
normalize relations. The statement makes reference both to the negotiation of a peace regime on the Korean peninsula and the exploration of
wider multilateral cooperation.

The document also outlines the inducements on offer. First, the five
parties would provide energy assistance, and South Korea reaffirmed
its commitment to a very specific proposal made in July 2005 providing
two million kilowatts of electric power to the DPRK. The document
also contained a euphemistic reference to the lifting of sanctions and the
provision of other economic assistance ("the Six Parties undertook to
promote economic cooperation in the fields of energy, trade and investment, bilaterally and/or multilaterally"). Light-water reactors entered
late in the negotiations, and threatened to derail them.[43] The statement
finessed the issue by affirming North Korea's right to a civilian nuclear
program, but the provision of such reactors by the five parties would
only be discussed "at an appropriate time."

However, the document also states quite explicitly that the proposed
measures would be implemented in a phased fashion, "in line with the
principle of 'commitment for commitment, action for action.'" Indeed,
it is not even clear that the statement of principles could be considered
an example of an "inducement," except in a declaratory or intentional
sense.

Despite the common perception of a dramatic shift in course by
the United States, the administration had by no means freed itself of
the internal divisions of the first term. These constraints were visible
almost immediately following the September statement of principles.
First, hawks within the administration crafted a statement that parsed
the agreement in a highly restrictive way, appearing to require full compliance with NPT obligations prior to the provision of any meaningful

[43] Funabashi (2007: 398–402).

inducements.[44] Discussion about LWRs would only occur after these actions had been taken, and normalization of relations remained contingent on discussion of the full range of issues vetted in the 2001 policy review and "bold approach." It took less than forty-eight hours for the North Korean foreign ministry to issue a statement explicitly rejecting the American interpretation of the agreement, and threatening that the United States "should not even dream of the issue of the DPRK's dismantlement of its nuclear deterrent before providing LWRs, a physical guarantee for confidence-building."[45]

A second major development that complicated negotiations was the gradual refinement of the Illicit Activities Initiative into a host of new financial restrictions on North Korea. The most significant of these new measures was the Treasury Department's naming of Banco Delta Asia as a "primary money laundering concern" on September 15, 2005, at almost the exact moment that the fourth round of the Six-Party Talks were reaching a conclusion. By April 2006 at least two dozen financial institutions had restricted or ended their financial dealings with North Korea, including banks in China and Vietnam. Despite very limited trade, investment, or financial relations with North Korea, the US Treasury had stumbled on a means for squeezing North Korea. Correspondent banking relations with American financial institutions are a *sine qua non* for virtually any foreign bank. These correspondent relations could be leveraged to limit North Korea's ability to conduct virtually any foreign transaction, from letters of credit to offshore deposits.

There is ample evidence that the BDA sanctions were viewed as a critical issue by the North Koreans, either for their direct effect on elite assets or – more probably given the small amount of money at stake, a mere $25 million – because of their wider consequences for North Korea's foreign economic relations. In April 2006, the North Koreans publicly tied a resumption of the talks to a resolution of the BDA issue.[46] Bilateral talks focused solely on, or including discussion of BDA were held in March and December 2006 and in January 2007, when a final deal was struck on the BDA funds.[47]

Constructing a balance sheet of the effects of a single policy measure like BDA is not straightforward. On the one hand, the keen interest of

[44] See "Statement of Assistant Secretary of State Christopher R. Hill at the Closing Plenary of the Fourth Round of the Six-Party Talks," September 19, 2005.
[45] "Spokesman for DPRK Foreign Ministry on Six-Party Talks," September 20, 2005, *Korean Central News Agency*, available at: www.kcna.co.jp/index-e.htm.
[46] "North Korean Offers Nuclear Talks Deal," *BBC News*, April 13, 2006, available at: www.news.bbc.co.uk/2/hi/asia-pacific/4905308.stm.
[47] National Committee on North Korea (2007).

the North Koreans in resolving the issue, and the speed with which the Six-Party Talks were able to resume and reach the first agreement on implementation of the joint statement following the October 2006 nuclear test, suggests a close link between BDA and North Korean behavior. On the other hand, the BDA measures were not adequate to deter North Korea from continuing to produce fissile material and undertaking the missile and nuclear tests of June and October 2006, even at the cost of a strongly-worded Security Council resolution on its missile program (UNSC 1695) and the first set of multilateral sanctions following the nuclear test (UNSC 1718).

Moreover, the sanctions "worked" only by being coupled with an adoption of tightly-phased approach of "actions for actions" in the two "roadmap" agreements of 2007.[48] A freeze on Yongbyon was exchanged for delivery of oil, a commitment to begin the process of removing the designation of the DPRK as a state-sponsor of terrorism and terminating the application of the Trading with the Enemy Act. During the first phase and the next phase, a complete declaration of all nuclear programs and disablement of all existing nuclear facilities would be exchanged for economic, energy, and humanitarian assistance up to the equivalent of one million tons of heavy fuel oil (HFO). The October 2007 agreement reiterated these commitments and set out a more precise timetable and further details on these exchanges.

Did the "actions for actions" approach work? The short answer is "no," but with derogations apparent on both sides. The February agreement to freeze the North's nuclear facilities was implemented roughly on schedule by October 2007, at which point second phase actions were to commence.[49] North Korea began implementing the October 3 Agreement by shutting down the five-megawatt nuclear reactor at Yongbyon. Although it missed the year-end deadline for both disablement – completing eight of eleven steps designed to make it inoperable for at least a year – this deviation was partly technical and not viewed as particularly serious.

The declaration and the linked issue of verification, however, posed stumbling blocks that led to the final collapse of the talks. The October agreement required North Korea to provide a "complete and correct declaration of all its nuclear programs." An early declaration provided in November fell well short of US and other intelligence estimates of the likely stock of fissile material, was lacking in detail, and made no mention of either HEU or proliferation activities. Proliferation concerns had

---

[48] "Initial Actions for the Implementation of the Joint Statement," February 13, 2007 and "Second-Phase Actions for the Implementation of the September 2005 Joint Statement," October 3, 2007.

[49] The following draws on the excellent account of Kim (2009).

become more pressing following the Israeli bombing of a reactor in the Syrian desert in September 2007 that had been constructed with North Korean support. Following three further rounds of negotiations in early 2008, North Korea promised a new declaration of the plutonium-based program and a confidential "acknowledgment" of US concerns about the North's HEU and proliferation activities. A massive compilation of documents was delivered to the United States in May and formally to the Chinese as chair of the Six-Party Talks in June.

Not coincidentally, a major food aid package with the United States was finalized at the same time, suggesting a tacit linkage between much-needed humanitarian assistance and progress on the talks. The United States responded as required by proceeding to lift restrictions applied to North Korea associated with the Trading with the Enemy Act and through President Bush's formal notice to Congress of his intention to remove Pyongyang from the list of state sponsors of terrorism. During the July round of talks, the six parties each agreed to fulfill "in parallel" their agreed commitments with respect to HFO shipments (or equivalents) and complete disablement by the end of October.

The statement of principles of September 2005 made reference to the fact that denuclearization would be "verifiable" and that North Korea would return to the NPT and IAEA inspections. But verification was not technically a component of the first two phases of implementation; in a narrow legal sense, the North Koreans were within their rights to push this issue into the next phase. Following bilateral negotiations on the issue, the parties issued a joint communiqué on July 12 outlining broad principles on the issue, including agreement that the initial inspection mechanism would involve experts from the six parties with the IAEA limited to "consultancy and assistance."

Both domestic political constraints within the United States and increasing disaffection on the part of South Korea and Japan (which had refused to supply fuel oil) – in short both credibility and coordination problems – undermined the tightly-scripted exchange of inducements and North Korean actions. As domestic political pressures mounted both outside and inside the Bush administration about the integrity of the North Korean declaration and the utility of the entire Six-Party process, the administration sought to mollify critics by moving verification efforts into phase two.[50] Following the joint communiqué the United States circulated a very tough draft verification protocol that included full access to all materials and all sites regardless of whether

[50] See Condeleeza Rice's "Remarks at Heritage Foundation on US Policy in Asia," June 18, 2008, available at: www.america.gov/st/texttrans-english/2008/June/2008061914 0227eaifas0.8862574.html.

included in the North's declaration or not, in effect, the equivalent of the IAEA special inspections protocol. Moreover, the United States demanded that IAEA inspectors would ultimately lead the implementation of the protocol, in line with expectations stated in the September 2005 joint statement that North Korea would return "at an early date" to the NPT and to IAEA safeguards. When North Korea rejected these efforts, claiming that full verification would come only at the end of the denuclearization process, the administration chose not to rescind North Korea's designation as a state sponsor of terrorism.

These events occurred exactly at the time that Kim Jong-il was subsequently believed to have suffered a stroke, compounding the difficulty of reaching any agreement. On August 26, a foreign ministry statement announced that North Korea would stop and then reverse the disablement process at Yongbyon.[51] On September 24 it removed IAEA seals and surveillance cameras from its reprocessing facility and restricted international inspectors from its reactor site in a virtual replay of the events of early 2003.

Realizing that the entire Six-Party process was in jeopardy, the administration reversed course, arguing that a verification agreement with North Korea had in fact been reached and that Pyongyang would be taken off the terrorism list. But nearly a month after this last minute concession was granted, North Korea questioned US interpretation of the details of the agreement. Two further rounds of negotiations in December proved unsuccessful. The Six-Party process had once again stalled.

A reprise: inducements and constraints in the Six-Party Talks

Several conclusions emerge from this narrative. First, the United States had limited success in turning the Six-Party Talks into a five-party cartel that would use economic-cum-political pressure to elicit concessions due to coordination problems. Although we are not privy to China's diplomacy with North Korea, Beijing's commitment to engagement with North Korea was a constant. Japan (roughly through the second Koizumi summit in 2004) and South Korea (through the end of the Roh administration in 2007) were also seeking to engage North Korea, even when the talks were not making progress. Ironically, coordination problems with South Korea and Japan resurfaced in 2008 but in reverse, placing constraints on US efforts to negotiate over the course of 2008.

---

[51] "Foreign Ministry's Spokesman on DPRK's Decision to Suspend Activities to Disable Nuclear Facilities," *Korean Central News Agency*, August 26, 2008, available at: www.kcna.co.jp/index-e.htm.

A second conclusion that would seem to follow closely is that the strategy of pressuring North Korea was not only futile but counter-productive.[52] North Korea responded to both military threats and economic pressure by accelerating their pursuit of weapons, most notably in early 2003, in 2006, and again in 2008–2009, leading ultimately to the second round of missile and nuclear tests in the first year of the Obama administration. Although internal political dynamics undoubtedly played a role, it is plausible that the onset of the crisis contributed to a broader shift in North Korean politics away from reform and toward greater military dominance.

However it is important to underscore that the evidence with respect to the utility of inducements is far from clear either. A willingness to offer inducements was crucial to the negotiations leading to the 2005 breakthrough, the resumption of talks in 2006, and the two agreements of 2007. Christopher Hill's strategy in 2008 was clear: focus on the production of plutonium in Yongbyon through an agreement on disabling the facility and finesse the issues of proliferation, HEU, accumulated stocks of fissile material and the weapons themselves until later rounds. Once the North Koreans saw the benefits to be gained from making concessions, they would be willing to deal on these questions as well.

But it is not clear that they were willing to deal on these questions. The deal made with respect to proliferation and HEU could be treated as an acknowledgment that they had engaged in such behavior in the past, but would not do so in the future. But the bitter fight over verification, even though technically not a part of phase two implementation, raised broader questions. At best, the events of 2008 suggest a prolonged round of further negotiations – and side payments – over verification, re-entry into the NPT, the readmission of IAEA inspectors, and the question of existing stocks of fissile material and weapons, during which time North Korea would effectively maintain a nuclear capability. The resistance to verification suggests that the North Koreans sought to maintain at least a minimal nuclear deterrent, and at worst may have been engaged in an elaborate exercise in strategic deception. It is simply impossible based on the evidence to distinguish between these two different interpretations; they are observationally equivalent.

The fundamental problems that we have identified: problems of coordination; a highly resistant target; and difficult sequencing problems – appear to be continuing under the Obama administration. Although it came into office promising to re-engage North Korea, the preparations for a long-range missile test were already visible by the time of

---

[52] Nincic, Chapter 4, this volume.

Secretary Clinton's first public comments on the issue during her trip to Asia in February 2009. Following the April 5 launch, the United Nations Security Council (UNSC) issued a Presidential Statement that strengthened sanctions under the earlier UNSC Resolution 1718 of October 2006. North Korea responded by withdrawing from the Six-Party Talks, resuming the reprocessing of spent fuel rods, and undertaking a second nuclear test on May 25. Following the nuclear test, the United States was able to coordinate passage of UNSCR 1874, imposing a much more robust sanctions regime than visible in UNSCR 1718. North Korea once again escalated by claiming that it would weaponize all recently reprocessed plutonium, commence a uranium enrichment program, and provide a "decisive military response" to any "blockade" against the country. Although the United States was able to coordinate an impressive political signal to North Korea, it remains unclear whether these sanctions have substantially affected trade with China and new trading partners in the Middle East and elsewhere in the developing world. Nonetheless, the recurrence of interdictions of banned materiel suggests that the sanctions are having at least some economic effect.

Translating those economic effects into a political response from North Korea proved an altogether different issue, particularly given the high level of political uncertainty associated with the succession process. Throughout this period, the United States sought to maintain a two-track policy. While orchestrating sanctions, the Obama administration also sought to hold out the promise of a package of incentives if North Korea came back to the negotiating table. As of this writing in late 2010, however, this prospective or conditional set of inducements had not succeeded in restarting the negotiations, let alone making concrete progress on denuclearization. Rather, tacit negotiations still focused on the confidence-inducing measures demanded by both sides to simply resume the talks.

Conclusion

Three points emerge from this analysis. The first has to do with domestic politics in North Korea and the causal mechanisms outlined in the introduction to this volume. The extraordinary repressiveness of the regime clearly calls into question the utility of broad commercial sanctions against North Korea, even assuming they could be coordinated. Although there is some evidence that financial sanctions brought the North Koreans back to the bargaining table in 2007, they did not deter the regime from testing its first nuclear device and only managed to resume a protracted negotiation process in which inducements had to be put on the table. The regime responded to external constraints by passing the costs onto its citizenry, even to the extent of allowing recurrent food shortages.

But evidence on North Korean willingness to cooperate is equally elusive. The same unaccountability to the general public which makes the regime impervious to broadly-based sanctions also has the effect of making it indifferent to rewards that do not directly benefit the regime and politically-connected groups. Moreover the trend during recent years has been toward a narrowing of regime support. Particularly after 2005, and culminating with the disastrous currency reform of 2009, resource allocation tilted toward military priorities and the market was viewed with increasing hostility. These domestic policy changes cannot be taken as firm evidence of a declining willingness to make trade-offs in the nuclear talks, but when coupled with a deteriorating security environment and recurrent statements about the perceived utility of developing and maintaining a deterrent, a more fundamental coalitional shift seems plausible.

From August 2008, these problems were compounded by Kim Jong-il's likely stroke and the onset of the succession process. It does not seem coincidental that this would coincide with a further "hardening" of the regime around core bases of support, a perceived importance of showing resolve, a preoccupation with security and a declining willingness to make trade-offs.

A second conclusion is that the efforts of the Bush administration to pressure North Korea were consistently undermined by severe coordination problems. China has been utterly unwilling to use its vast commercial and aid leverage to force a reckoning. Nor has China been the only constraint on a hardline approach. South Korea pursued a strategy of relatively unconditional engagement through 2007 and even Japan sought normalization until its policy was derailed by the abductee issue. Whatever the limits of an engagement approach, it is hard to see how the United States could – acting by itself – have brought more pressure to bear than it did.

This conclusion gains force through a consideration of the North Korean response to pressure and sanctions. There is little evidence from our narrative – at least to date – that ratcheting up pressure "worked"; to the contrary, it frequently served to poison negotiations. But inducements have had difficulty as well, in part because of recurrent credibility problems, and on both sides. Even when the United States had turned back to the provision of positive inducements, it extended them only in tandem with or after North Korea acting. Similarly, North Korea has reneged on commitments, used crises as a form of brinkmanship, and framed demands in ways that were either difficult to define (the United States ending its "hostile policy") or altogether unacceptable (withdrawal of troops; talks on normalization prior to progress on denuclearization). These broad political demands were coupled with the demand for quite specific economic payoffs, providing fodder for the interpretation that they are engaged in little more than an extended blackmail game.

There is some evidence that very tightly calibrated reciprocal actions worked in 2008 before the talks floundered on the issue of verification. But it is important to recognize that they "worked" only with respect to one, albeit important, component of the problem at hand, namely the production of fissile material at Yongbyon. Shutting down the Yongbyon complex would have been a worthy achievement, and might have lessened mistrust, provided a springboard into phase three negotiations and implementation and perhaps even set the stage for the negotiation of a "grand bargain," such as that proposed by the Lee Myung-bak government in late 2009.

But even shutting down Yongbyon completely would have still left a daunting agenda intact: the return to the NPT and IAEA inspections, proliferation, missiles, HEU, fissile material, and the weapons themselves. Particularly with changing political dynamics in North Korea and the cushion provided by its external economic relations, such a bargaining process would have effectively acknowledged a nuclear North Korea for some time, which is better off than we are today but perhaps only marginally so.

Postscript

Kim Jong Il died on December 17, 2011. In the year prior to his death, diplomacy around the Korean peninsula had taken place under the shadow of a second major North Korean provocation. In addition to the sinking of the Cheonan on March 26, 2010, North Korean military forces shelled Yeonpyeong Island on November 23, 2010. These events naturally made it difficult to restart the Six Party Talks, despite increasing signs of North Korean interest in doing so.

In the months prior to Kim Jong-il's death, diplomatic activity aimed at restarting multilateral negotiations had once again gained momentum, including through the staging of bilateral US-North Korean talks. The succession will further complicate nuclear diplomacy. Of particular concern are the political issues raised in this chapter: whether the young and untested Kim Jong Un will be even more beholden to the military than his father and whether this subtle shift in the coalitional base of the regime will reduce the prospects for restarting the talks and reaching an agreement.

9   Contrasting causal mechanisms: Iraq and Libya

David D. Palkki and Shane Smith

Introduction

In March 2003, the United States led an international military coalition to disarm Iraq of suspected weapons of mass destruction (WMD). While Saddam Hussein largely ended Iraq's WMD programs in 1991, Iraq's resistance to certain UN inspections and other measures led many to believe that it maintained WMD stockpiles and was reconstituting a nuclear weapons program. Nine months after the invasion of Iraq, Libya's leadership announced that it was "of its own free will" dismantling all of its WMD programs and would abide by the Nuclear Non-Proliferation Treaty. After thirty years of trying to acquire nuclear weapons, Muammar Qaddafi changed Libya's course to one of "building a new world void of WMD and void of all types of terrorism."[1]

For decades, both Saddam's Iraq and Qaddafi's Libya had sought nuclear weapons and found their countries the targets of unilateral and multilateral inducements. US-led economic sanctions and military threats were often employed as a coercive policy tool aimed in part at rolling back the illicit weapons programs. The intention was to punish or deny benefits to these leaders, for instance, by weakening their ruling coalitions and undermining their political and economic hold on power. Potential benefits associated with political and economic reintegration with the Western-oriented global system and assurances of regime survival, of varying credibility, went hand-in-hand with the sanctions. The United States and other countries offered these positive inducements as rewards for the leaders and their constituents interested

This chapter represents only the authors' personal views; it does not represent the views of the National Defense University or the Department of Defense. The authors wish to thank Christopher Alkhoury, Mohammed Baban, Donald Caldwell, John Caves, Etel Solingen, and Judith Yaphe for providing useful feedback and assistance.

[1] "Statement Released in the Name of Colonel Qadhafi", reprinted in Joseph (2009: 128).

in normalizing relations with the West, on condition that they would verifiably forgo WMD.

While scholars disagree over the relative effectiveness of these sanctions and positive inducements and have, of necessity, been forced to rely on a sort of Kremlinology to make sense of Iraqi and Libyan decision-making, new evidence promises to cast important light on these issues. When the United States invaded Iraq it captured millions of pages of Iraqi state records, including some 2,300 hours of taped meetings and telephone conversations in which Saddam was a participant. These new sources have the potential to transform Saddam's Iraq into one of the most transparent regimes of the previous century. This chapter draws on a portion of these captured records, digital copies of which are available to scholars at the National Defense University's new Conflict Records Research Center (CRRC).

This new data on Iraq enables important reassessments of earlier scholarship, though this chapter's findings are more exploratory than definitive. CRRC records present insightful views into Saddam's thinking and decision-making. At the time of this writing, however, only a small fraction of the captured records have made their way into the archive, leaving unknown what insights await and what reassessments will be in order as the archive grows. In the case of Libyan decision-making, the available data is much more limited. New accounts by regime officials provide important clues, yet Qaddafi's perceptions and decision-making remain frustratingly opaque and seemingly erratic.

In this chapter, we focus on *how*, as opposed to merely whether or to what extent, external inducements led to Iraqi and Libyan nuclear reversal decisions. While the evidence suggests that external inducements played a significant role in shaping both Iraqi and Libyan nuclear decisions, the primary focus here is on the inducements' domestic distributional effects, Qaddafi and Saddam's perceptions of these effects, and how all of this led to decisions to freeze or dismantle the two states' nuclear weapon programs.

Common reasons exist for why states seek and forgo nuclear weapons. As Solingen emphasized in the title of her previous book, however, nuclear acquisition and reversal decisions are guided as much by differing logics as any one, uniform, causal mechanism.[2] Similar external inducements involving economic sanctions and other factors persuaded Libya and Iraq to end their nuclear weapon programs, though the inducements, weapon programs, and paths taken were not identical.

---

[2] Solingen (2007a).

Nor, for that matter, were the reversal outcomes: Libya unambiguously disarmed, whereas Iraq's reversal was less clear. Scholars and policy-makers must understand the different denuclearization paths, and why states take one route over another, to craft inducements in the manner most conducive to altering target behavior.

Libya and Iraq's reversal decisions have much in common and provide useful comparisons. Each country's high dependency on oil exports left it vulnerable to economic embargoes. In each case the primary driver of negative external inducements was the United States, with other countries more inclined to offer positive inducements. Both countries were authoritarian regimes ruled by deeply suspicious dictators, though their sources of authority and institutions differed. For instance, the Iraqi regime derived ideological support from secular Baathism while the Libyan regime was based on Jamahiriya – a self-styled revolutionary neologism intended to convey a stateless society and political community managed directly by the people through consultation rather than representation.

While it is beyond the scope of this chapter to assess the relative sensitivity of democracies and autocracies to comprehensive inducements, the claim that democratic leaders are more susceptible to comprehensive inducements than authoritarian regimes strikes us as true.[3] Saddam found great pleasure in President George H.W. Bush's removal from office because of a slight dip in the US economy while he, by contrast, remained in power despite the decimating effects of sanctions on Iraq.[4] Clearly, leaders in Iraq and Libya were able to survive and in some aspects even thrive under sanctions for quite some time.

Nevertheless, a key finding from our research is that even in Saddam and Qaddafi's autocracies, comprehensive sanctions worked.[5] While Galtung derided comprehensive sanctions as "naïve" for the ostensible lack of a "transmission mechanism" whereby civilian suffering could translate into policy changes, we identify several such potential mechanisms.[6] Important evidence indicates that sanctions limited the ability to manage elite elements – particularly with regard to Libya. Perhaps equally significant, both Saddam and Qaddafi were sensitive to issues of legitimacy and morale among the masses out of concerns about their

---

[3] Discussed by Solingen in this volume.
[4] Woods, Palkki, and Stout (2011: 41–44).
[5] While the multilateral sanctions on Libya have often been characterized as "targeted" rather than "comprehensive," we argue later in this chapter that it is difficult to distinguish between the two when the target of sanctions is an industry representing 95 percent of a country's economy.
[6] Galtung (1967).

legacies and fears that disgruntled masses would offer fertile recruiting ground for opposition groups.

In the introduction to this volume, Solingen draws attention to timing and temporal sequences as important factors that condition the effect of external inducements on nuclear related decisions. Leaders might accept higher costs to retain mature nuclear weapons programs that benefit key constituencies and provide prestige than they would to keep unproductive programs or programs in their initial phases. While Saddam and Qaddafi had both long pursued nuclear weapons, their programs had produced little. Some evidence suggests that Qaddafi faced declining marginal returns – in terms of domestic political support, prestige, and security – on investments in Libya's illicit nuclear program the longer it continued without success. Saddam's Iraq, by comparison, faced a far smaller decline in these marginal returns given ambiguities over whether, and to what degree, it had actually reversed course.

This leads us to a final comparison. Leading scholar-practitioners have argued that whereas credible assurances of regime survival led Libya to verifiably disarm, insufficiently credible assurances led Saddam to adopt a hedging strategy aimed at persuading the United Nations that Iraq had disarmed, but leaving enough ambiguity to deter foreign or domestic attempts to overthrow the regime.[7] We argue, by contrast, that the assurances offered to Libya were not nearly as credible as commonly portrayed. Indeed, it is unclear to us that the United States offered any clear assurance in exchange for Libya's WMD, outside of the potential for better ties with the West. The 2011 US military intervention in Libya and lack of a perceived US concern with prior commitments, either public or private, only underscores the tenuous nature of the purported security assurance. Captured Iraqi records indicate that, at least in 1998, Saddam discounted US calls for regime change as insincere posturing for US domestic audiences. In any case, Saddam does not appear to have thought by the late 1990s that the United States was willing or able to overthrow his regime. In some instances, the Iraqi records suggest, Saddam accepted UN inspections and complied with disarmament-related demands precisely because he believed that noncompliance would undermine his ability to retain power – which he valued even more than WMD.

Libya's nuclear reversal

Shortly after taking power in 1969, Muammar Qaddafi's regime began seeking nuclear weapons. It approached China in 1970 in an effort to

---

[7] Litwak (2007).

buy them "off the shelf" but was rebuffed.[8] It turned to Pakistan in 1974, reportedly offering financial aid and uranium from Niger in the hope that Pakistan would share the results from its nuclear program.[9] Some reports also suggest Libya attempted to procure nuclear weapons from France in 1976, India in 1978, the Soviet Union in the late 1970s, and even sources on the black market in the mid 1970s.[10]

As these early efforts to acquire nuclear weapons outright proved unsuccessful, Libya sought the technologies for an indigenous "civil" program. After ratifying the NPT in 1975, it approached a number of countries about uranium exploration, conversion and enrichment capabilities, research and power reactors, as well as plutonium reprocessing/separation technologies. Qaddafi was most successful in getting assistance from the Soviet Union, which supplied Libya with a ten-magawatt research reactor. The reactor was operating by the early 1980s and eventually became the focal point for covert work on plutonium separation and uranium enrichment.[11] However, Libya's nuclear efforts were frustrated due to the reluctance on the part of most supplier countries to provide assistance.

In the 1990s, Libya's nuclear weapons program received a boost from A.Q. Khan and his global network of illicit suppliers. From about 1997 to 2003, the Khan network provided Libya with key technologies, such as those related to centrifuge enrichment, weapons design, and engineering as well as overseas training for Libyan personnel. Differing accounts suggest Libya spent between $100 and $500 million but most conclude that it was able to acquire most of the technical pieces for an indigenous nuclear program from Khan's suppliers.[12]

Despite successes exploiting the illicit network, Libya never made significant headway in building a nuclear weapon. This was due in part to the lack of managerial expertise and political leadership as well as a dearth of highly qualified, technical experts.[13] It was also likely due to the fact that A.Q. Khan's criminal network was not necessarily a reliable business partner. Reportedly, important requests were left unfulfilled, key parts and information were withheld, and delivered components

[8] Cirincione et al. (2005: 321).   [9] Spector and Smith (1990: 176).
[10] Bhatia (1988: 64–71), Mark (2002: 4), Feldman (1997: 63–65), and Specter and Smith (1990: 175–185).
[11] Bowen (2008: 333–337).
[12] Bowen (2006: 36–45), Bill Gertz, "Libyan Sincerity on Arms in Doubt," *Washington Times*, September 9, 2004, and Braun and Chyba (2004).
[13] For instance, Libyan officials claimed that they were not even able to assess the credibility of the nuclear weapons design they received due to the lack of qualified personnel (IAEA Report 2004).

were often unusable.[14] This is not to suggest that an eventual nuclear weapon was out of Libya's reach but it remained uncertain.[15]

After three decades and untold resources, Libya abandoned its nuclear ambitions. In March 2003, it sought discussions with the United States and Britain specifically on its WMD programs. Later that same year, however, the German cargo ship *BBC China* was intercepted en route to Libya carrying enrichment components manufactured in Malaysia and shipped through Dubai – such was the global nature of the Khan network. Despite or perhaps due to this interdiction, Libya announced its intention to immediately dismantle all WMD programs and abide by the NPT on December 19. It subsequently turned over its nuclear facilities and components to the United States and opened its doors to international inspectors.

The motivations underlying Qaddafi's decision to abandon his nuclear ambitions have been the subject of much debate.[16] Most analysts attribute significant influence to international inducements but there are differences of opinion over the relative causal weight the different inducements – positive and negative – had on Qaddafi's change of heart. This section explores the links between these external inducements and domestic politics that purportedly shaped Qaddafi's decision.

St. John characterizes Libya's decision to disarm as a lengthy, systematic, and complex process that started in the early 1990s.[17] Indeed, it was clear to some before the 9/11 terrorist attacks on the United States that Libya was ending its policy of confrontation and starting to meet many of the West's demands, suggesting it was on a path toward giving up its nuclear ambitions.[18] Over many years, several factors laid the groundwork for this change in direction, including a declining economic outlook, domestic challenges, diminished prestige, outside military pressure, and the international economic opportunity of a new approach.

External negative inducements

There were two types of external negative inducements: economic sanctions and military threats. By the time the United States designated Libya as a state sponsor of terrorism in 1979, it had already imposed

---

[14] Bowen (2006). One senior US official involved similarly described the technology as over-priced and under-advanced. See Mahley (2004).

[15] For a recent study of the capabilities Libya had amassed, see Albright (2010).

[16] For a sample of different views, see Bowen (2006), Jentleson and Whytock (2005/2006), Solingen (2007a), and Rublee (2009).

[17] St. John (2004: 401).   [18] Takeyh (2001).

export controls on military equipment and civilian aircraft, and withdrawn its embassy staff from Tripoli. Over the next seven years, a series of hostilities led to increasingly tough US sanctions. When the United States bombed Tripoli and Benghazi in April 1986 for Libyan complicity in the bombing of a Berlin discotheque, US sanctions had escalated to a total ban on direct import and export trade, commercial contracts, and travel-related activities. The United States had also frozen Libyan government assets in the United States.

During this period, Libya's economic performance steadily worsened. By some estimates, however, the direct economic impact of unilateral US sanctions between 1986 and 1992 was marginal. Libya was able to find alternative markets for its oil but the sanctions nonetheless heightened its vulnerability to the multilateral sanctions that would follow. For instance, the US ban impacted the country's investment patterns and forced it to abandon projects that would have encouraged diversification of its economy. US technology and companies had also been instrumental in building and maintaining Libya's oil industry since the 1950s. The ban on US imports hastened but by no means single-handedly caused deterioration of Libya's oil infrastructure during this time.[19]

In 1992, the United Nations joined the economic embargo after Libya refused to turn over suspects involved in the 1988 bombing of Pan Am flight 103 over Lockerbie. These multilateral sanctions proved much more damaging. Libya was no longer able to easily adjust by shifting to new markets/investments. Revenues began drying up. Levels of Libyan oil production in the 1970s were twice as much as in 2003.[20] Since the oil industry represents about 95 percent of the country's economy, this had significant impact across society despite the targeted nature of the multilateral sanctions.

Oil revenues provided the regime with the wherewithal for securing and maintaining domestic support. It did so by financing a robust welfare and education system as well as access to housing, healthcare, food, water, and electricity for its citizens.[21] The drop in oil income led to a freeze in public spending from 1982 to 2003 while inflation continued to rise (60 percent of state expenditure in Libya is reported to have been allocated to paying wages).[22] Moreover, the state could no longer incorporate people looking for jobs since its oil industry was not expanding. The result was an unemployment rate of approximately

---

[19] O'Sullivan (2003: 188–190). Libya's poor production capacity was likely the result of poor internal decisions as much as it was US sanctions, see Vandewalle (2006: 153).
[20] Vandewalle (2006: 188–189).   [21] Pargeter (2000: 29–31).   [22] Bowen (2006: 55).

25 percent by 2003 with a workforce that was growing by 4 percent every twelve months.[23]

Qaddafi's regime came under pressure. It was no longer able to fulfill basic needs or meet expectations. Declining living standards fed popular discontent, particularly among the younger populations that experienced high levels of unemployment and alienation from a political system they had little sentimentality for. Almost two generations had grown up since the 1969 revolution and many were impatient with their economic prospects and ongoing political experiments. Opposition groups grew. In short, the ability of the regime to provide welfare to the general population as well as economically reward domestic allies and punish challengers was in decline. These distributional effects on domestic politics are discussed further in the following section.

There is also a long history of the second type of external negative inducement – military threat. In 1981, the United States downed two Libyan aircraft over the Gulf of Sidra following Qaddafi's effort to impose a "line of death" in its territorial waters. Five years later, the United States bombed Tripoli and Benghazi after Libya's complicity in blowing up the Berlin discotheque, killing Qaddafi's adopted daughter, injuring two of his sons and about forty-five military and government officials. In 1989, the United States shot down two more Libyan aircraft over the Gulf of Sidra after another escalation of tensions.

While there were many threats over decades of US–Libya hostility, Libya's nuclear program was not necessarily the direct target of these inducements. Rather, they were more directly in response to Libya's sponsorship of terrorism. After 9/11, however, WMD in the hands of radical groups was identified by President Bush as the "gravest danger." The 2002 US National Security Strategy subsequently mapped out the rationale and issued military and diplomatic guidance for planning preemptive war against emerging WMD – particularly nuclear – threats.[24]

US leaders made the case for war against Iraq in 2002–2003 based largely on Iraq's suspected nuclear program. As it was moving forces into the Middle East to follow through on threats against Saddam, Libya approached the United Kingdom in an effort to engage in dialogue over WMD. The first secret meeting on the issue between US, UK, and Libyan personnel took place in April and discussions continued through September 2003 but there was little progress in terms of details on whether, when, and how Libya would surrender its program to international inspections.

---

[23] Pargeter (2000: 30).   [24] The White House (2002).

In October 2003, however, the *BBC China* was interdicted. Over the next month, the United States presented its evidence to Libya. Some argue that this had a dramatic effect on the Qaddafi regime by demonstrating the ability to disrupt the nuclear supply chain, driving down the potential for success, and increasing the risk of US/UK military action by removing doubt about Libya's intentions and actions.[25] Days after the interdiction, Libya accepted technical inspections and, by the end of the year, admitted to, renounced, and turned over its nuclear program to international scrutiny. Vice President Dick Cheney said that Qaddafi "watched what we did in Afghanistan and Iraq, and he decided maybe he might want to reconsider what he was all about. Five days after we arrested Saddam Hussein, Colonel Qaddafi went public and said, I give it up, come and get it, it's all yours."[26] Rep. Tom Lantos (D-Ca.) similarly said that the turnaround was due to what he termed the "pedagogic value" of the war in Iraq.[27]

Internal distributional effects

By the time multilateral sanctions against Libya were in place, its economy was already contracting as a result of directionless financial management, corruption, plummeting oil prices, and US sanctions. For instance, revenues declined from about $21 billion in 1980 to $6.5 billion in 1986. The subsequent impact of multilateral sanctions starting in 1992 was widely felt. Indeed, the distinction between comprehensive and targeted sanctions that Drezner discusses in Chapter 5 of this volume is less meaningful, when targeted sanctions are aimed at an industry comprising 95 percent of a country's economy and government revenue.[28]

Libya's economy grew only 0.8 percent a year between 1992 and 1999 and per capita GDP fell from $7,311 to $5,896.[29] In 1998 alone, just one year before Qaddafi looked to resolve issues over his past use of terrorism, export earnings had dropped to the lowest since the oil price crash of 1986 – roughly $7 billion. Agriculture and industrial production fell, unemployment hit 25 percent, and inflation rose dramatically. Between 1992 and 2001, Libya claimed that UN sanctions cost the country roughly $26.5 billion. Over that time, living standards noticeably declined.

---

[25] Jentleson and Whytock (2005/2006) and Joseph (2009).
[26] Office of the Vice President (2004).   [27] Lantos (2004).
[28] Discussed by Drezner in Chapter 5, this volume.
[29] EIU Country Profile: Libya 2001, 25.

In her earlier work, Solingen discusses the role of the global economy in domestic political survival strategies. Global markets, capital, investments, and technology, she argues, can influence individuals or groups through their impacts on employment, income, prices of goods and services, and provision of public services. Because these affect some groups more favorably than others, leaders attempt to manage their openness to global forces in a manner that maintains a sufficient domestic coalition for governing.[30] The evidence suggests this dynamic was under way in Libya well before 2003 as Qaddafi attempted to adjust to economic realities and changing political coalitions resulting from international sanctions.

To be sure, poor economic performance during the 1980s had made clear the deficiencies of a directed economic model. Qaddafi embarked on two major reform efforts in 1987 and 1990 aimed at liberalization and, in his own words, to "take the burden off public institutions" which were failing.[31] But, there were challenges to change. For one, the private sector was ill-prepared to survive without government support, particularly under the constrained conditions of international sanctions. Sustained liberalization would also encourage the rise of social inequalities and economic stratification that ran counter to Qaddafi's revolutionary promise of egalitarianism that could be exploited by opposition. At the elite level, Qaddafi had spent a great deal of effort supporting the economic fortunes of various groups – through tariffs, licensing requirements, and restrictions on imports and exports – to maintain a supporting coalition. Loosening these controls toward a market economy would cede a valued regime tool for rewarding elite supporters, punishing rivals, and managing the masses.

The move toward liberalization not only weakened Qaddafi's ruling coalition, it also revealed factions with different interests and power. Some of the early reforms in particular tended to benefit the consumer and entrepreneur classes as well as military and other government managers. Evidence soon emerged of a new generation of technocrats and intellectuals that strongly favored liberalization and rejoining the world economy if not community. This group would eventually be led by Qaddafi's own son, Saif al-Islam al-Qaddafi. But an early sign of a split occurred during a meeting in the mid 1990s, when a group led by General Secretary Umar al-Munstair and Energy Minister Abdallah Salim al-Badri reportedly pushed for more dramatic structural reforms and efforts to encourage international investments. This view did not go unopposed. Abd al-Salam Jallud, often thought to have been the second

---

[30] Solingen (2007a: 25).   [31] Quoted in Vandewalle (2006: 164).

most powerful figure in Libya for at least two decades, led opposition against domestic reforms and normalization as a new model.[32]

These groups vied for influence in Qaddafi's inner circle but, as Vandewalle explains, "the lack of institutionalization within the country's political system still left much of the process, as it lurched forward, subject to the vicissitudes of Qadhafi's own decisions."[33] He had to weigh liberalization and the perceived requirement of reconciliation with the West to revive Libya's broken economy against other pressures on regime survival, such as the legitimacy of adhering to the "revolution" and the impact of liberalization on his coalition of supporters.

Economic issues and regime survival merged over the 1990s. Opposition groups grew with the downturn in living standards across Libya. This helped push Qaddafi squarely in favor of liberalization and reconciliation with the West. Qaddafi had consistently viewed radical Islamist groups as a serious internal threat to his rule. In 1989, for example, he described them as "more dangerous than AIDS."[34] Shortly after taking power, he set about dismantling religious elites associated with the religious Sanusi movement aligned with his rival, King Idris. Throughout his reign, he treated suspects of underground Islamist opposition groups particularly harshly to dissuade would-be members.

Despite these efforts to root out political Islam, opposition groups began to mount. The economic and political malaise in Libya during the 1980s and 1990s provided radical groups not only with a growing number of potential recruits but also with a society that was more accepting of their presence. Many were attracted to the groups because they were able to provide social services and anti-corruption activities, where the government had ceded authority.

Throughout the 1990s, Qaddafi faced a series of uprisings. Some of the more dramatic were the Libyan Islamic Fighting Group's attempt to assassinate Qaddafi in 1996 and the armed resistance of the Islamic Martyr's Movement, both purportedly inspired and funded by al Qaeda.[35] The Muslim Brotherhood was also a serious concern for the regime. It espoused economic and political reforms in line with Islamic ideals, which were attractive to many blue-collar workers and junior civil servants. Its social welfare programs were appealing to urban and poor populations. Meanwhile, the National Salvation Front offered a broad-based movement aimed at accommodating secular and Islamic opponents.[36]

---

[32] Solingen (2007a: 222–223).   [33] Vandewall (2008: 216).   [34] Mattes (1995: 109).
[35] Solingen (2007a: 223–224).   [36] Bowen (2006: 55).

These movements were harshly repressed by Qaddafi's Revolutionary Committees – one of several informal institutions responsible only to Qaddafi and used from time to time to mobilize, indoctrinate, and police – rather than the regular army. This was a sign that Qaddafi had little confidence or trust in his armed forces. The memory of its embarrassing defeat against what has been described as ragtag Chadian forces in 1987 still loomed. Adding to this, the decline in economic conditions, Western sanctions on military hardware, and the collapse of a major arms supplier, the Soviet Union, led to a downturn in military procurements and left wages often unpaid for months.[37] To be sure, the sanctions created space for challengers to Qaddafi's rule and the constrained economic environment limited his ability to confidently mobilize the masses, elite, or even his armed forces against these challengers. The 2011 uprisings in Libya and defection of several regime leaders provide further evidence that Qaddafi and his supporters were vulnerable to broad-based domestic pressures.

While economic sanctions weakened Qaddafi's hold on power, some believe US military actions during the 1980s strengthened Qaddafi's hand in dealing with rivals inside government and quelling opposition.[38] St. John concludes that the 1986 bombings, for instance, did little to rally the masses around Qaddafi but invigorated a radical minority.[39] Others suggest that the raids led some in Qaddafi's inner circle to conclude that Libya could no longer afford to rouse American power and they began to question his confrontational approach. In the months after the 1986 raids, Joffe surmises that Qaddafi spent months rebuilding his alliances that were presumably weakened as a result of lost confidence in the regime's foreign policy direction.[40] This would suggest that perhaps the US military threat had a rallying effect among revolutionary zealots but engendered caution among more pragmatic elements.

During the 1990s, Qaddafi's support for international terrorism declined even while he increased efforts in the nuclear realm. US focus turned more directly to his suspected WMD program. Following 9/11 and particularly after the *BBC China* interdiction, Qaddafi's regime was again facing the prospect of US military attack. Evidence supports the view that this shook the regime. Qaddafi reportedly told Italian Prime Minister Berlusconi in a phone conversation after Hussein was toppled that "I will do whatever the Americans want, because I saw what

---

[37] Vandewalle (2006: 146–147).
[38] Schumacher (1986/1987) and Niblock (2001).
[39] St. John (2008: 132).   [40] Joffe (2008: 202–203).

happened in Iraq, and I was afraid."[41] Similarly, Qaddafi explained to congressional delegations in January and March 2004 that "one of the reasons … he was giving up the weapons was he did not want to be a Saddam Hussein, and he did not want his people to be subjected to the military efforts that were being put forth in Iraq."[42] With a severely weakened ruling coalition and little leverage to rally supporters – perhaps even his military – Qaddafi likely calculated that the odds of the regime surviving renewed US military pressure were not in his favor.

To be sure, it is difficult to discount the impact war had on cementing Qaddafi's strategic decision to abandon his program. This is not to argue that military threat was the sole or even the most important factor in the decision to disarm. The evidence suggests that economic sanctions played a major role over time in shaping Libya's longer term orientation back toward the global economy. However, it is difficult to conclude that a strategic decision had been made by Qaddafi to fully abide by NPT obligations until the end of 2003. The interdiction of the *BBC China* six months after he initially sought nuclear talks raises questions about the regime's earlier sincerity – a suspicion befitting Qaddafi's previous behavior. It is quite possible that Qaddafi was planning to use the *promise* of giving up his nuclear program as a negotiating tactic to secure benefits without fully surrendering his program. In fact, Libyan officials were sill bitterly rejecting claims that it even had a nuclear program prior to the *BBC China*. Libya's Foreign Ministry spokesperson, Hassouna al-Shawesh, dismissed an early 2003 CIA report by emphasizing that Libya was a member of the NPT and arguing that "These are allegations the CIA habitually puts out to serve interests hostile to the peoples" of other states.[43] This hardly seems the sentiment of a government determined to make amends over its illicit weapons effort.

The renewed prospect of military threat likely played a more immediate role in convincing Qaddafi that his nuclear ambitions had become too costly without clear benefits. At the same time, the costs and benefits of giving up Libya's nuclear program tilted the other way as coalitions favoring reform and global integration gained favor.

External positive inducements

As internal pressures mounted for Qaddafi as a result of years of sanctions, diplomatic isolation, and renewed military threat, two general

---

[41] R. Gedye, "Libya Agrees to Dismantle all WMD," *Telegraph*, December 20, 2003.
[42] Quoted in Joseph (2009: 40).
[43] Quoted in Mackby and Cornish (2008: 218).

types of positive inducements offered potential benefits for a new approach. One was the promise of normalized relations with the West, relief from sanctions, and much needed economic inflow. The other was the prospect not only of defusing the US military threat but also the potential of internationalizing the regime's fight against domestic Islamic opposition groups by joining the West and United States in the "war on terror."

Multilateral sanctions were suspended in 1999, when Libya effectively accepted responsibility for the Pan Am bombing. A modest increase in oil output that followed made clear that US markets, investments, and technology were needed to help Libya emerge from its stagnant economic situation created by the sanctions, failed reforms, and antiquated oil infrastructure.[44] And, the United States made clear that it required monetary compensation for the families of the Pan Am bombing, disavowal of terrorism as a foreign policy tool, and transparent resolution on WMD issues. As a result, the "carrot" of full political and economic reintegration remained.

A new outward looking model offered Libya a way to revitalize many areas of society. Notably, international firms were eager to invest in its oil sector once the uncertainty of sanctions and domestic stability could be resolved. In 2000–2002, international oil and gas executives continued to rank Libya as the top exploration spot in the world.[45] Three-quarters of Libya remained unexplored, while its natural gas reserves were widely thought to be enormous yet largely untouched. However, the unpredictability and stigma of working with Libya as well as the effects of the boycott and sanctions made investment there appear too risky for many. Libya's larger political issues and disputes with the West and the United States would have to be solved first.

Some suggest that Libya's decision to abandon nuclear weapons was part of a bargaining process. For instance, Saif noted in a December 20, 2003 interview that, "The truth is that this initiative is a political deal. This is not a secret. It is a political deal; give and take. We give you this much and you give me this much."[46] Similarly, there are recent reports that Saif and the Qaddafi regime used some of its remaining nuclear materials (5.2 kilograms of enriched uranium) to make demands on the United States, suggesting its nuclear program had been a bargaining chip all along.[47] However, this contradicts Qaddafi's previous claim that there was no "concrete reward" for giving up the nuclear program.[48] It

---

[44] St. John (2008: 138).   [45] Economic Intelligence Unit (2001).
[46] Quoted in Joseph (2009: 23).   [47] Fisher (2010).
[48] See, for instance, Braut-Hegghammer (2008: 68).

also contradicts the official Libyan statement that was released in 2003, stating its intention to eliminate its nuclear program of "its own free will." Senior US officials similarly hold that there was no quid pro quo of sanctions for Libya's nuclear program. Rather, it was put forth that relinquishing Libya's WMD programs would remove a major obstacle toward improved relations and related benefits.[49]

In addition to economic incentives, the attacks of 9/11 and the subsequent US "war on terror" offered Qaddafi an opportunity to get support for his own battle against domestic Islamic opposition. As mentioned above, he had a long history of battling domestic political Islamic groups and those with ties to international terror organizations such as al Qaeda.[50] Here, US and Libyan interest converged. He may have been looking to tie his fight against these groups to the US "war on terror" to get material assistance or to further legitimize his repression against opposition groups.

Lisa Anderson, a leading Libya scholar, sums up the impact of the 9/11 terrorist attacks as the moment when Qaddafi

saw an opportunity, because he heard loud and clear President Bush saying, "If you're not with us, you're with the terrorists." He said to himself, "This is my chance to say, 'I'm with you.'" So, [days later], the head of Libyan intelligence, Musa Kusa, who has also been involved in negotiating on the WMD issues, was meeting in Europe with people from the CIA, saying, "This is our list of suspects. These are the terrorists that we know that are connected to al Qaeda, who are operating out of Europe."[51]

Some also suggest there was a security assurance of sorts offered to the regime if it relinquished its WMD. For instance, Litwak argues that "The centerpiece of the Libyan deal was a tacit bargain entailing the Bush administration's assurance of security for the regime ... Without such a credible security assurance, Qadhafi would have had no incentive to relinquish his WMD arsenal."[52] The argument is that Qaddafi would have pushed forward rather than given up his nuclear efforts, had he thought the United States was determined to overturn his regime regardless of his decision. While it is difficult to assess the effects and perceived credibility of a tacit assurance, the evidence suggests that Libyan leaders believed relinquishing WMD would help defuse US security threats. In part, this may have been due to the decline in "regime change" language regarding Qaddafi among US officials since the 1980s and absence of Libya from President Bush's list of countries

---

[49] Joseph (2009: 23).   [50] Ronen (2002).
[51] Anderson (2003).   [52] Litwak (2007: 327).

belonging explicitly to the "axis of evil." As the 2011 US-led military intervention in Libya highlights, however, such tacit hints did not constitute credible commitments that the United States would no longer pursue regime change.

Internal distributional effects

Insolvent, diplomatically isolated, and facing a growing number of domestic challengers, Qaddafi's revolution had largely run its course by 2000. One astute Libya expert suggests "the energy of his revolution had dissipated beyond the possibility of rejuvenating it as an active force in the country's political life."[53] He was forced to consider a new model – the one offered by the West and the global economy. In January 2003, he reportedly spoke of this epiphany: "The history of mankind is not fixed," he offered, "and it does not go at one pace. Sometimes it moves at a steady pace, and sometimes it is very fast. It is very flexible all the time. The past stage was the era of nationalism – of the identity of one nation – and now, suddenly, that has changed. It is the era of globalization, and there are many new factors which are mapping out the world."[54]

The new model would reflect shifts in the domestic political landscape as Qaddafi looked to rebuild a ruling coalition of supporters. His nationalistic policies combined with international sanctions and isolation had left Libya's economy in ruins, the ruling coalition weak, and his regime vulnerable.[55] The new model and potential benefits offered a political lifeline for the regime and opportunity to orient political support around his second son and apparent successor, Saif. Educated at the London School of Economics and head of the Qaddafi International Foundation for Charity Associations, which conducted negotiations over the release of Western hostages in Africa and the Philippines and provided compensation to the families of previous terrorist bombing, Saif was thought to be an internationalist. As a leading advocate of reform, he publicly expressed in an interview that the "Libyan people want to modernize their economy, [and] they want to reform their system ... we [Libyans] want to bring foreign capital to Libya and we want to bring investment into our country, but we have our own model regarding privatization." This last part suggests that the regime – or at least some in the regime – may not have been fully ready to give up the leverage that came with controlling the economy as a tool for directing resources as rewards to a small group of domestic allies and away from challengers.

---

[53] Vandewalle (2006: 176).   [54] Anderson (2003: 33).   [55] O'Sullivan (2003).

The desire for investment and modernization was driven by the need to rebuild a ruling coalition of elite supporters as well as a need to repair the Qaddafi legacy. According to Chubin, the decision to disarm was directly related to rebuilding the regime's image in order to secure succession of power to Saif. To do so, she argues, "they must have recognized that it makes sense to bring Libya back into the fold of the international community", to "leave Libya in a slightly better position" by getting rid of "these useless weapons, which have created unnecessary distrust and suspicion on the part of its neighbors and, of course, the international community as a whole, including Britain and the United States."[56] Indeed, Libya's Prime Minister drew a similar connection, when he stated that "we thought this [giving up their WMD] would make us look better in the eyes of the world ... It's better that we concentrate on our economic development."[57]

Despite language coming out of Libya filled with globalization buzzwords associated with democracy and capitalism, few suggest there was a significant shift that matched the rhetoric. As one long-time regional expert suggests, "one thing has remained constant: Libya is thoroughly dictatorial with virtually no semblance of democratic life, whether within civil society or the state."[58] Vandewalle similarly suggests that "The fact that Saif al-Islam is seemingly emerging as a young oligarch himself, the fact that the major reform statement was made by someone who has no official standing within Libyan political life ... attest to the lingering personal politics and lack of institutionalization that still surround policy formulation in [Libya]."[59] Rather, there was limited reform primarily aimed at encouraging foreign investment and a monitored but burgeoning private commercial sector. Again, Libya's Prime Minister explained:

The strategies and initiatives that we are taking ... [to create] a new and comprehensive architecture for the national economy ... [includes] a lot of incentives to foreign investors, such as tax exemptions in the first few years, a major cut in corporate taxes, establishing a free zone in Misurata and opening the capital of public companies for foreign investors ... [and] to cut down mismanagement and corruption and of course bureaucracy.[60]

The evidence suggests that the regime was more interested in reforming its political-economic relationship with the international community, as a means to rebuild its oil-funded system of distribution and coercion that was the bedrock of its rule, than it was in reforming its

[56] Esfandiari (2003).   [57] Quoted in Solingen (2007a: 225).
[58] Entelis (2008: 175).   [59] Vandewalle (2006: 190).   [60] MEED (2004).

relationship with Libyan society. Indeed, the lack of domestic reforms helped feed the 2011 uprisings that continue (as of this writing) to challenge the regime. The evidence also suggests that the perceived need to reform its international relationships compelled the regime to reconsider its nuclear weapons program.

Iraq's nuclear reversal

External negative inducements: the domestic distributional effects of economic sanctions

Scholars from across the political spectrum have found that sanctions strengthened rather than weakened the Baathist regime vis-à-vis domestic competitors.[61] They correctly point out that sanctions enabled Saddam and his lieutenants to monopolize smuggling routes, manipulate the supply of scarce commodities, and reward regime loyalists.[62] The UN's oil-for-food program, critics suggest, strengthened the regime by institutionalizing it as the official gatekeeper of transactions overseen by the UN. Moreover, the rationing system, a countermeasure to the sanctions, intensified dependency on the state for food.[63] The sanctions decimated Iraq's middle class, thereby decreasing Iraq's already pitiful prospects for indigenous democratization.[64] Sanctions also provided Saddam with a useful scapegoat for Iraqi afflictions – the United States and the UN Special Commission (UNSCOM).[65]

While in some ways the sanctions strengthened Saddam's hold on power, other aspects were more destabilizing. A preliminary review of the captured Iraqi records indicates that Saddam and his senior advisors believed the sanctions undermined Iraqi morale, exacerbated social inequalities and class tensions, worked to delegitimize the regime, and created rifts among elite and influential circles. From Saddam's perspective, these effects were dangerous and undesirable.

Saddam and his advisors worried about the effects of Iraq's massive economic decline on morale. Saddam's closest advisors warned him that

---

[61] For examples, see Mazaheri (2010: 255 n4). For prominent exceptions, see Cortright and Lopez (2000: chapter 3), Cordesman and Hashim (1997: 357); O'Sullivan (2003: 136–37).

[62] Mazaheri (2010: 253–68), Byman and Waxman (2002: 112–13), Litwak (2007: 155), Cockburn and Cockburn (2002: 139–39), Drezner (1999: 1–2), and Urquhart (1999).

[63] Pollack (2002: 217), Mazaheri (2010: 257).

[64] Byman (2008: 611), Gause (1999: 55), Major and McGann (2005: 340), and Krasno and Sutterlin (2003: 145, 156).

[65] Tostensen and Bull (2002: 376), and Mazaheri (2010: 261).

the Iraqi masses would only tolerate their dismal standard of living for so long, and expected the regime to improve their situation. Saddam's Vice President once cautioned, "The impact of the economic decline on the Iraqi citizen" was a real problem that put at risk "the ability of the Iraqi citizen to tolerate the current situation."[66] Ali Hassan Abd al-Majid al-Tikriti, better known as "Chemical Ali," offered a more explicit warning:

The morale of our people, I believe, will not accept things to stay this way any longer without breaking down.[67]

For Saddam, maintaining Iraqis' morale was essential: "If the Iraqi loses his morale," he explained to advisors in late December 1990, "he is defeated."[68] Saddam believed he "[understood] the psychology of the people." He agreed that the Iraqi people had a right to see progress and told his advisors that the regime must take steps that would allow the Iraqis to hope for improvements to "the miserable life they are living" if they continue offering sacrifices.[69]

Saddam and his advisors were alarmed by the effects the economic sanctions were having on Iraq's middle class. They believed that massive wealth inequalities could lead to fissures in Iraqi society. As Saddam's Interior Minister observed, the pressure of "the sanctions have put tremendous pressure on the low income class while it is not affecting [*the rich*]. Sometimes, [*the sanctions*] are even becoming a tool for [*the rich*] to earn more at the expense of other levels in society. This relates to what Your Excellency was saying about how it has further ruptured our society … I am directly hurt and concerned about this issue as a citizen and as a government official responsible for solving social problems. Whenever these problems increase, so do my problems and likewise whenever these problems lessen." Saddam agreed that the wealthier strata needed to carry a heavier burden of the sanctions; he added, however, that the practicality of implementing measures to distribute economic pressures would need to remain a topic for further discussion.[70]

As many argue, the sanctions reinforced Iraqis' dependence on the regime for their livelihoods and daily sustenance. The regime's preferential ration allotments to government employees and regime supporters incentivized fealty, thus strengthening the regime.[71] This dependency,

[66] CRRC, SH-SHTP-A-001–187.
[67] CRRC, SH-SHTP-A-001–188.
[68] Woods, Palkki, and Stout (2011: 245). On the importance to Saddam of morale, see Woods *et al.* (2006) and Woods (2008).
[69] CRRC, SH-SHTP-A-001–188.   [70] CRRC, SH-SHTP-A-001–185.
[71] CRRC, SH-SHTP-A-001–192; Graham-Brown (1999: 169–170, 184).

however, had an underappreciated downside for the regime. Discontent over differential allocations risked leading much of the relatively disadvantaged population to blame the regime for their woes. This had the potential to undermine the regime's legitimacy and foster instability.

It is true that the regime accrued a degree of legitimacy for its willingness to confront the United States, yet from the perspective of some Iraqi leaders, the danger that mass suffering would undermine regime security more than offset these gains. For decades, Saddam and his party had sought legitimacy by industrializing Iraq, growing its economy, and improving living standards for average and underprivileged Iraqis.[72] As Vice President Ramadan noted, from the first days of the Baathist revolution the party had sought "to build Iraq, because that will reflect our power."[73] Even at moments of great peril in the war against Iran, the regime opted to maintain decent public services and living conditions rather than shift resources to the frontline.[74]

By 1993, sanctions, wartime destruction, and mismanagement of the economy had led Iraq's per capita GDP to plummet almost to 1960 levels, resulting in "the nullification of nearly half a century of growth and improvement in the living standards of the population."[75] As Izzat Ibrahim al-Duri told Saddam on May 2, 1995, every day the sanctions inflicted on Iraq "immeasurable losses." These losses, in turn, would stain the regime's legacy and undermine its future capabilities. He explained:

> If we form specialized economic, social, technical, political, and intellectual study groups to study this, they'll find out how much we are losing every year and every month in huge amounts. These losses are affecting the future of Iraq, its people, and the future of the Iraqi in every aspect of life. They will have a tremendous impact on the very existence of Iraqi individuals regarding their history, present, aspirations, morale, visions, principles, and traditions. All these things are being shattered by the continuation of the sanctions. We cannot let them continue draining us this way![76]

This point unquestionably resonated with Saddam, who later told his FBI interrogator that it was important to him what people would think of him 500 or 1,000 years in the future.[77]

Not only did the sanctions negatively affect the Iraqi masses, they also helped split Saddam's relatively small coalition of elite supporters. While Saddam masterfully played Iraqi security agencies, regime

---

[72] Marr (1985: 240–241, 248–252).   [73] CRRC, SH-SHTP-A-001–188.

[74] Baram (2000: 221).

[75] Graham-Brown (1999: 161). Graham-Brown is quoting Abbas Alnasrawi.

[76] CRRC, SH-SHTP-A-001–187.

[77] Federal Bureau of Investigation (2004b: Session Number 1, February 7, 2004, 2).

officials, and even wings of his own family against one another, infighting related to the sanctions occasionally got out of control. For instance, the long-time rivalry between Saddam's sons (Uday and Qusay) and the al-Majid wing of the family (Chemical Ali, Hussein Kamil, and Saddam Kamil) came to a head over smuggling operations and control of lucrative imported goods, contributing to the 1995 defection of Hussein Kamil and Saddam Kamil to Jordan. They subsequently briefed CIA officers and others on Iraq's prohibited weapon programs and, Saddam almost certainly worried, his personal security procedures. Saddam responded to the defection by relieving Uday of most of his positions and announcing a "disowning" of his relatives. He held a minimum of seven meetings with senior Iraqi officials to engage in damage control and to discuss how to prevent additional defections.[78] According to Abd al-Tawab Mullah Huwaysh, Hussein Kamil's replacement as director of the Military Industrial Commission, these defections greatly exacerbated Saddam's sense of insecurity.[79] Infighting among Saddam's lieutenants for spoils from sanctions and defections, however, continued.[80]

External positive inducements: Saddam's pursuit of foreign favors

Probably the best evidence of Saddam's aversion to the sanctions is found in the numerous strategy sessions he held with his inner circle dedicated to undermining the embargo. He sought, with a degree of success, to undermine and ultimately end the sanctions. In addition to manipulating distributional benefits at home, Saddam used Iraq's resources to encourage and strengthen friendly politicians and parties in foreign countries to help generate opposition to the sanctions.

Maintaining and increasing Russian support to remove the sanctions was, for Saddam and his inner circle, of paramount importance.[81] While the Iraqis believed it was in Russia's geopolitical interest to lift the sanctions,[82] they took no chances. Russian individuals

---

[78] CRRC record numbers SH-SHTP-A-000–565, SH-SHTP-A-000–762, SH-SHTP-A-000–828, SH-SHTP-A-000–833, SH-SHTP-A-000–837, SH-SHTP-A-001–189, and SH-SHTP-D-000–797.

[79] Central Intelligence Agency (2004: vol. 1, "Regime Strategic Intent," 21), Woods, Palkki, and Stout (2011: chapter 8). This Central Intelligence Agency report is referred to hereafter as the *Duelfer Report*.

[80] J. Borger, "Jordan Stops Iraqi Diplomats Leaving after Killings," *Guardian*, January 20, 1998.

[81] CRRC, SH-SHTP-A-001–196; CRRC, SH-SHTP-A-001–187; CRRC, SH-IMFA-A-D-000–545.

[82] CRRC, SH-SHTP-A-001–200.

and political parties were major recipients of Iraqi assistance. When President Boris Yeltsin ran for re-election in 1996, Saddam ordered his lieutenants to spend "three to four million from our weak skin" on his campaign.[83] For years, Yevgeny Primakov also benefited from under-the-table Iraqi financial support.[84] After Iraq accepted the UN Oil-for-Food (OFF) Program on December 10, 1996, it acquired the ability to sell oil, below market level prices, to countries based on their political support for the Baathist regime. As Aziz later described, Iraq sold oil only to individuals and companies that it considered "friendly." Russian companies received roughly one-third of the oil exported by Iraq under sanctions, with hundreds of millions of barrels allocated to Russia's Communist Party, the head of the Liberal Democratic Party, and the Party of Peace and Unity. Alexander Voloshin, Putin's Chief of Staff, received an allocation of some 4.3 million barrels.[85] The Iraqis also financially supported pro-Iraqi officials in France, Italy, and the United Kingdom, to name a few countries, as well as UN officials.[86]

The Iraqis also attempted to tie US companies' interests to the removal of sanctions. From Muhammad Tahir's perspective, the more incentives Iraq gave to US companies, the greater the pressure would be on the US administration to lift the sanctions. Other advisors observed, in 1992, that the United States needed money and might allow Iraq to purchase food, medicine, and perhaps agricultural products from American companies, thus undermining the sanctions.[87] Iraqi Vice President Taha Ramadan and Oil Minister Amir Rashid convinced Saddam to allocate oil to US companies in the hope that by tying the companies' interests to the lifting of sanctions, it would be able to generate a groundswell of domestic opposition in the United States to the sanctions regime.[88] Iraq reallocated the oil to Russian companies after seeing little change in US policy,[89] but it is unclear that they gave up hope in the approach. Shortly after George W. Bush's 2000 electoral victory, Aziz noted, perhaps optimistically, that the Bush family and Republican Party were "closer to the oil companies" than their Democratic counterparts.[90]

[83] Saddam does not specify the currency. See CRRC, SH-SHTP-A-001–200.
[84] Butler (2000: 106–107) and Duelfer (2009: 102).
[85] Volcker *et al.* (2005: 9, 27–28).
[86] Volcker *et al.* (2005: 48–98).
[87] CRRC, SH-SHTP-A-000–850.
[88] Volcker *et al.* (2005: 10).
[89] Volcker *et al.* (2005: 10).
[90] CRRC, SH-SHTP-A-001–197.

Iraqi assessments of positive external inducements

US inducements   As previously noted, some scholars have argued that a lack of credible US inducements was central to Iraq's failure to accede to international demands to comply with UNSC resolutions.[91] US announcements that it would pursue regime change and refuse to lift the sanctions regardless of Iraqi behavior, suggests Litwak, "priced the administration out of the reassurance market."[92] Some analysts have even concluded that Iraq's ambiguous disarmament stemmed from a desire to satisfy disarmament demands while maintaining enough ambiguity to deter a US attack.[93]

There is probably something to be said for this line of argument. Saddam and his advisors were perfectly aware of American leaders' statements indicating that the sanctions would remain as long as Saddam was in power, and suspected that no amount of Iraqi compliance would satisfy the United States.[94] Iraq could "have sanctions with inspectors or sanctions without inspectors," Saddam told his advisors.[95] Logically, the lack of rewards for good behavior would seem to undermine the efficacy of the disarmament effort.[96]

The empirical evidence, however, is mixed. Saddam had long suspected that the United States sought to overthrow the Baathist regime, even during the height of US support for Iraq in the Iran–Iraq War and the postwar years of US engagement.[97] From Saddam's suspicious perspective, the Americans had always been "conspiring bastards."[98] When US calls for military action and a regime change in Iraq increased in 1998, however, Saddam expressed belief that these were hollow threats and that US officials were grateful that the United Nations constrained it from attacking. He explained:

When we were kids, I saw a situation in Tikrit and I was surprised of it because I just came from the countryside. Two were fighting, and one of them tells the other, "Hold me, hold me," and he doesn't hit him, harassing him and

---

[91] UN Security Council Resolution 687 called on Iraq to verifiably give up its WMD and WMD related programs, as well as rockets with ranges in excess of 150km. Iraq was allowed to maintain its conventional weapons.

[92] Litwak (2003/2004: 28). See also Litwak (2007: 136–137), Malone (2006: 157), Mazaheri (2010: 255–256), and Jentleson and Whytock (2005/2006).

[93] Katzman (2009: 5) and Litwak (2007: 325).

[94] CRRC, SH-SHTP-A-000–850.

[95] *Duelfer Report* (2004: vol. 1, "Regime Strategic Intent," 61).

[96] On the importance of credible assurances, see Schelling (1966: 74–75).

[97] CRRC, SH-SHTP-A-000–554 and Brands and Palkki (2012).

[98] CRRC, SH-SHTP-D-000–567.

screaming. We have the same here. They are cursing and saying, "Hold me back, hold me back."[99]

Even in 2003, when US troops were preparing to invade, Saddam was surprisingly unconcerned. Aziz described Saddam as having been "very confident" the United States would not attack; if it did, Saddam reportedly believed, Iraq would defeat it.[100]

Rather than automatically taking US politicians' threats at face value, Saddam tended to assess the sincerity of Americans' threats and demands based on how he thought actions toward Iraq would affect US domestic political payoffs. As he explained to his advisors, Republicans in the US Senate pushed publicly for regime change in Iraq in the late 1990s "to make it difficult for Clinton … so that they can tell him he failed in achieving the goal, if the regime is not ousted." However, he continued, the White House understood that it was "unable to oust the regime." He believed that leading Republicans also knew "that the regime cannot be ousted, and because they are aware of this fact they raise the slogan of ousting the regime since they know that Clinton is not going to oust the regime." Republican leaders would not push so hard as to remove Clinton from power, he explained, since then Gore would enjoy incumbent advantages in the presidential election scheduled for two years hence.[101]

While scholars have decried US calls for Saddam's removal as harmful to US disarmament goals, it is unclear that the two were entirely incompatible. Senior Iraqi advisors advocated cooperating with UN inspectors to prevent the United States from using Iraqi obstructionism as justification for assassination attempts on Saddam.[102] When the risks of a US-backed regime change were objectively greatest, Iraq was relatively compliant. In the summer of 1991, when the risk was relatively high that the United States might resume hostilities against Iraq, Iraq appears to have destroyed the bulk of its WMD.[103] Iraqi compliance skyrocketed in 1995 following the defection of Saddam's sons-in-law and the perceived dangers it posed to the regime. In late 2002, with US-led troops preparing to invade, Iraq readmitted UN inspectors.

---

[99] CRRC, SH-SHTP-A-001–199.

[100] Woods *et al.* (2006: 28).

[101] Saddam also noted that the United States would not allow the emergence of a new state in Iraq's south or north, at least not at the moment, since the state would fall under Iranian influence. He also considered European opposition to a weak Iraq an important factor. See CRRC, SH-SHTP-A-000–756.

[102] Woods, Palkki, and Stout (2011: 259) and CRRC, SH-SHTP-A-001–186.

[103] *Duelfer Report* (2004: vol. 1, "Transmittal Message," 9).

Israeli and Iranian inducements As with the United States, neither Israel nor Iran offered tantalizing positive inducements to Saddam
to verifiably disarm. The Chief of the Royal Court in Jordan sent a message to Saddam indicating that reconciliation with Israel would lead the
United States to lift the sanctions, yet Saddam, who held deeply con-
spiratorial and anti-Israel views, was uninterested.[104] Even if his "revolutionary pragmatism" exceeded his anti-Semitism, the assassination
of Sadat for making peace with Israel provided a ready reminder of the
domestic consequences for pursuing such an unpopular approach.[105]
Baathist anti-Zionist ideology and Iraq's longstanding, hardline rejec-
tionist position toward Israel ensured that Saddam's regime would have
faced an internal legitimacy crisis had it abruptly shifted course in pursuit of Israeli carrots.

Iraq and Iran, by contrast, steadily improved relations and found
common cause in trading in violation of the UN sanctions and in
opposing Israel and the United States.[106] Intense hostility lingered from
the Iran–Iraq War, however, and Iran was waxing in strength relative to
Iraq and developing WMD and an active nuclear program of its own.
Saddam was obsessed with Iranian influence expanding in Iraq's predominantly Shia south, and had little reason to take steps that might
legitimize increased Iranian influence. In any case, the Iranians offered
no known incentives for verifiable Iraqi disarmament.

Some analysts have concluded that Saddam pursued a policy of "strategic ambiguity" to deter aggression by these traditional enemies while
simultaneously complying enough with disarmament demands to lift
the sanctions.[107] As evidence, they cite a June 2000 speech in which
Saddam said that if the Israelis "keep a rifle and then tell me I have the
right to possess only a sword, then we would say no. As long as the rifle
has become a means to defend our country against anybody who may
have designs against it, then we will try our best to acquire the rifle."
The Iraqi people would "view their right that lies on the horizon and the
right they have in their hand, and seek to achieve what is on the horizon
while protecting what they have in their hand," he continued.[108]

---

[104] Woods, Palkki, and Stout (2011: 316–317).
[105] On Saddam's "revolutionary pragmatism," see Post (2004: 215, 230–231).
[106] "Iran and Iraq Make Progress Toward Settling Their Differences," *New York Times*,
September 30, 2000 and Frank Gardner, "Thaw in Iran-Iraq Relations Continues,"
BBC News, October 1, 2000.
[107] The phrase "strategic ambiguity" comes from Lebovic (2007: 31).
[108] For the text of the speech, see "Saddam Says Iraq Ready to Destroy Weapons if
Others Reciprocate," 2000.

As further support, scholars cite FBI interrogation reports of Saddam and Chemical Ali. According to FBI Special Agent George Piro, Saddam told him that his June 2000 speech:

was meant to respond to Iraq's regional threat. Hussein believed that Iraq could not appear weak to its enemies, especially Iran. Iraq was being threatened by others in the region and must appear able to defend itself.

On the other hand, Piro continued, Saddam told him that the speech was also intended to demonstrate Iraq's compliance with UN disarmament demands.[109] According to Chemical Ali, he and other senior advisors "'pressed' Hussein to tell UNSCOM and the world that Iraq has no WMD," but Saddam refused, claiming that Israel would strike if it knew Iraq was disarmed.[110]

While space constraints prevent a thorough assessment of the "strategic ambiguity" argument in this chapter, several points are worth considering. First, the thrust of Saddam's June 2000 speech follows closely the pattern of Iraq's acceptance of UNSC Resolution 833, which required Iraq to recognize its border with Kuwait, and Iraq's acceptance of a UN demand for an air survey over Iraqi territory. In all three, Iraq declared its compliance while decrying the demands as unjust. When Iraq begrudgingly accepted Resolution 833, it announced: "Iraq does not agree; Iraq complies."[111] Saddam instructed his advisors that when they announced Iraq's acceptance of UN overhead flights, they should say, "Despite our conviction of our position, and the correctness of our position, etc., we will not hamstring aviation of this type if it is forced upon us."[112] In the June 2000 speech, Saddam criticized the double standard but confirmed Iraqi adherence by acknowledging that "Iraq does not have anything [WMD]." Iraq understood that it was currently unable to acquire WMD, yet reserved the right "on the horizon" (i.e., in the future) to pursue the same weapons its neighbors possessed. Saddam was not sending an ambiguous signal about Iraqi capabilities; rather, he was affirming Iraq's acquiescence to what he considered illegitimate and potentially unsustainable UN demands.

Second, it appears from the FBI interrogation report that Saddam didn't consider the June 2000 speech unique or important. When Piro first asked about the speech, and told Saddam "his own words could be taken as an admission that Iraq possessed WMD," Saddam replied that "his intention was for the region to be fully disarmed." Piro rejected this

---

[109] Federal Bureau of Investigation (2004b: Casual Conversation, June 11, 2004, 1).
[110] Federal Bureau of Investigation (2004a: January 31, 2004, 3).
[111] CRRC, SH-SHTP-A-000-791.
[112] Woods, Palkki, and Stout (2011: 260).

Contrasting causal mechanisms

287

response, however, telling the captive that "his speech did not project that message." Saddam, apparently unsure what exactly he had said, asked to review a copy of his speech before explaining its meaning.

When they returned to the subject a month later, giving Saddam ample time to come up with an acceptable response, Saddam blamed the United States' and Iraq's common enemy: the Iranians. While Piro took from the meeting that Saddam wanted to lead Iran to believe he retained WMD capabilities, his report indicates that the "major factor" behind Saddam's refusal to allow UN inspectors to return might have been concern that they would provide Iran with information on vulnerable Iraqi targets. The report reads:

Hussein stated he was more concerned about Iran discovering Iraq's weaknesses and vulnerabilities than the repercussions of the United States for his refusal to allow UN inspectors back into Iraq. In his opinion, the UN inspectors would have directly identified to the Iranians where to inflict maximum damage to Iraq. Hussein demonstrated this by pointing at his arm and stated striking someone on the forearm would not have the same effect as striking someone at the elbow or wrist, which would significantly disable the ability to use the arm.

Saddam knew that UN inspectors shared intelligence on Iraq with Baghdad's enemies, leaving it extremely unlikely that he would think he could lead UN inspectors or UN Security Council members to believe that he had disarmed but Israel or Iran that he had not.[113] Moreover, much of what Chemical Ali and Saddam told their interrogators was inaccurate and self-serving.[114] If Saddam sought to mislead Israel and Iran about Iraq's capabilities, implementation was abysmally ineffective. In private meetings, senior Iraqi officials informed Iranian interlocutors that Iraq had disarmed and expressed gratitude to UNSCOM inspectors for informing Israel of Iraq's compliance.[115]

Russian and French inducements While American calls for regime change regardless of Iraqi behavior might have undermined Iraqi incentives to comply with US disarmament demands, the Iraqis clearly saw incentives in accommodating Russian and French desires. Iraq's partial compliance was intended more to satisfy Russia and France and thereby divide the Security Council than it was to signal to some audiences that Iraq had disarmed but to others that perhaps it had not. As Saddam explained to his inner circle in fall 1991:

---

[113] Ritter (2005: 276–277).
[114] Woods, Palkki, and Stout (2011: 329–332) and *Duelfer Report* (2004: vol. 1, "Regime Strategic Intent," 2).
[115] CRRC, SH-MISC-D-000–203, 10 and Ritter (2005: 276–277).

we should not harass them [apparently Americans] with our refusal, nor harass them with our acceptance, but we should always place lines for them to cross, lines between refusal and acceptance. I mean, we should involve others, involve them in a manner that different opinions will emerge.[116]

The Iraqis understood that the Russians and French were far more willing to accept uncertainty about Iraqi WMD than were their American or British counterparts. As Aziz explained in a May 2, 1995 meeting of Saddam's inner circle, France's ambassador had told the UN Security Council, "The search for perfection is not a reality, you cannot achieve a point of 100 percent in every field." "From the Russian and French position," Aziz continued, it was possible to embarrass UNSCOM and the United States for pursuing unambiguous disarmament.[117] Iraq's incomplete compliance stemmed, at least in part, from the understanding that Russia and France would use this partial compliance to undermine calls for further Iraqi measures.

Senior Russian officials went much further than merely tolerating incomplete Iraqi compliance with international disarmament demands; at least from the perspective of some of Saddam's key lieutenants, they insisted upon it. When Iraqi officials were caught trying to import Russian gyroscopes for prohibited delivery systems, and cooperated with UN investigators, senior Russian diplomats reportedly complained to their Iraqi interlocutors that the information had portrayed Russia in an unfavorable light.[118] Such Russian messages seem not to have been lost on Saddam, who in late 1998 told his inner circle that Iraq should not provide UN inspectors with names of Iraq's earlier suppliers of WMD-related materials.[119] Saddam's subordinates appear to have faithfully implemented this guidance.[120]

Domestic consequences of compliance

External inducements from friends and foes unquestionably affected Iraq's disarmament behavior, though it seems highly unlikely that any package of foreign inducements would alter Iraqi behavior in ways Saddam perceived as threatening his hold on power. Saddam placed a high value on obtaining, maintaining, and exercising absolute power and almost certainly assessed potential positive (and negative) external inducements within the context of regime security.

Many scholars have written that Saddam refused to come completely clean for fear of appearing weak in the eyes of domestic opponents,

---

[116] Woods, Palkki, and Stout (2011: 261).   [117] Woods, Palkki, and Stout (2011: 277).
[118] Woods, Palkki, and Stout (2011: 282 n50).
[119] Woods, Palkki, and Stout (2011: 292–293).
[120] *Duelfer Report* (2004: vol.1, "Regime Strategic Intent," 64) and Woods *et al.* (2006: 95).

thereby inciting challenges to his regime.[121] Saddam had suppressed several Kurdish rebellions and beaten back Iranian invaders with chemical weapons. In a July 7, 1984 meeting with Iraqi air force officers, he extolled the coercive benefits of threatening but not launching unconventional weapons.[122] It appears that Chemical Ali ordered his lieutenants to drop flour on resisters during the 1991 Shia uprising as a means of terrifying them into submission with the appearance of a chemical strike.[123] According to an unconfirmed defector report, Iraqi security personnel, dressed in white uniforms and gas masks, terrified an angry Shia crowd in Najaf and compelled it to disperse with the implicit threat of chemical warfare following the assassination of Ayatollah Mohammed Sadeq al-Sadr in 1999.[124] If accurate, these examples reveal the utility the regime derived from bluffing before domestic audiences about its WMD capabilities and intentions.

Saddam might have sought to mislead his generals about Iraqi capabilities to avoid a deterioration of military morale. In late 2002, he told his generals he had "something up his sleeve," though it appears he was referring to an insurgency.[125] According to Aziz, the generals were surprised when he informed them in December 2002 that Iraq had no WMD, "because his boasting had led many to believe Iraq had some hidden capability." According to the *Duelfer Report*, "Military morale dropped rapidly when he told senior officers they would have to fight the United States without WMD."[126]

Saddam might also have favored incremental compliance with disarmament demands, in part, to preserve the morale and loyalty of employees and bureaucratic supporters of Iraq's WMD establishments. According to Saddam's FBI interrogator, Saddam acknowledged that some Iraq government employees were reluctant to cooperate with inspectors as they were dedicated to their work. He explained, "It was difficult for them to be told one day to open all of their files and turn over all of their work and government secrets to outsiders. It took time and occurred in steps."[127]

This might have been Saddam's way of shifting blame to his subordinates, yet Iraqi officials may, on various occasions, have violated UN *and* Iraqi prohibitions on weapons-related research and import

---

[121] Solingen (2007a: 163), Litwak (2007: 325), Hannay (2009/2010: 16–17), Gause (2010: 153), and Rohde (2010: 53).
[122] Woods, Palkki, and Stout (2011: 219).
[123] Federal Bureau of Investigation (2004a: April 9, 2004, 11).
[124] P. Cockburn, "Saddam Seizes the Moment," *Independent*, April 11, 1999.
[125] *Duelfer Report* (2004: vol. 1, "Regime Strategic Intent," 65).
[126] *Duelfer Report* (2004: vol. 1, "Regime Strategic Intent," 65).
[127] Federal Bureau of Investigation (2004b: Casual Conversation, May 13, 2004, 1).

activities. Amir Rashid explained to Saddam around November 1995 that Iraqi officials had imported prohibited gyroscopes through Jordan, without informing their superiors, since "some of the [Iraqi] specialists or others think that we are strict on them, especially Husam and I, concerning the issue of freezing the activity, and that is causing us a problem with the Special Commission." Saddam responded, "What is the truth? Where is the truth in this?"[128] While on later occasions Iraqi officials reportedly disregarded Saddam's orders to comply with inspectors out of belief that Saddam secretly wanted continued obstructionism, Saddam might well have seen in this merely the determination of patriotic, excessively dedicated officials.[129]

In any case, a good deal of evidence indicates that Saddam did not attempt to mislead senior regime officials about his WMD capabilities. In late August 1991 he told his advisors, "I have given them [the Americans] everything. I mean, I have given them everything: the missiles, and the chemical, biological and nuclear weapons."[130] In 1995 he told his inner circle, in a discussion about chemical and biological weapons, "We don't have anything hidden."[131] In August 1995, Saddam complained to his advisors that Iraq had presented everything required of it, and "We don't have anything left," yet the sanctions remained.[132] On a separate occasion he stated that the inspectors "destroyed the weapons," yet wondered, given the inspectors' demands for documents, whether Iraq could "guarantee that somebody didn't forget a file."[133]

In a meeting from around late November 1998, he recalled for his advisors a declaration he had ordered at a Council of Ministers meeting stating that Iraq had no WMD. He emphasized, "I am afraid, comrades, after all I said that you might think we still have hidden chemical weapons, missiles and so forth. We have nothing; not even one screw."[134] On a separate occasion he recalled that he once asked Amer Rasheed in a Council of Ministers meeting, "'In case I am not aware of something, do we have any missiles, biological research, chemical weapons, uranium production or armament?' He replied 'No, nothing is left.'"[135] In January 2002 Saddam asked his ministers, "What can they discover, when we have nothing?"[136] In late 2002, Saddam declared in meetings with his Revolutionary Command Council,

---

[128] Woods, Palkki, and Stout (2011: 280).
[129] *Duelfer Report* (2004: vol. 1, "Regime Strategic Intent," 9–10).
[130] Woods, Palkki, and Stout (2011: 254).   [131] CRRC, SH-SHTP-A-000–990.
[132] CRRC, SH-SHTP-A-001–201.   [133] CRRC, SH-SHTP-A-001–202.
[134] Woods, Palkki, and Stout (2011: 293).   [135] CRRC, SH-SHTP-A-001–198.
[136] *Duelfer Report* (2004: vol. 1, "Regime Strategic Intent," 62).

National Command, ministerial council, and military commanders that Iraq had no WMD.[137]

According to Saddam's FBI interrogator, Saddam "claimed on several occasions he held meetings with all of his ministers and asked them specifically if Iraq had WMD that he was unaware of. All of his ministers stated no, as they cited they knew Hussein's position on WMD matters clearly."[138] When he told his ministers in March 2003 to "resist one week and after that I will take over," it appears he was referring to an Iraqi insurrection against the US-led occupiers rather than a hidden WMD capability.[139] While Huwaysh wondered in 2002 if Iraq had completely disarmed, he attributed his doubts to Bush's accusations rather than Saddam's rhetoric or Iraqi behavior.[140] Similarly, General Raad Hamdani, who served from 1991 to 2003 as a Division Commander and Chief of Staff of Iraq's Republican Guard, believes that Saddam "used the technique of vagueness, i.e. deterrence through doubt, to avoid war, if possible." He came to this conclusion, however, because of reports in "our enemy's media outlets" of Iraqi WMD, as well as Saddam's firm political stances and high morale. While during this thirteen-year period Hamdani attended most Republican Guard meetings with Saddam, he makes clear that Saddam "never signaled the existence of WMD, neither in a statement of any kind nor by any hints."[141]

Iraqi concerns about regime security did lead to increased uncertainties about Iraq's WMD stockpiles and programs, yet the ambiguity might well have been little more than an unintended byproduct of policies intended to protect the regime. For instance, Iraq fiercely resisted certain UN inspections and intelligence collection techniques for fear that they would provide the United States with targeting information on the Baath leadership.[142] UNSCOM efforts to inspect Republican Guard, Special Republican Guard, and Iraqi intelligence facilities proved particularly contentious, as these groups had responsibilities not only for securing Iraq's WMD but also for protecting the regime.[143] The regime also opposed inspectors' interviews of scientists for fear that inspectors would obtain information endangering regime security.[144]

---

[137] *Duelfer Report* (2004: vol. 1, "Regime Strategic Intent," 65).
[138] Federal Bureau of Investigation (2004b: Casual Conversation, May 13, 2004).
[139] *Duelfer Report* (2004: vol. 1, "Regime Strategic Intent," 65–66).
[140] *Duelfer Report* (2004: vol. 1, "Regime Strategic Intent," 62).
[141] David Palkki's email correspondence with General Raad Hamdani, January 11, 2011. The authors are grateful to Khalid Seirafi for translating this correspondence.
[142] *Duelfer Report* (2004: vol. 1, "Regime Strategic Intent," 64), CRRC, SH-SHTP-A-000–786.
[143] *Duelfer Report* (2004: vol. 1, "Annex C: Iraq's Security Services," 85–95).
[144] *Duelfer Report* (2004: vol. 1, "Regime Strategic Intent," 62).

Compartmentalization of Iraq's WMD programs and security apparatus, intended largely to secure the regime, also led to a good deal of ambiguity. While Saddam's lieutenants told US interrogators that they were unaware of any remaining Iraqi WMD, some expressed uncertainty about whether other elements within the government might have maintained secret stockpiles or programs.[145] Coming clean would be extremely difficult, Hussein Kamil explained to Saddam and a handful of other senior advisors on May 2, 1995, since "Some of our teams are working in one direction, where another team does not know that they are working above in the same direction." Teams "not known to anyone" continued working on nuclear issues, he added, "even though everything is done and we are through with it."[146] Saddam might have done more to limit such bureaucratic compartmentalization and infighting, though it is far from clear that the resulting ambiguity was a goal as opposed to a mere byproduct of a bureaucratic structure and procedures designed to protect the Iraqi leader.

Conclusions

As we wrote at the outset, a good deal of intellectual humility is in order when writing about the internal dynamics of autocratic countries like Qaddafi's Libya or Saddam's Iraq. Notwithstanding newly released Iraqi records, on relatively few issues can one confidently proclaim, "We now know …" Emerging evidence at the CRRC and elsewhere will enable reassessments of our findings and new insights into the causal links between external inducements, distributional effects, and WMD decision-making. This is important, as much work remains.

Making sense of how inducements lead to nuclear reversal decisions is neither easy nor straightforward. The evidence from Iraq and Libya suggests that whatever effects inducements have, the relationship between inducements and denuclearization decisions is not necessarily a linear causal relationship. It is far too simple to view inducements as independent variables, denuclearization decisions as dependent variables, and domestic distributional effects as conditioning variables. For instance, Saddam and many other leaders have worked to deflect sanctions and manipulated the nature of external inducements by appealing to domestic constituencies in other countries. Inducing denuclearization involves strategic interactions, in which each side is both inducer

---

[145] *Duelfer Report* (2004: vol. 1, "Regime Strategic Intent," 62).
[146] Woods, Palkki, and Stout (2011: 275–279).

and target. Analysis is further frustrated by the need to take into account the perceptions of leaders as quixotic as Qaddafi.

Some of our findings are nevertheless worth highlighting. Common to both cases is strong evidence that comprehensive, multilateral sanctions had a significant role in shaping decisions over WMD. In Libya, sanctions were comprehensive by virtue of Tripoli's overwhelming dependence on oil and long-standing pariah status. While sanctions on Iraq became increasingly targeted over time, available captured audio files overwhelmingly indicate the effectiveness of sanctions during the earlier years. Contrary to scholarship suggesting that autocracies care about maintaining only a narrow group of domestic allies, sanctions' coercive effects were not limited to placing strains on the leadership's ability to retain a coalition of influential elites. The devastating effects of sanctions on the general populations weighed heavily on the leaders. Both Qaddafi and Saddam worried that declining standards of living for the average citizen would have a negative effect on the legitimacy and legacy of their respective regimes. Fear that disgruntled masses fed opposition groups was also an important concern.

Of course there are also important differences between the two cases. For one, Libya verifiably disarmed while Iraq's reversal was, at least at the time, more ambiguous. Some scholars suggest that Libyan leaders chose verifiable denuclearization in response to a tacit but nonetheless credible security assurance, whereas Saddam felt a need for an ambiguous deterrent since the United States had "priced itself out of the reassurance market" with its emphasis on regime change. Others argue that Libya's clear reversal stemmed from the "demonstration effect" of the US invasion of Iraq along with the interdiction of the *BBC China*. Unless better evidence emerges from Libya, this will likely remain an argument without end.[147]

Solingen's emphasis on temporal considerations evokes important questions regarding Libyan and Iraqi denuclearization decisions. Qaddafi had sought nuclear weapons for some three decades, with precious little to show for his efforts. Prestige, security, and other benefits seldom flow from failure. To the contrary, Qaddafi's inability after so many years to obtain nuclear weapons risked projecting weakness and incompetence. Meanwhile, his regime continued to pay a heavy price as a result of sanctions and isolation. To the extent that temporal factors played a role in Libya's disarmament, then, it is possible that with the passage of time Libya's nuclear program delivered steadily declining

---

[147] The phrase "argument without end" comes from Pieter Gayle's famous definition of history. See Dallek (1984: vii).

marginal returns. If so, this suggests the need to focus on progress in demonstrated capability rather than on temporal arguments, per se, that assume stepwise development of a nuclear program.

In the case of Iraq, it is unclear that the regime resisted complying with demands to verifiably scale back its nuclear program more when its program was advanced than when it was relatively basic. In part this might be because the regime faced a relatively small decline in its marginal returns given ambiguities over whether, and to what degree, it had actually reversed course. Baathist leaders, however, did fight tooth and nail to maintain the most basic dual-use chemical, biological, and nuclear facilities and know-how. Terrified that the United States and other states sought to de-industrialize Iraq, for the Iraqi leadership the most undesirable step down the proliferation ladder might well have been the bottom rung. Whatever the case, Solingen's emphasis on timing and temporal considerations provides scholars with much to chew on.

Part IV

Conclusions: understanding causal
mechanisms and policy implications

10   Ten dilemmas in nonproliferation statecraft

Etel Solingen

> In dealing with those nations that break rules and laws, I believe that
> we must develop alternatives to violence that are tough enough to
> change behavior – for if we want a lasting peace, then the words of
> the international community must mean something. Those regimes
> that break the rules must be held accountable. Sanctions must exact
> a real price. Intransigence must be met with increased pressure –
> and such pressure exists only when the world stands together as one.
> One urgent example is the effort to prevent the spread of nuclear
> weapons, and to seek a world without them ... It is also incumbent
> upon all of us to insist that nations like Iran and North Korea do
> not game the system. Those who claim to respect international law
> cannot avert their eyes when those laws are flouted. Those who care
> for their own security cannot ignore the danger of an arms race in
> the Middle East or East Asia. Those who seek peace cannot stand
> idly by as nations arm themselves for nuclear war ... I know that
> engagement with repressive regimes lacks the satisfying purity of
> indignation. But I also know that sanctions without outreach – and
> condemnation without discussion – can carry forward a crippling
> status quo. No repressive regime can move down a new path unless
> it has the choice of an open door. (President Barack Obama, Peace
> Prize Speech, Oslo 2010)[1]

Few topics are as critical to peace and international security as is nuclear
proliferation. The illegitimate pursuit of nuclear weapons featured
prominently as a justification for going to war in Iraq and will likely
remain a crucial challenge for any administration grappling with the
future of the Middle East, East Asia, and beyond. President Obama's
Nobel Prize speech echoes the view that different proliferation cases
entail different responses; that sanctions must be biting but a door to
dialogue should remain open; and that collective action (coordination
across senders) is key. A remarkable speech that in many ways reflects
state of the art thinking about statecraft in the early twenty-first century, it also mirrors some of the outstanding quandaries facing the

---

[1] Full transcript at www.msnbc.msn.com/id/34360743.

international community in its effort to stem nuclear proliferation. This concluding chapter highlights ten crucial dilemmas in nonproliferation statecraft.

Economic sanctions were traditionally considered the best alternative to military force. Yet growing perceptions that neither sanctions nor positive inducements have been effective in recent nonproliferation cases has fueled a re-thinking of options spanning the coercion-persuasion spectrum. This volume explored this range of instruments with special emphasis on their domestic distributional consequences on target states. There is ample divergence among authors over why, how, and whether comprehensive sanctions work; why, how, and whether targeted sanctions are more effective; why, how, and whether positive inducements are more valuable tools than negative ones; what causal paths underlie each of these inducements; and the possibility that all types may have proved futile in the last decade or so or, conversely, that they may have had more significant effects than suspected. The volume's primary aspiration was not to settle such disagreements – common in the social sciences – but rather to advance our understanding of the processes, causal mechanisms, and scope conditions that link particular inducements to specific outcomes. On the one hand our focus on causal mechanisms redirects the study of inducements beyond simple pronouncements on whether or not they "work," emphasizing no less the "why" and "how." On the other hand, efforts to unpack causal paths of inducements within target states reveal the complexity of the task, one that cannot in any case be forsaken. Outcomes are ultimately of crucial interest but a narrow focus on them comes at the expense of a deeper and more productive understanding of why different instruments may or not yield their expected effects under particular circumstances. Unintended and unexpected effects of inducements influence the distance between expectations and outcomes, raising several dilemmas of utmost significance for improving nonproliferation scholarship and practice.

Chapter 1 identified several causal logics linking various inducements to outcomes, including the target state's dominant models of political survival (inward-looking versus internationalizing), regime type (democratic versus autocratic), inducement type (positive or negative, targeted or comprehensive), and the importance of context, timing, sequences, and strategic interaction between senders and targets. Different chapters dwell on one or several causal mechanisms stemming from those logics. Together they raise at least ten dilemmas that, though discussed under separate sub-headings in this concluding chapter, are clearly intertwined analytically and empirically.

1 Most targeted but least vulnerable? Autocratic inward-looking models

The first dilemma emerging from this volume's focus stems from the following fact: domestic political economy models of regime survival closer to the inward-looking ideal-type tend to account for most cases of non-compliance with international commitments to eschew nuclear weapons in the last two decades.[2] Hence, regimes advancing such models have also been the most frequent targets of external inducements, particularly sanctions. The dilemma arises because the very structure, composition, preferences, and strategies of inward-looking models also make them most resistant to external inducements, particularly negative but even positive ones. The standard causal mechanism for sanctions in such contexts goes something like this: sanctions offer an opportunity for beneficiaries of economic closure to perpetuate and enhance their rents while invoking unity, solidarity, heroism, sacrifice, purity, and nationalist resistance to external intrusion, so that → the scarcity of any products in the target economy can be both blamed on such intrusion and offset through domestic substitution and smuggling, which in turn → enhances economic revenues for inward-looking constituencies, all of which → further concentrates their political power → making any concessions on their part futile and even counterproductive.

The standard causal mechanism for positive inducements is different but their outcome may not be. Positive inducements offer the prospect of additional rents but inward-looking ruling coalitions also regard them as sources of Pyrrhic gains and Trojan horse opportunities. This is so because positive inducements can → dilute these coalitions' credentials at home for "cooperating" with the very enemy erstwhile blamed for all problems, and → such inducements insidiously inject external influences into the domestic political economy → with deleterious short and longer-term effects on the ruling coalition, which → deter it from accepting positive inducements, and → allow it to dig its heels in non-compliant terrain. The basic incentive structures for both sanctions and positive inducements thus explain many a failure to persuade inward-looking regimes to renounce the pursuit of nuclear weapons.[3]

---

[2] Solingen (2007a). Inward-looking models provide only near-necessary but not sufficient conditions for non-compliance. Inward-looking models may comply with NPT and IAEA obligations more often than not but the probability of non-compliance is higher among them than among internationalizing models.

[3] Solingen (1994a, 1994b, 2007a) and Bernauer and Ruloff (1999).

As noted in Chapter 1, political economy models of regime survival (inward-looking versus internationalizing) and political regime type (democracy versus autocracy) are two separate analytical categories. Inward-looking models are conceptually and empirically distinguishable from autocratic ones.[4] On the one hand, democracies can adopt inward-looking political economy models and historically some have done so, as India and Israel, although both transcended those models once internationalization gathered sufficient political traction. On the other hand, autocratic regimes can advance internationalizing models and historically some have done so, as have South Korea, Taiwan, Chile, and others that later became democratic.

In the particular domain of NPT and IAEA violations, however, there is a high degree of confluence between inward-looking political economies and autocratic regime type, as evident in the cases of Iraq, Libya, North Korea, Iran, and Syria.[5] Chapter 1 elaborated on the logic of the finding that autocratic regimes are less vulnerable to sanctions and better able to channel their negative effects onto the population, particularly regime enemies.[6] A weakened and suppressed opposition, in turn, can hardly challenge the regime's nuclear policies through a free press or other means, nor can it accurately gauge its own mobilizing potential in the absence of freedom of assembly, speech, and independent polling. Those constraints can become self-reinforcing, stifling the opposition's incentives to confront the regime. Furthermore, sender states face particular difficulties in crafting targeted sanctions for autocratic regimes because the informational demands regarding crucial actors, coalitions, domestic institutions, and their respective leverages are particularly taxing.[7]

The convergence of autocratic regime types and inward-looking models thus yields targets that are especially resistant to, or hardened against, external inducements. This first dilemma thus points to the irony that the most frequent targets of external influence attempts

---

[4] For a detailed characterization of these models, and the distinction between them and regime types, see Solingen (1998, 2007b).

[5] On UNSC resolutions on all these cases, see Reynolds and Wan, Chapter 3. On Syria, see also Heinonen (2010), Spector and Berman (2010), and www.isis-online.org/uploads/isis-reports/documents/Syria_24May2011.pdf. On Iran, see www.isis-online.org/uploads/isis-reports/documents/Iran_24May2011.pdf. Some include Burma in this category, following unconfirmed reports that it sought nuclear weapons under an inward-looking autocracy (IAEA 2010; Engelberg 2010; www.isis-online.org/uploads/isis-reports/documents/Burma_Analysis_Bomb_Reactors_11April2011.pdf).

[6] See also Nooruddin (2002), Marinov (2005), Letzkian and Souva (2007), Allen (2008b), and Escriba-Folch and Wright (2010).

[7] Steve Krasner advanced this point at the Laguna workshop.

are also expected to be the least vulnerable to them.[8] As Haggard and Noland suggest, authoritarian inward-looking regimes are likely to be relatively indifferent to both sanctions and most positive inducements. The capacity of North Korea's regime to absorb the adverse effects of sanctions has proven extraordinarily high, enabling it to survive far greater challenges of widespread famine and death of possibly up to one million people. Palkki and Smith recount Saddam Hussein's ability to survive massive Iraqi losses in two major wars he had initiated, international sanctions, and decades of internal massacres of Shia and Kurdish communities, as well as Qaddafi's resilience to decades of sanctions and isolation. At the same time, the Libyan case suggests that even regimes defined by the double whammy of inward-looking autocratic models can become receptive to the right combination of inducements, positive and negative, with respect to nuclear weapons' acquisitions. Haggard and Noland consider inducements to be a very difficult but not an impossible strategy even in the North Korean context.

2   Do sanctions strengthen the dominant coalition? Type 1 unintended effects

Beyond the lower vulnerability of inward-looking autocracies to sanctions is the related question of whether or not sanctions actually *strengthen* regimes in target states more generally, an extension of the previous dilemma. I label this possibility Type 1 unintended effect given its prominence in the literature on sanctions. Several chapters discuss this general dilemma of economic statecraft whereby sanctions designed to weaken the dominant faction in target states end up buttressing it instead. They can do so directly, by allowing it to shift scarce resources to itself, and indirectly by further weakening opponents. Opponents that are most dependent on international economic openness tend to be most adversely affected by comprehensive sanctions, although not necessarily by targeted ones. Nader observes this dilemma in the Iranian context, where the regime did not bear the brunt of sanctions and in fact benefited from them financially through its control of state resources, especially oil revenues.[9] Monopoly over oil rents and over repression enabled regime hardliners to weather economic and political challenges, such as massive protests over allegedly

---

[8] Haass (1998). The flip side of this is that internationalizing democracies are hypothesized to be most vulnerable to external inducements, which may explain why they are less likely to embrace policies that would expose them to sanctions in the first place. See discussion of selection effects in the study of sanctions in Chapter 1.

[9] Shuster (2010).

fraudulent June 2009 presidential elections, while shifting the costs to the population, most recently through the removal of a massive subsidy system. While sanctions may have damaged Iran's economy overall, they are seen as enhancing the resources of the principlist faction and the IRGC, all vested in the status quo. Indeed, to reassure those constituencies of their continued monopoly of the economy, Ahmadinejad declared: "We welcome sanctions," while acknowledging that sanctions have made his camp stronger.[10]

Studies beyond nuclear proliferation found sanctions on human rights violations, particularly of the comprehensive type, to increase repression by authoritarian regimes, weaken democracy and human rights, and undermine press freedoms and the physical integrity of regime opponents.[11] The causal mechanisms are varied, for instance leading from sanctions to → threatening the stability of incumbent target leaders, which triggers → regime overreaction to the perceived insecurity and uncertainty induced by sanctions, thus encouraging → increased repression of challengers and dissenters. Although it might be difficult to measure variation in levels of repression by North Korea's regime over the last two decades, there has been greater variability in the Iranian case. This variability, however, may have been far more related to shifting domestic factional trends than to the effect of sanctions. Reformist president Khatemi was far less repressive even though sanctions remained in place during his tenure. Conversely, heightened repression under Ahmadinejad, particularly after June 2009, can be more easily traced to his radical inward-looking autocratic model than to sanctions. The penchant for closing down opposition media and websites, among many other measures of dramatically declining human and political rights in Iran, increased under Ahmadinejad. Whether dominant factions backed by IRGC and Basiji forces would have abstained from suppressing such political challenges in a hypothetical environment free of sanctions is questionable.

And yet sanctions help autocrats justify repression and maintain what Galtung labeled "pluralistic ignorance" or confusion about where the majority stands. In his words, "what matters is not so much what people think as whether they think there are many who share their treacherous thoughts."[12] Accurately gauging such potential is difficult, burdening the opposition's ability to ascertain its relative power vis-à-vis that of the regime. Autocracies come in different forms, however. Recent findings that personalist dictatorships are more vulnerable to sanctions

---

[10] Quoted in Guo (2009).   [11] Wood (2008) and Peksen and Drury (2009).
[12] Galtung (1967: 399).

than are single-party or military autocracies would suggest that North Korea is more vulnerable than Iran.[13] Yet, Haggard and Noland suggest that sanctions appeared to have had little effect on the stability of North Korea's personalist regime for decades. The same might be said of Saddam's Iraq, although Palkki and Smith find signs of competing causal mechanisms for sanctions, some strengthening Saddam's hold on power in the 1990s, others weakening it, as evidenced by Saddam's own expressed concerns as well as those of his aides. Sanctions helped Saddam monopolize smuggling routes, manipulate the supply of scarce commodities, reward regime loyalists, decimate Iraq's middle class, and undermine potential rivals. But Palkki and Smith also find that comprehensive multilateral sanctions played a significant role in shaping decisions over WMDs even in Iraq's (and Libya's) hardened inward-looking autocracies. As newly available records confirm, in the final analysis sanctions exacerbated Saddam's concerns with internal challenges and prevented him from developing nuclear weapons. Saddam and his lieutenants were deeply concerned with sanctions-induced declines in economic conditions, morale, regime cohesion, and legitimacy, all of which exacerbated Saddam's sense of insecurity. Contrary to the argument that autocratic leaders care only about a narrow group of domestic allies, Palkki and Smith find comprehensive sanctions to have weighed heavily on Qaddafi and Saddam, who feared that declining standards of living eroded their regimes' legitimacy and legacy, and strengthened the opposition. Those fears were justified and, in Qaddafi's case, popular deprivations rather than external intervention led to the onset of upheaval in early 2011.

Iran's corporate autocracy has been shaken by deeper internal cleavages more than anything else, but sanctions deepened those internal divisions and competition for spoils and rents. The regime has been able to rely on oil wealth (non-tax revenues) in good times to retain its hold on power but the vagaries of oil revenues exacerbated internal struggles. The increasingly adversarial relationship between Ahmadinejad on the one hand, and Khamenei and elements of the IRGC on the other, are a recent illustration. Nader and others note how sanctions enhanced domestic cleavages and stimulated broader debates over the nuclear program.[14] A 2009 *WorldPublicOpinion.org* poll revealed that two-thirds of Iranians polled would accept an agreement that precluded Iran's development of nuclear weapons; only one-third would negotiate away the right to enrich uranium and 38 percent favored

---

[13] Escriba-Folch and Wright (2010).
[14] See also Guo (2009), Crane (2010), and Chubin (2010a and 2010b).

nuclear weapons.[15] Though public opinion polls may be even less reliable in autocratic contexts and do not determine the outcome of Iran's elections in any event, domestic divisions can influence – and sometimes radicalize – the competitive outbidding among Iran's leaders.

In sum, the effect of sanctions on regime stability is mediated, to a large extent, by the dominant political economy model no less than by specific autocratic institutional forms. Most importantly, while sanctions indeed have the potential for strengthening the dominant coalition, it is not necessarily the case that increased repression, murder, harassment, imprisonment, and evisceration of the opposition's media are either a consequence of sanctions or an expression of regime strength. Repression is at least as often an expression of regime weakness, as the Libyan case clearly proved. Type 1 unintended effects are certainly authentic and reflected empirically in some cases but other instances – discussed below – suggest that sanctions do not inevitably strengthen regimes in power. As Stein notes, when sanctions are economically consequential, their political effects can range from strengthening state leaders to accelerating their downfall. A broader study found that economic sanctions do not always, or typically, empower dictators but rather reduce, on average, the chances of survival in office.[16] Deepening cleavages in Iran's dominant coalition, not easily separable from enhanced sanctions, seem to have indeed reduced Ahmadinejad's chances for survival in power.[17]

3   Do positive inducements weaken the opposition? Type 2 unintended effects

Chapters differ over the merits of positive inducements and their effects on target states' opposition. Stein notes that positive inducements fail in the same way that sanctions do unless the difficulties of forging state power and international cartels can be overcome, and elaborates on additional unintended effects of positive inducements. Reynolds and Wan point to the capturing of positive inducements in Iraq by a select few, and Palkki and Smith note Saddam's own mistrust of such inducements as potential threats to his hold on power. Nincic nonetheless makes the case for positive inducements, stipulating crucial scope conditions that

---

[15] Available at www.worldpress.org/Mideast/3424.cfm.
[16] Marinov (2005).
[17] Although Iran's revolution has always been plagued with cleavages, calls by supporters of Khamenei for "Death to opponents of the supreme leader" directed against Ahmadinejad, suggest that divisions within the regime may have reached unusual magnitude (Neil MacFarquar, "Power Struggle in Iran Enters the Mosque," *New York Times*, May 7, 2011, A5).

must be met for target regimes to be receptive to such inducements. First, the regime must feel insecure domestically and seek support from additional constituencies. Second, the domestic political economy must not be completely sealed from the international one, so that independent economic actors can favor closer links to the global economy. Third, positive inducements must directly benefit those independent actors being wooed by the regime. Fourth, the regime must value the support of new groups more than the policies it is asked to abandon. When all these conditions are met, he argues, positive inducements strengthen the opposition as they "help reconfigure interests and preferences ... so that new and moderate sources of regime support emerge."

Yet it may be hard to assess the point at which a regime's position is "insecure," as North Korea watchers have learned from decades of over-predicting its collapse. In addition, weakened and insecure leaders in the dominant coalition may have incentives to *avoid* granting competitors greater power that might dilute their own. Moreover, inducements that have enough in them for contradictory sets of opposition interests could be extremely hard to design. Inducements for those opposing confrontation are sometimes rejected as "tainted" by their would-be beneficiaries. Furthermore, there is always the risk that positive inducements end up buttressing the regime – now in command of additional resources to broaden its own support – rather than that of the opposition.[18] Finally, it is unclear how empirically frequent is the confluence – happy convergence – of all four conditions required for positive inducements to work on behalf of moderates or regime opponents.

North Korea offers not as promising a context for positive inducements, Nincic argues, given a closed state-run economy discouraging the emergence of independent economic actors and a complex civil society. But even there he does not rule out a possible turn to more moderate sources of support by North Korean leaders. Haggard and Noland, however, consider the combination of authoritarianism and the particular coalitional base of North Korea's regime to make it relatively indifferent to economic inducements. Such regimes, in their view, are only likely to be responsive to positive inducements over which they exercise direct control, or from which they profit directly, such as taxes, food and fuel transfers, fees from the Kaesong industrial park, or direct cash payments such as those that enabled the 2000 North–South summit. All those proceeds were controlled by, or worked for the benefit of, inward-looking constituencies, primarily a massive military-industrial complex.

---

[18] Singh (2009) addresses this worst-case scenario where positive inducements fail to deliver verifiable denuclearization while strengthening the dominant coalition in Iran.

Consequently, they argue, external benefits that might stream to constituencies favoring foreign trade, investment, or aid are unlikely to induce inward-oriented autocracies like North Korea's to adjust foreign policy in a more cooperative direction, because increased economic openness threatens the regime's existing rents and enables unwanted information inflows that weaken its power. Hence, even positive inducements by China and South Korea had few concrete benefits, foiled by the regime's "political imperviousness." Positive inducements were also offered during the 2005 breakthrough, the 2006 resumption of talks, the two 2007 agreements, and during Ambassador Christopher Hill's 2008 negotiations, which left unresolved issues of proliferation, HEU, fissile material accumulated stocks, and nuclear weapons themselves. Yet, it remains unclear, they suggest, whether North Korea was willing to deal on those issues eventually; bitter fights over verification raised broader questions about the regime's true intentions. North Korea sought to maintain a minimal nuclear deterrent at best, they conclude; at worst it may have been engaged in elaborate exercises in strategic deception. The potential for moral hazard – encouraging the same bad behavior that positive inducements are designed to forestall – could not be dismissed.

Nincic's proposals for Iran include positive inducements to *bonyads*, among the inward-looking constituencies under Khamenei's control, and perhaps to pragmatic conservatives. There is little indication, however, that leading "pragmatic" conservative Ali Larijani departs sharply or in the right direction from the nuclear preferences of Khamenei or Ahmadinejad. Indeed, Nader mentions Ali Larijani's opposition to the 2009 enriched uranium swap deal (shared by Khamanei), in effect out-radicalizing Ahmadinejad on the nuclear issue. And how interested some of Ahmadinejad's internal regime competitors – as opposed to the Green opposition – are in positive inducements to begin with remains unclear.[19] The sort of positive inducements they might be interested in could well concentrate the regime's power even further, foiling economic and political reform much as in Haggard and Noland's earlier depiction of moral hazard in North Korea's case. Positive inducements would then yield Type 2 unintended effects that

---

[19] As Secretary of the Supreme Council on National Security and Iran's top nuclear negotiator, Larijani threatened to discard the Additional Protocol in 2005. As Majlis Speaker, Larijani made equivocal statements regarding Iran's NPT membership in 2009 and declared in 2011 that the Majlis will definitely take up a bill that would sever diplomatic relations with the UK. See www.insideiran.org/nuclear-program/defiant-iran-rebuffs-iaea-and-escalates-tension-with-the-west. Thaler *et al.* (2010) include Larijani among principlists and Takeyh claims he is wrongly depicted as pragmatic (see Ray Takeyh, "Why Iran Remains Defiant on the Nuclear Bomb," *Washington Post*, December 8, 2011). Cortright and Väyrynen perceive the present regime as having little intention to cooperate effectively with external powers and international bodies.

weaken rather than empower the opposition. This should not be surprising given a policy that Nincic considers to be designed, by definition, to bolster domestic support for the regime. Indeed, if the strategy worked toward this very purpose, it could ironically siphon off support away from the Green opposition and into the dominant coalition from what are otherwise wavering members of the dominant faction.[20] Such potential unintended effects explain why even some latent supporters of positive inducements also consider them politically unpalatable, a theme developed in Stein's chapter.

Nincic invokes China's experience where some military officers embraced elements of a market economy. Such inducements, however, operated in a context where the Communist Party's dominant coalition itself cajoled the military toward international markets and improved relations with the West, in top-down fashion. This is not Iran's case in the foreseeable future, according to Nader, where the dominant coalition resists a similar opening. Indeed, as noted by another observer, "Obama's outreach is infuriating the Iranian leadership. They are at a loss. The last thing they want is to have the world's most powerful politician reach out to the people of Iran and undo years of Iranian efforts to portray the US as the 'Great Satan.'"[21] Similarly Karim Sadjadpour argues that "Iran's ruling clique cannot abandon animosity toward the US because it is an inextricable part of their revolutionary identity."[22] The Obama administration's open door policy to negotiations is thus said to keep Ahmadinejad off balance. Existing cleavages within the IRGC could arguably support a turn to moderation but this would hinge heavily on Iran's top leadership steering that shift, much as Chinese leaders have. As of 2011, the purge of reformist-oriented Guards by more radical peers points in the opposite direction.[23]

Even in the absence of ideal conditions, and even when the cat is out of the bag (i.e., target states have already become nuclear weapons states), Nincic finds it crucial to contain such regimes via "catalytic" strategies. Haggard and Noland, by contrast, find positive inducements to have strengthened North Korea's dominant coalition more often than not, making Type 2 unintended effects more the norm than the anomaly at least in that case. Such effects – dooming the rise of moderate, let alone

[20] Segments of the IRGC supported Mousavi in the 2009 elections. Nobel Peace Laureate Shirin Ebadi opposed World Bank aid to human rights violators, arguing that lending money to "well-kept dictators is to enslave their citizenry" (Shirin Ebadi and Amit Attarn, "When Politics Corrupts Money," *New York Times*, June 16, 2004, A19).

[21] "Congressional Action on Iran Imminent, Lawmaker Says," *Global Security Newswire*, March 23, 2010.

[22] Sadjadpour (2010b).

[23] Guo (2009), Ansari (2010a), and Thaler *et al.* (2010).

oppositional forces – also stem from regime efforts to cast those forces as "minions" of external powers, particularly when positive inducements benefit moderates and advance their aspirations for normal interactions with the rest of the world. This problem arises in a highly nationalistic Iranian context with a vengeance, leading many regime opponents to reject most external inducements except technologies to defeat the regime's monopoly over media and communications.[24] Drezner finds it unfeasible to even identify so-called "moderates" and, in any event, quite likely that moderates fall prey to accusations of external collaboration. Hence he proposes comprehensive positive inducements that might empower the opposition whereas targeted ones would not. Palkki and Smith suggest that positive assurances against regime change as the ones arguably extended to Qaddafi in 2003 – though deemed instrumental in securing denuclearization – undermined the opposition there as well. Yet Libya's opposition was re-energized by the broader Middle East upheavals in early 2011, at which time the opposition pleaded for external intervention to prevent ruthless repression by Qaddafi's forces.

Other circumstances of timing, sequence, and context raise the probability that positive inducements might – under certain conditions – benefit the opposition, thus overturning Type 2 unintended effects. In addition, negative security assurances (that the target state would not be attacked) can potentially strengthen the opposition in principle, by depriving dominant inward-looking leaders from a useful tool to coalesce domestic support for policies favoring protectionism, militarization, and nuclear weapons.

4   Too little or too much? Goldilocks in the world of inducements

Many disagreements over the relative merits of sanctions and positive inducements, the causal mechanisms they are supposed to concatenate, and their imputed outcomes stem from competing interpretations of the empirical record.[25] Some regard positive inducements proffered to target states to have been insufficient whereas others consider them to have been generous enough to have yielded the desired effects had they indeed worked as advertised. The same is true for sanctions, which are sometimes considered too-little-too-late or, conversely, far too exacting. Some of these discrepancies are evident across chapters in this volume,

---

[24] See, for instance, statement by Yousef Mollai, in "Iranian Troubles Seen Aiding West in Nuclear Dispute," *Global Security Newswire*, March 10, 2010.

[25] Experts differ not only in their predictions for the future but in their understanding of the past, even for the case of Libya. On drawing lessons from history that are

raising emblematic dilemmas entailed in calibrating between too-little and too-much so as to arrive at "just right."

4.1   Too little or weak sanctions

Various chapters address the dilution of UNSC resolutions to accommodate China and Russia. Within and beyond the UN context, the problem of collective action, coordination and discrepant individual (state and private) incentives mars the design and implementation of sanctions, a dilemma addressed more expansively below. In the context of the current discussion, coordination problems yield the net effect of attenuated (sometimes labeled "toothless") sanctions. For Drezner only sanctions that impose significant costs on the target economy are more conducive to concessions. Citing a broader literature largely based on statistical analysis, he argues that the cost of sanctions to target states is positively and significantly correlated with successful outcomes.[26] Similarly, on the basis of multilateral sanctions applied throughout the 1990s, others concluded that comprehensive sanctions were more effective than targeted ones, and their political effects most significant where economic and social impact have been greatest.[27] Although skeptical of the utility of financial sanctions, Drezner suggests that they too should have broad-based economic effects to enhance their likelihood of success. Another broader study of sanctions suggests that imposing more lenient sanctions initially, but far more robust ones later, has a higher chance to yield compliance.[28]

As Iran's largest trading partner, the EU was often reluctant to endorse stricter sanctions. The EU-3 (Britain, Germany, and France) took center stage in the negotiating process that followed the 2003 IAEA report on Iran's violations and resolution demanding full disclosure of nuclear activities and unrestricted access to facilities. Additional IAEA reports and resolutions found evidence that Iran had misled inspectors regarding illegal centrifuge procurement; shaping of uranium metal into hemispheres usable for explosive cores in nuclear weapons; testing conventional high explosives for use in an implosion-type nuclear weapon; designs to produce uranium tetrafluoride ("Green Salt"); "administrative connections" among the uranium project, high-explosives tests, and a re-entry vehicle design; and experiments with separation of

riddled with probabilistic loopholes and laced with contingencies, paradoxes, and implicit counterfactual assumptions, see Tetlock (2005).

[26] Dashti-Gibson et al. (1997), Morgan and Schwebach (1997), and Drezner (1999).
[27] Cortright and Lopez (2002).
[28] Hovi et al. (2005).

polonium-210 suitable for nuclear chain reaction.[29] Notwithstanding these unanswered questions, efforts to strengthen multilateral sanctions succumbed to private business and distributional differences within and among senders. From the standpoint of the glass-half-empty interpretation, too-little or weak sanctions explained the lack of progress and Iran's entrenched defiance. The 2009 discovery of the Fordow undeclared enrichment facility, suitable in size for increasing enrichment to weapons-level, pushed Russia and China to endorse a slightly more severe UNSC resolution. Iran rejected a plan backed by France, Russia, and the United States requiring the shipment of 1,200 kilograms of Iran's low-enriched uranium to Russia in exchange for material to fuel its medical isotope production reactor. The plan aimed at deferring Iran's ability to produce sufficient weapons-grade material for nuclear weapons while nuclear negotiations continued. In February 2010 Iran announced that it had begun efforts to enrich uranium to 20 percent, raising further questions about its intentions.[30]

The June 2010 UNSC Resolution 1929 was the strongest of the Chapter VII resolutions on Iran, calling it to comply with previous resolutions and address questions regarding the peaceful nature of its nuclear program while approving a fourth round of sanctions which tightened restrictions on shipping (including inspections) and financial activities; sanctioned IRGC members with connections to the nuclear program; and banned the sale of heavy weapons including battle tanks, large caliber artillery, combat aircraft, warships, missiles, and missile systems to Iran, the first such action against Iran. The United States went beyond the UNSC resolution in its 2010 Comprehensive Iran Sanctions, Accountability, and Divestment Act (CISADA), which threatened penalties on firms supplying Iran with gasoline and refined petroleum products, and further restricted financial transactions. The strongest EU sanctions imposed on Iran over its nuclear program followed, restricting sales of equipment for refining oil and producing gasoline, limiting financial transactions, preventing EU companies and insurers from transacting with Iranian state entities or affiliates, and curtailing the transfer of nuclear and dual-use items for Iran's nuclear program.[31] Canada, Australia, Japan, South Korea, Norway, and others restricted transactions with Iran's oil and gas sector, nuclear, missile, and dual-use goods. After years of overlooking UNSC resolutions, Gulf

---

[29] Arms Control Association (2010; www.iaea.org).
[30] Cortright and Väyrynen (2010). John Carlson, "Iran Nuclear Issue – Considerations for a Negotiated Outcome." Institute for Science and International Security, November 4, 2011.
[31] "Pressure Building," *NuclearIranNews*, July 29, 2010, available at: www.isisnuclear-iran.org/news/detail/424.

Cooperation Countries began scrutinizing transactions, with the UAE alone targeting about 40 companies trading with Iran in "dual-use" materials. This multilateral organization of market power, in Stein's terms, sent authoritative signals to private actors such as Schlumberger Ltd – among the last Western oil companies doing business with Iran and under US investigation for possible sanctions violations – which announced it would end activities once current contracts expired.[32] Accounting firms PricewaterhouseCoopers and Ernst & Young ended operations in Iran. Major US and European maritime insurers confirmed their preference for US business over underwriting oil shipments to Iran, burdening Iran's ability to import refined gasoline, which accounts for about 40 percent of its gasoline needs.[33] Fuel suppliers in the Middle East and Europe declined to refuel Iranian planes, and ships owned by the Islamic Republic of Iran Shipping Lines (IRISL) – no longer able to secure insurance – were seized.

This tightening elicited a flurry of opinion that, at long last, sanctions had started to have serious effects on Iran's economy.[34] Some reported massive discontent and low morale among high-level officials in Iran's nuclear program and elsewhere that presumably led to defections.[35] Others noted, however, that unlike the cases of Iraq and Libya, Iran's crude oil exports were not under sanctions partly for fear that they would undermine global economic recovery.[36] Upheavals throughout the Middle East deepened concerns with global economic repercussions. Yet, as Palkki and Smith suggest, depriving Libya of oil revenues for decades was a crucial component of Qaddafi's nuclear reversal as it diminished resources available to protect him against defections in his ruling coalition and from severe public discontent. By contrast, Iran could rely on economic and political support from China, Turkey, Zimbabwe, Brazil, Organization of Islamic States members, Russia, India and others who retained oil-related and other activities not proscribed by UNSC resolutions.[37] Labeling them "weak tea," some continued to

---

[32] Farah Stockman, "Oil Firm Says It Will Withdraw From Iran," *Boston Globe*, November 12, 2010.

[33] Thomas Erdbrink and Colum Lynch, "New Sanctions Crimp Iran's Shipping Business as Insurers Withhold Coverage," *Washington Post*, July 21, 2010.

[34] The Chairman of the Joint Chiefs of Staff, Admiral Michael Mullen, said: "I've certainly seen a body of evidence that indicates that the sanctions are taking their toll, much more rapidly than some had anticipated, more deeply" (quoted in Pessin 2010). On similar assertions by Secretary of State Hillary Clinton, see Mark Landler, "US Says Sanctions Hurt Iran Nuclear Program," *New York Times*, January 10, 2011.

[35] "Iranian Nuclear Insiders Providing More Information," *Global Security Newswire*, April 26, 2010.

[36] Pickering (2010).

[37] Erdbrink and Lynch, "New Sanctions Crimp Iran's Shipping Business."

dismiss the impact of economic sanctions on Iran's behavior.[38] This was also a far cry from the diplomatic isolation that had suspended South Africa's membership in international institutions and withheld recognition.[39] Even while ranked at the bottom in world public opinion surveys, Iran's status as the fifth-largest oil producer worldwide protected it from the kind of isolation endured by Libya and Iraq, despite similar internal repression, human rights abuses, support for terrorism, and threats to other states. Yet, according to President Obama's nonproliferation advisor Gary Samore, as the costs and risks become high enough Iran could still accept suspension of enrichment activities.[40]

Sanctions on oil-poor North Korea went far beyond those imposed on Iran, making it more difficult – but not impossible – to argue that "weak tea" accounted for North Korea's failure to comply. As Haggard and Noland show, sanctions did not prevent growing Chinese and South Korean trade with North Korea, accounting for between 55 and 80 percent of its total trade. China's compliance with sanctions was reportedly selective and inconsistent, and North Korea's regime remained resilient. As for targeted financial sanctions, after naming BDA a primary money-laundering concern, at least two dozen financial institutions – including Chinese and Vietnamese ones – either ended or limited transactions with North Korea. These measures brought North Korea back into negotiations, argue Haggard and Noland, but only helped make some progress toward denuclearization in the context of positive inducements. The BDA experience may have been "just right" although it did not prevent the 2006 nuclear test and may have even borne some responsibility for it. Indeed, consistent with his embrace of positive inducements, Nincic traces North Korea's missile tests to the BDA affair as a totally counterproductive measure, a view I turn to next.[41]

4.2   Too much or too harsh sanctions

Counter to the glass-half-empty perspective is one suggesting that sanctions have in fact been too harsh, too extensive, or too extended over time. A distinct literature assesses these claims from various ethical standpoints.[42] This volume's focus, however, is on whether, how, and why sanctions may have unleashed the kinds of causal mechanisms and expected effects anticipated by senders. Harsh sanctions have

---

[38] Wall (2010).
[39] Klotz (1995) and Crawford and Klotz (1999).
[40] David E. Sanger, "Harder Push to Stop Iran From Making Nuclear Fuel," *New York Times*, December 11, 2010.
[41] See also Chinoy (2008).   [42]Lopez (1999).

unintended effects, including the potential for undermining civil society; some studies suggest that declines in democracy and human rights have been more pronounced under comprehensive than under targeted sanctions.[43] Cortright and Vyrynen find that coercive disarmament (prior to 2003) worked only in the exceptional case of Iraq, which was both defeated in the 1991 war and subject to draconian multilateral sanctions. Mueller finds sanctions aimed at preventing nuclear proliferation to enhance the likelihood that nuclear weapons will be sought.[44]

Reluctance to hurt constituencies that might be part of the solution has been a partial justification for avoiding sanctions on Iran's oil exports and for diluting proposed measures under the 2010 UNSC resolution, which froze the IRGC's international holdings and assets, and banned travel for some of their leaders. China and Russia vehemently opposed harming "the Iranian people" or "normal trade," decrying sanctions beyond the UN system.[45] "Sanctions should be effective and ... smart," argued President Medvedev, "not lead to humanitarian catastrophe" lest they move Iran's public to hate the entire world. "They should force ... the Iranian leadership to think about what's next" but not cause suffering.[46] Opposed to sanctions on banks, China allowed only one bank to be targeted. Proposals for banning international cargo shipments by Iran Air and IRISL were blocked, allowing inspection only if they were found in violation of previous UNSC resolutions.[47] Proposals prohibiting non-Iranian companies from insuring transport contracts were replaced with "additional steps" to implement existing penalties on insurance for Iran's oil. Proposals to bar non-Iranian entities from buying Iranian state bonds were replaced with calls for "vigilance" in transactions. Even these dilutions, however, evoke objections that "the stick side has been emphasized so much that it is hard for Iran to hear anything positive."[48]

Similar views suggest that sanctions have failed to make North Korea more pliable at the negotiating table and that "strategic patience" would risk waiting an eternity.[49] Sanctions have been an impediment to a negotiated resolution because, in this view, North Korea has demonstrated

---

[43] Wood (2008) and Peksen and Drury (2009).
[44] Mueller (2010).
[45] Neil MacFarquhuar, "UN Approves New Sanctions to Deter Iran," *New York Times*, June 9, 2010.
[46] Quoted in *Good Morning America*, April 9, 2010, transcript at http://abcnews. go.com.
[47] "Insiders See Iran Sanctions Proposal Watered Down," *Global Security Newswire*, March 25, 2010.
[48] Paul Pillar, quoted in "Complications Seen in Nuclear Diplomacy with Iran," *Global Security Newswire*, November 16, 2010.
[49] See, for instance, Sigal (2010).

in no uncertain terms that it would never bow to sanctions and that only US reconciliation with North Korea might change this course. Since these views dovetail with a strong endorsement of positive inducements, I turn to that position next.

4.3   Too little or timid positive inducements

The flip side of the debate over sanctions as glass-half-full or half-empty measures is whether or not positive inducements have been meaningful enough or too timid to yield desired outcomes. Nincic argues that positive inducements offered to Iran have been insufficient to make firm statements about their effects and hence "there is little reason to think they would make matters worse." Modest inducements provided little incentive to give up a nuclear pursuit in this view, one that also concedes that positive inducements should not be considered successful by default, only because sanctions have presumably not worked. Nader suggests that expanded diplomatic and trade relations had a moderating effect on Iran's foreign and national security policies under Rafsanjani and Khatemi. Reynolds and Wan note a secret US diplomatic olive branch to Khatemi and other positive overtures in the late 1990s, and UK and EU restoration of full diplomatic ties with Iran as well as extensive economic exchange.

Yet Nincic sees opportunities not acted upon by sender states under Khatemi, acknowledging that "one cannot be sure that a favorable response from the West would have halted Iran's nuclear program, but the possibility cannot be dismissed." Nader, instead, points to Khamenei's empowerment of the IRGC in security, intelligence, and vigilante organizations that blocked Khatemi's agenda and physically suppressed reformers. This explains inconsistent implementation of nuclear commitments under Khatemi according to Reynolds and Wan, questioning Khatemi's ultimate authority over the program and foiling the effects of external positive inducements.[50] Receptivity to positive inducements declined further with the resurgence of hardliners, according to Nader, who rejected the 2009 P5+1 offer to supply fuel for Tehran's research reactor in exchange for Iran's transfer of a portion of its low-enriched uranium stockpile to Russia for fuel fabrication. While asserting that positive inducements have so far failed, Cortright and Vayrynen propose that more substantive ones could have greater impact, though they do

---

[50] Rowhani (2005) admits that when ratification of the Additional Protocol came along, some argued that "accepting that protocol would amount to treason. Others believed that the Majles must approve it with triple urgency. There were differences of opinion between the factions, and this made the differences between factions even wider."

not specify the domestic circumstances that would enhance such receptivity to external inducements. For Drezner, even the domestic conditions of early 2011 – peak dominance of hardliners – seem suitable for comprehensive engagement that might empower the opposition.

The view that positive inducements might have been too timid surfaces for North Korea as well. Whereas some viewed the US extension of negative security guarantees in the 2005 Joint Statement and in the 2010 US Nuclear Posture Review as a clear positive inducement, others argued that "the United States did not make a sovereign, reliable commitment to not use nuclear weapons against the DPRK if it denuclearized."[51] Only a treaty commitment approved by the US Senate would count, in this view, while acknowledging that "no-one knows if the DPRK would accept this framework." Support for North Korea's economic reconstruction and the development of nuclear power could be withheld until acceptance of a nuclear-weapons-free-zone, presumably leading eventually to North Korea's nuclear disarmament. Others viewed the easing of sanctions to have elicited positive responses from North Korea. The Clinton administration's promise to end sanctions under the Trading with the Enemy Act arguably led to the 2000 first-ever North–South summit. The Bush administration made a similar promise that arguably led to the disabling of nuclear facilities at Yongbyon. Regrettably, in this view, neither promise by the United States was ever fully implemented.[52] The Bush administration was blamed for wasting the opportunity to deal with a healthy, confident Kim Jong-il and for letting internal US divisions over verification prevail.[53]

Finally, the initiative to abolish the nuclear arsenals of all nuclear weapon states, the leitmotif of the speech by President Obama quoted at the beginning of this chapter, could arguably be considered an indirect positive inducement. Article VI, however, is hardly the main driver for nuclearization of new states. As Schelling (2009: 131) argues, "concern over North Korea, Iran, or possible non-state violent entities is justified, but denuclearization of Russia, the United States, China, France, and the United Kingdom is pretty tangential to those prospects." At the same time, serious progress in the road to zero nuclear weapons would signal a valuable erosion of their

[51] Hayes (2010). The 2010 Nuclear Posture Review stipulates that the United States will not use or threaten to use nuclear weapons against non-nuclear weapons states that are party to the NPT and in compliance with their nuclear nonproliferation obligations.

[52] Sigal (1998, 2010).

[53] Jeffrey Lewis, quoted in Martin Matishak, "U.S. Should Reconsider North Korea Strategy, Experts Say," *Global Security Newswire*, December 7, 2010; Chinoy (2008).

value. Ironically, this may not be regarded as positive an inducement by inward-looking regimes interested in the development of nuclear weapons because it would deprive them of an oft-cited excuse, a subterfuge for developing their own nuclear weapons in violation of their NPT commitments. Their actual reasons for doing so – the nature of their regime survival model – would thus become even more apparent. Progress toward a global zero, instead, might strengthen the case of domestic constituencies receptive to both denuclearization and internationalization.

4.4   Too much positive inducements

In contrast to the preceding section, others see too many positive inducements to have been proffered to no avail, breeding moral hazard and deceit. In response to a question by a member of the Supreme Cultural Revolution Council, who asked why Iranian nuclear activities were not done in secret, Supreme National Security Council Secretary Hassan Rowhani said: "This was the intention; this never was supposed to be in the open. But in any case, the spies exposed it. We did not want to declare all this … We had kept some things secret and thought nobody knew about them," adding that "It … became evident that the IAEA knew about some secret tests we had conducted a number of years earlier."[54] Rowhani, associated with pragmatic conservatives, also acknowledged to Iran's newspaper *Kayhan* that Tehran had achieved brilliant results in technical, legal, political, propaganda, and national security spheres while negotiating with the EU-3. "It may seem on the surface that we have accepted the suspension. But in reality, we have used the time to alleviate many of our shortcomings. We continued building centrifuges until the Paris Accord. After June, we doubled our efforts to make up for the suspension. We have not suspended work in Isfahan, even for a second. Arak has not been suspended at any time."[55] Other Iranian officials added that the EU-3 process also enabled large oil and gas contracts with India, China, Pakistan, and the UAE.

Reynolds and Wan find positive inducements to have been used at a much higher rate in general since 1995, particularly between 1995 and 1999. Their Table B3.8 indicates an increase in the number and diversity of positive inducements vis-à-vis Iran under Khatemi, during the P5+1 process, and following President Obama's election, which

[54] Rowhani (2005).
[55] Interview with *Kayhan*, July 23, 2005, cited in *Global Security: Iran – Fifth Report of Session 2007–08*, House of Commons Foreign Affairs Committee, March 2, 2008.

reinvigorated US diplomatic outreach despite Ahmadinejad's hardline positions. Iran's business deals multiplied, particularly in the oil sector, even after new revelations of long-standing illegal nuclear activities. Yet Iran rejected P5+1 offers of economic, technological, and security incentives conditioned on the suspension of uranium enrichment. Reynolds and Wan highlight that notwithstanding UNSC resolutions demanding such suspension, President Obama offered to negotiate without that precondition. Even Pakistan's former foreign minister Qureshi, representing a country where domestic support for Iran's nuclear efforts is among the highest in the world, acknowledged that the Obama administration "has been extending the olive branch" and that Iran should "make use of it. Engage the world."[56] Iran's public, particularly the young, reportedly considered President Obama's offer of unconditional dialogue a "fair shake" that would make it easier to blame Iran's regime for future sanctions rather than the United States.[57] Critics of this outreach point to their futility, given subsequent revelations of yet another undeclared enrichment facility (Fordow), Iran's commitments to additional ones, its rejection of the 2009 P5+1 offer, its announcement that it began enrichment to 20 percent bringing it closer to a nuclear weapons capability, and more specific IAEA findings regarding suspected military dimensions to Iran's nuclear program.[58]

Reynolds and Wan identify declines in sanctions and a rise in positive inducements vis-à-vis North Korea between 1995–1999 and 2005–2009. The 1994 Agreed Framework stipulated gradual normalization; US security assurances not to use nuclear weapons against North Korea; replacement of North Korea's sensitive reactor with light-water reactors through the Korean Peninsula Energy Development Organization (KEDO); and provision of oil to North Korea in exchange for freezing its reprocessing facility, promising not to build new ones and store fuel rods, resuming talks with South Korea, and allowing unimpeded IAEA inspections. In 1999 former Secretary of Defense William Perry

---

[56] Quoted in "Iran Doesn't Need Nuclear Weapons: Pakistan," *AFP*, October 18, 2010. On Obama's unprecedented outreach, see also Maloney (2009).

[57] Bahman Baktiari, quoted in "Obama Signs Iran Sanctions Legislation," *Global Security Newswire*, July 2, 2010.

[58] On Iran's indifference to positive inducements and how they openly deride security guarantees, see Lindsay and Takeyh (2010: 34) and Takeyh and Maloney (2011). On IAEA findings, see www.isis-online.org/uploads/isis-reports/documents/Iran_24May2011.pdf. Former IAEA deputy director Elli Heinonen declared "We protested officially, but they tricked and misled us, and used the time creatively to keep pushing forward. My former boss and good friend Mohamed ElBaradei never understood that it's too late to act if Iran has violated all agreements, has touched the nuclear material and its weapons program is already in its final stages." See www.spiegel.de/international/world/0,1518,790042,00.html.

proposed normalization of diplomatic relations, relaxation of economic sanctions and other positive opportunities for North Korea. Some restrictions associated with the Trading with the Enemy Act were lifted, easing some trade and travel sanctions, particularly following the 2000 North–South Joint Declaration. In another important landmark, Secretary of State Madeleine Albright visited North Korea.

Yet both sides failed to fulfill commitments and North Korea's 2002 acknowledgment of secret enrichment activities led to the US abandonment of the Agreed Framework, North Korea's expulsion of IAEA inspectors, and its withdrawal from the NPT.[59] Following a tense period under the Bush administration, the September 2005 Joint Statement of Principles issued by Six-Party Talks participants included not only positive commitments to provide food, energy, economic aid, and eventually diplomatic normalization but also negative security guarantees against nuclear or conventional attack on North Korea by the United States, seen as a significant gesture.[60] In 2008 the United States also removed North Korea from the list of state sponsors of terrorism (much to the chagrin of its ally Japan), a concession designed to salvage a deal that would not even require North Korea to accept verification of other nuclear weapons facilities, including enrichment. As Haggard and Noland point out, positive inducements did not preclude continued illicit activities (including counterfeiting), nuclear tests in 2006 and 2009, several rounds of ballistic missile tests, and, as confirmed in late 2010, the construction of a state-of-the-art enrichment facility skirting UNSC sanctions and arguably undetected by US intelligence.[61] Even proponents of positive inducements note that Pyongyang's obstructionism was systematic, applied to major and minor issues, and ultimately made it difficult for external powers to sustain such inducements, a theme clearly highlighted by Haggard and Noland.[62] North Korea also continued its illegal exports of missile and other sensitive technologies to Iran and others, including a nuclear reactor to Syria.

4.5   *Domestic politics, grand bargains, and observational equivalence*

Whether positive inducements are too-little or too-much hinges to a large extent on their domestic distributional consequences. Cortright and Vyrynen note that coercive disarmament failed in most cases because in

---

[59] Wit *et al.* (2004). On North Korea's deception over uranium enrichment, see Gallucci (2011).
[60] Cortright and Väyrynen (2010).
[61] David E. Sanger and William J. Broad, "US Concludes N. Korea Has More Nuclear Sites," *New York Times*, December 14, 2010.
[62] Cortright and Väyrynen (2010).

the final analysis the domestic calculus of expected costs and benefits is decisive for the outcome. Distributional considerations were evident, for instance, in the 2009 P5+1 offer to Iran, rejected by a domestic pincer movement from both so-called pragmatic conservatives and reformists, including Ali Larijani, Mir Hossein Mousavi, and Mehdi Karroubi, all of whom sought to protect themselves from accusations of "sellout" to the outside world. Mousavi's position, however, was quite different from that of conservatives, pragmatic or otherwise. He criticized Ahmadinejad for brushing off the effects of sanctions on Iran's security and economy; decimating Iran's private sector through statization; "hardships arising from demagogic policies" including unemployment, inflation, and growing developmental gaps with Iran's neighbors; "political hallucinations and unbalanced remarks" that have made Iran vulnerable even in its own region; and uncompromising nuclear stands bound to push Iran into total international isolation.[63] In North Korea's case, former US negotiator Victor Cha argued that the view that presumes that all the United States needs to do is provide a peace agreement, energy, food, and diplomatic recognition ignores that North Korea's aggressive military actions have very little to do with sanctions or US negotiating positions and everything to do with domestic regime transition.[64] Drezner argues that its domestic structure makes North Korea's regime more vulnerable to comprehensive sanctions and that negative externalities of increased sanctions in that case stem not from the possibility that they would not work but rather that they *would*, threatening massive population overflows into neighboring countries.

Transcending the "too little of either" debate are proposals for "grand bargains" offering both very attractive positive inducements and very unpleasant negative ones.[65] The empirical record offered in Reynolds and Wan's appendices suggest that positive and negative inducements are designed more often than not to be complementary. Many strong supporters of either sanctions or positive inducements believe they should not be applied in isolation. As Palkki and Smith, Drezner, and Haggard and Noland argue, combining both types of inducement appears most effective.[66] Cortright and Vyrynen emphasize both stronger positive

---

[63] Michael Slackman, "Possibility of a Nuclear-Armed Iran Alarms Arabs," *New York Times*, October 1, 2009; "World Powers Weigh Reply to Iranian Talks Offer," *Global Security Newswire*, July 8, 2010; "Wikileaks Disclosed Iran's Weak Foreign Policies, Says Opposition," *Middle East World News*, December 12, 2010.

[64] Victor Cha, "Belligerence and Internal Weakness," *New York Times*, November 24, 2010.

[65] Riedel and Samore (2008: 125), Pritchard and Tilleli (2010), and Blechman and Brumberg (2010).

[66] See also Foran and Spector (1997).

inducements while reserving a role for sanctions to raise the price of non-compliance and slow down progress toward weapons development. Similarly Reidel and Samore endorse what they label "bigger carrots" but doubt they alone will be effective, arguing instead that tougher multilateral and unilateral sanctions, focused diplomacy, and credible military contingencies must all be part of the nonproliferation statecraft toolkit.

Competing accounts of the Goldilocks dilemma abound, drawing rather different conclusions from experiences with proliferating states. Haggard and Noland suggest that claims that positive inducement strategies are doomed to failure and that they could generate denuclearization cannot be true simultaneously. The fact that the behavior predicted by these two competing narratives is often observationally equivalent presents an intractable methodological problem in assessing the effects of positive inducements. It is nearly impossible to distinguish between responses to positive inducements that are not deemed credible or large enough by target regimes from the behavior of opportunists forever seeking more concessions. In the end, whether inducements of either kind were too little, too much, or just right, has much to do with the observer; the kinds of demands imposed on targets; how reasonable they seemed to different constituencies; and whether they appear to be aimed at regime or policy change. The Goldilocks dilemma is also intertwined with dilemmas of coordination and compounded by the observation that most states engaged in proscribed nonproliferation activities are also transgressors in other areas, a dilemma I explore next.

5   "To link or not to link?" Dealing with serial transgressors

As Reynolds and Wan document for Iran, Iraq, Libya, and North Korea, violators of nonproliferation commitments have also been involved in human rights violations, extensive repression, terrorism, narco-trafficking, money laundering or other illicit behaviors. Hence, they are subjected to sanctions on account of other violations prior to, or in tandem with, sanctions related to nuclear proliferation.[67] Syria fits this profile as well. Libya was suspected of seeking nuclear weapons as early as 1970 and designated a state sponsor of terrorism by the United States in 1979.[68] Multilateral sanctions were only imposed after terrorist attacks

---

[67] For the four countries, Reynold and Wan find nearly 80 percent of sanctions and 56 percent of positive inducements to have been nuclear-related.

[68] Albright (2010).

on Pan Am and UTA flights, leading to UNSC resolutions in 1992 and 1993, neither of which included explicit nuclear-related restrictions because Libya successfully concealed its nuclear program until 2003, when it was caught red-handed importing proscribed enrichment equipment from the A.Q. Khan network. Multilateral sanctions were imposed on Qaddafi's domestic human rights violations only in February 2011, when the regime violently suppressed an initially peaceful uprising. Saddam's stranglehold on Iraq since the early 1970s entailed horrific and large-scale human rights abuses, including the use of chemical weapons on minorities and the invasion of Iran leading to massive deaths of noncombatants among many other international transgressions. Yet Iraq only came under comprehensive sanctions following its 1990 invasion of Kuwait, UNSC resolutions, and the US Iraq Sanctions Act. And only after the 1991 occupation of Iraq uncovered the depth of Saddam's illegal nuclear activities did UNSC resolutions tie nuclear proliferation to existing sanctions, demanding the destruction of Iraq's WMD programs and compliance with international inspections.

North Korea's 1950 invasion of South Korea and China's intervention led President Truman to invoke the 1917 Trading with the Enemy Act; declare North Korea a threat to US national security and apply the Treasury Department's Foreign Assets Control Regulations forbidding financial transactions with it. The ruthless autocratic inward-looking regime guided by *juche* ideology and autarky mistrusted even the Soviet Union and China, both of which provided it with material support and war-tested security guarantees. Thus North Korea began searching for nuclear weapons arguably as early as the 1950s, efforts that may have escaped the attention of US nonproliferation estimates until decades later.[69] The bombing of Korean Airlines flight 858 in 1987 led the United States to designate North Korea a state supporter of terrorism and impose rigorous trade controls. The United States subsequently targeted North Korean firms involved in missile proliferation to Iran, Syria, Pakistan, and Yemen. Even after the 2002 revelation of North Korea's clandestine enrichment program and its 2003 NPT withdrawal, the UNSC abstained from resolutions sanctioning North Korea. Only the 2006 long-range ballistic missile tests triggered a UNSC resolution, followed by North Korea's nuclear test and another UNSC resolution. Multilateral sanctions related to North Korea's nuclear program were thus imposed rather recently despite its decades-long record of illegal nuclear activities. As in the previous three cases, sanctions on Iran initially had no connection to nuclear proliferation. The 1979–1980 US

---

[69] Solingen (2007a); see also Mazarr (1995).

embassy takeover and support for terrorism, narco-trafficking, and money laundering throughout the 1980s triggered unilateral sanctions against Iran's oil and military sectors, which expanded to a comprehensive trade and investment ban by 1987. US sanctions escalated in the 1990s due to concerns with WMD proliferation but UNSC sanctions on proliferation activities were first applied only in 2006, years after Iran's long-standing illicit program was more fully revealed.

Serial transgressions by nuclear proliferators raise the dilemma of whether sender states should link compliance in one issue area with other issue areas, demand acquiescence with international expectations across the board on all issues, or create a hierarchy of issues that must be complied with in some sequential order. The dilemma "to link or not to link" came to the fore, for instance, as President Obama considered whether or not to pressure Iran's hardliners for their violent repression following the June 2009 elections. The decision to abstain from more direct intervention might have been guided either by efforts to protect the opposition from accusations of acting on behalf of foreign agents or by a strategy placing the nuclear issue – rather than domestic repression – at the top of the transgression hierarchy.[70] The dilemma led to a flurry of contradictory advice, some discouraging linkages across issues, others favoring a strategy of sensitizing the Iranian public to the links between individuals and entities advancing nuclear defiance and those engaged in repression.[71] Some advocated raising human rights issues in negotiations with Iran and in US public statements whereas others prodded the United States to provide strong support for Iran's democratization while minimizing pressures on the nuclear issue.[72] Nobel Peace Laureate Shirin Ebadi warned against additional sanctions, claiming that they would harm Iran's population rather than the regime, drawing attention to the need to prevent corporations such

---

[70] Mohsen Milani and Suzanne Maloney, "Foreign Affairs Live: Iran in Crisis," July 23, 2009, available at: www.youtube.com/watch?v=d1JyQ_6CVF8. A few months after the height of the repression President Obama declared in his Nobel Peace Prize speech: "We will bear witness to ... the hundreds of thousands who have marched silently through the streets of Iran." About 20,000 people were reportedly arrested on the thirty-first anniversary of the Islamic Revolution (Nazila Fathi, "Iranian Authorities Close 2 Opposition Publications," *New York Times*, March 2, 2010).

[71] Askari (2010), Wright (2010), and Levitt (2010). In October 2010 the Obama administration targeted eight Iranian officials charged with human rights abuses for violations in the nuclear proliferation area.

[72] Singh (2009) and Milani (2010a) criticized US policy for its lack of encouragement of Iranian democrats opposed to nuclear weapons; unrealistic ultimatums on the nuclear issue; and repeated change of course. Rafsanjani reportedly argued that "it will be helpful if the West spoke out against the election fraud and human rights violation that followed" (quoted in Milani 2010b). See also Ray Takeyh, "The Downside of Sanctions on Iran," *International Herald Tribune*, June 26–27, 2010, 6.

as Nokia-Siemens from providing technology aiding in the regime's repressive behavior, and to avoid negotiating with Ahmadinejad in the wake of his ruthless repression.[73] In 2010 President Obama signed an executive order imposing sanctions against Iranian officials and entities responsible for human rights violations since the June 2009 elections.

Echoing some of these prescriptions, some groups around the world viewed Iran's human rights abuses as a far more powerful mobilizing force than its nuclear defiance. In Brazil, for instance, Iran's decision to stone a woman accused of adultery to death was arguably more effective in mobilizing grassroots Brazilian criticism of the Islamic Republic than its nuclear designs (Iran's response to this criticism was to change the verdict to "hanging").[74] Brazil's lame duck president Lula da Silva may have ignored Iran's human rights violations in his nuclear overtures to Iranian leaders but over 60 percent of Brazilians expressed negative opinions of Iran's regime.[75] Human rights violations also appear to have been more costly to Iran's rulers among Arab public opinion than its nuclear designs, as suggested by polls discussed below. Remarks by Iranian leaders in "support" of the 2011 popular protests in the Arab world only highlighted their duplicitous endorsement of rights denied to its own citizens.

6   Good or bad timing? Good or bad sequence? Inducements in temporal context

Several dilemmas discussed so far are intertwined with yet another: packages of sanctions and positive inducements may be adequate in some circumstances but not others. Furthermore, packages of positive inducements often require sequential implementation, falling prey to shifting domestic and international contexts. Various chapters reflect a widespread view that combinations of inducements allowing target regimes a choice are most effective. President Obama's Nobel speech reflects the broad contours of that consensus: "We must try as best we

---

[73] Remarks at Asia Society Headquarters, March 3, 2010, available at: www.asiasociety.org; see also Akbar Ganji, "Money Can't Buy Us Democracy," *New York Times*, August 1, 2006 and Singh (2009). The US Congress adopted the "Iran Digital Empowerment Act" to facilitate mass internet communications and the "Reduce Iranian Cyber-Suppression Act" authorizing the President to ban US government contracts with foreign companies that sell technology that enables government control and monitoring of the internet. Siemens announced in 2010 that it would not sign new business agreements with Iran.

[74] At least two other women were stoned to death recently and eight more await the same fate (Joel Brinkley, "Ban Ki-Moon's Leadership Fails UN, World," *San Francisco Chronicle*, November 14, 2010).

[75] Pew Research Group, June 17, 2010.

can to balance isolation and engagement ... I know that engagement with repressive regimes lacks the satisfying purity of indignation. But I also know that sanctions without outreach – and condemnation without discussion – can carry forward a crippling status quo. No repressive regime can move down a new path unless it has the choice of an open door." The consensus begins to break down once attention shifts to designing packages that are attentive to domestic distributional effects, timing, context, and other dilemmas discussed above and below.

Timing and sequence are crucial because the domestic political landscape in target states has an independent dynamic that is not always derivative of external circumstances. Domestic struggles for power lead to time inconsistency, or changing preferences over time about the relative value of inducements, positive or negative. A given sequence appropriately designed at a certain point in time can be derailed by domestic dynamics down the road. Indeed, domestic dynamics have often unleashed critical causal mechanisms that shifted North Korea's behavior from collaboration to defection and back, sometimes irrespective of the external context. Many characterize these shifts as erratic and random and some shifts are that indeed. Others regard domestic economic reform, the policy of *son'gun cho̅ngch'i* ("military first"), and nuclear behavior to be more organically or systematically related.[76] Haggard and Noland point to a relatively reformist phase after 1998 leading to partial reforms in 2002 and a North Korean opening missed by a Bush administration preoccupied with North Korean enrichment activities. The demise of reform after 2005, culminating with the devastating currency reform of 2009, entrenched a "military first" model inimical to the implementation of previous commitments. Domestic disaffection with reversed reforms and military shows of force following Kim Jong-il's stroke intruded into nuclear negotiations.

Sequential implementation can also succumb to the competitive nature of incentives for senders and targets, each of which prefers front-loading or realizing their own benefits prior to delivering concessions. The Agreed Framework suffered from this tension, leading to more conscious efforts to design a balanced sequence through the Six-Party Talks. Haggard and Noland depict both North Korean and US moves in those terms, designed to secure the other side's delivery of concessions first while delaying its own irreversible actions until a distant future. This "actions for actions" approach failed as well, in their view, due to derogations on both sides and problems of credibility

---

[76] Solingen (2007a) and McEachern (2008).

and senders' coordination that plagued the tightly-scripted exchange of inducements. Furthermore, they argue, as the regime's cost-benefit calculus vis-à-vis nuclear weapons shifted over time, positive inducements became even more questionable. Some of the same dynamics applied in Iraq, according to Palkki and Smith.

The Iranian case too illuminates difficulties inherent in designing optimal packages and sequences, and how contingent their implementation is on the proclivities of different ruling coalitions at specific points in time. The United States removed its veto on Iran's application for WTO membership as a positive incentive directed at Khatemi, adding to the EU+3's extension of valuable technology, fuel, trade, and security concessions in exchange for Iran's voluntary (and temporary) suspension of uranium enrichment and implementation of the Additional Protocol. Some describe this period as a market failure that aborted a more stable collaborative relationship. Yet these sequential moves on both ends reflected some commitment to "specific (conditional) reciprocity" under the Clinton and Khatemi administrations.[77] Subsequently Iran's domestic context did not countenance "specific reciprocity" in response to President Obama's unprecedented and unconditional overtures to Iran which, as Reynolds and Wan note, were a significant departure from past US policy. Two personal letters by President Obama to Khamenei calling for improving US–Iranian relations went unreciprocated, dismissed by Khamenei as a conspiracy to delegitimize the 2009 vote.[78] This response, characterized by Sadjadpour as "cynical," was followed by revelations of yet another undeclared enrichment facility; Iran's rejection of the uranium-for-fuel exchange deal and its escalation into 20 percent uranium enrichment and other defiant steps.[79]

Libya's case is often considered a sanctions success for leading Qaddafi to renounce nuclear weapons against a background of declining resources, disaffected Jamahiriyyah revolutionaries and other domestic challenges to his rule, and a prospective shift from an inward-looking to a very embryonic internationalizing model.[80] As Palkki and Smith and Drezner note, however, Libya's reversal was the product of the concurrent application of different tools including not only comprehensive sanctions on

---

[77] On "conditional reciprocity," see Keohane (1986).

[78] Ewen MacAskill, "Obama Sent Letter to Khamenei Before the Election, Report Says," *Guardian*, June 24, 2009.

[79] Sadjadpour (2010c) finds Khamenei's contempt for the United States to be consistent throughout three decades of writings and speeches.

[80] Saif al-Islam, "The New Gadhafi," 60 Minutes, CBS News, March 10, 2004. See also Niblock (2001), Jentleson and Whytock (2005/2006), Bowen (2006), Litwak (2007), and Solingen (2007a).

oil exports but also diplomacy, the Proliferation Security Initiative, the *BBC China* interception, and the tacit demonstration effect of the 2003 Iraq War. All operated at a timely conjuncture to unleash several desired causal mechanisms leading to verifiable denuclearization. Libya's surrender of nuclear materials was nearly simultaneous with expected external rewards, which began streaming shortly thereafter. Other relevant temporal sequences are Qaddafi's prior efforts to re-insert Libya in the global economy through *infitah* (economic reform) leading to denuclearizing commitments. Furthermore, although negotiations over the nuclear program began prior to the 2003 Iraq War, the war buildup may have enhanced Qaddafi's urgency to come clean on his nuclear designs.

Addressing the virtues of positive inducements, Nincic recalls the experiences of Egypt and Vietnam. Those two, however, had abandoned inward-looking models for "*infitah*" and "Dôi Mói" (economic opening) earlier, changing the context for extending them positive inducements.[81] This was not the case with Iraq, Iran, North Korea, or Syria for that matter. Prior commitments to economic reform can pave the way for positive inducements, particularly where nuclear weapons have not yet been acquired. Japan, Taiwan, and South Korea had embarked on internationalizing trajectories before endorsing the NPT.[82] Once nuclear thresholds – nuclear tests, breakout, expelling inspectors, renouncing the NPT – have been crossed, the insights of audience costs and prospect theory illuminate why renouncing actual weapons might be more difficult, but not impossible. A regime's consideration of what constitutes appropriate timing and sequences for negotiating nuclear concessions is related to how it perceives its own chances of political survival, and to the potential audience costs it could incur in deciding one way or another. As discussed in Chapter 1, leaders sustain audience costs – potential removal from office for instance – when they renege on their own public commitments. Different chapters confirm leaders' sensitivities to such costs, prominently in Iran where Ahmadinejad made commitments to uranium enrichment a central – if not *the* most central – feature of his continued hold in power. Chapter 1 also introduced principles of prospect theory to illuminate leaders' incentives to accept higher risks in order to retain existing nuclear weapons ("endowments") than programs leading to future *potential* acquisition. Leaders and publics presumably value more what they already have than what they might get in the future.

---

[81] On the connections between Libya's and Egypt's *infitah* and nuclear postures, see Solingen (2007a).

[82] For a detailed analysis of these cases, see Solingen (1998, 2007a).

Combining prospect theory and audience costs arguments suggests that concessions may be easier for autocratic leaders in states that have not yet achieved weaponization. And domestic shifts to internationalizing models facilitate such concessions. But neither Iran nor North Korea seems close to this ideal combination of circumstances and context. North Korea has not only tested nuclear weapons but has also rejected China or Vietnam-style reforms thus far, although there are some signs of possible efforts in that direction as of early 2011.[83] Both nuclear tests and resistance to reform increased North Korea's distance from a more favorable context for denuclearization. Its existing (nuclear) "endowment" had arguably made concessions prohibitive for Kim Jong-il given his main audience: hardline supporters of an inward-looking "military first" economy. Barely three days into the Kim Jong-un era it is unclear whether or not Kim Jong-il's recent efforts to strengthen the party will hold beyond his death. Absent nuclear testing and weaponization, an Iranian leader would arguably face lower audience costs for nuclear concessions. Yet, as Nader and others argue, a shift toward an internationalizing model does not seem to be forthcoming anytime soon.[84] And recent IAEA reports cited earlier hint that Iran's nuclear weapons-related activities have not necessarily stalled.

In sum, a given causal mechanism may have different effects under different spatial and temporal contexts. The timing, circumstances, and sequence in the application of inducements of any sort are crucial.[85] Comprehensive sanctions on all imports of refined oil products may not be as effective under normal conditions, when the population rallies around the regime to condemn external intervention. However, under different conditions – following rigged elections and heightened repression in Iran – such measures gained broader acceptability as a means to weaken the regime. Despite a poor historical track record of sanctions in Iran, Sadjadpour senses greater receptivity – especially by democracy activists – to targeted sanctions against the repressive

---

[83] Mazarr (2011) also points to the emergence of something akin to a self-interested North Korean "middle class" with interests that sometimes differ from those of the regime, a group that should be offered prospects of inclusion in a post-transition scenario.

[84] Ahmadinejad approved hundreds of no-bid construction and petrochemical contracts for IRGC conglomerates and their smuggling networks, said to net $12 billion a year, according to an Iranian lawmaker (Guo 2009). Other projects were also transferred to the IRGC under the cover of "privatization." See "The Revolutionary Guards' Looting of Iran's Economy," *Iran Briefing*, October 24, 2010, available at: www.aei. org/outlook/100969.IRGC.

[85] On the importance of the interaction between causal mechanisms and context in causal explanations, see Falleti and Lynch (2009).

apparatus including the IRGC, labeled "a mafia of sorts."[86] By contrast, Nincic considers positive inducements to be especially effective when the regime's domestic position is insecure, making the aftermath of the 2009 elections a particularly suitable timing. This would have been the worst possible timing from the vantage point of dilemmas involving serial transgressors, however, signaling utter disregard for human rights.

7   Elusive boundaries: regime or policy change? Quid pro quo or transformational strategies?

The 900-pound gorilla present in many of the dilemmas described thus far is the question of whether or not sender countries share clearly defined and/or homogeneous preferences regarding the outcomes expected from external inducements. Is the objective regime change or a change in policy, the latter defined as verifiable renunciation of nuclear weapons? In actuality a broader hierarchy of objectives may be under consideration, from destabilizing the economy, to changing distributional outcomes of economic activities, reshuffling the broad political landscape, catalyzing new coalitions, changing nuclear policies, and replacing the regime altogether. As Litwak's (2007) landmark study suggests, the war designed to replace Saddam Hussein has left a particularly poignant legacy of skepticism about regime change as a strategy for dealing with nuclear proliferators.

But regime change as an objective is not always pursued through military means or sanctions. In their study of positive inducements, Kahler and Kastner (2006) differentiate between conditional engagement strategies (where positive inducements require quid pro quos) and unconditional strategies (where positive inducements aim at transforming the context of target states). They find the latter to be more effective for democratic targets but, as evident from our first dilemma analyzed above, the universe of cases violating nonproliferation commitments is chiefly autocratic. Furthermore, chapters in this volume suggest that it is not always easy in practice to discern between purely quid pro quo and transformational strategies. Haggard and Noland relay that positive inducements were cast as quid pro quos for North Korea but had sometimes an implicit longer-term objective of transforming the regime. Given its inward-looking and autocratic nature, however, North Korea never allowed inducements such as Kaesong to exert any transformational influence on its domestic politics (or nuclear policy), using positive inducements simply as sources of rents to replenish regime coffers.

---

[86] Sadjadpour (2010a), Guo (2009), and Ansari (2010a, 2010b).

For Nincic positive inducements imply that regime change via sanctions is not on the cards, at least within an acceptable time frame,
and consequently some variant of the incumbent regime will remain
as interlocutor over the foreseeable future. His exchange model seems
closer to a quid pro quo and his catalytic model to a transformational
strategy, yet even the latter does not imply a "complete regime overhaul" or a transformed "architecture of power" but rather a foreign
policy change only, one that enables the regime to retain power. Indeed
his endgame tolerates Iran becoming nuclear under "less alarming"
leadership. Either way the operation of different causal mechanisms
with unexpected and unintended effects makes it difficult for senders
to calibrate policies so as to achieve merely exchange or more ambitious
transformational goals. Furthermore, targets are often unable (and
even more frequently unwilling) to differentiate between the two strategies. Inward-looking autocracies, as argued, thrive by wielding foreign
intervention – invariably depicted as attempts at regime change – as a
way to enhance internal cohesion. What may seem like paranoia is also
a coherent strategy for retaining and maximizing power.[87] The shadow
of the past, or precedents like the coup against Mossadegh, is of critical
value for domestic mobilization. In some cases neither senders nor targets can genuinely recognize or calibrate the boundaries between quid
pro quo and transformational strategies.[88]

Even strong advocates of positive inducements acknowledge that a
definitive solution to North Korea's nuclearization might be difficult
to achieve short of a fundamental change in the nature of the regime.[89]
Others, more skeptical of positive inducements, find incentives and
security assurances to be futile in contexts where the regime regards
nuclear weapons as a guarantee of its own survival while stalling on
China-style reforms with potential to hasten its demise.[90] At issue is
whether or not nuclear weapons are prized for protecting the regime
largely from *within* rather than from external attack. Either way, North
Korea's demand to Ambassador Christopher Hill that the United States
grant it nuclear weapons status similar to that of India's may signal a
commitment to retain them, in line with expectations from prospect

---

[87] Riedel and Samore (2008: 125) favor an explicit US commitment renouncing regime
change in exchange for Iran's compliance but acknowledge that neither this guarantee
nor political and economic normalization are attractive to regime hardline elements.
[88] On the role of cognitive distortions in interpreting others' intentions in international
relations, see Jervis (1976) and Schelling (1966).
[89] Cortright and Väyrynen (2010). On positive incentives as neither necessary nor sufficient for denuclearization, see Bernauer and Ruloff (1999).
[90] Victor Cha, "Up Close and Personal, Here's What I Learned," *Washington Post*, June
14, 2009. Fitzpatrick (2011).

theory. Genuine changes in North Korean policy would compel it to freeze and irreversibly degrade and disable its nuclear program as stipulated in UNSC resolutions and Six-Party Talks. Whether or not this could be achieved without regime change is a matter of great contention no less in South Korea, Japan, China, and beyond than in the United States.[91] The passing of Kim Jong-il renews this debate.

As for sanctions, Drezner concludes that those imposing comprehensive costs have a greater likelihood to result in regime change.[92] Marinov finds sanctions to increase the probability that leaders in target states are replaced. Escribà-Folch and Wright find personalist authoritarian regimes particularly vulnerable to serious sanctions and internal coups, arguably making them more compliant.[93] Palkki and Smith's account validates this finding for the case of Libya, and even Iraq, prior to 2003. Drezner concludes that only regime change – not North Korea's current personalist leadership – is more likely to lead to concessions. Others argue that "waiting around for significant political change in Pyongyang to solve our problems is the longest of long shots. North Korea as we know it isn't going to disappear any time soon, and the problems that flow from its anomalous policies won't lessen if Washington keeps banging its collective head against the same old wall."[94] Disagreements regarding the longevity of North Korea's regime have been the staple of debates over appropriate tools of statecraft for that case and are exacerbated by the sudden death of Kim Jong-il.

The Escribà-Folch and Wright findings suggest that sanctions would have limited effects on regime stability if Iran was defined as a single-party or a military regime. But Iran is also largely driven by personalities, the *faqih* who has final authority, and the President, although some consider the IRGC to have become the decisive source of power behind Khamenei. Either way the regime has endured decades of sanctions and war. The June 2010 UNSC sanctions' stated objectives were to enhance political pressure on Iran to change its nuclear policy; suspend uranium enrichment; comply with previous UNSC resolutions; and resolve outstanding issues with the IAEA through transparency, inspections, and verification assurances that no nuclear weapons are developed. The stated objectives of US sanctions conformed to UNSC

---

[91] On domestic debates regarding North Korea's nuclearization in Northeast Asia, see Solingen (2011b).

[92] Dashti-Gibson *et al.* (1997).

[93] Escribà-Folch and Wright (2010). McGillivray and Stam (2004) found that a change in leadership in authoritarian states, in turn, increases the likelihood that sanctions are terminated by thirty-eight times.

[94] Lewis and Carlin (2010). On the pitfalls of building on the assumption that North Korea is monolithic, see Mazarr (2011) and Solingen (2007a).

resolutions: "We can't expect a change of heart from a regime founded in violence, and in violent disregard for world opinion – but we can demand a change of behavior."[95] National security advisor James Jones, however, declared that tougher sanctions *could* well trigger a regime change.[96] Documents revealed by Wikileaks confirm what was already known. Not only Western countries but most – though not all – of North Korea's and Iran's neighbors would not mourn the passing of the two regimes even though this is only rarely explicitly advocated, let alone through violent means. But neither is the latter strategy altogether absent, as learned from alleged remarks by the Saudi monarch exhorting the United States to attack Iran and sever "the head of the snake" before it is too late.[97]

Whether or not senders pursue regime or policy change is also a function of their perception of domestic support for those regimes within target states. Yet, as the 2011 popular uprisings in the Middle East confirm, precise levels of support for autocratic inward-looking regimes are extremely hard to gauge for reasons explored earlier, leading to wide-ranging assessments. Drezner argues that because of greater domestic support for Iran's regime (relative to North Korea), comprehensive sanctions are less likely to work. Nader challenges the extent of such support arguing that Iran lacks enough coherence and unity to reach agreement on nuclear matters. Sadjadpour declares "ideological fatigue" to have set in, enabling US policies to expedite – though not to engineer – political change.[98] From their carefully-researched study of an even more opaque case, North Korea, Haggard and Noland infer that the post-2005 trend has been toward narrowing regime support, particularly after the 2009 disastrous currency reform. However, they remain skeptical that narrowing support will lead to fundamental political change from below. Again, the picture is even less clear under the sudden succession to Kim Jong-un.

In sum, analysts differ in their estimation of "the shadow of the future" or whether senders will continue to interact with incumbent regimes in the near, medium, or longer term. Senders craft sanctions and positive inducements – quid pro quo or transformational policies – that are not always easily differentiated, either by design – as a way of hedging – or because of their unintended effects and unpredictable causal mechanisms.

[95] Former House Majority Leader Steny Hoyer, in "Congressional Action," *Global Security Newswire*, March 23, 2010.

[96] "Western Powers Target Iranian Oil Exports," *Global Security Newswire*, February 16, 2010.

[97] Meris Lutz, "MIDDLE EAST: Arab Media Play Down WikiLeaks Reports of Support for Iran War," November 29, 2010, available at: www.latimesblogs.latimes.com.

[98] Sadjadpour (2010c); Ganji (2009) argues that the majority of Iran's population oppose the "fundamentalist" regime.

Most frequent targets of nonproliferation efforts – inward-looking autocracies – have built-in incentives to blur differences between the two strategies, labeling most policies – including positive inducements – efforts
at regime change ("velvet revolutions"). Armed with newly available
evidence, Palkki and Smith defy the conventional wisdom that Saddam
found US calls for regime change in 1998 credible. Saddam believed that
members of the Republican Party in the United States advanced regime
change as sheer posturing for domestic audiences, to discredit President
Clinton for not embarking on a policy that would be difficult to carry
through in any event. Conversely, Palkki and Smith find that assurances of regime survival offered to Libya were not nearly as credible as
commonly portrayed, yet led to Libya's compliance in 2003.[99] Whether
regime behavior or regime change becomes the objective is also influenced by the extent to which promised compliance becomes transparent.
Palkki and Smith, and Litwak, compare Libya's verifiable compliance
with Iraq's hedging strategy aimed at persuading the UN that Iraq had
disarmed while leaving significant ambiguity, presumably an unintended
byproduct of policies intended to protect the regime.

8   *E Pluribus Pluribus?* The perennial coordination problem

Many dilemmas explored thus far are the product of, contribute to, or
are intertwined with the perennial sender coordination or collective
action problem, a frequent subject in the study of sanctions.[100] Virtually
all chapters address this problem in one form or another. Stein's in particular dwells on the difficulty of acquiring and wielding market power,
the key to effective sanctions and positive inducements. Senders seek to
marshal together their own domestic economic interests to wield collective market power but different domestic and state actors have incentives to foil that objective. Most chapters detail how competing state
interests have made crafting tougher sanctions on Iraq, Libya, North
Korea, and Iran more difficult. Collective action problems afflict both
the negotiation and the credibility of implementation of sanctions and
positive inducements.

Target regimes are far from inert objects of persuasion or coercion
and seek to exploit senders' heterogeneity of interests. Saddam Hussein's
ability to exploit such divisions was legendary – as Palkki and Smith

---

[99] Litwak (2007) mentions only tacit assurances by the United States, and Palkki and
Smith cite Libya's absence from the "axis of evil" speech.

[100] See, for instance, Martin (1992a) and, sensitive to domestic distributional costs
among senders, Mansfield (1995) and Morgan and Bapat (2003).

document – and Iran's regime perfected that strategy to an art form. Haggard and Noland dissect North Korea's skill to deepen cleavages among senders and gravitate toward trading partners that placed least restrictions. They find UNSC Resolution 1718 to have had little impact on Chinese behavior, increasing its luxury goods and total exports to North Korea despite its two nuclear tests. Positive inducements proffered by China and – until recently – South Korea cleaved the Six-Party Talks, which have yet to yield their nonproliferation objectives. China's compliance with multilateral sanctions has been selective, reluctant, and intermittent, often relying on linguistic and behavioral contortions to justify inconsistencies.[101] China allegedly provided a transshipment site for ballistic missile and enrichment components for Iran and North Korea.[102] As European firms ended contracts with Iran, China's National Petroleum Corporation stepped in to develop the South Pars gas field, attracted by potentially lucrative liquefied natural gas exports.[103] Japan, the EU, China, and India have been important recipients of Iran's exports and reluctant to endanger them. Firms from Turkey, Malaysia, Kuwait, the UAE, China, Ukraine, the UK, Japan, South Korea, Switzerland, Singapore, Israel, and Taiwan have been directly or indirectly involved in proscribed transactions, refined oil sales, transshipment, and other activities.[104] Iran's Shahid Bagheri Industrial Group sought inputs from Germany through front companies and intermediaries that route goods through the UAE.[105] A 2010 UN report revealed that 111 of 192 UN members had not submitted reports on their implementation of UNSC resolutions against North Korea.[106]

This perceived weakness of multilateral sanctions and their brittle implementation have led the United States and others to impose additional constraints through unilateral sanctions, which some – Turkey and Brazil, for instance – reject as illegitimate.[107] Yet, despite skepticism regarding the ability to overcome coordination problems, cumulative sanctions imposed by the UNSC, the United States, the EU, and others are estimated to have had significant effects on Iran's economic

---

[101] On China's approach to sanctions on Iran and North Korea, see Solingen (2012).
[102] Stricker (2010), US Government Accountability Office (2007), "More Nations Sidestep Iranian Atomic Tour," *Global Security Newswire*, January 14, 2011.
[103] Christian Oliver, "US Tells China Not to Exploit Sanctions on Iran," *Financial Times*, August 2, 2010.
[104] Doyle McManus, "A Nuclear Iran? Not so Fast," *Los Angeles Times*, January 21, 2011; Michael R. Gordon and Andrew W. Lehren, "US Strains to Stop Arms Flow," *New York Times*, December 6, 2010; US Government Accountability Office 2010 (GAO-10–967R); Katzman (2011).
[105] Stricker (2010).   [106] *The Korea Herald*, June 14, 2010, 2.
[107] Turkish State Minister for Foreign Trade Zafar Caglayan, quoted in www.presstv.ir/detail/145167.html.

wherewithal. For all its public vacillation, China's alleged vast invest-ments in Iran's gas and refining infrastructure appear to be mired in actual difficulties or perhaps in purposeful efforts to slow them down. Private providers of gasoline, including Shell, Total, and BP have retreated from Iran as have public and private providers of insurance, reinsurance, shipping, technology, and other services.[108] And there have been occasional limits to senders' gullibility to targets' divide-and-rule strategies. President Sarkozy, for instance, while supporting a US pol-icy of "extended hand" vis-à-vis Iran also asked "what have these pro-posals for dialogue produced for the international community? Nothing but more enriched uranium and more centrifuges."[109]

Domestic public opinion in sender states influences states' positions on inducements and the ability to overcome collective action prob-lems. A Pew study conducted before the June 2010 UNSC vote and the November 2011 IAEA report, found that in nineteen of twenty-two countries polled, majorities of those who opposed Iran's nuclear weapons program expressed approval for tougher international eco-nomic sanctions to prevent it from developing nuclear weapons. This included 67 percent in Russia, 66 percent in Japan, and 58 percent in China.[110] Majorities or pluralities in eighteen of twenty-two countries expressed unfavorable opinions of Iran, 86 percent in Germany, 81 per-cent in France, 75 percent in Japan, 60 percent in China, 66 percent in Egypt, 63 percent in Jordan, 60 percent in Lebanon, and 58 per-cent in Turkey. Only majorities in Pakistan and Indonesia were more favorable.[111] Majorities in Egypt, Jordan, Lebanon, and Turkey lacked confidence in Ahmadinejad to do the right thing in world affairs and majorities opposed Iran's acquisition of nuclear weapons, including 66 percent in Egypt, 63 percent in Turkey, 88 percent among Christians and Sunni in Lebanon, and 60 percent in Indonesia but only 53 per-cent in Jordan.

A German Marshall Fund study found little support for accepting Iran's acquisition of nuclear weapons without efforts to stop it (6 per-cent among EU countries and 4 percent in the United States).[112] Only a significant Turkish minority (25 percent) among countries polled was

---

[108] The Economist Intelligence Unit (2010).
[109] "French Atomic Pique," *Wall Street Journal*, September 29, 2009.
[110] About 62 percent of polled Pakistanis *opposed* such measures, as did 49 percent of Indians (Pew Research Center, June 17, 2010).
[111] About 58 percent favored Iran's pursuit of nuclear weapons in Pakistan, rising to 91 percent among Lebanese Shia. See Bruce Stokes, "Iran's Nuclear Program: The Public Speaks," *The Daily Star* (Lebanon), October 4, 2010.
[112] Stokes, "Iran's Nuclear Program."

willing to accept a nuclear Iran. Whereas 35 percent of Europeans surveyed preferred offering positive economic incentives to Iran, 40 percent of Americans preferred economic sanctions. Only 6 and 9 percent of Europeans and Americans respectively favored military action over other actions. However, when facing a choice between military action and a nuclear Iran, a plurality of Europeans (43 percent) and a majority of Americans (64 percent) favored a military strike. British (57 percent) and Turkish respondents (54 percent) favored a nuclear-armed Iran over military action. Among those opposing a nuclear Iran, military force was supported by 55 percent in Egypt, 53 percent in Jordan and pluralities in Lebanon (44 percent) and Indonesia (39 percent). Yet 55 percent in Japan and 34 percent in China rejected military means. In sum, the two cited polls confirm considerable public support among key senders for preventing a nuclear-armed Iran. The usual caveats apply, however; polls can be highly contingent on the questions asked and highly volatile in response to events. Whereas less than 30 percent supported military action in South Korea against the North after the *Cheonan* sinking, nearly 70 percent supported limited military actions following the shelling of Yeonpyeong Island.[113] Polls are even more questionable in autocratic contexts. The 2011 upheavals in the Middle East, and Iranian leaders' response to them, particularly regarding Syria, have led to dramatic declines in support for Iran's policies throughout the region.

Coordination problems among Iran's immediate neighbors at the leadership level have gained attention through Wikileaks which, despite much fanfare, only confirmed known support for sanctions and even military action among some of Iran's neighbors. Saudi Foreign Minister Saud al-Faisal declared that while "sanctions are a long-term solution ... we see the issue in the shorter term because we are closer to the threat" needing "immediate resolution rather than gradual resolution."[114] UAE Crown Prince Sheik Mohamed bin Zayed al-Nahyan reportedly warned American officials since 2006 that Iran's nuclear program should be dealt with "this year or next," that Ahmadinejad was "going to take us to war," and that he was Hitler.[115] The UAE Ambassador to the United States Yousef al-Otaiba reportedly stipulated that "the benefits of bombing Iran's nuclear program

[113] Poll from *The Chosun Ilbo*, November 29, 2010. For polls among Northeast Asian countries regarding North Korea, see Solingen (2011b).
[114] "Western Powers Target Iranian Oil Exports," *Global Security Newswire*, February 16, 2010.
[115] James Kitfield, "Iran Nuclear Crisis Forges Coalition for Containment," *Global Security Newswire*, December 17, 2010; Lutz, "Middle East."

outweigh the short-term costs."[116] Although another UAE official
refuted that report, others suggested the ambassador's views were common among UAE and Saudi officials.[117] Bahrain's Ambassador to the
United States reportedly expressed that "sanctions never had a chance
of working" and clearly hadn't worked before, casting doubt that the
2010 sanctions would have better results.[118] Qatar purportedly agreed
to grant basing rights for an attack on Iran to eliminate its nuclear capabilities, and pay 60 percent of maintenance costs for the Al-Udeid airbase, in return for US guarantees that operations at the jointly-owned
Qatari-Iranian South Pars natural gas field would not be threatened.[119]
Qatar's Prime Minister Sheikh Hamad bin Jassim al-Thani allegedly
expressed that Washington shouldn't be "upset" about Qatar's ties to
Iran: "They lie to us, and we lie to them." Others, including the Saudi
Foreign Minister, called for far more severe US and international sanctions on Iran without ruling out military pressure.[120] Extensive military
purchases are another indication of Arab Gulf regimes' lack of trust
of Iran's intentions. The alleged attempted assassination of the Saudi
ambassador to the United States by Iranian operatives exacerbated
Saudi-Iranian tensions.

Former President Mubarak's piercing assessment, shared by other
regional leaders in his view, was that his Iranian interlocutors "are
big, fat liars and justify their lies because they believe it is for a higher
purpose."[121] Popular uprisings have deposed the Mubarak regime and
the secular Tunisian regime and weakened other opponents of Iran
but also its allies (Iran has contributed to Bashar Assad's repression
of the Syrian uprising). The US ability to coordinate policy vis-à-vis
Iran among its Gulf neighbors will hinge on unfolding developments in
the region, prominently in Syria and Egypt. In a relatively more stable
Northeast Asia, China remains North Korea's main recourse for cir-
cumventing sanctions.

As of early 2011, the costs of staying the non-compliant course have
been more tolerable for inward-looking autocrats in Iran and North

---

[116] Eli Lake, "UAE Diplomat Mulls Hit on Iran's Nukes," *The Washington Times*, July 6, 2010.

[117] "World Powers Weigh Reply."

[118] Ben Birnbaum, "Iranian Nukes Worry Neighboring Bahrain," *The Washington Times*, October 7, 2010.

[119] Jack Khoury, "WikiLeaks Cable: Qatar Okays Use of Airbase for US Attack on Iran," *Haaretz*, November 30, 2010.

[120] Documents available at: www.guardian.co.uk/world/us-embassy-cables-documents/150519.

[121] Grim (2010); Margaret Coker, "Leaked Papers Show Arab Leaders Critical of Iran, Neighbors," *The Wall Street Journal*, November 29, 2010.

Korea than the costs of complying with multilateral demands. Cleaving senders has been these regimes' primary tool for diluting the costs of non-compliance but their tendency to overshoot occasionally yields greater coherence among senders. Yet even the Obama administration's impressive efforts to raise the costs of non-compliance have not been immune to resistance by other states and private firms. The rise of emerging powers may further reduce the ability of Western countries to wield market power in the crafting of inducements.[122] Domestic actors can undermine that ability as well, as noted in a 2010 report by the US Government Accountability Office identifying sixteen companies selling refined oil products to Iran since 2009.[123] A *New York Times* study revealed that seventy-four foreign and multinational firms with business ties to Iran – including in oil and gas – had been awarded over $100 billion in US federal contracts.[124]

9   Is perfect the enemy of the good? When sanctions trump no action

Voltaire's dictum that "perfect is the enemy of the good" acquires particular significance in the study of nonproliferation statecraft, where choices are more frequently not between good and bad but between bad and worse. Even so, Palkki and Smith suggest, sanctions have had expected effects in Libya and Iraq though nothing appears to yield fruit in North Korea and Iran according to others. Our overview brings to relief the many dilemmas underlying the design and implementation of sanctions and positive inducements, all of which render them imperfect instruments, as most tools of statecraft are. The inevitable question that must be posed in any consideration of inducements is the "relative to what" question, oftentimes ignored in the assessment of sanctions. As Baldwin's (1985, 1998) seminal work reminds us, the utility, usefulness, or efficiency of any instrument can only be estimated when the costs and benefits of all alternatives are taken into account. That may leave sanctions as the most appropriate option relative to their alternatives in some circumstances, even when they cannot yield the precise

---

[122] Referring to reported Turkish ties to an Iranian bank under sanctions, Senator Robert Menendez told a Senate Banking Committee that "a sanctions regime that ultimately goes largely unenforced or to low-level players, sends the message of a toothless tiger" (in David Lauder, "U.S. Treasury Nears Iran Sanctions on Foreign Banks," *Reuters*, May 3, 2011).

[123] US Government Accountability Report 2010. See also Feaver and Lorber (2010) and Katzman (2011).

[124] Jo Becker and Ron Nixon, "US Enriches Companies Defying its Policy on Iran," *New York Times*, March 6, 2010.

desired outcomes. "Even when the expectation of success is very low," argues Baldwin, "sanctions are justified if there is no policy alternative with a higher expectation of success."[125]

Most chapters, including our discussion of dilemmas thus far, have explored alternatives to sanctions in the form of positive inducements, including suspension of sanctions, normalization, political and diplomatic reassurance, economic engagement, security assurances or guarantees, and other forms documented in charts and appendices to the Reynolds and Wan chapter. As Baldwin suggests, however, in order to address the question of whether or not economic sanctions are a useful substitute for military force one must compare the utility of sanctions and force using the same analytical framework and notion of success, taking into account costs and benefits associated with each instrument. What policy-makers most want to know, argues Baldwin (1998: 194–195) is the conditions under which economic sanctions are likely to have more utility than military force. This question cannot be answered by merely comparing the relative effectiveness of military force and economic sanctions. The primary argument against using nuclear weapons to oust Saddam Hussein, Baldwin argued, would not be their lack of effectiveness but rather their excessive costliness relative to economic sanctions. The invasion of Iraq certainly put an end to Saddam's ability to develop nuclear weapons but many question that this was the most desirable or cost-effective option. This logic renders sanctions more useful even if they are less effective than force (which, many argue, was not the case in Iraq).

What about the costs and benefits of "doing nothing?" None of the chapters seem to endorse this alternative, perhaps because it is deemed unlikely to yield the desired change in behavior barring dramatic internally-driven transformations. The inward-looking autocracies that have provided the main focus here have been quite determined to thwart such transformations. Furthermore, the negative utility of doing nothing – allowing unimpeded nuclearization – includes the possibility of seriously harmful externalities. As argued in Chapter 1, not sanctioning NPT violators has demonstration effects relevant to the integrity of the nonproliferation regime. States faithfully matching their behavior with their international commitments must be reassured that other states' violations have real consequences.[126] This terrain is well treaded in the literature on international institutions, compliance, and

---

[125] Baldwin (1999/2000: 92).
[126] The flip side of this, when positive inducements create moral hazard, has demonstration effects of a different sort. See Bernauer and Ruloff (1999).

nonproliferation, and won't be rehearsed here. As one study puts it, imposing sanctions is unfortunately an inevitable part of maintaining the nonproliferation regime's credibility in the face of Iran's persistent violations of safeguards agreement, IAEA resolutions, and legally binding UNSC Chapter VII resolutions.[127] Herein lies a crucial antidote to the coordination dilemma, explaining why target states sometimes overplay their ability to cleave senders and underestimate the latter's collective resolve to prevent diffusion of nuclear capabilities.[128] One example of such underestimation was Iran's selective invitations to would-be supporting countries – largely declined – to visit chosen nuclear sites.

Nor should reputational costs associated with UNSC and IAEA violations be underestimated. The do-nothing option lowers those reputational costs for target states and heightens them for sender states which had privately or publicly extended warnings against the dangers of unimpeded proliferation. Audience costs become part and parcel of senders' considerations of costs and benefits. Expectations that democracies are more vulnerable to such costs perhaps place Western powers at higher risk than China and Russia for not following through. However, there is evidence that China's failure to prevent North Korea's escalating provocations has domestic audience costs as well, perhaps explaining China's departure from its long-standing opposition to sanctions and support for UNSC resolutions.[129] Some popular support for sanctions on Iran in Russia – though not a prominent issue – might increase domestic audience costs there as well. Sanctions thus are sometimes regarded as less damning than no action, even when the probability of success is low, and can even be artfully undertaken with limited intent to implement them, at a cost. One way to minimize audience costs is to acknowledge the imperfect nature of sanctions, paralleled by the imperfect nature of most alternatives to them. President Obama warned that there is no guarantee that sanctions will change Iran's behavior even as he organized market power with the expectation that steady international pressure might alter the regime's nuclear calculations.[130]

---

[127] Goldschmidt (2010) and Crane (2010).

[128] Rowhani (2005) warned his own compatriots that "when it comes to the nuclear fuel cycle, there is a kind of consensus [among foreign powers]." European states, he added, compete over "insignificant matters, and we [Iran] can use that competition to our advantage" but "it is not easy to create a gap between them."

[129] Feng (2010) and Solingen (2012).

[130] Quoted in *Good Morning America*, April 8, 2010, transcript available at: abcnews.go.com. Admiral Mullen expressed that the 2010 sanctions were not likely to persuade Iran to give up its atomic aspirations.

Galtung's seminal piece on sanctions addressed the drawbacks of "doing nothing" as "tantamount to complicity," arguing that "something has to be done to express morality" when military action is impossible, as a clear signal of disapproval.[131] Even when they fail to serve instrumental purposes, he argued, sanctions still have an expressive function. Even when falling short of their primary objective of preventing nuclear weapons' acquisition, sanctions can weaken serial transgressors in more than symbolic fashion. Baldwin suggests that the infliction of costs for noncompliance has been a common standard for measuring success even when sanctions fall short of their optimal outcome.[132] Stein posits that the whole point of economic sanctions is to impose economic hardships on target states. CIA director Leon E. Panetta reflected this view when he argued that targeted economic sanctions on Iran probably will not deter the regime from seeking a nuclear capability but the tighter 2010 sanctions could create serious economic problems and weaken the regime.[133] Furthermore, as Marinov found in a broader study of sanctions, sanctioned leaders have a higher probability of being ejected from power.

At the end of the day few scholars and practitioners believe sanctions are silver bullets for preventing proliferation.[134] More often than not, as Reynolds and Wan's appendices illustrate, sanctions are one component in assorted packages that also include positive inducements, diplomacy, and military threats and actions, all of which unleash different causal effects and domestic distributional consequences. The particular consequences of military threats for the domestic politics of target states have rarely been studied systematically in the context of nuclear proliferation, and are the subject of our tenth and final dilemma.

10   Military threats or paper tigers? Domestic implications in target states

Although several chapters address military threats in the context of broader discussions of inducements, Kreps and Pasha extend the volume's concern with distributional effects into a dedicated exploration of military threats as tools of nonproliferation statecraft. Many argue that

---

[131] Galtung (1967: 411).
[132] Baldwin (1998: 193). On "suboptimization," see Schelling (1966: 110).
[133] "CIA Director Skeptical of Iran Sanctions," *The Washington Times*, June 27, 2010.
[134] Goldschmidt (2010), for instance, argues that sanctions alone, at any level, will not deter Iran from pursuing its course. The primary objective of UNSC resolutions was to slow down Iran's progress towards an eventual nuclear weapons capability and enable a diplomatic compromise. See also Bruno Tertrais, "History Teaches That Iran Will Choose Nuclear Weapons," *The National* (UAE), January 16, 2011.

credible threats of force are essential for successful diplomatic strategies and that whether or not the United States is ultimately prepared to use military force it must convince proliferating states that it is willing to do so if all acceptable diplomatic resolutions are rejected.[135] Similarly, a Middle Eastern foreign minister reportedly suggested that the best way to *avoid* striking Iran was to make Iran think that the United States is about to strike it.[136] Others have made analogous arguments regarding North Korea. French President Nicolas Sarkozy threatened Iran with military force if it developed the bomb in his first major foreign policy speech as President. Palkki and Smith conclude that when US threats were highest – in 1991, 1995, and 2002–2003 – Saddam was more likely to comply.

Even as inward-looking autocrats (sometimes misguidedly) doubt the credibility of such threats, they benefit from exposing them as tools to rally domestic support. Declassified correspondence between Kim Il-sung and Stalin suggests that even the older Kim was not as concerned with potential use of nuclear weapons by the United States during the Korean War.[137] In 1977 Kim declared that the United States and South Korea could not use nuclear weapons on the peninsula because they would be killed too.[138] Despite the potential demonstration effect of the 2003 attack on Iraq, US overextension in Iraq until recently, and Afghanistan has further diluted the credibility of an attack on North Korea. As Wit puts it, "fifty years of history, if not just pure logic, tell Kim Jong Il that the United States and South Korea will not risk escalation."[139] Yet while demanding a peace treaty with the United States that would codify abstention from use of force, it remains unclear whether the Kims' regime intends to forfeit its own nuclear weapons thereafter, given the domestic rationale examined here and elsewhere.[140] And given that same rationale, external threats may benefit supporters of the "military first" economy over its alternatives.

Though not addressing military threats specifically, Haggard and Noland surmise that a deteriorating external environment strengthened military dominance in North Korea and influenced shifts away from economic reform. They conclude that both military threats and economic pressure appear futile and counterproductive but recognize that purely internal political dynamics could not be discounted as a more fundamental driver of North Korea's behavior. The same outcome – including

---

[135] See, inter alia, Riedel and Samore (2008: 122) and Lindsay and Takeyh (2010: 34).
[136] Goldberg (2010).   [137] Mansourov (1995).
[138] Ha (1978: 1142). See also Hayes (1991).   [139] Wit (2010).
[140] Chanlett-Avery and Taylor (2010: 6). Mazarr (2011) argues that North Korea will not abandon its nuclear weapons anytime soon.

two nuclear tests – might have obtained even in the absence of external threats.[141] Negative security assurances that North Korea would not be attacked appear not to have helped either, possibly because, despite public declarations to the contrary, inward-looking autocrats beholden to their military are conflicted about assurances that foil the rationale for a military-first economy while privileging economic reforms.[142] Proponents of *songun* can lean on the 2011 intervention in Libya to dismiss any positive inducements but this hardly hides their instrumental use of events to retain a policy embraced for decades to hang on to power.

Iran's illicit nuclear program since the 1980s had little to do with fears of a US attack for at least the first two decades.[143] Covert nuclear activities preceded the "axis of evil" speech by at least sixteen years.[144] According to Chubin and Litwak, the nuclear program in the 1990s was not rooted in any security imperatives but in nationalism, prestige, and domestic drivers; Iran had no historic enemies, existential threats or giant, hostile neighbors once Iraq was contained militarily and economically through massive sanctions.[145] When asked about the prospects of war between Iran and the United States in 1995, Foreign Minister 'Ali Akbar Velayati saw absolutely no reason for concern. After unconfirmed reports that US commandos were selecting targets for attacks on Iran in early 2005, President Khatemi considered the likelihood of an attack to be "very negligible."[146] Even Ahmadinejad's Deputy Interior Minister for Security Affairs Muhammad Baqer Zolqadr – a Revolutionary Guard – declared that the United States was only capable of soft threats but incapable of launching military operations against Iran, adding that US threats were designed to create instability and tension inside Iran in a transparent acknowledgment of fears of *regime* change rather than an actual military attack on Iran.[147] Ahmadinejad himself declared to Al-Jazeera that "America is not interested in sparking a military confrontation." "Do you believe an army that has been defeated by a small

---

[141] Conversely, despite prior threats to retaliate with fury if South Korea conducted military exercises in late 2010, North Korea was conciliatory in their aftermath, perhaps with an eye on domestic commitments to celebrate the 2012 centennial of Kim Il-sung's birth as a "Strong and Prosperous Nation." On the argument that the most likely catalysts of change are internal, see Mazarr (2011).

[142] According to Davis (2000), a leadership genuinely concerned with external vulnerability is more receptive to assurances.

[143] Solingen (2007a) and Kreps and Pasha (Chapter 6, this volume).

[144] Normark *et al.* (2005).

[145] Chubin and Litwak (2003). See also H. Blix, "Nuclear Options," *Guardian*, February 25, 2009.

[146] "US Attack 'Madness,' Says Khatami," *BBC*, January 20, 2005.

[147] "Newsline – April 27, 2007," Radio Free Europe/Radio Liberty, available at: www. rferl.org/content/article/1143861.html.

army in Iraq can enter into a war with a large and well trained army like the Iranian army?" he asked rhetorically.[148]

Military threats in the Iranian–Israeli context are a more recent development as well. Even as Iran pursued secret nuclear capabilities since the 1980s there is no evidence of military threats against Iran except from Iraq, until the latter's nuclear disarmament and containment in 1991. Throughout the 1990s the view of Israel as a threat to Iran was considered to have only "propagandistic elements ... [that] may not fully accord with Tehran's deepest threat perceptions."[149] In the early 2000s, Takeyh (2005) surveyed Iranian official speeches and commentaries on nuclear weapons and was surprised "by how seldom Israel actually features into these deliberations," and by how the clerics do not seem "inordinately concerned about Israel's nuclear monopoly." Rather, in his view, Iran's alarmist rhetoric about an "Israeli threat" was designed to satisfy extremist nationalist and anti-Israel domestic and regional constituencies, including Hezbollah. The advent of Ahmadinejad's hardline coalition; its threats to obliterate Israel; and Holocaust denials inaugurated a period of heightened reciprocal threats between Iran and Israel.[150] Yet Supreme National Security Council secretary Larijani dismissed Israeli warnings of a military strike, advising "not to take these things so seriously. This is because Iran is a powerful country and has the necessary power. It is a hard target ... [Such threats] have never been taken seriously."[151] Israeli threats became more credible toward the end of the decade but Ahmadinejad reiterated the view – to Al-Jazeera – that "Israel is too weak to face up to Iran militarily," adding that Jerusalem did not have "the courage to do it ... I do not think its threat is serious."[152] Iranian Brig. Gen. Ahmad-Reza

---

[148] Quoted in www.lebanonwire.com/1008MLN/10082315HZ.asp. Following the end of the US military presence in Iraq, Iran's Defense Minister declared that the US is unable to maintain a successful presence anywhere in the world.

[149] Jones (1998: 42). See also Kaveh L. Afrasiabi, "The Myth of an Israeli Strike on Iran," *AsiaTimes Online*, April 7, 2005.

[150] Regarding Ahmadinejad's threats, Thomas Schelling (2006: 51–52) argued that "the president of Iran was recently quoted as saying that Iran still intended to wipe Israel off the face of the earth. My guess is that if they think about it, they are not going to try to do it with nuclear weapons. Israel ... would be able to launch a counterattack if its existence is threatened. Iran does not want to invite a nuclear attack ... an invitation to national suicide." Ahmadinejad also expressed that "if we want to make a bomb we are not afraid of anyone and we are not afraid to announce it, no one can do a damn thing." While adding that Iran doesn't want to acquire weapons, he also named a nuclear weapons expert to head the Atomic Energy Organization of Iran (www.isis-online.org).

[151] Islamic Republic of Iran News Network, Tehran 1055, December 5, 2005.

[152] Quoted in www.lebanonwire.com/1008MLN/10082315HZ.asp.

Pourdastan added that "today no enemy has the requirements *and the desire* [my emphasis] to carry out a military attack against the powerful Iran and military aggression against Iran is highly unlikely and even impossible and is synonymous with the suicide of the aggressor."[153]

Against this background, Kreps and Pasha examine the impact of US military threats against Iran between 2002 and 2009. Whereas studies of military threats often blackbox target states, theirs is a novel effort to probe into domestic distributional effects of threats. Their focal causal mechanism hinges on the assumption that threats have differential effects on domestic ruling coalitions with different orientations to the global political economy, a central hypothesis in this volume. Threats arguably strengthen inward-looking coalitions – wary of integrating into the global economy – that privilege protectionism, import substitution, and the military-industrial complex, including the nuclear program. As argued, even low credibility threats offer inward-looking leaders useful ammunition for promoting their constituencies, broadening domestic support, and justifying increased expenditures under the mantle of "national security."[154] Conversely, Kreps and Pasha expect threats to undermine internationalizing constituencies favoring increased private and foreign investment and trade, and decreased spending on military-industrial complexes (which are often import-substituting competitors of private and foreign capital). Threats thus arguably weaken domestic proponents of more conciliatory nuclear policies.

Kreps and Pasha interpret their quantitative indicators to suggest that as the credibility of US threats began to decline after 2007, lagged effects of threats may partially explain low levels of Iranian trade and investment freedom. However, those levels could also be traced to independent effects of favored inward-looking economic strategies by Ahmadinejad, Khamenei, and their IRGC allies, and to increased sanctions, despite ample seepage. Kreps and Pasha carefully flag problems of multiple causation, validity, and reliability. Indicators for the dependent variable – trade and investment levels, military expenditures – are only potential expressions of deeper shifts in the relative power of competing inward-looking and internationalizing coalitions. Yet changes in trade, investment, and military spending may not necessarily be indicative of such shifts. Furthermore, changes in relative coalitional strength are often the result of factors unrelated to military threats. Military threats

---

[153] "Iran Sanctions Bill Introduced in House," *Global Security Newswire*, April 21, 2011.

[154] Marinov (2005) found that military action increased the duration of the government in power.

are thus neither necessary nor sufficient for changing the balance of power between competing domestic coalitions.

Kreps and Pasha complement their study with qualitative analysis probing the domestic beneficiaries of external threats. Intensifying US threats in 2005–2006 may have been endogenous, triggered by a newly-elected hardline Majlis (2004) and a newly-elected hardline president (2005) following extensive repression of reformists. Ahmadinejad skillfully manipulated presumed external threats to mobilize support beyond the IRGC and *basiji* that brought him to power. As Kreps and Pasha conclude, however, domestic factors may have played a more central role than threats or sanctions in sustaining this coalition favoring economic "self-reliance," import substitution, and rejection of foreign investment. Warning against an overemphasis on external dynamics, they point out that Iran's 2009 elections and repressive aftermath deepened the inward-looking faction's hold on power far more than external threats, which had largely ceased by 2009. As Sadjadpour put it, "Iran's sense of siege is a self-fulfilling prophecy ... The looming foreign enemy is needed to justify domestic suppression."[155] The greatest fear of Iran's hardline coalition is American seduction, not American attack, argues Clawson.[156] Secretary of State Hillary Clinton declared in Qatar in late 2010 that the United States had no plans to carry out a military strike against Iran. Defense Secretary Robert Gates reiterated that a military attack would be only a "short-term solution" that could not stop Iran from getting nuclear weapons and Admiral Mullen acknowledged that a military strike would open a "third front" with serious ripple effects throughout the region.[157] These statements can erode US credibility, of crucial concern in the Kreps and Pasha framework, but can also corrode Iranian hardliners' opportunities to amplify external threats.

Finally, Palkki and Smith find the evidence for distributional effects of US military threats against Qaddafi to have been mixed in the 1980s (their study ends prior to the momentous events of 2011). He may have strengthened his hand vis-à-vis rivals and emboldened some revolutionary zealots but there were small rally-round-the-flag effects, and doubts about his confrontational approach increased within his inner circle and among more pragmatic elements. Palkki and Smith also find military threats to have been eminently credible and consequential for Qaddafi, particularly in 2003, in contrast to Saddam Hussein, who doubted the

---

[155] Sadjadpour (2010c).   [156] Clawson (2010).
[157] The statements here are in Mark Landler, "Clinton Raises US Concerns of Military Power in Iran," *New York Times*, February 16, 2010; "Iranian Nuclear Program Would Outlive Attack, Gates Says," *Global Security Newswire*, November 17, 2010.

credibility of US threats even as some of his advisors, quietly, took them more seriously. Military threats have questionable credibility even under normal conditions, and the circumstances in the second decade of the twenty-first century have eroded that credibility further. NATO's military intervention in Libya to prevent a potential genocide by Qaddafi's forces may well be an exception that proves a countervailing trend.

Some concluding thoughts

Debates regarding comprehensive and targeted sanctions, positive inducements, the different causal mechanisms through which they operate, and their ultimate effectiveness are bound to continue unabated.[158] Former weapons inspector Hans Blix concluded that sanctions by themselves may not lead to results in Iran but they had big effects in Iraq and Libya.[159] In the late 1990s and even later, however, many thought sanctions had failed in Iraq even though Saddam and his lieutenants knew otherwise, according to new evidence detailed by Palkki and Smith.[160] Many continue to believe that neither sanctions nor positive inducements have had expected effects on nuclear capabilities and designs in North Korea or Iran although they appear to have hurt the economy and access to international financial, shipping, and other services. Iran's own ruling coalition releases equivocal statements on the effects of sanctions, ranging from Ahmadinejad's dismissal of sanctions as an inconsequential "used handkerchief" to Khamenei's stern demand to "put away the sanctions."[161] By late 2011, however, the strongest yet IAEA report on Iran's violations led to several Congressional initiatives calling, among other things, for sanctions on entities doing business with Iran's Central Bank. These, in turn, led various Iranian officials – including the foreign minister and the governor of the central bank

[158] A newer wave of targeted inducements came in the form of the Stuxnet worm, the distributional implications of which (for senders and targets) are yet unknown.
[159] Lee Michael Katz, "Attack On Iran Would Be 'Disastrous,' Blix Says," *Global Security Newswire*, August 9, 2010. On Iraq, see also O'Sullivan (2003), Lopez and Cortright (2004), Duelfer (2004), and Lebovic (2007).
[160] Haass (1997), Pape (1998), Gause (1999), and Mueller and Mueller (1999).
[161] "Iranian Leader Sets Demands for Talks With US," *Global Security Newswire*, August 19, 2010. Yet in 2011 Ahmadinejad declared that Iran's banks "cannot make international transactions anymore," www.gsn.nti.org/gsn/nw_20111103_9144.php. Rowhani (2005) acknowledged that as far back as 2005, the transfer of Iran's nuclear file to the UNSC for possible sanctions "had a great impact on [Iran's] economy ... the value of the shares on our stock market goes down. Therefore, this issue affects the economy, public opinion, and, unfortunately, our security." In a speech to influential clerics, Rafsanjani expressed: "I would like to ask you and all the country's officials to take the sanctions seriously and not as a joke." *Time Magazine*, September 27, 2010.

– to acknowledge the gravity of sanctions. Iran's *rial* plunged in value by more than 50 percent in 2011 and especially sharply after President Obama signed into law measures that could curtail Iran's oil exports. Some Iranian leaders threatened to shut the Straits of Hormuz if those sanctions were adopted while others expressed a willingness to renew negotiations. These actions suggest both that political effects of sanctions cannot be dismissed and that those effects continue to elicit different responses from different constituencies.

In principle, the probability that sanctions would have desired effects in the nuclear realm is burdened by at least three factors. First, the most frequent targets of these sanctions – inward-looking autocracies – are also expected to be the least vulnerable to them. Second, sanctions are expected to surface only when targets believe that concessions would risk regime survival more than defiance, but this is a biased sample. Cases where targets are receptive to inducements, pre-empting sanctions altogether, are often excluded in studies on the effects of sanctions. These selection effects concentrate the analysis of sanctions largely on inward-looking autocracies, where sanctions are least expected to work. Inward-looking autocracies, in other words, appear to be endogenous to why sanctions emerge as tools of statecraft to begin with.[162] Third, perhaps because inward-looking autocracies provide limited tangible public goods beyond hyper-nationalism, they may price nuclear weapons particularly highly as legitimating substitutes for other public goods, making such regimes even more resistant to comply with external demands regarding their nuclear designs.

All these premises deserve further scrutiny but, taken together, they lower the probability that sanctions may yield desired effects, prima facie. However, to the extent that sanctions have actually unleashed such effects – as various chapters document for two or three of the four major cases since the 1990s, and perhaps others before that – the rate of success is far from negligible. Such incidence of success may be even more remarkable given that nuclear proliferation is among the toughest realms for tools of statecraft to prove effective. It is also the case, perhaps, that nuclear proliferation may make it easier for senders to overcome collective action dilemmas, although this is far from consensual knowledge in the scholarly and policy communities. Notwithstanding continued differences and problems of implementation, the degree of consensus regarding sanctions on Iran since 2010 has been higher than ever before. Indeed, some European countries were pressing most

---

[162] The logic of these selection effects and the sources of this endogeneity are described in Solingen (2007a).

forcefully for measures against Iran, reaching an agreement to ban Iranian crude oil imports into the EU. Disputes led China to halve its oil imports from Iran and replace them with Russian and Vietnamese supplies. Some Russian firms appeared to be backtracking on oil investments in Iran as well. Even Turkey intercepted materials that Iran could have used to advance its nuclear program, and its ambassador to the US declared that Turkey would never resign itself to an Iranian bomb. And Iran's threats to shut the Straits of Hormuz broadened the space for multilateral cooperation further than ever before.

On the positive inducements side of the ledger, various chapters find them to have largely benefited the regime more than moderate oppositions, though in some cases inducements were deemed to have been rather timid. Yet, Qaddafi's response to the 2011 popular uprising also suggests that the showering of a repressive autocracy with rewards since 2004 had negative unintended effects from a human rights standpoint. And yet the possibility of a Qaddafi with nuclear weapons – absent the 2003 agreement – would have entailed high costs as well. Finally, sender's abstention from military threats may be considered a positive inducement short of security assurances that can nonetheless deprive targets of the opportunity to manipulate such threats to advance nuclear weapons programs. And, as Robert Gallucci (2011) suggests, threats of regime change are particularly ill-advised as the delicate transition to Kim Jung-un begins, just as this book goes to press. It remains unclear whether and when negotiations to renew US food aid in exchange for North Korea's acceptance of international inspections of retired nuclear facilities will resume.

Beyond any definitive assessment of the role of various inducements forms, the chapters sought to explore causal mechanisms that may explain how inducements operate in the domestic context of target states, and how, in turn, target states exploit gaps in senders' distributional considerations. A research agenda along these lines both opens productive new paths and raises difficult questions. Disentangling the effects of domestic developments from external inducements can be very challenging methodologically. There is a danger of imputing too much weight to sanctions in instances where causal dynamics are largely domestic. There is also the reverse danger of overstating purely domestic factors that can never be fully isolated from external inducements.

Political economy models of regime survival – a crucial focus in this volume – offer an important mechanism linking different domestic constituencies to competing incentives and variable receptivity to external inducements. Inward-looking models are a powerful identifier of prevailing incentives regarding inducements. The more inward-looking the target's ruling coalition, the lower its receptivity to inducements of any kind. Autocratic regime forms reinforce resilience against external inducements. At the extreme, this combination enhances the primacy of Innenpolitik, where nuclear behavior can be virtually sealed from external influences. Yet, as pre-2003 Iraq and Libya suggest, resilience is not invulnerability. Often considered the most autarkic case, even North Korea's "military first" model can be susceptible to external influences. But inward-looking models also make it difficult to isolate the effect of sanctions from the model's inherently inefficient economic management. Leaders blame sanctions very effectively as the culprit for all problems yet North Korea's dire predicament – and even Iran's, softened by oil revenues – is no less the very product of inward-looking autocratic models. The four main cases discussed in this volume had both built-in barriers against effective economic performance and high predisposition to economic predation. Methodologies for disentangling the effects of external factors from those of the models themselves remain an important research frontier.

Our understanding of outcomes may improve with more detailed knowledge of particular mechanisms and scope conditions, and with their further identification and testing.[163] Yet mutual interactions among multiple mechanisms also introduce highly contingent pathways connecting the threat/offer of inducements with compliant or non-compliant outcomes. Tetlock (2005) accurately warns against predicting outcomes with large stochastic components. As Stein notes with respect to sanctions, however precise their targets, they remain blunt instruments whose consequences hinge on a complex set of strategic interactions. Multiple actors with diverse incentives within sender and target states compound complexity and the likelihood of unintended and unpredictable consequences.[164] Multifaceted targets – rather than monoliths – anticipate and foil the very effects sought by senders, and vice versa. Second, third, and nth-order effects can unleash counterintuitive mechanisms, different from what might have seemed the obvious ones. Additionally, closed and autocratic targets heighten inherent information asymmetries, providing senders with much less knowledge about the target's domestic landscape than the other way round. All this suggests that the ability to map causal mechanisms with somewhat greater precision should not lead to the illusion that one can either fully uncover such knowledge or translate it into foolproof policy all that easily. The alternative to complexity – stylized and overly-simplified

---

[163] Hedström and Ylikoski (2010).
[164] Jervis (1997, 2010), Tetlock (2005), Katzenstein and Sil (2010) and Lebow (2010).

assumptions – has merit at times but, as Tetlock's (2005) masterful treatise on prediction suggests, parsimony can be the enemy of accuracy, a substantial liability in real-world forecasting.

Many lessons about inducements, causal mechanisms, domestic models, regime types, and unintended or unexpected effects may be applicable to the study of statecraft beyond nuclear proliferation. The distributional consequences of inducements across different issue areas may certainly differ but many of the causal mechanisms might resemble the ones explored here. The absence of a universal law of inducements does not imply that there are no recurrent features in some causal logics.[165] Haggard and Noland's findings regarding pernicious effects of aid to North Korea, for instance, resonate with recent findings that aid tends to stabilize dictatorships.[166] At the same time, differences in the overall objective of statecraft may limit the transferability of some lessons from the special domain of nuclear proliferation. Persuading regimes to abandon nuclear weapons may trigger different distributional considerations than persuading them to improve their human rights record or to abstain from terrorist activities. Whether target regimes perceive the renunciation of nuclear weapons as entailing higher costs than yielding on human rights or democratization is another outstanding riddle worthy of further investigation. Comparative studies of statecraft across issue areas may also gauge the extent to which persuasion or coercion are more effective or more difficult in some issue areas than others, and if so why.

Nonproliferation statecraft will increasingly be influenced by overarching changes in the underlying configuration of international financial, economic, and diplomatic power and influence required for wielding market power. The conventional wisdom views rising China, Brazil, Russia, India, Turkey, and others as more reluctant to endorse sanctions. But even China's once strict opposition to them has been superseded by its unprecedented endorsement of UNSC resolutions sanctioning North Korea and Iran. Russia's opposition to sanctions could wither away under new circumstances. Brazil's strong endorsement of Iran's policies under Lula may not endure given domestic debates over Iran's human rights and Brazil's own newly-discovered oil reservoirs. Shifting positions on nonproliferation statecraft among

---

[165] Tilly (2003, citing his 1993) expressed similar skepticism for Laws of Revolution even as he identified the centrality of a basic polarization within regimes around the monopoly of coercion; also in interview with Daniel Little, December 15, 2007, available at: www.youtube.com/watch?v=PP900JiYFr8.

[166] Morrison (2009).

senders cannot be discounted in light of the domestic distributional effects that this volume placed at the center of analysis. If the domestic organization of market power needed for applying sanctions is more difficult for market-oriented democracies than for market-oriented autocracies, Chinese leaders would be advantaged on their home turf, at least in theory. However, presumed difficulties facing democracies in the organization of market power have not resulted in trivial rates of reliance on sanctions, whether geared to prevent acquisition of nuclear weapons or enhance human rights. Indeed, democracies have proven more rather than less inclined to rely on sanctions than other regime types, particularly sanctions on autocracies and even under the difficult circumstances of 2011.[167] Furthermore, autocracies are themselves evolving polities (not merely in target states), and they too must consider domestic audience costs. Whether or not autocracies are better positioned to organize multilateral monopoly or monopsony in the twenty-first century adds another important dimension to the research agenda on nonproliferation statecraft and beyond.

Finally, international power, always an elusive concept, should not be overestimated as the single most important determinant of when, how, why, and what sanctions or inducements might be applied. Paradoxically, a US administration presiding over the most adverse economic and political circumstances since World War II also mustered more successful collective action vis-à-vis Iran and North Korea than might have been expected given a precarious US position in the aftermath of the Great Recession. The US organization of multilateralism could differ from a future one reflecting changing power distributions, but some of its features could well endure. The dilemmas explored in this book suggest that the pathways of inducements have always been, and will remain, hard to predict. And even the future's arrival will leave plenty of room for disagreement over the definitive outcomes of those inducements.

[167] Cox and Drury (2006).

References

Abedin, M. 2006. Iranian Public Opinion and the Nuclear Stand-Off. *Mideast Monitor* 1 (2): 2–8.

Acemoglu, D., and J. Robinson. 2005. *Economic Origins of Dictatorship and Democracy*. Cambridge University Press.

Acton, J. 2009. Extended Deterrence and Communicating Resolve. *Strategic Insights* 8 (5): 1–7.

Adler-Karlsson, G. 1968. *Western Economic Warfare, 1947–1967*. Stockholm: Almquist & Wiksell.

Albright, D. 2010. *ISIS Special Report: Libya: A Major Sale at Last*. Washington, DC: Institute for Science and International Security.

Albright, D., and M. Hibbs. 1991. Iraq's Nuclear Hide-and-Seek. *Bulletin of the Atomic Scientists* 47 (7): 14–23.

Albright, D., and J. Shire. 2009. ISIS Report: IAEA Report on Iran. November 16.

Albright, D., P. Brannan, and J. Shire. 2009. ISIS Report: IAEA Report on Iran. August 28.

Albright, M. 2003. *Madam Secretary: A Memoir*. New York: Hyperion.

Alfoneh, A. 2008. The Revolutionary Guards' Role in Iranian Politics. *Middle East Quarterly* 15 (4): 3–14.

Allen, S.H. 2005. The Determinants of Economic Sanctions Success and Failure. *International Interactions* 31 (2): 117–138.

2008a. Political Institutions and Constrained Response to Economic Sanctions. *Foreign Policy Analysis* 4 (3): 255–274.

2008b. The Domestic Political Costs of Economic Sanctions. *Journal of Conflict Resolution* 52 (6): 916–944.

Alnasrawi, A. 2001. Iraq: Economic Sanctions and Consequences, 1990–2000. *Third World Quarterly* 22 (2): 205–218.

Amirpur, K. 2006. The Future of Iran's Reform Movement. *Iranian Challenges*, edited by Walter Posch, Chaillot Paper No. 89, European Union Institute for Security Studies, 32.

Amuzegar, J. 2002. Khatami's First-Term Presidency. *The SAIS Review*. Johns Hopkins University Press.

2010. Iran's Economy in Turmoil. *International Economic Bulletin*. March. Washington, DC: Carnegie Endowment for International Peace.

Anderson, J.L. 2010. After the Crackdown. *The New Yorker*. August 16.

352

Anderson, L. 2003. Libyan Expert: Qadhafi, Desperate to End Libya's Isolation, Sends a "Gift" to President Bush. Interview with Bernard Gwertzman. Council on Foreign Relations. December 22.

Anderson, S. 2003. The Makeover. *New York Times Magazine*. January 19.

Andreas, P. 2005. Criminalizing Consequences of Sanctions. *International Studies Quarterly* 49 (2): 335–360.

Andrews, D.M., ed. 2006. *International Monetary Power*. Ithaca: Cornell University Press.

Ang, A.U., and D. Peksen. 2007. When Do Economic Sanctions Work? *Political Research Quarterly* 60 (1): 135–145.

Ansari, A. 2010a. The Revolution Will Be Mercantilized. *The National Interest* 105: 50–60.

2010b. The Mafia State. *The National Interest*. February 19.

Aref, B., and B. Farahany. 2010. The Guards. *Middle East Online*. March 10.

Arms Control Association (ACA). 1998. Congress Okays KEDO Funding. *Arms Control Today*. October. Online.

2007. Chronology of Libya's Disarmament and Relations with the United States. Available at: www.armscontrol.org/factsheets/LibyaChronology.

2009a. Chronology of U.S.-North Korean Nuclear and Missile Diplomacy. Available at: www.armscontrol.org/factsheets/dprkchron.

2009b. History of Official Proposals on the Iranian Nuclear Issue. Available at: www.armscontrol.org/factsheets/Iran_Nuclear_Proposals.

2010. Questions Surrounding Iran's Nuclear Program.

Art, R.J. 2003. Introduction. In *The United States and Coercive Diplomacy*, edited by R.J. Art and P.M. Cronin. Washington, DC: United States Institute of Peace, 3–20.

Asher, D.L. 2007. The Impact of U.S. Policy on North Korean Illicit Activities. Heritage Lectures No. 1024, April 18. Washington, DC: Heritage Foundation.

Asia Society Center on US-China Relations and The University of California Institute on Global Conflict and Cooperation. 2009. *North Korea Inside Out: The Case for Economic Engagement*.

Askari, H. 2010. Iran's Economic Health and the Impact of Sanctions. Washington, DC: Carnegie Endowment for International Peace.

Axelrod, R., and R.O. Keohane. 1985. Achieving Cooperation Under Anarchy. *World Politics* 38 (1): 226–254.

Baily, M.N. 1974. Wages and Employment Under Uncertain Demand. *The Review of Economic Studies* 41 (1): 37–50.

Baldwin, D.A. 1971a. The Power of Positive Sanctions. *World Politics* 24 (1): 19–38.

1971b. Thinking About Threats. *Journal of Conflict Resolution* 15 (1): 71–78.

1985. *Economic Statecraft*. Princeton University Press.

1998. Evaluating Economic Sanctions. *International Security* 23 (2): 189–195.

1999/2000. The Sanctions Debate and the Logic of Choice. *International Security* 24 (3): 80–107.

2003. Prologamena to Thinking About Economic Sanctions and Free Trade. *Chicago Journal of International Law* 4 (2): 271–281.

Baram, A. 2000. The Effect of Iraqi Sanctions. *Middle East Journal* 54 (2): 194–223.

Barro, R.J. 1977. Long-term Contracting, Sticky Prices, and Monetary Policy. *Journal of Monetary Economics* 3 (1): 305–316.

BBC News Persian. 2009. Zendegi e Namzadha: Mir Hussein Mousavi. (The Candidates' Lives: Mir Hosseun Mousavi.) May 21.

Beach, W.W., and T. Kane. 2007. *Index of Economic Freedom*. Washington, DC: Heritage Foundation.

Becker, C.M. 1987. Economic Sanctions Against South Africa. *World Politics* 39 (2): 147–173.

Bengio, O. 2000. How Does Saddam Hold On? *Foreign Affairs* 79 (4): 90–103.

Bennett, W.L., and D.L. Paletz, eds. 1994. *Taken By Storm*. London: University of Chicago Press.

Bernauer, T., and D. Ruloff, eds. 1999. *The Politics of Positive Incentives in Arms Control*. Columbia: University of South Carolina Press.

Betts, R.K. 2003. Striking First. *Ethics and International Affairs* 17 (1): 17–24.

Bhatia, S. 1988. *Nuclear Rivals in the Middle East*. New York: Routledge.

Bianchi, A. 2007. Assessing the Effectiveness of the UN Security Council's Anti-terrorism Measures. *European Journal of International Law* 17 (5): 881–919.

Biersteker, T.J. 2004. The Emergence, Evolution, Effects, and Challenges of Targeted Solutions. Paper prepared for the conference *Sanctions Economiques: Vers de Nouvelles Pratiques*. Paris, France. June 14.

Biersteker, T.J., S. Eckert, A. Halegua, and P. Romaniuk. 2005. Consensus from the Bottom Up? In *International Sanctions: Between War and Words in the International System*, edited by P. Wallensteen and C. Staibano. London: Routledge, 15–74.

Blechman, B., and D. Brumberg. 2010. *Engagement, Coercion, and Iran's Nuclear Challenge: Report of a Joint Study Group on U.S.-Iran Policy*. Washington, DC: The Henry L. Stimson Center.

Bolks, S., and D. Al-Sowayel. 2000. How Long Do Economic Sanctions Last? *Political Research Quarterly* 53: 241–265.

Bolton, J. 2007. *Surrender Is Not an Option*. New York: Threshold Editions.

Bonds, T., D. Baiocchi, and L. McDonald. 2010. *Army Deployments to OIF and OEF*. Arlington: Rand Corporation.

Boothroyd, P., and P. Xuan Nam, eds. 2000. *Socioeconomic Renovation in Viet Nam: The Origin, Evolution, and Impact of Doi Moi*. Singapore: Institute of Southeast Asian Studies.

Bornstein, M. 1968. Economic Sanctions and Rewards in Support of Arms Control Agreements. *American Economic Review* 58 (2): 417–427.

Bowen, W.O. 2006. *Libya and Nuclear Proliferation*. International Institute for Strategic Studies, Adelphi Papers 380.

2008. Libya. In *Nuclear Safeguards, Security and Nonproliferation: Achieving Security with Technology and Policy*, edited by James Doyle. New York: Elsevier Inc.

Bracken, P. 2007. Financial Warfare. *Orbis* 51 (4): 685–696.

Brands, H., and D. Palkki. 2010. Conspiring Bastards: Saddam Hussein's Strategic View of the United States, accepted for publication in *Diplomatic History*.

Braun, C., and C.F. Chyba. 2004. Proliferation Rings. *International Security* 29 (2): 5–49.

Braut-Hegghammer, M. 2008. Libya's Nuclear Turnaround: Perspectives From Tripoli. *The Middle East Journal* 62 (1): 55–72.

Brooks, R.A. 2002. Sanctions and Regime Type. *Security Studies* 11 (4): 1–50.

Broz, J.L., and J. Frieden. 2006. The Political Economy of Exchange Rates. In *The Oxford Handbook of Political Economy*, edited by B.R. Weingast and D. Wittman. New York: Oxford University Press, 587–597.

Bruno, G. 2009. Backgrounder: Iran's Revolutionary Guards. Council on Foreign Relations. June 22.

Brzoska, M. 2003. From Dumb to Smart? *Global Governance* 9 (4): 519–535.
    2008. Measuring the Effectiveness of Arms Embargoes. *Peace Economics, Peace Science and Public Policy* 14 (2): Article 2.

Buchta, W. 2000. *Who Rules Iran? The Structure of Power in the Islamic Republic.* Washington, DC: The Washington Institute for Near East Policy and the Konrad-Adenauer-Stiftung.

Buck, L., N. Gallant, and K.R. Nossal. 1998. Sanctions as a Gendered Instrument of Statecraft. *Review of International Studies* 24: 69–84.

Buell, R.L. 1932. Are Sanctions Necessary for a Successful International Organization? *The Annals of the American Academy of Political and Social Science* 162: 93–99.

Bueno de Mesquita, B., and R.M. Siverson. 1995. War and the Survival of Political Leaders. *American Political Science Review* 89 (4): 841–855.

Bueno de Mesquita, B., J.D. Morrow, R.M. Siverson, and A. Smith. 1999. An Institutional Explanation of the Democratic Peace. *American Political Science Review* 93 (4): 791–807.
    2003. *The Logic of Political Survival.* Cambridge, MA: MIT Press.

Burr, W., and J. Richelson. 2001. Whether to Strangle the Baby in the Cradle. *International Security* 25 (3): 54–99.

Butler, R. 2000. *The Greatest Threat: Iraq, Weapons of Mass Destruction, and the Growing Crisis of Global Security.* New York: PublicAffairs.

Byman, D. 2008. An Autopsy of the Iraqi Debacle. *Security Studies* 17 (4): 599–643.

Byman, D., and J. Lind. 2010. Pyongyang's Survival Strategy. *International Security* 35 (1): 44–74.

Byman, D., and M.C. Waxman. 2002. *The Dynamics of Coercion: American Foreign Policy and the Limits of Military Might.* London: Cambridge University Press.

Carter, B.E. 1987. International Economic Sanctions. *California Law Review* 75 (4): 1159–1278.
    1988. *International Economic Sanctions.* New York: Cambridge University Press.

Casey, G. Jr. 2009. The Army of the 21st Century. *Army*: 25–40.

Central Intelligence Agency. 2004. *Comprehensive Report of the Special Advisor to the DCI on Iraq's WMD*, Vols. 1–3. Langley: Central Intelligence Agency.

Chan, S., and A.C. Drury, eds. 2000. *Sanctions as Economic Statecraft*. London: Macmillan; New York: St. Martin's.

Chang, S. 2007. Economic Sanctions Against North Korea. Paper presented at the AEA-KAEA Session, Chicago.

2008. Why Has North Korea Responded Positively to the Nuclear Talks in 2007? *North Korean Review* 4 (2): 6–15.

Chang, S., and S.H. Kim. 2007. *Economic Sanctions Against a Nuclear North Korea*. Jefferson: McFarland & Company, Inc.

Chanlett-Avery, E., and M.A. Taylor. 2010. *North Korea: U.S. Relations, Nuclear Diplomacy, and Internal Situation*. Congressional Research Service (CRS) Report for Congress. November 10.

Chinoy, M. 2008. *Meltdown*. New York: St. Martin's Press.

Choi, J. 2009. Why is North Korea so Aggressive? Nautilus Institute Policy Forum Online 09–062A. July 30.

Chubin, S. 2010a. The Iranian Nuclear Riddle After June 12. *The Washington Quarterly* 33 (1): 163–172.

2010b. *The Domestic Politics of the Nuclear Question in Iran*. Aspen European Strategy Forum Paper.

Chubin, S., and R. Litwak. 2003. Debating Iran's Nuclear Aspirations. *The Washington Quarterly* 26 (4): 99–114.

Cirincione, J., J.B. Wolfstahl, and M. Rajkumar. 2005. *Deadly Arsenal: Nuclear, Biological, and Chemical Threats*, 2nd edn. Washington, DC: Carnegie Endowment for International Peace.

Claire, R. 2004. *Raid on the Sun*. New York: Broadway.

Clark, H.L., and L.W. Wang. 2007. Foreign Sanctions Countermeasures and Other Responses to U.S. Extraterritorial Sanctions. Dewey Ballantine LLP report for USA*Engage. August.

Clawson, P. 2010. *The Perfect Handshake With Iran*. Washington Institute Strategic Report. Washington, DC: The Washington Institute for Near East Policy.

CNN. 1998. Transcript of Interview With Iranian President Mohammad Khatami. January 7.

Cockburn, A., and P. Cockburn. 2002. *Saddam Hussein: An American Obsession*. London: Verso.

Cohen, E.A. 2003. *Supreme Command: Soldiers, Statesmen, and Leadership in Wartime*. New York: The Free Press, Simon & Schuster, Inc.

Collier, D. 1995. Translating Quantitative Methods for Qualitative Researchers. *American Political Science Review* 89 (2): 461–466.

Conflict Records Research Center (CRRC), Washington, DC.

SH-IMFA-D-000–545, "Letters from the Ministry of Foreign Affairs to the Administrative Office of the Presidency Concerning the Relationship between Iraq and Russia," 2000.

SH-MISC-D-000–203, "Report on an Iraqi Delegation Visit to Russia and France," April 6, 1996.

SH-RVCC-A-001–184, "Saddam Hussein Meeting with Ba'ath Party Members," July 25, 1996.

SH-SHTP-A-001–185, "Saddam Hussein Meeting with Ba'ath Party Members Discussing the State of the Country," August 2, 1992.

SH-SHTP-A-001–186, "Saddam Hussein Meeting with Ba'ath Party Members Discussing the UN Inspection Process in Iraq," July 23, 1992.

SH-SHTP-A-001–187, "Saddam Hussein Meeting with High-ranking Officers about UN Security Council Resolutions," May 2, 1995.

SH-SHTP-A-001–188, "Saddam Hussein Meeting with Some Advisors Concerning the Defector Hussayn Kamil and Other Issues," April 5, 1995.

SH-SHTP-A-001–189, "Plans for a Press Report about Husayn Kamil," August 28, 1995.

SH-SHTP-A-001–192, "Saddam Hussein Attending an Iraqi Government Meeting with High Officials Discussing the Ration Cards," July 19, 1995.

SH-SHTP-A-001–196, "A Meeting Between Saddam and Unidentified Iraqi Leaders," undated (circa July 1994).

SH-SHTP-A-001–197, "Meeting Between Saddam and his Inner Circle," March 1, 2001.

SH-SHTP-A-001–198, "Saddam and his Advisors Discuss the Rules of the UN Security Council," undated.

SH-SHTP-A-001–199, "Saddam Hussein Meeting Discussing United Nations Reports," July 21, 1998.

SH-SHTP-A-001–200, "Saddam Meeting with Ba'ath Regional Command Members Discussing Sanctions, Russia/Soviet Politics, Primakov, and American Air Strikes," circa February 23, 1998.

SH-SHTP-A-001–201, "Iraqi Leaders Discuss Oil Sales, Ekeus, a Possible Biological Project, and the Iraqi Media," undated.

SH-SHTP-A-001–202, "Saddam Hussein Meeting with the General Command of the Armed Forces," undated.

SH-SHTP-A-000–554, "Meeting between Saddam Hussein and Iraqi Officials regarding the Political Relationship between Iraq, Iran and the USA," September 17, 1988.

SH-SHTP-A-000–565, "A Meeting between Saddam Hussein and Unidentified High Ranking Officials regarding US Plans to Attack Iraq, Irrigation Projects, and other Military Issues," undated.

SH-SHTP-A-000–756, "Proceedings of a Meeting of the Revolutionary Command Council," February 9, 1998.

SH-SHTP-A-000–762, "Meeting between Saddam, Iraqi Ministers, and Unidentified Individuals," August 1995.

SH-SHTP-A-000–791, "Meeting Between Saddam Hussein and the Council of Ministers Regarding Russia, France, and Arab Countries' Positions toward the Sanctions," undated.

SH-SHTP-A-000–828, "Meeting Between Saddam and unknown Individuals Regarding Husayn Kamil and Other Issues," undated.

SH-SHTP-A-000–833, "Iraqi Leaders Discuss Husayn Kamil," undated.

SH-SHTP-A-000–837, "Saddam Hussein Discusses Husayn Kamil's Behavior with his Advisors," undated.

SH-SHTP-A-000–850, "Revolution Command Council and Regional Command Meeting," February 29, 1992.

SH-SHTP-A-000–990, "Meeting between Saddam Hussein and Senior Advisors," 1995.

SH-SHTP-D-000–567, "Meeting between Saddam Hussein and Baath Party Officials," October 5, 1985.

SH-SHTP-D-000–797, "Meeting between Saddam Hussein and Iraqi Commanders on Weapons Inspections and how the United States Intends to Continue the Sanctions on Iraq," undated (probably 1994).

Cooper, J.H. 1989. On Income Distribution and Economic Sanctions. *South African Journal of Economics* 57 (1): 14–21.

Cordesman, A.H., and A.S. Hashim. 1997. *Iraq: Sanctions and Beyond.* Boulder: Westview Press.

Cortright, D. 2001. A Hard Look at Iraq Sanctions. *The Nation.* November 3.

Cortright, D., and G.A. Lopez. 1995. The Sanctions Era. *The Fletcher Forum of World Affairs* 19 (2): 65–85.

1999. Are Sanctions Just? *Journal of International Affairs* 55 (2): 735–755.

2000. *The Sanctions Decade.* Boulder: Lynne Rienner Publishers, Inc.

eds. 2002. *Smart Sanctions: Targeted Economic Statecraft.* New York: Rowman & Littlefield.

Cortright, D., and R. Väyrynen. 2010. *Towards Nuclear Zero.* New York: Routledge.

Cox, D.G., and A.C. Drury. 2006. Democratic Sanctions: Connecting the Democratic Peace and Economic Sanctions. *Journal of Peace Research* 43 (6): 709–722.

Crane, K. 2010. Iran and International Sanctions: Elements of Weakness and Resilience. In *The Strategic Implications of the Iranian Nuclear Program*, edited by J. Krause and C.K. Mallory IV. Germany: Aspen Institute.

Crawford, N.C., and A. Klotz, eds. 1999. *How Sanctions Work: Lessons From South Africa.* New York: St. Martin's Press, Inc.

Crumm, E.M. 1995. The Value of Economic Incentives in International-Politics. *Journal of Peace Research* 32 (3): 313–330.

Cummings, J. 2006. New Study Reports Use of U.S. Unilateral Sanctions on the Rise (Press Release). USA*Engage. October 27.

Dallek, R. 1984. *Ronald Reagan: The Politics of Symbolism.* Cambridge, MA: Harvard University Press.

Damrosch, L.F. 1994. The Collective Enforcement of International Norms Through Economic Sanctions. *Ethics and International Affairs* 8 (1): 59–75.

Danilovic, V. 2001. The Sources of Threat in Extended Deterrence. *Journal of Conflict Resolution* 45 (3): 341–369.

Dashti-Gibson, J., P. Davis, and B. Radcliff. 1997. On the Determinants of the Success of Economic Sanctions. *American Journal of Political Science* 41 (2): 608–618.

David, S.R. 1991. Explaining Third World Alignment. *World Politics* 43 (2): 233–256.

Davis, J.W. Jr. 2000. *Threats and Promises.* Baltimore: Johns Hopkins University Press.

Davis, L., and S. Engerman. 2003. History Lessons – Sanctions. *Journal of Economic Perspectives* 17 (2): 187–197.

Davis, P.A. 1999. *The Art of Economic Persuasion.* Ann Arbor: University of Michigan Press.

Dehghanpisheh, B. 2010. Smugglers for the State. *Newsweek*. July 10.

Desch, M. 2007. Bush and the Generals. *Foreign Affairs* 86 (3): 97.

Dorn, W.A., and A. Fulton. 1997. Securing Compliance with Disarmament Treaties. *Global Governance* 3 (1): 17–40.

Dorussen, H. 2001. Mixing Carrots With Sticks. *Journal of Peace Research* 38 (2): 251–262.

Doxey, M.P. 1971. *Economic Sanctions and International Enforcement*. New York: Oxford University Press.

Dreze, J., and H. Gazdar. 1992. Hunger and Poverty in Iraq, 1991. *World Development* 20 (7): 921–945.

Drezner, D.W. 1998. Conflict Expectations and the Paradox of Economic Coercion. *International Studies Quarterly* 42 (4): 709–731.

1999. *The Sanctions Paradox*. Cambridge University Press.

1999/2000. The Trouble with Carrots: Transaction Costs, Conflict Expectations, and Economic Inducements. *Security Studies* 9 (1–2): 188–218.

2000. Bargaining, Enforcement, and Multilateral Sanctions. *International Organization* 54 (1): 73–102.

2007. *All Politics Is Global*. Princeton University Press.

2010. Sanctions Sometimes Smart. *International Studies Review* 12 (4).

Drury, A.C. 2001. Sanctions as Coercive Diplomacy. *Political Research Quarterly* 54 (3): 485–508.

Duelfer, C. 2004. "Comprehensive Report of the Special Advisor to the Director of Central Intelligence on Iraq's Weapons of Mass Destruction." Available at: www.cia.gov/library/reports/general-reports-1/iraq_wmd_2004/index.html.

2009. *Hide and Seek: The Search for Truth in Iraq*. New York: PublicAffairs.

Dunn, L.A. 1998. On Proliferation Watch. *The Nonproliferation Review* 5 (3): 59–77.

Dyson, T. 2009. New Evidence on Child Mortality in Iraq. *Economic and Political Weekly* 44 (2): 56–59.

Early, B.R. 2009. Sleeping With Your Friends' Enemies. *International Studies Quarterly* 53 (1): 49–71.

Eaton, J., and M. Engers. 1992. Sanctions. *Journal of Political Economy* 100 (5): 899–928.

Eberstadt, N. 2004. The Persistence of North Korea. *Policy Review* 127. Hoover Institute Stanford University. October 1.

Eckert, S. 2008. The Use of Financial Measures to Promote Security. *Journal of International Affairs* 62 (1): 103–111.

The Economist Intelligence Unit. 2001. *Country Report: Libya*. London: The Economist Intelligence Unit.

2010. *Country Report: Iran*. London: The Economist Intelligence Unit.

Eisenberg, L. 1997. Editorial: The Sleep of Reason Produces Monsters–Human Costs of Economic Sanctions. *New England Journal of Medicine* 336 (17): 1247–1250.

Elliott, K.A. 1998. The Sanctions Glass. *International Security* 23 (1): 50–65.

2002. Analyzing the Effects of Targeted Sanctions. In *Smart Sanctions: Targeting Economic Statecraft*, edited by D. Cortright and G.A. Lopez. New York: Rowman & Littlefield.

Elster, J. 1989. *Nuts and Bolts for the Social Sciences*. New York: Cambridge University Press.

Engel, J.A. 2005. Of Fat and Thin Communists. *Diplomatic History* 29 (3): 445–474.

Engelberg, S. 2010. Experts, Intelligence Agencies Question a Defector's Claims About Burma's Nuclear Ambitions. *ProPublica*. November 12.

Entelis, J.P. 2008. Libya and Its North African Policy. In *Libya Since 1969*, edited by D. Vandewalle. New York: Palgrave Macmillan.

Escribà-Folch, A. 2007. Economic Growth and Potential Punishment Under Dictatorship. *Kyklos* 60 (2): 187–210.

Escribà-Folch, A., and J. Wright. 2010. Economic Sanctions and the Duration of Civil Conflicts. *Journal of Peace Research* 47 (2): 129–141.

Esfandiari, G. 2003. Libya: Analysts Say Decision On WMD Inspired By Economics, Worries About Succession. RFERL. December 22.

Estelami, H. 1999. A Study of Iran's Responses to US Economic Sanctions. *Middle East Review of International Affairs* 3 (3): 51–61.

Etemad Melli. 2010. Goftegoo ba rais e commosion e vizhe asl 44 majles. (A discussion with the head of the commission for the implementation of article 44.)

Falleti, T.G., and J.F. Lynch. 2009. Context and Causal Mechanisms in Political Analysis. *Comparative Political Studies* 42 (9): 1143–1166.

Farmer, R.D. 1999. The Domestic Costs of Sanctions on Foreign Commerce. Congressional Budget Office Study. March.

2000. Costs of Economic Sanctions to the Sender. *The World Economy* 23 (1): 93–117.

Fearon, J.D. 1994a. Domestic Political Audiences and the Escalation of International Disputes. *American Political Science Review* 88 (3): 577–592.

1994b. Signaling versus the Balance of Power and Interests. *Journal of Conflict Resolution* 38 (2): 236–269.

1997. Signaling Foreign Policy Interests. *Journal of Conflict Resolution* 41 (1): 68–90.

Feaver, P.D., and E. Lorber. 2010. *Coercive Diplomacy: Evaluating the Consequences of Financial Sanctions*. London: Legatum Institute.

Federal Bureau of Investigation. 2004a. *Ali Hassan al-Majid (aka "Chemical Ali") and Sabir Abdul-Aziz al-Duri*. Washington, DC: Federal Bureau of Investigation.

2004b. *Written Interviews*. Washington, DC: Federal Bureau of Investigation.

Feffer, J. 2010. North Korea: Why Engagement Now? *38 North*. August.

Feldman, S. 1997. *Nuclear Weapons and Arms Control in the Middle East*. Cambridge, MA: Center for Science and International Affairs.

Feng, Z. 2010. China's Policy Toward North Korea. *PacNet No. 60*. Washington, DC: Center for Strategic and International Studies.

Fiedorowicz, G. 1936. Historical Survey of the Application of Sanctions. *Transactions of the Grotius Society* 22: 117–131.

Fisher, M. 2010. A Nuclear Standoff with Libya. *The Atlantic*. November 27.

Fitzpatrick, M. 2006. Iran and North Korea. *Survival* 48 (1): 61–80.

2010. Preventing Nuclear Dangers in Southeast Asia. International Institute for Strategic Studies. *Strategic Dossier*, March 24: 1.

2011. North Korean Security Challenges: A Net Assessment. *Strategic Dossier*, July 21.

Foot, R. 2007. The United Nations, Counter-Terrorism, and Human Rights. *Human Rights Quarterly* 29: 489–514.

Foran, V.I., and L.S. Spector. 1997. The Application of Incentives to Nuclear Proliferation. In *The Price of Peace*, edited by D. Cortright. Lanham: Rowman & Littlefield.

Ford, C.A., J. Yuan, and D. Choubey. 2009. Book Review Roundtable. *Asia Policy* 7: 113–158.

Førland, T.E. 1990. An Act of Economic Warfare? *The International History Review* 12 (3): 490–513.

1991. "Economic Warfare" and "Strategic Goods." *Journal of Peace Research* 28 (2): 191–204.

1993. The History of Economic Warfare. *Journal of Peace Research* 30 (2): 151–162.

Foroohar, K. 2010. Dubai Helps Iran Evade Sanctions as Smugglers Ignore U.S. Laws. *Bloomberg*. January 25.

Frieden, J.A., and R. Rogowski. 1996. The Impact of the International Economy on National Policies. In *Internationalization and Domestic Politics*, edited by R.O. Keohane and H.V. Milner. New York: Cambridge University Press, 25–47.

Fruchart, D., P. Holtom, D. Strandow, P. Wallensteen, and S. Wezeman. 2007. *United Nations Arms Embargoes*. Stockholm: SIPRI.

Fuhrmann, M., and S. Kreps. 2010. Targeting Nuclear Programs in War and Peace: A Quantitative Empirical Analysis, 1941–2000. *Journal of Conflict Resolution* 54 (6): 831–859.

Funabashi, Y. 2007. *The Peninsula Question*. Washington, DC: The Brookings Institution.

Gallucci, R. L. 2011. "What to Do, and Not Do, About North Korea," *The New York Times*, December 21, 2011.

Galtung, J. 1967. On the Effects of International Economic Sanctions. *World Politics* 19 (3): 378–416.

Ganji, A. 2009. Rise of the Sultans. *Foreign Affairs*. June 24.

Garrett, G., and B. Weingast. 1993. Ideas, Interests and Institutions. In *Ideas and Foreign Policy*, edited by J. Goldstein and R.O. Keohane. Ithaca: Cornell University Press.

Gas Matters. 2010. Iran's Latest Export/Import Options. *Gas Matters*, April: 1–7.

Gause III, F.G. 1999. Getting it Backward on Iraq. *Foreign Affairs*. May/June.

2010. *The International Relations of the Persian Gulf*. New York: Cambridge University Press.

Gawdat, B. 2007. The Proliferation of Weapons of Mass Destruction. *Arab Studies Quarterly* 29 (2): 21–36.

George, A.L., and R. Smoke. 1974. *Deterrence in American Foreign Policy*. New York: Columbia University Press.

George, A.L. 1992. *Forceful Persuasion*. Washington, DC: United States Institute of Peace.

George, A.L., and A. Bennett. 2005. *Case Studies and Theory Development in the Social Sciences*. Cambridge, MA: MIT Press.

Gershenson, D. 2002. Sanctions and Civil Conflict. *Economica* 69: 185–206.

Ghajar, S. 2010. Sanctions: The Unexpected Losers and Beneficiaries. *Inside Iran*. July 27.

Gierbolini, L. 1997. The Helms-Burton Act. *Journal of Transnational Law and Policy* 6 (2): 289–321.

Goldberg, J. 2010. The Point of No Return. *Atlantic Magazine*. September.

Goldemberg, J., and H.A. Feiveson. 1994. Denuclearization in Argentina and Brazil. *Arms Control Today* 24 (2): 10–14.

Goldschmidt, P. 2010. Preventing the Iranian Nuclear Crisis from Escalating. Paper prepared for joint workshop in Brussels. Washington, DC: Carnegie Endowment for International Peace.

Goodkind, D., and L. West. 2001. The North Korean Famine and its Demographic Impact. *Population and Development Review* 27: 219–238.

Gordon, J. 2010. *Invisible War*. Cambridge, MA: Harvard University Press.

Gottemoeller, R. 2007. The Evolution of Sanctions in Practice and Theory. *Survival* 49 (4): 99–110.

Graham-Brown, S. 1999. *Sanctioning Saddam*. New York: I.B. Tauris.

Grim, R. 2010. Egyptian President in WikiLeaks Docs. *The Huffington Post*. November 29.

Gulal, S.A. 2001. How Saddam Gained Upper Hand. *Economic and Political Weekly* 36 (32): 3026–3029.

Guo, J. 2009. Letter From Tehran: Iran's New Hard-Liners. *Foreign Affairs*. September 30.

Ha, Y. 1978. Nuclearization of Small States and World Order. *Asian Survey* 18 (11): 1134–1151.

Haass, R.N. 1997. Sanctioning Madness. *Foreign Affairs*. November/December.

1998. *Economic Sanctions and American Diplomacy*. New York: Council on Foreign Relations Press.

Haass, R.N., and M. O'Sullivan, eds. 2000. *Honey and Vinegar: Incentives, Sanctions, and Foreign Policy*. Washington, DC: The Brookings Institution.

Hafezi, M., A. Mostashari, and R. Alvandi. 2004. The Impact of U.S. Sanctions on Iran. Iranian Studies Group at MIT. June.

Haggard, S., and M. Noland. 2007. *Famine in North Korea*. New York: Columbia University Press.

2008. North Korea's Foreign Economic Relations. *International Relations of the Asia-Pacific* 8 (2): 219–246.

2009a. North Korea in 2008. *Asian Survey* 49 (1): 98–106.

2009b. Sanctioning North Korea: The Political Economy of Denuclearization and Proliferation. *Asian Survey* 50 (3): 539–568.

2010a. The Winter of Their Discontent. *Policy Brief 10–1*. Washington, DC: Peterson Institute for International Economics.

2010b. Sanctioning North Korea. *Asia Survey* 50 (3): 539–568.

2010c. Economic Crime and Punishment in North Korea. *Working Paper WP 10–2*. Washington, DC: Peterson Institute for International Economics.

Haggard, S., and M. Noland. 2011. "Engaging North Korea: The Role of Economic Statecraft." Honolulu: East-West Center Policy Studies #59.

Haggard, S., and D. Pinkston. 2010. Guarding the Guardians: North Korea's Political Institutions In Comparative Perspective. Paper prepared for Conference on Authoritarianism in East Asia, City University of Hong Kong, June 29–July 1.

Hannay, D. 2009/2010. Three Iraqi Intelligence Failures Reconsidered. *Survival* 51 (6): 13–20.

Harris, V., S. Hatang, and P. Liberman. 2004. Unveiling South Africa's Nuclear Past. *Journal of Southern African Studies* 30 (3): 457–476.

Harrison, S.S. 2001. Time to Leave Korea? *Foreign Affairs* 80 (2): 62–78.

2002. *Korean Endgame*. Princeton University Press.

2005. Did North Korea Cheat? *Foreign Affairs* 84 (1): 99–110.

2010. The New Faces of Reform in North Korea. *Boston Globe*. October 13.

Hart, R.A., Jr. 2000. Democracy and the Successful Use of Economic Sanctions. *Political Research Quarterly* 53 (2): 267–284.

Hawkins, D., and J. Lloyd. 2003. Questioning Comprehensive Sanctions. *Journal of Human Rights* 2 (3): 441–454.

Hayes, P. 1991. *Pacific Powderkeg*. Seoul: Han-ul Press.

2010. DPRK Enriched Uranium Highlights Need for New US DPRK Policy. Policy Forum. Nautilus Institute for Security and Sustainability. November 22.

Hedström, P., and P. Ylikoski. 2010. Causal Mechanisms in the Social Sciences. *Annual Review of Sociology* 36: 49–67.

Heinonen, O. 2010. The Case for an Immediate IAEA Special Inspection in Syria. *PolicyWatch No. 1715*. Washington, DC: The Washington Institute for Near East Policy.

Hendrickson, D.C. 1994/1995. The Democratist Crusade. *World Policy Journal* 11 (4): 18–30.

Hersh, S. 2003. The Cold Test. *The New Yorker*. January 27.

Hibbs, M. 1987a. Iraqi Attack on Bushehr Kills West German Nuclear Official. *Nucleonics Week* 28 (47): 1.

1987b. Bushehr Construction Now Remote after Three Iraqi Air Strikes. *Nucleonics Week* 28 (48): 5.

1991. Bonn will Decline Teheran Bid to Resuscitate Bushehr Project. *Nucleonics Week* 32 (18).

Hinnebusch, R.A. 1993. The Politics of Economic Reform in Egypt. *Third World Quarterly*. 14 (1): 159–171.

House of Commons Foreign Affairs Committee. 2008. *Global Security: Iran – Fifth Report of Session 2007–08*. House of Commons Foreign Affairs Committee. March 2.

Hovi, J., R. Huseby, and D.F. Sprinz. 2005. When Do (Imposed) Economic Sanctions Work? *World Politics* 57 (4): 479–499.

Hufbauer, G.C., and B. Oegg. 2000. Targeted Sanctions. *Law and Policy in International Business* 32: 11–20.

Hufbauer, G.C, J.J. Schott, and K.A. Elliott. 1990a. *Economic Sanctions Reconsidered, II Edition*. Washington, DC: Peterson Institute for International Economics.

1990b. *Economic Sanctions Reconsidered: Supplemental Case Histories*. Washington, DC: Peterson Institute for International Economics.

2007. *Economic Sanctions Reconsidered, III Edition*. Washington, DC: Peterson Institute for International Economics.

2009. *Economic Sanctions Reconsidered, III Edition (Softcover with CD)*. Washington, DC: Peterson Institute for International Economics.

Hughes, L., and S.J. Kreyling. 2010. Understanding Resource Nationalism in the 21st Century. *Journal of Energy Security*. July.

Huntington, S. 1981. *The Soldier and the State: The Theory and Politics of Civil-Military Relations*. Cambridge, MA: Harvard University Press.

Hymans, J.E.C. 2006. *The Psychology of Nuclear Proliferation*. New York: Cambridge University Press.

Ikenberry, G.J. 1988. An Institutional Approach to American Foreign Policy. *International Organization* 42 (1): 219–243.

2000. *After Victory*. Princeton: Princeton University Press.

Ilias, S. 2010. Iran's Economic Conditions. Congressional Research Service (CRS) Report for Congress, RL34525. April 22.

Institute for Cuban and Cuban-American Studies. 2006. The Cuban Military in the Economy (Staff Report). *Focus on Cuba* 46. August 11.

Institute for Science and International Security (ISIS) Reports. 1999. Documents Assessing the Organizational Structure of FEDAT. December 14.

International Atomic Energy Agency (IAEA). 2004. *Implementation of the NPT Safeguards Agreement of the Socialist People's Libyan Arab Jamahiriya: Report by the Director General*.

2010. *Implementation of the NPT Safeguards Agreement and relevant provisions of Security Council resolutions 1737 (2006), 1747 (2007), 1803 (2008) and 1835 (2008) in the Islamic Republic of Iran: Report by the Director General*.

Iranian Human Rights Documentation Center. 2007. Murder at Mykonos: Anatomy of a Political Assassination.

Islamic Republic News Agency. 2007. Iran: Supreme Leader Calls for Acceleration of Privatization Program. February 19.

James Martin Center for Nonproliferation Studies (CNS). 2010. Nuclear Chronology. *Nuclear Threat Initiative: Country Profiles*. Monterey Institute of International Studies.

Jentleson, B.W., and C.A. Whytock. 2005/2006. Who "Won" Libya? *International Security* 30 (3): 47–86.

Jervis, R. 1976. *Perception and Misperception in International Politics*. Princeton University Press.

1980. The Impact of the Korean War on the Cold War. *The Journal of Conflict Resolution* 24 (4): 563–592.

1997. *System Effects: Complexity in Political and Social Life*. Princeton University Press.

2010. *Why Intelligence Fails: Lessons From the Iranian Revolution and the Iraq War*. Ithaca: Cornell University Press.

Joffe, G. 2008. Prodigal or Pariah? In *Libya Since 1969*, edited by D. Vandewalle. New York: Palgrave Macmillan.

Jones, P. 1998. Iran's Threat Perceptions and Arms Control Policies. *The Nonproliferation Review* (Fall): 39–55.

Joseph, R.G. 2009. *Countering WMD*. Fairfax: National Institute Press.

Kaempfer, W.H., and A.D. Lowenberg. 1988. The Theory of International Economic Sanctions. *American Economic Review* 78 (4): 786–793.

    1992. *International Economic Sanctions*. Boulder: Westview Press.

    1999. Unilateral Versus Multilateral International Sanctions. *International Studies Quarterly* 43 (1): 37–58.

Kaempfer, W.H., A.D. Lowenberg, and W. Mertens. 2004. International Economic Sanctions Against a Dictator. *Economics and Politics* 16 (1): 29–51.

Kahler, M., and S.L. Kastner. 2006. Strategic Uses of Economic Interdependence. *Journal of Peace Research* 43 (5): 523–541.

Katzenstein, P.J., and N. Okawara. 2001/2002. Japan, Asian-Pacific Security, and the Case of Analytic Eclecticism. *International Security* 26 (3): 153–185.

Katzenstein, P.J., and R. Sil. 2010. *Beyond Paradigms: Analytic Eclecticism in the Study of World Politics*. New York: Palgrave Macmillan.

Katzman, K. 2002. *Iraq: Compliance, Sanctions, and U.S. Policy*. Issue Brief for Congress.

    2009. *Iraq: Former Regime Weapons Programs and Outstanding UN Issues*. Congressional Research Service (CRS) Report for Congress.

    2011. *Iran Sanctions*. CRS Report for Congress.

Keohane, R.O. 1986. Reciprocity in International Relations. *International Organization* 40 (1).

Khatami, M. 1998. *Islam, Liberty, and Development*. Birmingham: Institute of Global Cultural Studies, State University of New York.

Kim, S.Y. 2009. The Torturous Dilemma. In *SAIS U.S.-Korea Yearbook 2008*. Washington, DC: Johns Hopkins University.

Kirshner, J. 1995. *Currency and Coercion*. Princeton University Press.

    1997. The Microfoundations of Economic Sanctions. *Security Studies* 6 (3): 32–64.

Klebnikov, P. 2003. Millionaire Mullahs. *Forbes.com*. July 21.

Klotz, A. 1995. *Norms in International Relations: The Struggle Against Apartheid*. Ithaca: Cornell University Press.

Knorr, K. 1977. International Economic Leverage and Its Uses. In *Economic Issues and National Security*, edited by K. Knorr, and F.N. Trager. Lawrence: Regents Press of Kansas, 99–126.

Koh, B.C. 2005. "Military-First Politics" and Building a "Powerful and Prosperous Nation" in North Korea. Nautilus Institute Policy Forum Online 05–32A.

Krasner, S.D. 1977a. Domestic Constraints on International Economic Leverage. In *Economic Issues and National Security*, edited by K. Knorr and F.N. Trager. Lawrence: Regents Press of Kansas, 160–181.

    1977b. US Commercial and Monetary Policy. *International Organization* 31 (4): 635–671.

Krasno, J.E., and J.S. Sutterlin. 2003. *The United Nations and Iraq*. Westport: Praeger.

Kreps, S., and M. Fuhrmann. 2011. Attacking the Atom: Does Bombing Nuclear Facilities Affect Proliferation? *Journal of Strategic Studies* 34 (2): 161–187.

Lacy, D., and E.M.S. Niou. 2004. A Theory of Economic Sanctions and Issue Linkage. *Journal of Politics* 66 (1): 25–42.

Lankov, A. 2008. Staying Alive. *Foreign Affairs* 87 (2): 9–17.

2009. Pyongyang Strikes Back. *Asia Policy* 8: 47–71.

Lantos, T. 2004. Interview by Robert Siegel, *All Things Considered*. National Public Radio. January 30.

Larson, E.V., and B. Savych. 2005. *American Public Support for US Military Operations*. Arlington: Rand Corporation.

Lavoy, P.R. 1993. Nuclear Myths and the Causes of Nuclear Proliferation. *Security Studies* 2: 192–212.

Leamer, E.E. 1995. The Heckscher-Ohlin Model in Theory and Practice. *Princeton Studies in International Finance* 77. Princeton.

Lebovic, J.H. 2007. *Deterring International Terrorism and Rogue States*. New York: Routledge.

Lebow, R.N. 2003. *The Tragic Vision of Politics*. New York: Cambridge University Press.

2010. *Forbidden Fruit: Counterfactuals and International Relations*. Princeton University Press.

Lee, A.R., H. Lee, J.Y. Lee, and I.G. Kim. 2009. The Paradox of North Korea's Ideological Radicalism. *North Korean Review* 5 (1): 46–61.

Lee, S. 2003. Food Shortages and Economic Institutions in the Democratic People's Republic of Korea. Unpublished doctoral dissertation. Department of Economics, University of Warwick.

Lektzian, D.J., and M. Souva. 2007. An Institutional Theory of Sanctions Onset and Success. *Journal of Conflict Resolution* 51 (6): 848–871.

Lenway, S.A. 1988. Between War and Commerce. *International Organization* 42 (2): 397–426.

Levitt, M. 2010. Iran's Economic Health and the Impact of Sanctions. Washington, DC: Carnegie Endowment for International Peace.

Levy, J.S. 2000. The Implications of Framing and Loss Aversion for International Conflict. In *Handbook of War Studies II*, M.I. Midlarsky, ed. Ann Arbor, MI: University of Michigan Press: 193–221.

Lewis, J.W., and R. Carlin. 2010. The Six-Party Talks. *Bulletin of the Atomic Scientists*. March 17.

Liberman, P. 2001. The Rise and Fall of the South African Bomb. *International Security* 26 (2): 45–86.

Lim, J. 2009. *Kim Jong Il's Leadership of North Korea*. New York: Routledge.

Lindsay, J. 1986. Trade Sanctions as Policy Instruments: A Re-Examination. *International Studies Quarterly* 30 (2): 153–173.

Lindsay, J., and R. Takeyh. 2010. After Iran Gets the Bomb. *Foreign Affairs* 89 (2): 33–49.

Liss, J. 2007/2008. Making Monetary Mischief. *World Policy Journal* 24 (1): 29–38.

Litwak, R.S. 2002/2003. The New Calculus of Preemption. *Survival* 44 (4): 53–80.

2003/2004. Non-proliferation and the Dilemmas of Regime Change. *Survival* 45 (4): 7–32.

2007. *Regime Change*. Washington, DC: Woodrow Wilson Center Press.

Loeffler, R. 2009. Bank Shots. *Foreign Affairs* 88 (2): 101–110.

Lopez, G.A. 1999. More Ethical Than Not: Sanctions as Surgical Tools. *Ethics & International Affairs* 13 (1): 143–148.

Lopez, G.A., and D. Cortright. 2004. Containing Iraq: Sanctions Worked. *Foreign Affairs*, July/August.

Lowe, V. 1997. US Extraterritorial Jurisdiction. *International and Comparative Law Quarterly* 46 (2): 378–390.

Mackby, J., and P. Cornish. 2008. *U.S.-U.K. Nuclear Cooperation After 50 Years*. Washington, DC: Center for Strategic and International Studies.

MacLachlan, A. 1986. Iran Seeking Way to Finish Bushehr Plant but Bonn Denies Exports. *Nucleonics Week*. October 30.

Macleod, S., and N. Siamdoust. 2004. Iran, Still Defiant. *Time Magazine*.

Mahley, D. 2004. Dismantling Libyan Weapons. *The Arena* 10: November.

Major, S., and A.J. McGann. 2005. Caught in the Crossfire. *Journal of Conflict Resolution* 49 (3): 337–359.

Makhmalbaf, M. 2010. Secrets of Khamenei's Life. Homylafayette (blog). January 1.

Malloy, M.P. 2006. Study of New U.S. Unilateral Sanctions, 1997–2006. USA*Engage and National Foreign Trade Council.

Malone, D.M. 2006. *The International Struggle over Iraq*. New York: Oxford University Press.

Maloney, S. 2009. Iran Sanctions: Options, Opportunities and Consequences (Transcript). Testimony before the Subcommittee on National Security and Foreign Affairs, Committee on Oversight and Government Reform. December 15.

2010. Sanctioning Iran. *The Washington Quarterly* 33 (1): 131–147.

Mansfield, E.D. 1995. International Institutions and Economic Sanctions. *World Politics* 47 (4): 575–605.

2004. Conflict, Statecraft, and National Security in the Global Economy. In *International Conflict and the Global Economy*, edited by E.D. Mansfield. Cheltenham: Edward Elgar Publishing, 9–17.

Mansourov, A.Y. 1995. In Search of a New Identity: Revival of Traditional Politics and Modernisation in Post-Kim Il Sung North Korea. *Working Paper No. 1995/3*. Canberra, Australia: Research School of Pacific Studies, Australian National University.

Maoz, Z. 1983. Resolve, Capabilities, and the Outcomes of Interstate Disputes. *Journal of Conflict Resolution* 27 (2): 195–229.

Maramoto, M. 2008. North Korea and the China Model. *On Korea* 1: 98–117.

Marinov, N. 2005. Do Economic Sanctions Destabilize Country Leaders? *American Journal of Political Science* 49 (3): 564–576.

Mark, C.R. 2002. *Libya: CRS Issue Brief for Congress*. Washington, DC: Library of Congress.

Marks, S.P. 1999. Economic Sanctions as Human Rights Violations. *American Journal of Public Health* 89 (10): 1509–1513.

Marr, P. 1985. *The Modern History of Iraq*. Boulder: Westview Press.

Martin, L.L. 1992a. *Coercive Cooperation*. Princeton University Press.

1992b. Institutions and Cooperation. *International Security* 16 (4): 143–178.

1993. Credibility, Costs, and Institutions. *World Politics* 45 (3): 406–432.

Martinez, L. 2007. *The Libyan Paradox*. New York: Columbia University Press.

Mastanduno, M. 1988. Trade as a Strategic Weapon. *International Organization* 42 (1): 121–150.

2008. Economic Statecraft Revisited. In *Foreign Policy: Theories, Actors, and Cases*, edited by S. Smith, A. Hadfield, and T. Dunne. New York: Oxford University Press, 171–187.

Mattes, H. 1995. The Rise and Fall of the Revolutionary Committees. In *Qadhyafi's Libya 1969 to 1994*, edited by D. Vandewalle. New York: St. Martin's.

Mazaheri, N. 2010. Iraq and the Domestic Political Effects of Economic Sanctions. *Middle East Journal* 64 (2): 253–268.

Mazarr, M.J. 1995. Going Just a Little Nuclear. *International Security* 20 (2): 92–122.

2007. The Long Road to Pyongyang. *Foreign Affairs*. September/October.

2008. The Folly of "Asymmetric War." *The Washington Quarterly* 31 (3): 33–53.

Mazarr, M.J., and the Study Group on North Korean Futures. 2011. Preparing for Change in North Korea: Shifting Out of Neutral. Korea Economic Institute (KEI) Academic Paper Series 6.3.

McDermott, R. 1998. *Risk Taking in International Relations*. Ann Arbor: University of Michigan Press.

McEachern, P. 2008. Interest Groups in North Korean Politics. *Journal of East Asian Studies* 8 (3): 235–258.

McGillivray, F., and A. Smith. 2008. *Punishing the Prince: A Theory of Interstate Relations, Political Institutions, and Leader Change*. Princeton University Press.

McGillivray, F. and A. C. Stam. "Political Institutions, Coercive Diplomacy, and the Duration of Economic Sanctions," *Journal of Conflict Resolution* (2004).

MEED. 2004. Tripoli Talks but Can It Walk? June 4.

Mehr News Agency. 2010a. Iran's Lavan Refinery Produces One Million Liters of Gasoline Per Day. January 17.

2010b. Iran's Nuclear Program Will Follow Japanese Model: Larijani. February 25.

Mercer, J. 2005. Prospect Theory and Political Science. *Annual Review of Political Science*: 1–21.

Meyer, S.M. 1984. *The Dynamics of Nuclear Proliferation*. University of Chicago Press.

Milani, A. 2010a. Truths in Tehran. *The New Republic*. December 16.

2010b. The Shah's Atomic Dreams. *Foreign Policy*. December 29.

Miller, T., and A.B. Kim. 2010. *2010 Index of Economic Freedom*. Washington, DC: Heritage Foundation.

Milner, H., and K. Kubota. 2005. Why the Move to Free Trade? Democracy and Trade Policy in the Developing Countries. *International Organization* 59 (1): 107–143.

Mohamedi, F. 2010. Iran's Economic Health and the Impact of Sanctions. Washington, DC: Carnegie Endowment for International Peace.

Moon, W.J. 2009. The Origins of the Great North Korean Famine. *North Korean Review* 5 (1): 105–122.

Mora, F.O. 2002. Raul Castro and the FAR. Paper presented at the conference, *Cuba: Integration into the International System.* The Pell Center for International Relations and Public Policy, Newport, RI: March 21–24.

Morgan, T.C., and N.A. Bapat. 2003. Imposing Sanctions: States, Firms, and Economic Coercion. *International Studies Review* 5 (4): 65–80.

Morgan, T.C., and V.L. Schwebach. 1996. Economic Sanctions as Instruments of Foreign Policy. *International Interactions* 21 (3): 247–264.

1997. Fools Suffer Gladly. *International Studies Quarterly* 41 (1): 27–50.

Morley, M.H. 1984. The United States and the Global Economic Blockade of Cuba. *Canadian Journal of Political Science* 17 (1): 25–48.

Morrison, K.M. 2009. Oil, Nontax Revenue, and the Redistributional Foundations of Regime Security. *International Organization* 63 (1): 107–138.

Morrow, J. 1989. Capabilities, Uncertainty, and Resolve. *American Journal of Political Science* 33 (4): 941–927.

Moslem, M. 2002. *Factional Politics in Post-Khomeini Iran.* Syracuse University Press.

Mueller, J. 2010. *Atomic Obsession.* New York: Oxford University Press.

Mueller, J., and K. Mueller. 1999. Sanctions of Mass Destruction. *Foreign Affairs* 78 (3): 43–53.

Nader, A. 2009. Punish Iran's Rulers, Not Its People. *Foreign Policy.* December 14.

Naji, K. 2008. *Ahmadinejad.* Los Angeles: University of California Press.

Nakdimon, S. 1987. *First Strike.* New York: Summit Books.

Nanto, D.K., and E. Chanlett-Avery. 2009. *North Korea: Economic Leverage and Policy Analysis.* Washington, DC: Congressional Research Service. August 14.

National Association of Manufacturers. 1997. A Catalog of New US Unilateral Economic Sanctions for Foreign Policy Purposes 1993–96. USA*Engage. March.

National Committee on North Korea. 2007. In the News: North Korea and Banco Delta Asia. June 26.

Newnham, R.E. 2000. More Flies With Honey. *International Studies Quarterly* 44 (1): 73–96.

2002. *Deutsche Mark Diplomacy.* University Park: Pennsylvania State University Press.

Niblock, T. 2001. *"Pariah States" and Sanctions in the Middle East.* Boulder: Lynne Rienner.

Niksch, L.A. 2002. *North Korea's Nuclear Weapons Program.* CRS Report for Congress.

Nincic, M. 2005. *Renegade Regimes.* New York: Columbia University Press.

2010. Getting What You Want. *International Security* 35 (1): 138–183.

2011. *The Logic of Positive Engagement*. Ithaca: Cornell University Press.

Nincic, M., and P. Wallensteen, eds. 1983. *Dilemmas of Economic Coercion*. New York: Praeger.

Noël, P. 2010. Is Europe Shooting Itself in the Foot (To Russia's Benefit)? *The Race for Iran*. July 1.

Noland, M. 2004. *Korea after Kim Jong-il*. Washington, DC: Institute for International Economics.

2005. Famine and Reform in North Korea. *Asian Economic Papers* 3 (2): 1–40.

2009a. Telecoms in North Korea. *North Korea Review* 5 (1): 62–74.

2009b. The (Non) Impact of UN Sanctions on North Korea. *Asia Policy* 7: 61–88.

Nooruddin, I. 2002. Modeling Selection Bias in Studies of Sanctions Efficacy. *International Interactions* 28 (1): 57–74.

Normark, M., A. Lindblad, A. Norqvist, B. Sandström, and L. Waldenström. 2005. *Israel and WMD: Incentives and Capabilities*. Swedish Defence Research Agency, NBC Defence User Report.

North Korea Leadership Watch. 2010. Pak Pong Ju's Return. August 23.

Nossal, K.R. 1989. International Sanctions as International Punishment. *International Organization* 43 (2): 301–322.

Nourbakhsh, A.A. 2005. Khatami & Rafsanjani. *Payvand Iran News*. May 20.

Nye, J.S. 2008. Public Diplomacy and Soft Power. *The Annals of the American Academy of Political and Social Science* 616 (1): 94–109.

Office of the Vice President. 2004. *Vice President Participates in a Q&A at the Boone County Lumber Company in Columbia, Missouri*. White House Archives.

O'Sullivan, M.L. 2003. *Shrewd Sanction*. Washington, DC: Brookings Institution Press.

Oye, K.A. 1985. Explaining Cooperation Under Anarchy. *World Politics* 38 (1): 1–24.

Pant, H.V. 2010. Energy Security Multipolarity. *Journal of Energy Security*. July.

Pape, R. 1997. Why Economic Sanctions Do Not Work. *International Security* 22 (2): 90–136.

1998. Why Economic Sanctions Still Do Not Work. *International Security* 23 (1): 66–77.

Pargeter, A. 2000. Anglo-Libyan Relations and the Suez Crisis. *Journal of North African Studies* 5 (2): 41–58.

PBS. 1999. Chaos in Iran. July 13.

Peksen, D. 2009. Better or Worse? *Journal of Peace Research* 46 (1): 59–77.

2010. Coercive Diplomacy and Press Freedom. *International Political Science Review* 31 (4): 449–469.

Peksen, D., and A.C. Drury. 2009. Economic Sanctions and Political Repression. *Human Rights Review* 10 (3): 393–411.

Perkovich, G. 2009. Nuclear Quagmire with Iran. Washington, DC: Carnegie Endowment for International Peace.

Perry, G. 1971. *Political Elites*. Colchester: ECPR Press.

Pesaran, H.M. 2000. Economic Trends and Macroeconomic Policies in Post-Revolutionary Iran. In *The Economy of Iran: Dilemmas of an Islamic State*, edited by P. Alizadeh. New York: I.B. Tauris.

Pessin, A. 2010. Top US, Israeli Military Leaders Meet Amid Iran Controversy. *Voice of America*. November 17.

Peterson, Scott. 2009. Iran's Revolutionary Guard tightens grip. Christian Science Monitor, December 9.

Pew Research Group. 2010. Muslim Disappointment: Obama More Popular Abroad Than at Home, Global Image of U.S. Continues to Benefit. The Pew Global Attitudes Project. June 17.

Pickering, T.R. 2010. The Iranian Quagmire. *Bulletin of the Atomic Scientists* 66 (6): 88–94.

Pinkston, D.A. 2003. Domestic Politics and Stakeholders in the North Korean Missile Development Program. *The Nonproliferation Review* 10 (2): 51–65.

Pinkston, D.A., and L.S. Spector. 2007. Six Parties Adopt Steps for North Korean Denuculearization but Uraniam Enrichment Remains a Major Obstacle. *WMD Insights*, April.

Pollack, J.D. 2003. The United States, North Korea, and the End of the Agreed Framework. *Naval War College Review* 56 (3): 11–49.

Pollack, K.M. 2002. *The Threatening Storm*. New York: Random House.

2004. *The Persian Puzzle*. New York, NY: Random House.

Post, J.M. 2004. *Leaders and Their Followers in a Dangerous World: The Psychology of Political Behavior*. Ithaca: Cornell University Press.

Potter, W.C., and G. Mukhatzhanova. 2008. Divining Nuclear Intentions. *International Security* 33 (1): 139–169.

Potter, W.C., with G. Mukhatzhanova, eds. 2010a. *Forecasting Nuclear Proliferation in the 21st Century: Volume I, The Role of Theory*. Palo Alto: Stanford University Press.

2010b. *Forecasting Nuclear Proliferation in the 21st Century: Volume II, A Comparative Perspective*. Palo Alto: Stanford University Press.

Press, D.G. 2005. *Calculating Credibility*. Ithaca: Cornell University Press.

Pritchard, C.L. 2007. *Failed Diplomacy*. Washington, DC: The Brookings Institution.

Pritchard, C.L., and J.H. Tilleli Jr. 2010. Task Force Report: *US Policy Toward the Korean Peninsula*. New York: Council on Foreign Relations Press.

Qaddafi, M. 1976. *The Green Book*. London: Martin, Brian, and O'Keefe.

Radio Zamaneh. 2010. Opposition Leader Says Revolutionary Guards Will Benefit from Iran Sanctions. July 11.

Ragin, C.C. 2000. *Fuzzy-Set Social Science*. London: University of Chicago Press.

Ramberg, B. 2006. Preemption Paradox. *Bulletin of the Atomic Scientists*. July/August.

Reardon, Robert J. 2010. Nuclear Bargaining: Using Carrots and Sticks in Nuclear Counter-proliferation. Ph.D. dissertation. Department of Political Science, Massachusetts Institute of Technology.

Redd, S.B. 2002. The Influence of Advisers on Foreign Policy Decision Making. *Journal of Conflict Resolution* 46 (3): 335–364.

Redick, J.R., J.C. Carasales, and P.S. Wrobel. 1994. Nuclear Rapprochement. *The Washington Quarterly* 18 (1): 107–122.

Reiss, M. 1988. *Without the Bomb*. New York: Columbia University Press.

1995. *Bridled Ambition*. Washington, DC: Woodrow Wilson Center Press.

Reiss, M., and R. Galucci. 2005. Red Handed. *Foreign Affairs*. March/April.

Reiss, M., and R.S. Litwak. 1994. *Nuclear Proliferation After the Cold War*. Washington, DC: Woodrow Wilson Center Press.

Reiter, D. 2005. Preventative Attacks Against Nuclear Programs and the "Success" at Osiraq. *Nonproliferation Review* 12 (2): 255–371.

2006. Preventive Attacks against Nuclear, Biological, and Chemical Weapons Programs. In *Hitting First, Preventive Force in US Security Strategy*, edited by W.W. Keller and G.R. Mitchell. Pittsburgh University Press.

Rennack, D.E. 2005. *North Korea: Economic Sanctions*. Congressional Research Service (CRS) Report for Congress.

Riedel, B., and G. Samore. 2008. "Managing Nuclear Proliferation in the Middle East." In *Restoring the Balance: A Middle East Strategy for the Next President*. Washington, DC: Brookings Institution Press.

Ritter, S. 2005. *Iraq Confidential: The Untold Story of America's Intelligence Community*. New York: I.B. Tauris.

Rodman, K.A. 1995. Sanctions At Bay? *International Organization* 49 (1): 105–137.

2001. *Sanctions Beyond Borders*. Lanham: Rowman & Littlefield.

Rohde, A. 2010. *State-Society Relations in Ba'thist Iraq*. New York: Routledge.

Ronen, Y. 2002. The Lockerbie Endgame. *Middle East Quarterly* (Winter): 53–59.

Rosecrance, R. 1981. Reward, Punishment, and Interdependence. *Journal of Conflict Resolution* 25 (1): 31–46.

Rowe, D.M. 2001. *Manipulating the Market*. Ann Arbor: University of Michigan Press.

2010. Economic Sanctions and International Security. In *The International Studies Encyclopedia*, edited by R.A. Denemark. Blackwell Publishing. Blackwell Reference Online.

Rowhani, H. 2005. Text of speech to the Supreme Cultural Revolution Council. "Beyond the Challenges Facing Iran and the IAEA Concerning the Nuclear Dossier." *Rahbord*, 7–38.

2008. 20 Years Perspectives and a Progressive Foreign Policy. *Persian Journal*. February 28.

Rozen, L. 2010. U.S. Sanctions IRGC Engineering Firms. *Politico.com*. February 10.

Rublee, M.R. 2006. Egypt's Nuclear Weapons Program. *The Nonproliferation Review* 13 (4): 555–567.

2009. *Nonproliferation Norms*. Athens, GA: University of Georgia Press.

Sadjadpour, K. 2010a. Dealing With Iran. Washington, DC: Carnegie Endowment for Internation Peace. *CNN Newsroom*. February 10.

2010b. Domestic and International Pressures Build in Iran (Radio). Washington, DC: Carnegie Endowment for International Peace.

2010c. Iran's Economic Health and the Impact of Sanctions. Washington, DC: Carnegie Endowment for International Peace.

2010d. 5 Minutes With Benjamin Netanyahu. *The Atlantic*. August 24.

2010e. The Sources of Iranian Conduct. *Foreign Policy*. November.

Sadjadpour, K., and A. Milani. 2009. Testimony before the House Committee on Foreign Affairs (Transcript). Serial No. 111–31. July 22.

Sadjadpour, K., S. Bakhash, R. Cohen, and H. Esfandiari. 2009. Iran: A Conversation About the Elections, Protests, and the Future (Transcript). Washington, DC: Carnegie Endowment for International Peace. July 15.

Sagan, S.D. 1996/1997. Why Do States Build Nuclear Weapons? *International Security* 21 (3): 54–86.

Schelling, T.C. 1960. *The Strategy of Conflict*. Cambridge, MA: Harvard University Press.

1966. *Arms and Influence*. New Haven: Yale University Press.

1976. Who Will Have the Bomb? *International Security* 1 (1): 77–91.

2006. Nuclear Deterrence for the Future. *Issues in Science and Technology*: 50–52.

2009. A World Without Nuclear Weapons? *Daedalus* 138 (4): 124–129.

Schultz, K.A. 2001. *Democracy and Coercive Diplomacy*. New York: Cambridge University Press.

2005. The Politics of Risking Peace. *International Organization* 59 (1): 1–38.

Schumacher, E. 1986/1987. The United States and Libya. *Foreign Affairs* 65 (2).

Security Council Report. 2010. DPRK (North Korea) Historical Chronology. April 29, available at: www.securitycouncilreport.org/site/c. glKWLeMTIsG/b.2705183.

Selden, Z.A. 1999. *Economic Sanctions as Instruments of American Foreign Policy*. Westport: Praeger.

Setadnet. 2010. Hemayat e 59 nafar as farmandehan e sepah asbgh va arshad e sepah e pasdaran az mir Hussein mousavi. (The support of 59 former Revolutionary Guards commanders for Mousavi.) Mihan (Blog).

Shagabutdinova, E., and J. Berejikian. 2007. Deploying Sanctions While Protecting Human Rights. *Journal of Human Rights* 6 (1): 59–74.

Shehabaldin, A., and W. Laughlin Jr. 1999. Economic Sanctions Against Iraq. *International Journal of Human Rights* 3 (4): 1–18.

Shen, D. 2010. "Can Sanctions Stop Proliferation?" The Washington Quarterly, Vol. 31, No. 1 (January), pp. 89–100.

Shuster, M. 2010. Amid Iran's Economic Woes, Sanctions Begin to Bite. *NPR*. October 28.

Siddiqi, A. 2005. Khatami and the Search for Reform in Iran. *Stanford Journal of International Relations* 6 (1).

Sigal, L.V. 1998. *Disarming Strangers*. Princeton University Press.

2002. North Korea Is No Iraq. *Arms Control Today*. December.

2005. Misplaying North Korea and Losing Friends and Influence in Northeast Asia. *The North Korean Nuclear Crisis: Regional Perspectives*. Social Science Research Council (SSRC): July 12.

2009. Punishing North Korea Won't Work. *Bulletin of the Atomic Scientists*. May 28.

2010. Looking for Leverage in All the Wrong Places. *38 North*. August.

Sil, R., and P. J. Katzenstein. "Analytic Eclecticism in the Study of World Politics: Reconfiguring Problems and Mechanisms across Research Traditions," in *Perspectives on Politics* 8 (June 2010): 411–431.

Singh, M. 2009. The Hidden Costs of the Nuke Deal with Iran. *Foreign Policy.*
    October 21.
Skålnes, L.S. 2000. *Politics, Markets, and Grand Strategy.* Ann Arbor: University
    of Michigan Press.
Slavin, B. 2005. Iran on the Eve of the Presidential Election. Address to the
    Woodrow Wilson International Center for Scholars. May 23.
    2007. *Bitter Friends, Bosom Enemies.* New York: St. Martin's Press.
Smith, A. 1995. The Success and Use of Economic Sanctions. *International
    Interactions* 21 (3): 229–245.
Solingen, E. 1994a. The Political Economy of Nuclear Restraint. *International
    Security* 19 (2): 126–169.
    1994b. The Domestic Sources of International Regimes: The Evolution of
    Nuclear Ambiguity in the Middle East. *International Studies Quarterly* 38
    (4): 305–337.
    1995. The New Multilateralism and Nonproliferation. *Global Governance* 1
    (1): 205–228.
    1998. *Regional Orders at Century's Dawn.* Princeton University Press.
    2001. Mapping Internationalization. *International Studies Quarterly* 45 (1):
    517–555.
    2007a. *Nuclear Logics: Contrasting Paths in East Asia and the Middle East.*
    Princeton University Press.
    2007b. Pax Asiatica versus Bella Levantina: The Foundations of War and
    Peace in East Asia and the Middle East. *American Political Science Review*
    101 (4): 757–780.
    2009a. The Global Context of Comparative Politics. In *Comparative Politics*,
    edited by M.I. Lichbach and A.S. Zuckerman. New York: Cambridge
    University Press, 220–259.
    2009b. "Of Theory, Method, and Policy Guideposts," Author's Response,
    Asia Policy, No. 7 (January 2009), pp. 139–151.
    2010. Domestic Models of Political Survival. In *Forecasting Nuclear
    Proliferation*, edited by W.C. Potter. Palo Alto: Stanford University Press,
    38–57.
    2011a. Hindsight and Foresight in South American Non-proliferation
    Trends. In *Over the Horizon Proliferation Threats*, edited by P. Lavoy and J.
    Wirtz. Palo Alto: Stanford University Press. (Forthcoming.)
    2011b. Northeast Asian Approaches to North Korea's Nuclearization, East
    Asian Institute, *Working Paper Series* No. 24, Seoul, South Korea.
    2012. Three Scenes of Sovereignty and Power. In *Back to Basics: Rethinking
    Power in the Contemporary World*, edited by M. Finnemore and J. Goldstein.
    (Forthcoming.)
Solingen, E., and A. Wolf. 2009. Economic Statecraft and Domestic Politics
    (ms., Department of Political Science, University of California Irvine,
    March 15).
Sørensen, V. 1989. Economic Recovery Versus Containment. *Cooperation and
    Conflict* 24 (2): 69–97.
Sotomayor Velazquez, A.C. 2000. Civil Military Affairs and Security
    Institutions in the Southern Cone. *Latin American Politics and Society* 46
    (4): 29–60.

Spector, L., and D. Berman. 2010. The Syrian Nuclear Puzzle. In *Forecasting Nuclear Proliferation in the 21st Century: Volume II, A Comparative Perspective*, edited by W.C. Potter with G. Mukhatzhanova. Palo Alto: Stanford University Press, 100–130.

Spector, L., and J. Smith. 1990. *Nuclear Ambitions: The Spread of Nuclear Weapons, 1989–1990*. Boulder: Westview.

St. John, R.B. 1983. The Ideology of Mu'ammar Al-Qadhafi. *International Journal of Middle Eastern Studies* 15 (4): 471–490.

2004. Libya is Not Iraq. *Middle East Journal* 58 (3): 386–402.

2008. The Libyan Economy in Transition. In *Libya Since 1969*, edited by D. Vandewalle. New York: Palgrave Macmillan.

Steil, B., and R. Litan. 2006. *Financial Statecraft*. New Haven: Yale University Press.

Stein, A.A. 1976. Conflict and Cohesion. *Journal of Conflict Resolution* 20: 143–172.

1980. The Politics of Linkage. *World Politics* 33 (1): 62–81.

2003. Trade and Conflict: Uncertainty, Strategic Signalling, and Interstate Disputes. In *Economic Interdependence and International Conflict*, edited by E.D. Mansfield, and B. Pollins. Ann Arbor: University of Michigan Press.

Stremlau, J. 1996. Sharpening International Sanctions: Toward a Stronger Role for the United Nations. A Report to the Carnegie Commission on Preventing Deadly Conflict, Carnegie Corporation of New York. November.

Stricker, A. 2010. ISIS Reports: State Department Cables: Stopping Iran's and North Korea's Illicit Procurement for their Nuclear and Ballistic Missile Programs. Institute for Science and International Security. December 10.

Takeyh, R. 2001. The Rogue Who Came In From the Cold. *Foreign Affairs* 80 (3): 62–72.

2003a. Iran's Nuclear Calculations. *World Policy Journal* 20 (2): 21–28.

2003b. Iran's Municipal Elections. The Washington Institute for Near East Policy. March 6.

2006. *Hidden Iran*. New York: Times Books.

Takeyh, R., and N.K. Gvosdev. 2004. Pragmatism in the Midst of Iranian Turmoil. *The Washington Quarterly* 27 (4): 33–56.

Takeyh, R., and S. Maloney. 2011. "The self-limiting success of Iran sanctions." *International Affairs* 87:6 (2011) 1297–1312.

Takishita, K.M. 2005. U.S. Economic Sanctions Against North Korea. *Pacific Rim Law & Policy Journal Association* 14 (2): 515–544.

Targeted Financial Sanctions Project. 2004. Background Paper on Targeted Sanctions. Prepared for the Workshop on United Nations Sanctions. Brown University, Watson Institute for International Studies, July 16–17.

Tetlock, P.E. 2005. *Expert Political Judgment: How Good is It? How Can We Know?* Princeton University Press.

Thaler, D.E., and A. Nader. 2010. Deep-Seated Entanglements: The Web of Iranian Leadership Can Be Negotiated, Not Unraveled. *RAND Review* 34 (1).

Thaler, D.E., A. Nader, S. Chubin, J.D. Green, C. Lynch, and F. Wehrey. 2010. *Mullahs, Guards, and Bonyads*. Santa Monica: RAND Corporation.

Thielmann, G. 2010. The UN Sanctions' Impact on Iran's Military. *Arms Control Association*. Issue Brief 1 (7). June 11.

Tierney, D. 2005. Irrelevant or Malevolent? *Review of International Studies* 31 (4): 645–664.

Tilly, C. 2003. *The Politics of Collective Violence*. Cambridge University Press.

Toloraya, G. 2008. The Economic Future of North Korea. Korea Economic Institute. *On Korea* 1: 32.

Tomz, M. 2007. Domestic Audience Costs in International Relations. *International Organization* 61 (4): 821–840.

Tostensen, A., and B. Bull. 2002. Are Smart Sanctions Feasible? *World Politics* 54 (3): 373–403.

United Nations Press Release. 2006. Security Council Imposes Sanctions on Iran for Failure to Halt Uranium Enrichment. UN Security Council. December 23.

United States General Accounting Office. 1992. *Economic Sanctions: Effectiveness as Tools of Foreign Policy*. Report to the Chairman, Committee on Foreign Relations, U.S. Senate. Washington, DC.

United States Government Accountability Office. 2004. *Recovering Iraq's Assets: Preliminary Observations on U.S. Efforts and Challenges*. Testimony before the Committee on Oversight and Investigations, Committee on Financial Services, House of Representatives. Washington, DC.

    2007. *Iran Sanctions: Impact in Furthering U.S. Objectives is Unclear and Should Be Reviewed*. Report to the Ranking Member, Subcommittee on National Security and Foreign Affairs, House Committee on Oversight and Government Reform. Washington, DC.

    2010. *Exporters of Refined Petroleum Products to Iran*, GAO-10–967R. Washington, DC.

Urquhart, B. 1999. How Not to Fight a Dictator. *The New York Review of Books*. May 6.

US Energy Information Administration. 2010. Statistics on Iran: Oil.

Vandewalle, D. 2006. *A History of Modern Libya*. Cambridge University Press.

VanWagenen, P. 2000. U.S. Economic Sanctions. *Law and Policy in International Business* 32: 239–261.

Volcker, P.A. 2005. *Manipulation of the Oil-for-Food Programme by the Iraqi Regime*. Independent Inquiry Committee into the United Nations Oil-For-Food Programme.

Volcker, P.A., R.J. Goldstone, and M. Pieth. 2005. *Independent Inquiry into the United Nations Oil-for-Food Programme*. New York: United Nations.

von Lutterotti, L. 2002. The US Extraterritorial Sanctions of 1996 and the EU Reaction. In *External Economic Relations and Foreign Policy in the European Union*, edited by S. Griller and B. Weidel. New York: Springer.

Wall, C.R. 2010. Weak Tea. *Foreign Policy*. June 8.

Wallensteen, P. 1968. Characteristics of Economic Sanctions. *Journal of Peace Research* 5 (3): 248–267.

    2000. A Century of Economic Sanctions. Uppsala Peace Research Papers No. 1. Uppsala University, Department of Peace and Conflict Research.

Wallensteen, P., and C. Staibano, eds. 2005. *International Sanctions*. London: Routledge.

Walt, S. 2010. Sleepwalking With Iran. *Foreign Policy* (Blog). May 26.

Weeks, J.L. 2008. Autocratic Audience Costs. *International Organization* 62 (1): 35–64.

Wehrey, F., J.D. Green, B. Nichiporuk, L. Hansell, R. Nafisi, and S.R. Bohandy. 2009. *The Rise of the Pasdaran*. Santa Monica: RAND Corporation.

Weschler, W. 2001. Follow the Money. *Foreign Affairs* 80 (4): 40–57.

White House. 2002. *The National Security Strategy of the United States of America*.

Wickman, S.B. 2002. *North Korea's Perennial Diet of Carrots and Sticks*. Washington, DC: National Defense University, National War College.

Wilkinson, S. 2009. Just How Special is "Special." *Diplomacy and Statecraft* 20 (2): 291–308.

Williams, B.H. 1943. The Coming of Economic Sanctions Into American Practice. *American Journal of International Law* 37 (3): 386–396.

Wintrobe, R. 1990. The Tinpot and the Totalitarian. *American Political Science Review* 84 (3): 849–872.

Wit, J.S. 2010. Time to Get Serious About North Korea. *Foreign Policy*. December 13.

Wit, J.S., D. Poneman, and R.L. Gallucci. 2004. *Going Critical*. Washington, DC: Brookings Institution Press.

Wood, R.M. 2008. A Hand Upon the Throat of the Nation. *International Studies Quarterly* 52 (3): 489–513.

Woods, K.M., and M.E. Stout. 2010. Saddam's Perceptions and Misperceptions. *Journal of Strategic Studies* 33 (1): 5–41.

Woods, K.M., M.R. Pease, M.E. Stout, W. Murray, and J. Lacey. 2006. *Iraqi Perspectives Project: A View of Operation Iraqi Freedom from Saddam's Senior Leadership*. Washington, DC: Joint Center for Operational Analysis.

Woods, K.M., D.D. Palkki, and M.E. Stout. 2010. *A Survey of Saddam's Audio Files, 1978–2001*. Washington, DC: Institute for Defense Analyses.

Wright, R. 2010. Domestic and International Pressures Build in Iran (Radio). New York: Carnegie Endowment for International Peace.

Yonhap News Agency. 2003. *North Korea Handbook*. Seoul: Yonhap News Agency.

Yoon, D.Y., and B.O. Babson. 2002. Understanding North Korea's Economic Crisis. *Asian Economic Papers* 1 (3): 69–89.

Yoon, S. 2007. An Economic Perspective of Keasong Industrial Complex in North Korea. *American Journal of Applied Sciences* 4 (11): 938–945.

Zarate, J. 2009. Harnessing the Financial Furies. *The Washington Quarterly* 32 (4): 43–59.

Zeev, M. 1983. Resolve, Capabilities, and the Outcome of Interstate Disputes, 1816-1976, *Journal of Conflict Resolution*, 27(2): 195–229.

Zweiri, M. 2010. What To Do About Iran – American & Gulf Perspectives (Event). Foreign Policy, Brookings DOHA Center, and Saban Center for Middle East Policy Event. May 5.

Index